PULL HARD!

PULL HARD!

FINDING GRIT AND PURPOSE ON COUGAR CREW, 1970–2020

DAVID ARNOLD

WSU PRESS

Washington State University Press
Pullman, Washington

Washington State University Press
PO Box 645910
Pullman, Washington 99164-5910
Phone: 800-354-7360
Email: wsupress@wsu.edu
Website: wsupress.wsu.edu

Library of Congress Cataloging-in-Publication Data

Names: Arnold, David, 1966- author.
Title: Pull hard! : finding grit and purpose on Cougar crew, 1970-2020 /
    David Arnold.
Description: Pullman, Washington : Washington State University Press, 2021.
    | Includes bibliographical references and index.
Identifiers: LCCN 2021033653 | ISBN 9780874224085 (paperback)
Subjects: LCSH: Washington State University--Rowing--History. |
    Rowers--Washington (State)--Biography.
Classification: LCC GV807.W37 A76 2021 | DDC 797.12/309797--dc23
LC record available at https://lccn.loc.gov/2021033653

The Washington State University Pullman campus is located on the homelands
of the Niimíipuu (Nez Perce) Tribe and the Palus people. We acknowledge their
presence here since time immemorial and recognize their continuing connection
to the land, to the water, and to their ancestors. WSU Press is committed to
publishing works that foster a deeper understanding of the Pacific Northwest and
the contributions of its Native peoples.

On the cover: Cover image by Robert Hubner, WSU Photo Services.
        Cover design by Jeffry E. Hipp

For my mom, Patricia Deisher, who eagerly read every chapter and offered absolutely no criticisms or suggestions for revisions. She loved every word of it. Everyone needs a mom like that.

CONTENTS

ILLUSTRATIONS

INTRODUCTION

A History of Grit

In rowing...I found a sport that demanded some skill, granted, but placed a much higher premium on plain hard work and persistence.

—Harry Parker, Harvard crew coach, 1963–2013

You can learn a lot about life at the end of an oar.

—Bob Orr, WSU crew head coach, 1971–1973

I titled this book *Pull Hard* not just because that is what you do when you row (and there is also a nice alliteration with Pullman) but because it is the name of the newsletter that the Washington State University rowing club has published "somewhat irregularly"—as the masthead of the first issue announced—since 1973. Today, in 2020, *The Pull Hard* is a beautifully produced quarterly gazette, the work of current rowers and an alumni editor, that informs the entire republic of Cougar Crew (students, alumni, parents, the WSU administration) about the current happenings of the club. It is the vital mouthpiece of a thriving, self-perpetuating club community, giving voice to the aspirations of current student rowers and their coaches while also articulating the shared interests of the club alumni.

Like Cougar Crew itself, the existence of *The Pull Hard* is remarkable and unique—very different in its origins and process than, for example, a newsletter from a university-funded team, where staffers and secretaries report on recruiting, scheduling, and team performance. Because *The Pull Hard* emanates from a student club rather than an administrative bureaucracy, it is a messier, more democratic process, with uneven results. That in itself summarizes the difference between a club sport and a university-funded athletic program.

Since the first issue was printed in 1973, *The Pull Hard* has sometimes been published quarterly, sometimes once, twice, or three times a year, and sometimes not at all. During the 1990s, it stopped printing for an entire decade. The journal has thus served as an indicator species, like salmon or beaver, of the health of the larger ecosystem that surrounds it. It is the "canary in the coal mine" of Cougar Crew—if *The Pull Hard* perishes or becomes sickly, it is an indication of

1

systemic problems. If it thrives—as it does today in 2020—it suggests that the community of organisms that makes up the Cougar Crew ecosystem is healthy and strong.

I could think of no better title for a book about the history—and life cycle—of a student rowing club than the name of its hallmark species. As longtime coach Ken Struckmeyer pointed out in the magazine's second edition, in 1974, "The term 'Pull Hard' implies that the student oarsmen are working hard to bring WSU crew into equal status with the major rowing schools of the country." But, he noted, "If you reverse the term, you have Hard Pull, which indeed it is and has been."[1]

Originally, I wanted to call this book *A History of Grit*, because the history of Cougar Crew over five decades is fundamentally one of perseverance in the face of adversity. Fifty years ago, the WSU students who founded the rowing club had no money, no coach, no equipment, no boathouse, and no body of water within a forty-minute drive from campus. Never having rowed a stroke in their lives, they conceived a plan and carried it through, designing and building a shell house and then rebuilding it after a windstorm blew it down. They obtained hand-me-down equipment and drove thirty winding miles every day through the Palouse to the Snake River Canyon. There, they blistered their hands and soaked their cotton shirts with sweat and backsplash from their rough, untutored rowing style.

When they finally competed, they lost badly and were ridiculed as outsiders and hayseeds in a sport that was, and still is today, as self-consciously elitist as any other in college sports. Why did they persist? Why did they show such fidelity to a sport that offered them no glory and an abundance of hardship? Why do these rowers, fifty years later, still see their participation in Cougar Crew as one of the formative experiences of their lives, and perhaps the most important piece of their education at WSU?

Those founding oarsmen at WSU were followed by generations of student rowers who embodied the same values of grit and tenacity. The first women arrived at the boathouse in 1974, insisting that they too be allowed an equal right to physical suffering and hardship. In 1979, the first WSU national championship crew traveled to Syracuse, New York, borrowed a heavy training shell from Brown University, and refused to believe they were inferior to their more polished East Coast competitors. The first WSU rower to make an Olympic team, Kristi Norelius, never considered herself an athlete until she joined the rowing club, but she later won an Olympic gold medal. Paul Enquist, who rowed at WSU from 1973 to 1977, embarked on a remarkable odyssey that took him to the pinnacle of the rowing world. Oarsmen kept

The WSU Rowing Club assembles for the very first team photo in the 1971 *Chinook*. While they spearheaded the construction of the first shell house, most of them never rowed. Row One, from left to right: Lynel Bortles, Rick Norberg, unidentified, Darrel Lau. Row Two: David Emigh, Jim Verellen, Dave Atherton, Jan Koal, Ed Arnold, Clam Sowder, Rich Stager. Row Three: Paul Kennedy, George Sutch. Russ Rome, Ken Fielder, Tom Ardell, Gene Chouinard, Gary Hubbard, Bill Raisner. Source: *The Chinook* (1971), 144, courtesy of WSU Manuscripts, Archives, and Special Collections.

the men's club alive in the 1990s when its existence was in peril. Nameless hundreds of club rowers, men and women who never won championships or even races, spent their fall Saturdays setting up and taking down tables, chairs, and tents before and after football games or selling their labor in "rent-a-rower" fundraisers so that they could spend their afternoons on the Snake River pushing themselves to their physical limits.

Generations of WSU club rowers, with their "hang-in-there posture toward a challenge," have embodied what psychologist and MacArthur fellow Angela Duckworth refers to as "grit." Duckworth's research shows that grit, which she defines as a "combination of passion and perseverance," matters far more than talent or ability when it comes to realizing one's goals in life.[2] There is no better word to characterize a successful college student than grit, nor to describe the student rowers, men and women, who were changed by club rowing at WSU and then carried that experience into the rest of their lives.

WSU club rowers have never been funded by the university—there were no scholarships, paid travel, free gear, or college credits to gain. Club rowers paid to row with their time, money, and sweat. They fundraised continuously, adding countless hours to the ones already spent training. Moreover, rowing is not "fun" in the conventional sense. There are no balls to kick or throw, goals to be scored, games to be won or lost in last-minute heroics, no hills or mountains to triumphantly ascend or daringly descend, no individual glory to be gained. There is only the purposeful toil of moving backward over a body of water, striving to make each stroke better than the last, with the goal of surrendering your personal ambitions to the collective will of the boat.

Duckworth emphasizes that the Latin root word for passion, *pati*, means "to suffer." In essence, those who can suffer without quitting have what it takes to succeed in life. The same was, and is, true for Cougar Crew. In fifty years, thousands of WSU students have tried their hand at rowing during those lovely fall days on the Snake River when the club is courting new recruits. Only a small portion of them remained on the crew as fall rowing on the glorious Snake gave way to the harsh reality of winter training, which entailed morning weights and afternoon sessions charging up stadium stairs, racing across snowy hills, running to the airport in subfreezing temperatures, or pulling endless hours on rowing machines. Why did some students persist when most did not? Who would make such a sacrifice? Kathleen Randall, who rowed in the late 1970s, defined Cougar club rowers simply as "non-quitters." What compelled these "non-quitters" to exhibit such "ferocious devotion"—in Duckworth's words—to Cougar Crew?

According to its first constitution, written in 1971, the WSU Rowing Club was "strictly a non-politically aligned organization" dedicated to cultivating "team unity among individuals and all campus groups represented on the team."[3] Those "groups represented" were mostly white, but they came from diverse backgrounds—urban and rural, middle-class and working-class, liberal and conservative, religious and secular, athletic and bookish.[4] Some of them rowed because of a desire to compete and prove themselves athletically, some because they needed a break from their studies (and from Pullman), some because they were drawn by the sublime natural environment of the Snake River Canyon, and some to simply become part of something bigger than themselves. All of them, however, told me that whatever might have attracted them initially, it was the human community that kept them coming back.

Upon arriving at the shell house, they found themselves surrounded by others who were not always like-minded but who shared with them an affinity for sitting in a rowing shell and propelling themselves through the water. It was an inclusive community that invited anyone to join who was willing to "pull hard" and also dedicate themselves to sustaining the club through fundraisers and self-governance. This community looked different over time: in the

1970s, it was a community of long-haired renegade workout maniacs in cotton shorts; in the 1980s and 1990s, Lycra-wearing workout maniacs; and in the 2000s, workout maniacs with smart phones. They all shared the common thread of being just a little bit mad and willing to do things—like traveling to the Snake River every day to ritually engage in communal suffering—that marked them as kindred spirits.

A college education is substantially about exploring (and perhaps finding) one's identity and also establishing oneself within a community. Research shows that students who become engaged in the life of their school beyond their courses are more likely to succeed academically.[5] If they participate in extracurricular activities that connect them with other students, professors, and mentors, they are much more likely to flourish and finish their degrees. Understanding this, colleges and universities today attempt to establish such connections for incoming students, designing orientations, like WSU's "Alive," that shower freshman with opportunities to explore various communities of interest. Long before these programs existed, Cougar Crew established a community of interest that helped thousands of student rowers find themselves—or at least learn more about themselves—and produced a learning experience that was, for many, the most meaningful of their university education.

While talking to former rowers, I expected to learn about the hardships of balancing academics with rowing. After all, the time commitment of Cougar Crew is beyond the scope of any normal club. However, I rarely heard that crew negatively impacted academics. What I heard more often was that Cougar Crew helped students make it through school—some even claimed they never would have graduated had it not been for rowing. Not only did rowing help students manage their time more effectively, it imbued their education with purpose and meaning, motivating them to work even harder. Though it's true that some former rowers who received degrees in general studies (or history) essentially majored in rowing, a substantial number of my interviewees were in fields like engineering, premed, or pre-veterinarian, and they credited crew with helping them succeed academically and navigate the challenges of their lives and careers beyond WSU.

There is plenty of fodder here regarding the history, philosophy, and technical aspects of rowing, including my own biased opinions about what makes fast boats (answer: lots of dedicated rowers), what makes a great rowing coach (answer: one who recruits and retains lots of dedicated rowers), and what technical approach yields the fastest boats (answer: it doesn't matter as long as you do it in perfect unity). But this is *not* a history of *rowing* at WSU. It is a history of *club rowing* at WSU. Unlike the sports programs in WSU's athletic department, Cougar Crew, throughout its history, has welcomed all comers and allowed many non-gifted athletes the opportunity to push their limits and find their community. My initial conception for this project revolved around this question: what role did club rowing at WSU play in the education, personal growth, and subsequent lives of the many hundreds of students who participated in Cougar Crew? The final product reflects that emphasis. This history of Cougar Crew is fundamentally about education, especially the power of a college club—an intentional community of student volunteers who work together, despite their differences—to strive toward common objectives.

The themes that anchor the book are what one might expect from a sport that prides itself on the absence of notoriety and an abundance of pain: grit, hardship, resilience, volunteerism, sacrifice, failure, transformation, and triumph. Underneath these themes, there is one overarching through line: the exhausting democratic process of building and maintaining a community of students and alumni bound together by the love of something shared. If this sounds corny, like the generic corporate posters of a rowing squad touting "teamwork," my answer is twofold: first, the corny stuff is most often the good stuff when it comes to education, athletics, and perhaps life itself; second, this history of Cougar Crew, as you will see, gives depth and humanity to the corporate clichés about teamwork and sacrifice. It is the real thing—even if the words used are the same ones that populate our clichés.

I interviewed over ninety former rowers, coaches, and administrators—only about five percent of the number of those involved in Cougar Crew since 1970. I took pieces of their various stories, along with parts of newspaper accounts and other written sources, and assembled them into a patchwork that began to make coherent sense. The resulting narrative, whether you call it an argument or a story, is not objective *truth* but rather my perspective, informed by the questions I asked and the sources I consulted. Some will disagree with my interpretations, but I hope my narrative is representative enough that every former rower will see their own experiences reflected in these pages.

That might be more difficult in the sections that chronicle the gold medal exploits of Kris (aka Kristi) Norelius and Paul Enquist. But even their stories reflect the shared spirit of Cougar Crew—arguably Paul's more than Kristi's, since he graduated from WSU while she rowed for her first two years at WSU before rowing for and graduating from the University of Washington (UW). Even so, after interviewing Kris Norelius, I believe that Cougar Crew has every right to claim her as one of their own, and her story, like Paul Enquist's, deserves more attention than I was able to give it here. I am sensitive to the optics of writing an entire chapter on the male gold medalist while dedicating only a section to the female gold medalist, but Norelius's full Olympic journey from WSU to UW and then to the Olympic podium is beyond the scope of this book.

I am not a dispassionate scholar of this history. I have a personal stake in Cougar Crew. A skinny seventeen-year-old distance runner from the suburbs of Seattle, I arrived in Pullman in fall 1984 seeking a community of kindred spirits. I might have found my people in a fraternity, student government, or intramural sports. Instead, like so many others, I found them on the grass in front of Bohler Gymnasium, where the WSU rowing club had placed two ergometers—rowing machines—as a means of recruiting lonely prospects such as myself. Two seasoned rowers, shirtless and lean, pulled so powerfully on the machines that it seemed the flywheels might lift off into the ether. Their motion, from their initial leg drive through the finish of each stroke, appeared effortless. I stood mesmerized amidst a small crowd of tanned, chiseled oarsmen clad in the Lycra tights that were de rigueur for endurance athletes in the 1980s. I had found my people. That Saturday, I squeezed myself into an old Chevy van captained by a towering figure called Coach Struckmeyer, traveled nearly thirty miles through the wheat fields, and entered into an alternate reality of sun, wind, river, and bluffs that served as the anchor of my daily routine for the next four years. As a history major, I should have joined the History Club, and probably would have, had I not been spending three hours every afternoon in a distant river canyon sitting backward in a long, narrow rowing vessel with eight teammates, pulling an oar through the water as the evening sun disappeared behind the Snake River breaks.

I was one of two lightweights to make the first frosh boat that year, which was coached by a laconic, tobacco-chewing rowing legend called Kash Van Cleef, whom we regarded with reverence. We took our lumps but also walked away with victories over the University of Southern California (USC) and San Diego State University (SDSU) at the West Coast Conference Rowing Championships in Sacramento. I was hooked.

The next year, I found myself rowing two seat on the varsity lightweight crew that beat UW—a perennial rowing powerhouse—and won the Pac-10 Conference Rowing Championships, taking second on the West Coast behind the SDSU crew that itself finished second to Princeton University in the national championships later that year. My senior year, I stroked the lightweight eight that raced in Istanbul, Turkey, on the Golden Horn. Despite these achievements, there was no sport at WSU that earned less notoriety than rowing. We were an underfunded club sport that most people didn't even know existed. "WSU has a rowing team? Where do you row—in the wheat fields?"

Today, many more people know about Cougar Crew, not just in Pullman but across the nation. It is one of the strongest college rowing clubs in the country and has been for decades. It is the only "varsity sport club" on the WSU campus, a status that acknowledges not only its size and success but the degree of commitment from its members, who are driven to compete at the highest levels, even against university-funded athletic programs. But it is still a club, meaning that the students govern themselves through their elected officers and pay their own way through fundraising and by forging strong connections with their loyal alumni base. The fact that Cougar Crew is a club means that securing funding and managing the fortunes of the team is tenuous and difficult, but most members of the club would not have it any other way. As former rower and club adviser Roger Crawford said in 2000, "I don't view our club status as a detriment: the team creates its own destiny, just as it did when we were rowing. The viability of the team during its years of formation and early growth was a function of what we did as athletes and officers, and that is still the case."[6]

Most former WSU rowers see their participation in Cougar Crew as the most transformative element of their education, if not their lives. That is why this project is not simply a history of a club—it is a meditation on the value of amateur athletics, on the capacity of endurance and physical hardship to change lives, and on the enduring value of building community through shared sacrifice. It is a story of struggle, adversity, and grit. It is a classic WSU story, chronicling a team that cultivated an identity as poor underdogs and outsiders but whose ambitions were not limited by paltry resources or their own lack of experience. It is a story that illuminates the best traditions of club sports—the epitome of amateur athletics—showing that the voluntary pursuit of excellence through hard work, absent financial rewards or notoriety, is perhaps the most enduring value of a well-rounded education.

Rich Ray (1976–80)

For me, rowing was this island of social and mental stability that made it possible to navigate the crisis I was having in my academic life.... Ken and Marj Struckmeyer and the crew gave me a reason to figure out an alternative route and to stay [in school], and I really owe them a lot.

I totally disagree with the "winning is the only thing" approach to sports. I just don't see very much value in it. The value for me is the cohesive social bonds that people make when they're trying to do something together that's really difficult and really challenging and doesn't pay anything. It's almost impossible to verbalize that kind of thing while you're going through it. Certainly the challenge of beating the UW is a huge one, and I totally understand why people get so worked up about it; but for me, winning will never be the important focus for building this crew, because I want the maximum number of people to have the opportunity to experience what I did. Some of them will obviously be Paul Enquists and Kristi Noreliuses, but most of us are kind of average. It doesn't mean we shouldn't have the opportunity to row, because it's a terrific opportunity and it shouldn't be reserved for elite athletes.

Mike Klier (1971–75)

If meaning can be found only on the podium, most of those who row are destined for perpetual meaninglessness. Bringing meaning to rowing is then, in fact, what most oarsmen must do, even the bulk of those who crew at the universities that dominate the sport. It is no surprise that people leave it moved in subtle and profound ways, carrying with them a nagging, unshakable, troubling sense that something vital has come, and gone.

CHAPTER ONE

"Best Crew by a Dam Site!" 1970–1973

Nobody in their right mind would do what we did. There was no running water there. There was no toilet there. No electricity. We drove down in beat-up old cars. Sometimes we had to pay for our own gas. We had improper clothing. We didn't know anything. Everything came out of our own pocket. It was forty-five minutes one way just to get to the water. So it was a huge commitment of time. Sleep deprived because you're going to class. It's crazy. Who would do that? I know for myself, I wanted to be a part of something.

—Mike Klier (1971–75)

It takes a strong back and a weak mind to sit on your ass and go backward.

—Bob Orr, Cougar Crew head coach, 1971–73

The founding of a rowing team at Washington State University (WSU) was so improbable, so unforeseen, that Rick Coffman, sportswriter for the *Daily Evergreen*, used it as a punch line in his January 1969 sports column, "Jock It to 'Em." Coffman's column that week was a tongue-in-cheek satire prophesizing the "top events" in sports for 1969, each one more outrageous than the last. He predicted, for instance, that the Baltimore Colts would beat the New York Jets 73–0 in the Super Bowl and that Joe Namath's flight back to New York would be hijacked to Havana, where he would "try to explain to Fidel Castro the advantages of shaving one's beard off with the new Schick razor." After forecasting that the Los Angeles Lakers would trade Wilt Chamberlin to a professional team in Newfoundland, the jocular student journalist made a prediction that he supposed was just as unlikely: On April 30, 1969, "WSU's first crew team was launched today following approval by the Pacific-8. Coach Ernie Kegel states that the workouts through the Palouse wheat fields are progressing nicely but 'you should see those guys go when they hit the water.'"[1]

To Coffman and his readers, the prospect of a rowing team at WSU was a lark, just as funny and improbable as WSU's skinny, long-distance running phenom, Gerry Lindgren, being drafted by the Buffalo Bills—his next prediction. After all, where would a WSU crew row? The wheat fields, har har? That Coffman could use the prospect of a rowing team in the Palouse as fodder for his send-up revealed just how improbable the founding of Cougar Crew really was.

In fact, a rowing team was not created at WSU in 1969. As one would expect from an over-the-top student satire, none of Coffman's outrageous predictions came true in 1969. Indeed, none of them ever came to fruition, except for one—and it happened the very next year. On November 12, 1970, sixty-three foolhardy students and three advisers met in the Compton Union Building (CUB) at seven that evening to establish a rowing club, despite the fact that WSU had no lakes or navigable rivers close to campus, no facilities to accommodate such a team, and no funding to make it happen. Inexplicably, its members' sole mission was to pile into an old Volkswagen van (and any other available vehicles) and wind their way through twenty-six miles of narrow farm roads—including ten miles of unpaved gravel—to the magnificent but unpredictable Snake River with the hope of "sitting on their asses and going backward" in long, narrow boats. Even more improbably, that student club rapidly grew to become one of the largest, most active student clubs in the history of the university.[2]

There were no great impersonal forces pushing for the birth of rowing at WSU in 1970. In fact, the tides of the time pushed against it. Athletic budgets were down. WSU's athletic department did not have the resources or the desire to take on a new sports team, especially one as costly as rowing. WSU's football team was in a demoralizing slump, and the athletic department, according to one snarky *Daily Evergreen* reporter, had a reputation as the "armpit of the Pac-8."[3] Meanwhile, the nation was mired in the Vietnam conflict; student protests escalated on university campuses nationwide, including WSU's. In May 1970, news of U.S. bombing raids on Cambodia touched off another wave of dissent on college campuses, culminating in the tragedy at Kent State University, when National Guard troops killed four unarmed protesters.

The WSU Rowing Club emerged at a time when young men had to consider the future very carefully. The new club transported its racing shells to its new shell house on October 22, 1971, the same day the *Daily Evergreen* reported a meeting in the CUB Auditorium of the WSU Draft Advisory Board, where its chairman, Reverend John Butler, provided young men at the university with alternatives to Vietnam.[4] When the WSU Rowing Club rowed its first race in April 1972, President Nixon was ordering the mining of North Vietnamese ports and the bombing of Cambodia in an attempt to force North Vietnam to the bargaining table. At the same time, the Citizens Mobilization Committee to End the War, an antiwar group at WSU, was demanding that food services in the CUB boycott Wonder Bread because the company that manufactured it was promoting "mechanized warfare" in Vietnam with its production of sensor devices for the U.S. Air Force.

In May 1972, WSU rowed against UW for the very first time, while Arab hijackers seized a Belgian airliner in Tel Aviv, congressmen called for Nixon's impeachment over his escalation of the Vietnam conflict, and WSU antiwar students occupied the CUB in protest.[5]

Within this crucible of national crisis, a little-known band of student volunteers created a rowing club with no money, no facilities, no coach, no tradition, no experienced prep school rowers, and no support from WSU's athletic department. While few people were paying attention, the fledgling WSU Rowing Club, with the support of a few sympathetic administrators and volunteer coaches, built a program that would have remarkable durability, growth, and success. Their do-it-yourself rowing club, which turned no one away, would shape the education of thousands of WSU students over the next half century.

Improbable Origins

It is hard to create anything from scratch, but founding a new student club at a university comes with unique challenges: bureaucracy, student apathy, time constraints, competition from other clubs, finances, and a shortage of eager faculty and staff advisers. These challenges exist for clubs dedicated to watching sci-fi movies or making homecoming banners; but imagine a student club that seeks to build a boathouse thirty miles from campus, populate it with fragile, sixty-foot-long racing shells, and send those delicate vessels—crewed by headstrong young men who have never rowed a stroke in their lives—out on the unpredictable currents of the Snake River. This is precisely what junior engineering student Rich Stager proposed to do in 1970.

Having watched competitive rowing on television during the 1968 Summer Olympics, Stager was intrigued. He had never rowed before, but there was something about the sport that called to him—perhaps the angles and mechanics of rowing appealed to his analytical mind. His father worked at the Lower Granite Dam construction site on the Snake River, so Stager at least knew there was a body of water in the general vicinity of Pullman. By fall 1970, he was determined to start a rowing club at WSU, though he didn't know if anyone else would be interested.

Stager began by posting notices across campus for an organizational meeting.[6] He then informed the *Daily Evergreen* of his intentions, calmly acknowledging "the problems involved in an undertaking of this nature" but professing his confidence that the Snake River was a "possible place" to row and all other problems could be solved if there was enough interest.[7] The first meeting far exceeded Stager's expectations. He knew that only twelve people had showed up at the first meeting to establish a rowing club at the University of Oregon, but his meeting had attracted sixty-three students and three possible advisers—all of them, like Stager, undaunted by the fact that WSU did not have a rowing program and that starting one would be risky, costly, and logistically problematic. He was ecstatic. The attendees founded the Washington State University Rowing Club. Deciding they would worry about such particulars as obtaining boats and oars later, they formed a committee tasked with writing a constitution and scheduled a second meeting.[8] And so it began.

There was no student at WSU better situated to create the WSU Rowing Club and make it a reality than the tall, rangy, fair-haired Rich Stager. A civil engineering student and a problem solver fascinated with overcoming obstacles, he was an analytical young man who moved purpose-driven through the world, his hair carefully parted to one side and a pocket protector in his shirt containing a notebook and mechanical pencil. Stager could be seen walking around campus with a slide rule, his mind contemplating the next problem to solve. He was less interested in the athletic side of rowing than, as Mike Klier—coxswain of WSU's first varsity eight—recalled, the "logistics, programmatics, engineering, and organization associated with rowing."[9]

Stager became the prime organizer of the student work parties that built the first shell house on weekends. Every week, he contacted club members to arrange travel to the Snake River. He also obtained each student's meal ticket number so that he could order sack lunches from the dining halls to send with them to the river.[10] This was Stager's great strength—organizing students and materials to complete a project—and the current project involved planning and building a facility to house those delicate sixty-foot shells.

It was helpful, to say the least, that the founder of Cougar Crew was an engineering student and a problem solver, but the serendipity did not end there. Dave Pratt, one of WSU's engineering professors, had rowed at the UW in the 1950s and coached rowing at the U.S. Naval Academy for six seasons in the late 1950s and early 1960s, even guiding the Navy freshmen to a national championship in 1963.[11] Pratt had no intention of becoming head coach or even the primary adviser of the rowing club at WSU—he was an ambitious professor whose plans did not include spending his career in Pullman—but he brought important connections to the table. For one, he was close friends with Dick Erickson, UW's head rowing coach.[12] This friendship proved invaluable, as Erickson willingly donated cast-off rowing shells to the WSU start-up program in those first years.

Even more importantly, by 1970, Pratt had become an assistant dean, and he used his position to promote rowing from within WSU's Voiland College of Engineering and Architecture. He convinced Dave Scott, chair of the Architectural Engineering Department, that senior architecture students should design the first shell house.[13] When the shell house was built, Pratt encouraged his engineering colleagues, among them Professor Jack Kimbrell, to spread the word among their students that the rowing club was looking for eager volunteers, especially tall ones. This proved crucial in recruiting key members of WSU's first varsity crews. Mike Kimbrell—Jack Kimbrell's son—and Steve Porter were both engineering students, as was Paul Enquist, a freshman mechanical engineering student in the fall of 1973 who went on to win an Olympic gold medal in rowing. He first learned of the rowing club when his engineering professor wrote "Crew" on the chalkboard during the first day of class. In so many ways, the engineering school informally sponsored the rowing club, especially during the construction phase of that first year.

Dave Pratt also contributed another crucial connection: he had rowed at UW not only with Dick Erickson but also with Ken Abbey, WSU's assistant vice president of business and finance. While Pratt did not have time to be a full-time adviser for the fledging crew, Abbey became fully committed to building the WSU program, even though he was skeptical at the outset. When he first heard of Stager's ambitions, he thought the idea was "nuts." Abbey warned Stager, "There are lots of good reasons why you can't have a crew at WSU, and the main one is it's in the middle of a bunch of wheat fields."[14] But neither Abbey nor Pratt could resist Stager's enthusiasm. They both attended Stager's organizational meeting in the CUB, where Stager learned that Abbey had started the crew club at the University of Oregon. The pieces were falling into place. It seemed to Dave Pratt that "old oarsmen" were appearing "as if by magic from the woodwork" to help establish WSU's rowing club.[15]

Ken Abbey, a bespectacled chain-smoker who wore white dress shirts and polyester slacks, looked every bit the backroom bureaucrat from the early 1970s. He liked to say that WSU had "lots of little pockets of money for very specific purposes, and I know where they all are!"[16] From his position in WSU's Office of Business Affairs, Abbey became the binding force behind WSU rowing, even while generations of rowers had no idea of the role he played behind the scenes. Abbey, in Mike Klier's words, kept "everything going, getting the money, shaping the whole thing, cutting some red tape, and none of us knew it."[17] Indeed, Abbey's experience founding the rowing team at Oregon gave him an understanding of the obstacles they faced, and his connections in the French Administration Building allowed him to help other university officials see the benefits of supporting a rowing program at WSU.[18] It was no small thing to ask a university administration to allow students to take on such a risky project. A prudent administrator might nip such reckless plans in the bud, but Abbey championed rowing from the inside, smoothing the bureaucratic path, and, just as importantly, he located financing for the cash-strapped club.

Connections inside the French Administration Building, however, could only take them so far—perhaps to the rolling wheat fields at the edge of campus. Once the club reached the Snake River Canyon, there was a different bureaucratic institution calling the shots: the U.S. Army Corps of Engineers. By 1970, the Corps was pushing to complete the last, and most upstream, of four giant dams on the lower Snake River that Congress had authorized in 1945.[19] When completed, the dams would provide hydroelectric power to the Pacific Northwest but, more importantly, they would allow large barges and tugs to navigate the Snake River all the way inland to Lewiston, Idaho, so that wheat farmers in the Palouse could ship their harvest to distant points around the globe. Those dams, by transforming the wild-flowing Snake into a series of slack-water reservoirs, would also enable a rowing team to safely navigate the river. The completion of the Little Goose Dam in 1970 created Lake Bryan, which was pronounced to be "rowable water" by Bob Orr, Cougar Crew's aptly named first head coach.[20]

To take advantage of Lake Bryan, Stager's band of "potential oarsmen," as Dave Pratt called them, would need to build a shell house on the Snake River. That required the Corps' assistance or, at the very least, a piece of government property. Amazingly, they obtained both, thanks again to Rich Stager, whose fortuitous connections made everything possible. Because Stager's father was managing the building of the Lower Granite Dam just above Boyer Park, where they wanted to erect the first shell house, Ken Abbey reached out to him on behalf of WSU's administration. Remarkably, the Corps not only allowed the rowing club to erect its boathouse on federal property, it donated materials—and poured the concrete slab—for the structure itself, which WSU architecture students designed and WSU Rowing Club members began building in spring 1971.[21]

It was the kind of arrangement that seems inconceivable today: students and professors from various departments, university administrators, and federal agencies all working in unison toward a common goal and with extraordinary speed. Every weekend throughout the winter and spring of 1971, teams of students armed with hammers and sack lunches rattled their way down to the Snake River Canyon to build the boathouse from the ground up. Dave Emigh, a junior from Walla Walla, remembered that they would work all morning "until the noon Lower Granite Dam whistle sounded time to eat those delicious sack lunches."[22]

Many of the student volunteers who built that first shell house would never sit in a boat or pull an oar through the water. Some were seniors who had no hope of rowing, while others "were friends who just wanted to get out of Pullman and do something different on a Saturday."[23] Emigh and Jim Verellen remained on the team and reaped the benefits of their own labor when the club began rowing late in 1971. But even for those two, their labor was an act of faith—they had never rowed before and were dedicating themselves to a sport they had yet to experience. Bob Orr, who later became their coach, was amazed: "They'd never rowed a stroke in their lives. But they built their boathouse. And they built their dock. It took a good year before we got boats and put them in the water. They did the whole thing on faith."[24]

With the shell house under construction, the next step was finding boats to fill it. Abbey and Pratt turned to their old friend and former teammate Dick Erickson. As head rowing coach at the University of Washington, Erickson had no reason to be generous to the start-up program. After all,

Rich Stager organized weekend work crews to build the shell house at Boyer, such as this one, assembling in front of Neill Hall and preparing to leave campus in February 1971. From left to right: Tom Ardell, Ken Fielder, Gary Hubbard, Paul Kennedy, and Russ Rome. Photo Credit: Rich Stager.

WSU was UW's archrival in every other sport. Why help? But Erickson was unique. Even though he was at the helm of arguably the greatest rowing program in the nation, he wasn't interested in monopolizing rowing in the Pacific Northwest. In fact, he was more interested in promoting *college* rowing than *UW* rowing. He was eager and willing to use UW's considerable resources to nurture programs throughout the region, and this was to Cougar Crew's great benefit in those first years. While later rowers at WSU often saw UW as a privileged powerhouse—a rival team with lots of money and towering athletes—UW under Erickson was anything but an evil empire. He became one of WSU's patrons from the very beginning, even coming to Pullman to speak to the first club members in February 1971.[25] Erickson pledged to give WSU two eight-man shells—the *101* and the *Winlock W. Miller*.[26] The boats were a little tired, but they floated and even kept out most of the water. Now all the young club needed was a coach—and he walked through Ken Abbey's office door in the fall of 1971.

Orr's Men

Bob Orr—like Ken Abbey and Dave Pratt—was a former Husky oarsman. His father had rowed at UW in the 1920s, and Orr himself had rowed for famed coach Al Ulbrickson in the late 1950s. After his undergraduate work, Orr was drafted into the military. Starting out as a private in the rear ranks, he then attended officer training school, after which he became a first lieutenant paratrooper infantry platoon leader. Becoming a paratrooper "was a stupid thing for me to do," he later said. The Vietnam War was just ramping up; Orr knew that if he stayed on he would find himself fighting in Southeast Asia. When his tour ended, he turned down an appealing invitation to extend his service with a transfer to the Third U.S. Infantry, known as the "Old Guard," which is the army's official ceremonial unit and escort to the president, where "you march all the parades and escort beautiful young ladies to various events." Instead, he went back to graduate school. In fall 1971, he took a sabbatical from teaching public school in Auburn to attend WSU and earn his PhD in education. When he heard about the start-up rowing program, he wrote to Ken Abbey, "I'm coming over, and I'd like to be involved." Arriving on campus in August, he walked into Abbey's office and said, "Here I am. I'd be happy to help." "Ok," Abbey responded. "You're the coach."[27]

The start-up program could not have found a better first coach than Bob Orr. His Washington rowing pedigree gave him legitimacy while his military career and teaching background gave him an aura of authority. He was hyper-organized, which allowed him to work on his thesis, attend his courses, and manage the crew. The latter included recruiting athletes, designing workouts, and repairing the well-worn equipment that WSU had inherited from UW. His discipline and competence earned him the confidence of his young oarsmen.

The man, the myth. Bob Orr, Cougar Crew's first head coach, poses, stopwatch in hand, for his friend and fellow WSU graduate student, Len Mills. Mills took beautiful, professional-quality photographs for the crew in 1972 and 1973 that often appeared in the *Evergreen* and *Chinook*. Photo Credit: Len Mills.

"Everybody really liked him because they could see that he knew what the heck he was doing and they trusted him a lot," remembered Len Mills, a good friend of Orr's who was attending WSU graduate school at the same time and became the team's unofficial photographer.[28] More than that, Orr had chutzpah and a theatrical nature that endeared him to his rowers. He would walk to the edge of the dock at the beginning of practice and declare, "Rowable Water!" no matter how poor the conditions, and his faithful oarsmen would, in the words of Bob Appleyard, "dutifully get into boats and row out on the river and get swamped."[29] He always had a quip, and he always looked for ways to "motivate and inspire and encourage" the rowers in his unique, charismatic, and amusingly caustic way.[30]

As he assessed his novice crew that fall, Orr could be forgiven if he had second thoughts. Only seven of the nineteen original club members had returned. Those who did—Rich Stager, Dave Emigh, Jim Verellen, Dave Atherton, Paul Kennedy, Gary Hubbard, and Bill Raisner—had yet to pull an oar. They were joined by new recruits Bob Appleyard, Jim Rudd, Mike Klier, Steve Rowlett, Bruce Warninger, Walt Cowart, Doug Kee, and a couple dozen others who had seen a sign posted or been cajoled into attending the fall organizational meeting by a dorm mate. Most had never seen rowing before, even on television.

Bob Appleyard remembered them as an unruly bunch—a wild mix of personalities. Many of them had played sports in high school, but, according to Appleyard, "this was not your collection of star jock athletes."[31] Some, like Stager, were more interested in solving engineering problems than rowing. Others, such as Dave Emigh, had never participated in high school athletics—earning his Eagle Scout badge had kept him too busy. But Emigh, like the others who showed up in 1971, had a fiercely competitive personality. He was the kind of Boy Scout who trained for hiking so that he could beat everyone else to camp on the first night of the annual backpacking trip. He didn't have the dexterity for baseball or basketball, but he was a kid who liked to bicycle on the edge of his anaerobic threshold until he felt the burn in his thighs.[32] Rudd, Appleyard, and Verellen had been serviceable high school athletes, but they were all looking to participate at the college level. "It was a real mix of personalities, but the binding force," Appleyard recalled, was that everyone "just liked being out in the elements doing hard physical work."[33]

Orr's Men: His crew gives Bob Orr their rapt attention before they take to the water. It is safe to say that Coach Orr garnered the full respect of his young charges. From left to right: Jim Rudd, Bruce Warninger, Doug Kee (in back), unidentified, unidentified, Glade Austin. Photo Credit: Len Mills.

It was a good thing they loved working hard in the elements because those first rows in early December 1971 primarily involved working very hard, getting very wet and cold, and going nowhere fast. Unlike established programs, they did not have the advantage of a rowing barge, tank, or simulator, where you could teach novices how to row in stable conditions. There were no VCRs or Internet available for showing the young rowers instructional videos. They didn't even have the advantage of upperclassmen to demonstrate how it was supposed to look. Bob Orr remembered his first time rowing at UW: the varsity oarsmen lifted their boat out of the shell house, slapped it in the water, put their oars in, and rowed away while Orr and his fellow freshman looked on in awe, thinking, "Man, that was really cool. I want to do that!" But this was different—no one on the WSU team had ever pulled a stroke. "Heart in hands," they gingerly carried the *Winlock W. Miller* out of the boathouse. Orr and Pratt fixed the boot stretchers and showed the young men how to feather an oar blade. Then, very carefully, they christened the shell in the waters of the Snake, pushing eight novice oarsmen out into the fast-running current.[34]

During that first practice and the ones that followed, the team mostly rowed by pairs and fours, allowing the idle rowers to sit with their oars on the water and stabilize the boat. It was an exercise, as Mike Klier remembered, of "lurch and jerk."[35] Jim Rudd called it "splashing and thrashing." Rowing well is hard work in the best circumstances, but "when you're rowing poorly, it's twice as much work as when you are rowing well." Rudd remembered practice after practice spent pursuing the possibility that they might put ten strokes together in perfect unison.[36] It was a hard slog. The boats were weathered and leaky, but more water was coming over the gunwales from the splashing of oar blades.

In the first week of December, Dave Emigh remembers lifting the boat from the river and, as the water cascaded over their heads and down their backs and legs, their shoes beginning to freeze to the dock.[37] It was late in the year to be rowing on the Snake, but they hadn't gotten on the water until after Thanksgiving, and Orr hoped that this taste of real rowing—even in poor conditions—would carry them through the drudgery of winter training. It worked; his rowers left for winter break enthusiastic to keep in shape and return in the spring for WSU's first ever rowing season.

Then disaster struck. In early January 1972, a seventy-mile-an-hour gale ripped up the Snake River Canyon, collapsing the boathouse and demolishing everything inside—and nearly the program itself. Ken Struckmeyer, then assistant coach, lamented later that the crew had "lost two shells worth $9,000, a couple of oars, and our pride."[38] The situation was grim. Bob Orr and Walt Cowart surveyed the damage the next day with an *Evergreen* photographer in tow. The image on the front page of the *Evergreen* captured the desolation of the moment—both men stood, hands in pockets, in front of a torn fragment of racing shell that lay on the ground, dismembered, underneath fallen roof shingles.[39] Both sixty-foot shells and Orr's cedar single were destroyed. Nothing was insured. In the photo, Cowart is looking at Orr as if to say, "What now?" Orr, wearing a dark pea coat and a serious look, seems to be already pondering his next move.

This might have been the time to call it quits. The young club now had no money and no boats. Again. One violent windstorm had erased a year's worth of organization and effort. How long would it take to put the pieces back together? Certainly, the season could not be salvaged. "That's too bad," thought Bob Appleyard when he saw the story about the decimated boathouse in the *Evergreen*. "I kind of liked doing that crew thing."

When Appleyard and other crew members attended a club meeting after the disaster, many of them expected simply to be told that the season was lost. "I was figuring, this is all done."[40] What they heard was just the opposite: Orr stood up and told his men that they would be rebuilding immediately. Plans were already underway. Rich Stager's father and his Lower Granite Dam construction crew had pledged materials and labor to rebuild the fallen structure. Also, Orr and Stager contrived to display the smashed shells on campus and sell buttons, using the disaster as a fundraiser.[41] Finally, Abbey, Pratt, and Orr were on the telephone with Dick Erickson, who was pledging three more UW boats so the Cougars could get back on the water.[42] Among the shells Erickson sent was the *Loyal Shoudy*, a storied vessel that broke the course record on the Montlake Cut when it was christened in 1940 and in which UW later rowed to a national championship. Three decades later, it was headed to the Palouse.[43]

Everyone did their part in the undaunted collective effort. Erickson sent boats. The team fundraised and kept training. The Army Corps of Engineers came with materials and men. Orr and his rowers expected to rebuild the boathouse themselves, but an old, grizzled construction foreman told the team, "You boys are pretty long on theory but short on practical experience. We're going to frame this thing so that it will never fall down."[44] And they did. By late March, Rich Stager reported that "the shell house has been completely rebuilt and is reinforced more than before the storm."[45]

It was a triumph of the spirit that WSU rowing had a season at all in 1972. It began with Class Day, a tradition that Orr had brought from UW. During a week where the *Daily Evergreen* ran headlines that proclaimed, "McGovern Predicts Victory," "Anti-War Activity to Be Continued," and "Hot Pants Will Be Judged" (not, apparently, on a moral basis but contested on "appearance and originality"), the newspaper also carried news of Cougar Crew's first rowing race in team history, which pitted a junior/senior boat against the freshmen/sophomores.[46] On Saturday, April 22, 1972, around 150 spectators stood on the banks of the Snake River to watch as the upperclassmen "jumped off to a fast start and rowed to an easy 4 1/2-length win" over the frosh/sophomore boat, which was "never able to overcome the initial advantage lost at the start of the race."[47]

The fledgling team had completed its first race, but they still hadn't seen anyone row besides themselves. That happened the very next weekend when they traveled to Corvallis to race against seventeen West Coast crews in their first ever intercollegiate regatta. It was exciting but intimidating. The young crew was perhaps "exceeding their capabilities by having the gall to participate in a competition after being on the water for all but a few weeks," remembered Mike Klier. "We didn't know anything. We could spell regatta, maybe. Other than that, we were completely ignorant."[48] On Wednesday night, the club had its weekly meeting in Cleveland Hall. They talked about the logistics of the upcoming weekend—whose cars they would drive, where they would stay, the schedule for the large two-day event. Then they spent the remainder of the meeting watching crew races on an old projector.[49] As they watched, they wondered to themselves, were they ready?

Ready or not, the Cougars lined up on the Willamette River for the first heat of the Lightweight coxed four (four rowers and a coxswain) on Friday evening, April 28, 1972—the first time a WSU boat raced against other college crews. They were in lane three. Santa Clara University was in lane one. UC Santa Barbara had lane two. The starter's gun went up: "Are you ready? Ready all, row!" And off they went in a clamor of spray and noise, as the coxswains hollered their commands and pounded the gunwales. Just that week, Bob Orr had, for the first time, told his rowers to take their blades off the water during the recovery. This meant the boat would be less stable—keeping their oars on the water helped the shell maintain an even keel—but the drag of the blades slowed the boat down. It was like rowing with training wheels—safe, stable, and slow. With his order to take the training wheels off, the shell felt unsteady and dangerous, but also sleek and smooth. It glided through the water on the recovery. It was like flying. They had never felt anything like it. Bob Appleyard remembered thinking, "We're really hot stuff here." But that was in an eight-man shell, which was much steadier than the smaller, tipsy four-oared shell they were rowing now.

When they seated themselves in that borrowed four and pushed out onto the Willamette, they immediately felt wobbly and decided, "Blades stay on the water!" Now, even in the race, they dragged their blades on the water because they were afraid of tipping over. But amid the chaos and splashing, something remarkable was happening. Appleyard and his teammates could see the other two boats slipping farther behind. They kept dragging and pulling until, finally, they had covered the 2,000-meter course. It was only a heat, but somehow, they were the first boat to cross the finish line. They were elated and surprised. Appleyard had absolutely no idea how the other crews "could have been worse than us, but we actually won it!"[50]

The rest of the regatta was more predictable. In the finals the next day, the lightweight four managed to defeat the University of Oregon (Oregon) but lost to three other crews. The Cougar heavyweight eight competed in the novice race and was soundly defeated by crews from Oregon State University (OSU) and Pacific Lutheran University (PLU). When the scores were totaled up, WSU finished thirteenth out of seventeen crews, behind the likes of Holy Names High School of Oakland, which scored fifty points to WSU's eight, but ahead of the Portland Rowing Club, PLU, University of Puget Sound (UPS), and Mills—a women's college.[51] Dave Emigh joked that, despite their performance, they were nonetheless the "best crew by a dam site!"

Two weeks later, they were in Seattle racing mighty UW and other Northwest crews in the Steward's Cup. They finished fifth out of five in each of the three races they entered. The snide sportswriter for the *Seattle Post-Intelligencer* joked, "The Cougars of the Palouse, making their debut in rowing circles here," showed remarkable consistency. "They were last on each occasion." The writer particularly relished sending up the Cougar frosh four that was so far back it "should have been equipped with running lights." He estimated they came in twenty-seven lengths behind the winning UW boat, finishing "while the other boats were returning to the beach." Even more dispiriting, the WSU four was nearly swamped by the officials' launch as it followed the lead boats. "It's easy to sympathize with the Cougars," the reporter quipped. "The least they could have done was disqualify the launch."[52]

Despite the demoralizing losses, simply having fielded a crew in 1972 was a victory. Even so, Bob Orr and his young club had far greater designs for the 1972–73 school year. Some of his rowers did not return, including Rich Stager, who focused instead on finishing his civil engineering degree and maintaining his perfect 4.0 GPA. "Once he got boats on the water and organized the crew," Mike Klier remembered, Stager "had satisfied what he wanted to accomplish." But the ones who did return—such as Klier, Rudd, Verellen, and Emigh—were even more hungry to compete, and they were joined by some promising new recruits, including Steve Rowlett and Eric Anderson, who were accomplished high school athletes. Another freshman,

Jim Austin, had even rowed before. Growing up on Mercer Island, Austin was already familiar with UW rowing. The summer he became a high school senior, a UW oarsman had commandeered an eight-man shell, which he stored on Mercer Island all summer so he could give rowing lessons to the local kids. Austin spent his summer afternoons learning how to row from a Husky oarsman. When Bob Orr found out, he moved Austin into the stroke seat, which he occupied until his senior year.[53]

The young crew's rising hopes were partially validated in fall 1972 when the team visited Seattle for the Head of the Lake Regatta, a three-mile timed interval against UW and other Northwest programs. Rowing in the junior varsity event—since they were still a start-up program—the Cougars officially finished seventh in a fifteen-boat field, but they later learned that an error had added an extra minute to their time, meaning that they had actually finished third behind UW and UPS.[54] This promising showing propelled them into an ambitious winter conditioning schedule that was Rocky-esque. Clad in their baggy gray sweat suits, Orr had his men running "seven to eight miles at a crack" on "Pig Road" toward the Pullman Airport, lifting weights, and sprinting up "25 flights of stairs in Martin Stadium."[55] Sometimes their regimen included carrying a teammate piggyback as they climbed the twelve flights of the Physical Sciences Building.[56] Orr even had them "pushing cars."[57]

Winter training included pounding the steps at Martin Stadium as well as lifting weights and running on "Pig Road." Pictured here in the winter before the 1973 racing season are Eric Anderson, front, and Steve Rowlett. Photo Credit: Len Mills.

Solemn faces as the varsity heavyweight eight prepares to launch from the Husky boat-house for the Head of the Lake regatta in November 1972, only the second time WSU raced beyond Almota. They are wearing the second style of WSU racing jerseys, with distinctive stripes. Bow to cox: Doug Kee, Rick Mosloff, John Reynolds, Brent Youlden, Dave Emigh, Eric Anderson, unidentified, Steve Rowlett, coxswain Craig Illman (feet shown). Photo Credit: Len Mills.

Back on the water in February 1973, Orr kept the pressure on, sending his men on twelve-mile rows punctuated with shorter pieces at race pace. He was a harsh taskmaster, and he gave his orders with a devilish glint in his eye while chuckling to himself. Standing in his launch, he exhorted his rowers, "Pop that catch," instilling in them the same "Conibear stroke" that he had learned at UW. In 1973, the Cougars would not be kidding around. Orr had scheduled an ambitious spring season that included hosting Seattle Pacific University (SPU), PLU, and UW in Pullman, rowing against Western Washington University (WWU) in Bellingham and UW in Seattle, traveling to the Corvallis Invitational Regatta in Oregon, as well as competing in the Western Sprints Regatta in Los Gatos, California. This was, according to Orr, the "first real effort by WSU to boat competitive crews."[58] He was optimistic. In March, Orr pronounced his team "1,000 percent better when compared with last year."[59]

Then disaster struck, again—this time in the form of a surprise squall that snuck up the Snake River Canyon while Orr had his crew rowing far upstream above the Lower Granite Dam construction site. It was the Thursday of spring break, and, as would become tradition thereafter, while most WSU students decamped for home or distant vacations, rowing club members were spending their holiday on the Snake River, suffering through grueling two-a-day practices. On this morning, the sky was blue and the river calm as three boats rowed above the dam site toward Lewiston for a long paddle—they were putting in heavy miles in preparation for the racing season. They reached a lovely, sandy shore where they debarked and "enjoyed a moderate time of rest, lounging on the beach in the sun."[60] Suddenly, the temperature dropped drastically and a vicious gale swept up the canyon, catching the crew off guard.

Orr told his crew to head back toward the shell house, but already they were being swamped with two-foot whitecaps pouring over the gunwales. In the double-hulled *Titanic*, coxswain Craig Illman wisely ordered his oarsmen to row half slides and take shorter strokes into the wind. Doug McBride, also rowing in the *Titanic*, was nervous: "The boat was full of water, and oarsmen randomly took turns trying to bail it as we proceeded downriver." By this time, everyone was worried for their safety. Illman guided them to shore just short of the dam, where they emptied the boat before attempting the dangerous passage "through the bridge pilings just upriver of the dam." Illman maneuvered his crew through the pilings expertly, cautiously alternating short strokes from his bow and stern pairs while using his center four rowers for balance and ballast. When they came to the bridge, Illman had his rowers pull in their oars. As they swept past the pilings in the whirl of wind and current, McBride was "looking at the face of the dam and praying that we didn't get wind-blown too close and get sucked down by the current hitting the face of the dam."[61] Illman's crew arrived safely at the shell house, boat and rowers intact, but they were the only ones who did.

Meanwhile, upriver, as Mike Klier was guiding the *Loyal Shoudy*, he realized the situation was dire. They were taking on water and starting to sink. A seam had opened in the port side gunwale, and every time stroke seat Steve Rowlett applied pressure to his oar, water poured into the shell. Mike Kimbrell, rowing behind Rowlett in the seven seat, saw him turn around and yell, "Row hard, because we're going down!" They weren't going to make it back to the boathouse. Klier immediately pointed them toward shore. By the time they neared the steep, rocky shore, the boat was already submerged. The young men tumbled out of the shell into the cold Snake River and struggled to get the boat ashore and empty the water without smashing it to pieces.

The same fate awaited the rowers in the *Tyee*, who also found themselves swamped on the rocky beach opposite the shell house above the dam. Men in both boats double-teamed each shell and managed to get them upright and drained in time for Coach Orr to arrive in his launch and order them to row back to the boathouse. As much loyalty and fondness as they felt for their intrepid leader, whom they regarded much as Revolutionary War foot soldiers regarded George Washington, this time they were not crossing the Delaware with him. Once on dry land, no one was willingly going back into that cold, raging river. Coach Orr would have to tow them to the shell house.[62]

Orr successfully towed the *Tyee* back. Then he and Philip Irvin tied a line to one of the *Shoudy's* riggers and tried pulling the shell back to the boathouse behind the coach's launch. It might have worked had the line been fixed to the bow nose of the shell; instead, the long hull jackknifed, and Irvin watched the shell "turn perpendicular to the direction of the tow and cut through the water with all the grace and beauty of a 90-foot-wide gang plow." The *Shoudy* didn't make it. The national championship-winning shell died one month shy of its thirty-third birthday.[63] The rowers from all three boats returned to carry its dismembered corpse back to the shell house. When they had finished their funerary march, it was already half past four. Coach Orr assembled his crew, still wet and shivering from the day's disaster, and told them with his best droll delivery: "Afternoon practice is cancelled."[64]

After this latest debacle—remembered thereafter as "Black Thursday"— the crew appealed once again to Dick Erickson for more equipment. And once again, he lent material support, sending more old UW hulls to the Palouse. When the retired Erickson visited Pullman a decade later to deliver the keynote address at Class Day, Bob Appleyard had the opportunity to ask him, "Coach, we kept wrecking your boats, and you kept sending over more… what's the deal?" Erickson replied, "Well, shit, those alumni of mine kept buying me new boats, and I had to make room for them in the boathouse."[65]

The Cougars didn't miss a single race in the spring of 1973, and they didn't win a single race. They could thank Coach Erickson for every loss. More directly, they could thank him for the trouncing they received from the Huskies when UW visited Pullman in early May. After showing "definite improvement" and drawing "praise from the competition" when they visited Seattle to race the Huskies in late April, UW's visit to Boyer Park in May was, in Coach Orr's mind, "the biggest disappointment of the year." WSU crews performed poorly and "the results overwhelmingly went to Washington in both races."[66]

The WSU Rowing Club finished its 1973 season racing in the Western Sprints for the first time. This was the highlight of the Cougars' second spring of competition and, once again, Orr's crew was "plagued by bad luck." Since this was still technically its first *full* year of competition, the WSU heavyweight crew competed in the junior varsity event. In the heats, the crew rowed an inspired

The lightweight men pose on the dock at Boyer in spring 1973 for one of the first team photos in their hallmark black shirts, the third style of WSU racing livery, worn because the University of Washington wore white. Stroke to Bow from left to right: Jim Saldine, Bruce Warninger, Bob Appleyard, Walt Cowart, Doug McBride, Gary Hubbard, Mike Craft, Jim Rudd. Front: Coxswain Craig Illman. Photo Credit: Len Mills.

The first heavyweight varsity team photo at the Boyer dock. Stroke to bow from left to right: Unidentified, Mike Kimbrell, Eric Anderson, Ken Bartline, Steve Rowlett, Ron Neal, Brent Youlden, Doug Kee. Front: Coxswain Mike Klier. Photo Credit: Len Mills.

race, starting to move and trading strokes with the University of California, Berkeley (Cal Berkeley) for the lead when a lane marker drifted into their shell and, according to Orr, "effectively eliminated the boat from the race."

Coach Orr filed a protest, and Dick Erickson—coming to WSU's aid once again—encouraged race officials to allow the Cougars to compete in the junior varsity final the next day. In their first final at the Western Sprints, the Cougars fought hard. They were never out of the race and they made a play for the lead at 500 meters and again at the halfway mark. They finished seventh out of seven, but Orr believed he saw something in his heavyweight crew—they "had come of age."[67]

Conclusion

Bob Orr finished his graduate work in Pullman and headed back to Auburn in the fall of 1973. He ended his short career with the unyielding loyalty of his rowers. Before he left, he rhapsodized about his "glorious memories" of the "old crimson and gray crew" with its "gr-e-a-t spirit(s) and traditions, our handsome coaches, and our burly, bouncing oarsmen."[68] Orr spoke fondly of his rowers, like Dave "Flex" Emigh ("elected Mr. Body Beautiful"), Jim Verellen ("a man of humble origin"), Mike Klier ("talents unlimited") and the "rocking, riotous events" of a "BIG year," where they went to Western Sprints, "chloroformed the Huskies, served tea to California, and drank warm beer in our shell house."[69] Even though the Cougars had not been victorious that year, one thing was clear: they had fun.

Those first two years of Cougar Crew were filled with many disappointments for such a hypercompetitive bunch. They had wanted to win shirts from their competitors—a time-honored rowing tradition—but all they had done was give theirs away. In looking back at the 1972–73 season, Mike Kimbrell lamented that they lost every single race they rowed, heavyweight and lightweight—"That's a lot of shirts!"[70] Despite the losses, the story of what Orr and his men accomplished was as remarkable as it was improbable. The WSU Rowing Club had evolved from an idea inside the head of one engineering student to a club that was enthusiastic, growing, and developing a sense of itself as uniquely audacious and gritty.

The hardships the club faced and the adventures they had were becoming part of an emerging identity. They were a cash-starved, struggling, embattled program amid the wheat fields. If UW could, as Bob Orr liked to say, "roll out of their beds and into their rowing shells," the daily grind for WSU rowers began with the long drive to the river and ended only when they had raised

Eric Anderson (left) and Craig Illman (right) near the Husky docks in November 1972, clad in their new Cougar Crew letter jackets based on the University of Washington style. You can see Ken Struckmeyer in the background, wearing a letter jacket, and Bob Orr with his back to the camera. Photo Credit: Len Mills.

enough money to pay their debts, which was never. The fact that Cougar oarsmen were paying dearly for their torture made their sacrifices even more virtuous. They didn't win any races; but by year's end, Orr believed his team had "won quite a bit of respect."[71]

Orr's signal achievement was to give the program a set of established traditions, which he imported directly from the University of Washington—something that was often lost on future Cougar rowers. By the end of the decade, the rituals of Class Day, spring break, the annual banquet, and winter workouts were so well established that it appeared to freshman oarsmen as though they had existed for decades. Those traditions—and even the design of the letter jackets they wore—were drawn from Orr's experience at UW. The generations of WSU rowers that followed often did not realize the important role that former UW rowers—and one UW coach—played in shaping the early program.

Perhaps Bob Orr's greatest lasting accomplishment had simply been to keep them going when it might have been easier to quit. "He was never daunted by anything," remembered Bob Appleyard. "To actually put us on the water, to keep us going, that took a real force of effort." Appleyard credited Orr "with having the drive to point us all in a direction" and keep us moving toward our goals.[72] In that sense, Cougar Crew was already proving to be an education unto itself, instilling lessons that club members would carry with them throughout their lives.

The coup de grâce of the 1973 season was the first annual banquet at Boyer Park, where UW coach Dick Erickson gave the keynote address. He likened the beginnings of WSU crew to the founding of the sport at UW, Cal Berkeley, Harvard, and Yale. All those great programs started on shoestrings, just like WSU's—with a group of eager oarsmen, a couple of old boats, and "a shed to throw the darn things in." His message was clear: the WSU Rowing Club already had everything it needed to be as good as those programs. The rest was up to the rowers—how good did they want to be? "Look at what you guys have started," Erickson told the young men. "You guys come back here in fifty years and you won't believe what this has grown into."[73]

Dick Erickson speaks to the crew at their first banquet at the end of the 1973 racing season. Without Erickson's generosity and material support, Cougar Crew might never have survived those first years. Photo Credit: Len Mills.

Bob Appleyard (1971–75)

Bob Orr would come down, stand on the dock, stare out at the river, and say, "Rowable water!"...To him, it was always "rowable water." To actually put us on the water, to keep us going, that took a real force of effort on his part. I really credit him with having the drive to point us all in a direction, and we were all just a crazy bunch of guys, so we went along with it. We all looked like pictures of college kids from the early 1970s. This was not your collection of star jock athletes—we were kind of like anti-jocks getting together. It was a real mix of personalities, but the binding force was that everyone seemed to enjoy being out in the elements doing hard physical work. We would not have connected other than being in the boat together. I really doubt that we even would have known each other if it hadn't been for rowing. But everybody was competitive. We probably knew that we weren't that good, but I remember the competitiveness and wanting to go out from the very beginning and race Washington and get a shirt off a Washington rower. That was the drive, and I think that was the common bond. Everybody thought, "Yeah, let's go out and try to win a race!"

Jim Verellen (1971–73)

One of my main memories of Ken Abbey is one day during my senior year in 1973 when he came by the meeting spot where we would divide up into cars to drive down to the river. He grabbed me and had me go with him to a meeting of what was called the Recreational Budget Committee or something like that, because he was making a pitch to them for money to help us get a boat or... something. So I went in my rowing clothes, which were kind of grubby things. We sat in there—by this time we had been to a few races—and they were asking us questions like, how big are the boats? So, I'm kind of describing the boats, and I said, "Yeah, we were kind of surprised when we went to our first crew race down at Oregon State, the Oregon State Invitational, because we saw that their boats were really brown, but ours were mostly gray from duct tape." My recollection is they laughed at that, and then they asked if it would it make more sense to have a four if you're going to buy a boat instead of an eight, because then that gives you more flexibility if you don't have two full boats. I said, "Well, eights are the main competition—that's what races are—so I think we're better off with an eight. We can always row a six in it for a workout if we need to." I also remember, when we were short a coxswain one time—I think this was probably a Saturday—Ken Abbey jumped in as a substitute coxswain, wearing his full slacks and everything. You could just see he was loving it—the idea of getting back in a boat—he just couldn't contain himself.

CHAPTER TWO

The Boys in the Boat in the Wheat Fields, 1973–1979

I look forward to those days in the fall and spring when our boats pulse and glide through the water and people say, "Who won? Washington State? I didn't know they had a crew!"

—Ken Struckmeyer, Cougar Crew head coach, 1973

When Washington State University took up rowing a few years ago, there were chuckles among the traditional powers of crew racing. The Cougar oarsmen—and lately, oarswomen—had to scout out a distant practice course—a straight stretch on the crooked Snake River—and put as much mileage on rubber tires as on their seat slides.

—Georg N. Meyers, *Seattle Times*, 1979

Steve Wells grew up in Ames, Iowa, where his dad was a professor in the Communications Department at Iowa State University. He graduated high school in 1968 and went off to Grinnell College, where he dropped out after one quarter. His girlfriend at Grinnell, who later became his wife, liked to say that Steve's semester had ended in October while everyone else's went until December. He left Iowa and headed to Fairbanks, Alaska, seeking his fortune on the oil pipeline they were building. He lost his wallet with his draft card and, "like an idiot," he wrote the draft board asking for a new one. They wrote back immediately with one question: why are you in Fairbanks when our records show you're attending college in Iowa? Steve knew he had "screwed that one up," so he went to the draft recruiter and enlisted. By spring 1971, he was at Fort Lewis, Washington, waiting for embarkation orders to Vietnam, when his unit was assembled and told, "We've got bad news for you boys: we are winding down our combat role in Vietnam, so we don't need any combat troops at the moment and we're reassigning you all to Alaska or Germany." Steve spent the remainder of his tour of duty in Alaska, where he had begun.

From there it was more tramping around the American West, looking for purpose. He found it first in ski bumming and road bike racing in Salt Lake City. By then, his father, Donald Wells, had taken a job at Washington

State University, where he became chair of the Communications Department. Steve ended up in Pullman in fall 1974 and enrolled at WSU, but he was completely directionless and dropped out again. In spring 1975, he was still racing his road bike and looking for purpose when he attended a dinner party and met Vance Smith, a graduate student and former MIT lightweight who was currently helping with the rowing club. Smith planted a seed in Steve's mind—he should turn out for the crew.

That fall, Steve reenrolled at WSU, went down to the Snake River, and found his tribe. He was already an outsider—a bearded, lanky, twenty-four-year-old married student with a fierce independent streak and a penchant for wandering, or riding his bike, off the beaten path. He found a group of guys like himself who were also pushing themselves in ways that were not normal. They weren't countercultural in a political sense, but they were outsiders when measured against conventional standards. He saw them immediately as kindred spirits.

"We were all countercultural to a certain degree," he remembered, "because you're in a club sport and you're not in the main line and you're off doing weird stuff." Joining the crew gave Wells "a group and an identity." His entire social life became the rowing club and, without his new community, Wells might not have made it through college: "I'd have made another semester or two and gone, 'What the heck am I doing here?' and dropped out again." Joining the crew made it easier to "keep plugging along" with his studies. He rowed for three years, was elected club commodore for the 1977–78 year, served as an assistant coach for one year, and finished his general studies degree in 1979. For someone who didn't naturally gravitate toward academics, Wells learned a critical lesson about college retention: "You've got to find that one group that you make into your community; otherwise, college really sucks."

When Wells began rowing in fall 1975, he was taken by two things. First, although the club had only been around a handful of years, it was already a "good, solid organization" that seemed well-established. Second, he realized that the cornerstone of that stability was "the total devotion" of a young landscape architecture professor who was coaching the team on his own time and his own dime. Wells was amazed. Not only was the coach working for free, but he was also "taking money out of his own pocket to help fund it." As an older, married student who had "been around the block a few more times than the wide-eyed eighteen-year-olds," Wells understood instantly that club sports "lived or died based on whether or not they have that one person who will devote an absurd amount of time and resources to it and keep it going year after year." It was clear to Wells that for Cougar Crew that person was Ken Struckmeyer.[1]

After defeating the University of Washington in the dual on the Snake River, the 1978 heavyweight varsity crew pose with the white Husky racing shirts they just won draped over their shoulders. From the left: Bruce Giddens, Rich Ray, Kelvin Eder, Doug Engle, Chris Gulick, John Leendertsen, Steve Ranten, Steve Wells, and coxswain Al Fisher, front. Photo Credit: Dave Emigh.

Steve Wells implicitly understood that student clubs rise and fall precipitously depending on their ever-changing leadership. The most successful clubs thrive during periods when they find stable, devoted leadership, but that is hard to achieve in the university environment. Student leaders come and go. Club advisers—usually young, untenured professors—also come and go, since these unpaid positions are long on commitment and short on professional rewards.

When Bob Orr left Pullman after the 1973 rowing season, all the club needed was a new volunteer coach willing to devote countless hours to running practices, repairing equipment, organizing fundraisers, crafting a racing schedule, and managing the logistics of taking dozens of club rowers to regattas up and down the West Coast. The lucky candidate would have to use their own vehicle, spend thousands of dollars yearly on gas and maintenance, and forego numerous other professional opportunities. All this for the chance to work daily with headstrong young men who lacked attention but had an abundance of energy and half-baked ideas—the gap between what they knew and thought they knew was wider than the Snake River Canyon. No problem.

Amazingly, after a "five-minute national search," the crew club found that person in the form of Ken Struckmeyer, a Scandinavian giant whose weathered, permanently tanned face and gentle smile became synonymous with WSU rowing for generations of Cougar oarsmen. Struckmeyer had arrived on campus in August 1971, an assistant professor of landscape architecture from Wisconsin, sporting a Mark Spitz mustache. That fall he noticed a sign advertising an informational meeting for the rowing club. The young professor stood in the back, but he immediately caught the eye of Bob Orr. Struckmeyer was hard to miss. He stood six and a half feet tall and had the broad shoulders of a rower. Orr approached him eagerly. "You should row!" he said. Struckmeyer told Orr that he had rowed as an undergraduate at the University of Wisconsin, one of nation's top programs. "I'm sorry, but I've already used my eligibility," said Struckmeyer. "Then it's settled," decided Orr. "You'll be a coach."[2]

Men end their practice at the Boyer dock in spring 1973. Assistant Coach Ken Struckmeyer is in the foreground on right, wearing a Cougar Crew letter jacket. On left, Doug Kee, Gary Hubbard, Eric Anderson, Steve Rowlett, Stroke Bob Appleyard, and Cox Craig Illman. Bob Orr is in the dark shirt and white pants facing away from the camera. Photo Credit: Len Mills.

In summer 1973, as Struckmeyer prepared to assume the role of head coach, he sent a memo to all returning WSU oarsmen that indicated his seriousness about building a winning program. Even though they were a club that would turn no one away, Struckmeyer wanted his men to know that it was not just about participating—it was also about winning. Struckmeyer told his oarsmen he "wanted nothing to do with a program which didn't have as its top goal to establish a winning tradition." If his oarsmen kept themselves in "excellent physical condition," increased their strength, and perfected their technique, then "we shall win," he promised them. "Let us challenge Washington this year," exhorted the young head coach.[3]

Oarsmen in later years often saw Struckmeyer as a kindly, doting, teddy bear of a man with the permanent peaceful grin of a Scandinavian Buddha. He was approachable, with an easy smile and a disarming playfulness. "He was a true mentor to all of us," remembered Doug Engle, who rowed on the varsity boat in the late seventies. His oarsmen appreciated their coach's funny sayings, such as "s-tragedy planning" and "take a long walk off a short dock," delivered in his droll Wisconsin accent. When Struckmeyer drove the team van to the river for practices, he was generally quiet, allowing his young rowers space to chatter, but when the bunkum piled up too high, Struckmeyer's hand would shoot to the ceiling so that he could "protect his watch" because it was "getting too deep in here." He loved being around his athletes as well as his students. Engle regarded him as a "student's professor," and he was certainly a rower's coach.[4] Struckmeyer's oarsmen developed a special fondness for their gentle leader.

But what many of his rowers missed on first blush was Struckmeyer's competitive nature. Once committed to becoming the head coach, Struckmeyer had ambitious plans for the upstart club program, and he had high expectations for his oarsmen. He declared that "no man will row who cannot run three miles in twenty minutes or less the first day of fall turnout." He demanded that "all participants must attend 95 percent or better of all turnouts in order to row" and that "no man will row who does not turn out from the beginning of the season." He asked his men to dedicate themselves to rowing. "We just cannot have a successful intercollegiate rowing program with an intramural attitude and attendance," he admonished. "We would rather have nine guys dedicated to rowing than twenty-two who are rowing as a lark."[5]

Struckmeyer's clubs would far exceed those numbers. By the time Steve Wells arrived in the mid-1970s, the club already had nearly forty members and fielded a varsity eight, a lightweight eight, a junior varsity eight, and a freshman eight. By that time, "nobody was worrying about the crew disappearing."[6] Over the course of that first decade, Struckmeyer and his rowers struggled for recognition, respect, and funding but nonetheless built a program that could boast remarkable achievements, including an Intercollegiate Rowing Association (IRA) national championship as well as victories over well-established Pac-8 (and later Pac-10) varsity-funded crews. This was all done without cutting athletes or turning anyone away. Adhering to the club ethos, Struckmeyer gave generations of young WSU rowers the opportunity to push themselves physically and develop themselves emotionally. He also provided them the opportunity to find themselves and their community.

The Other UW: Wisconsin

Ken Struckmeyer had never considered that he would become the head coach of a university rowing program until Ken Abbey came to him in the late spring of 1973. With Bob Orr leaving, it seemed natural that Struckmeyer, who had been assisting Orr for two years, would assume the lead role. But for Struckmeyer, it was something unforeseen. He had never participated in athletics in high school, and his identity was that of someone "who was not really that athletic at any time in my life." He had rowed for four years at Wisconsin, the other UW, but even then he was always a junior varsity oarsman. So now, to claim the title of "head coach" for a growing university rowing team seemed somewhat strange and improbable. But if not him, then who?

Struckmeyer had already developed a tremendous sense of obligation to the kids in the rowing club. So many of them reminded him of his younger self, casting about for meaning, purpose, and a sense of identity. Rowing at Wisconsin, he had found these things, and much more. "Rowing at Wisconsin taught me about myself and taught me things I could do that I had never ever in my life thought I could do," remembered Struckmeyer. Could he give the same gift to these young men? He had always wanted to be a professor—that role came easily to him. And what was a coach but a teacher and mentor?[7]

Rowing at Wisconsin had changed Struckmeyer's life—maybe even saved it. He hadn't realized how much until he found himself in the remote jungle of Nigeria after graduation. He was working with a University of Wisconsin team on a U.S. Agency for International Development (USAID) contract, building a campus deep in the tropical forest. The contaminated water, poor sanitation, and tropical climate took their toll. Struckmeyer contracted a terrible sickness. He could hold nothing down. The hulking oarsman dropped from 220 to 170 pounds, his face became gaunt, and he could barely stand. He didn't fully recover his physical health for nearly two years. He had worms in his digestive tract, but that was not the worst of it. He was also diagnosed with malaria, a disease that afflicted him for the rest of his life, occasionally incapacitating him with bouts of severe illness. But it was that time in Nigeria when he had realized how much he owed to rowing. He believed he might not have made it through his year there without the strength and fortitude rowing had given him.

At Wisconsin, Struckmeyer had never made the varsity or even the second team. He was a third boat oarsman, albeit for a team whose third boat was better than most college varsity crews. But he stuck it out for four years of rowing. Coach Randy Jablonic, who was Struckmeyer's freshman coach and who later became Wisconsin's head coach and guided the Badgers for twenty-eight years, made a distinct impression on him. There were many practices when Struckmeyer was convinced that he could not go on. An inner voice would tell him, "I can't do it anymore." But Jablonic told him—told all of them—that they could do it, that they must do it. He demanded that they give their utmost, and Struckmeyer responded. He didn't quit. And gradually his inner voice began to agree with Coach Jablonic. He could do it. With every interminable, agonizing, oxygen depleting row, Struckmeyer could feel something in him growing. Grit. Confidence. The ability to endure pain and overcome it is what transforms rowers from mere participants in a sport to a tightly bonded community of survivors. It was a community that Struckmeyer could not leave.

As a coach, Struckmeyer borrowed from another Wisconsin head coach, Norm Sonju, whose theory of rowing was to put eight big corn-fed farm kids into a boat and tell them to pull hard. But it was Coach Jablonic with whom he regularly conferred about training and technique, as well as another UW coach, Dick Erickson, at the University of Washington. Erickson once told Ken, "Rowing is not fun, but it is fulfilling." Struckmeyer repeated that line often. He knew it to be true, and it was a truth that he wanted to spread to young men who, like his undergraduate self, needed to face a little adversity to develop themselves. In the 1970s, everyone went to college to "find" themselves—what quicker way than to leave campus, strip down, grab a wooden oar, stare at the back in front of you, and row through the starkly magnificent Snake River Canyon until you reached the edge of delirium, until your legs bulged, your lungs burned, and your eyes stung. It was akin to a daily vision quest, where each rower returned to civilization a new man. It was an experience that Struckmeyer hoped to give to as many students as possible.

Struckmeyer was confident that his oarsmen would make their mark in the spring of 1974, his first season as head coach. On summarizing the prospects of his inexperienced team to a *Daily Evergreen* reporter, he simply said, "We're going to win." After two seasons of being trounced, even by small schools, his men were ready to assert themselves. The 1974 campaign began on March

23 with PLU and UPS traveling to Pullman, a regatta where Struckmeyer predicted, "We stand a good chance of winning."[8] He was right: his varsity eight and his lightweights breezed to open water wins in the team's first-ever outright victories. No matter that these triumphs came against small-school teams. The elation of the Cougars was barely contained. "'I've never seen them win in two years,' exclaimed the wife of one heavyweight oarsman as she watched the WSU boat finish far ahead of second-place Pacific Lutheran."[9] After two seasons of bringing up the rear, it was a new and heady feeling.

Buoyed by that first taste of success, it was a confident group of rowers that traveled to Madison, Wisconsin, in April 1974, to race against Struckmeyer's alma mater and other Big 10 schools in the Midwestern Sprints. Going to Wisconsin was more than just another regatta—it was an epic trip across the country to race one of the nation's most dominant crews. But more than that, it was a pilgrimage home for Ken Struckmeyer, who reminded his men that "only one other crew [in the country] has a Wisconsin graduate as head coach, that being the University of Wisconsin itself." This was Struckmeyer's chance to show his oarsmen the motherland and stamp his unique imprint upon WSU rowing—to make the team his own. Ken Abbey, Dave Pratt, and Bob Orr—the three men most responsible for Cougar Crew's existence to that point—were all former UW oarsmen who were still, in many ways, in the thrall of the mighty Huskies, as was everyone else in the Pacific Northwest. Struckmeyer, his tongue firmly in his cheek, called them "three sterling examples of Husky manhood" who might bestow their "divine help" upon him, "a man of humble origin" whose "rowing background [was] not the best."[10]

Struckmeyer knew that the University of Washington wasn't the only mecca of rowing, and he was determined to show his rowers that there was another UW to which they—through him—were connected. A journey to Wisconsin would not only give his rowers an unparalleled experience but liberate them, at least for a week, from the subordinate shadow of the University of Washington. Struckmeyer had been making regular calls to Jablonic since taking the reins. "How do you do this drill? What are you looking for in that drill?" When Jablonic mentioned the Midwestern Sprints, Struckmeyer jumped at the opportunity. Jablonic was more than happy to extend an invitation to his former rower's new team. Upon their arrival in Madison, the Wisconsin coach rolled out the red carpet, giving the WSU rowers the best boats and altogether treating them like equals. It was a show of respect that the young program and its young coach craved more than anything else. "The Wisconsin coach has named us as the team to beat," Struckmeyer beamed.[11] This meant something, coming as it did from the coach of one of the premier programs in the country, a crew that had beaten the University of Washington twice the previous summer in Nottingham, England, as the two crews were preparing to race at the Royal Henley Regatta—a fact that Struckmeyer repeatedly reminded his rowers and anyone else who would listen.

The journey to Wisconsin was epic in many ways, beginning with an itinerary that had them leaving Spokane by train at 11:50 Tuesday night and arriving in Madison on Thursday at noon. On the train ride to Wisconsin, whenever the gangly, oversized oarsmen draped their legs across the aisles and tried to stretch out and sleep, the train conductor kicked their legs off. They passed Glacier Park and the scenic parts of the trip in the dead of night, stopping in the early morning in Havre, Montana, where the famished young men got their workout sprinting to a Dairy Queen. On Thursday, they arrived deep in the heart of Struckmeyeravia. The rowers were divvied up in twos and threes among Struckmeyer's relatives and friends, who fed and lodged them. "This was Ken's old stomping grounds," remembered Jim Rudd, "and he knew everybody." Rudd was impressed. "We met Coach Randy Jablonic, who is basically the Dick Erickson of Wisconsin, and he treated us like royalty."[12]

There was a dream-like quality to the trip. A luxurious heatwave was just hitting the upper Midwest. It was late April, but it felt like the first day of summer. The boys from Pullman found themselves dazzled by everything—the lively town of Madison, the Wisconsin girls in summer dresses, the enviable rowing facility with its impressive rowing tanks, Lake Mendota, where you could row right past the student union building, which served beer to students over eighteen. Brad Sleeper, a first-year lightweight, was in awe. The Wisconsin boathouse was "the real deal," with a "tank and everything!" At their Thursday afternoon practice, they rowed along the shoreline of Lake Mendota, right in the center of campus. Then Sleeper and his teammates charged off to the student union where they had "beer and brats and sat outside on the spring day watching girls."[13] To Jim Austin, it seemed like "all the girls were running around with no clothes on."[14] The next morning, one of Struckmeyer's rowers told his teammates that State Street in Madison was the most amazing place he had ever seen. "I was sitting on the curb at four o'clock in the morning," he said, "and things were still going crazy!" Struckmeyer just shook his head and rolled his eyes, thinking to himself, "What the hell were you doing sitting on a curb at four in the morning!"[15]

The beautiful dream continued on race day. On a morning that dawned cloudy and windy, Struckmeyer watched with delight as his lightweights won first place in both the four and the eight and his varsity heavyweights and freshmen placed a strong second behind Wisconsin, which he reminded everyone had been the intercollegiate national champion the previous year and was a favorite to repeat as champion this year. The young coach was giddy. He could barely contain his enthusiasm. "We're extremely elated!" he told the *Daily Evergreen*.[16] WSU had lost to Wisconsin, which was expected, but they had defeated crews from Notre Dame, Nebraska, Minnesota, Purdue, and Kansas State. Struckmeyer proclaimed, without hyperbole, that "Washington State rose to the finest performance in its history."[17]

It was a benchmark showing in more ways than one: not only had the WSU rowers proved themselves on the water, but their young coach was able to impress upon his team his own, distinct identity as a former Wisconsin—not Washington—rower. It was a validating experience for Struckmeyer and the entire team, especially "to be treated the way Wisconsin treated us, as an equal." They had beaten everyone but Wisconsin and, Struckmeyer thought, it was kind of like, "What's Washington doing here? No! Washington State! Well, what's the difference?"[18]

The long train ride back to Pullman—punctuated this time by beer runs—was a happy one. But with little rest, WSU returned to Pullman to race UW the very next weekend. The varsity heavyweights—perhaps weary from the long trip to Madison—did not achieve the longed-for breakout victory over UW, but their performance was respectable. WSU rowed well but lost in the varsity and frosh races. However, the WSU lightweight boat beat UW, which was another significant landmark—"the first time a WSU boat has ever defeated a Husky shell since the beginning of Cougar Crew," noted an article in the *Daily Evergreen*.[19]

Struckmeyer's crews had achieved wins in three consecutive regattas. His first year as head coach was already an astounding success. If the first two seasons of Cougar Crew were remarkable because the club simply managed to take to the water and compete, 1974 was noteworthy for signaling to WSU rowers that hard work and suffering were not always just an end in themselves but sometimes a means of achieving something more—recognition, respect, and even rewards, in the form of their competitors' shirts.

The Lightweight Mafia

The Wisconsin trip was a breakthrough on several fronts. It gave the young team and its coach confidence—perhaps even a little swagger. The shared experience had strengthened their bonds and given them memories to last a lifetime. And one more thing—the WSU lightweight boat emerged from the Wisconsin race with a new sense of themselves. After Wisconsin, the lightweights became the first truly competitive varsity crew at WSU. In doing so, they also helped forge an irreverent, renegade (and sometimes abrasive) mentality that became one strand of an emerging Cougar Crew identity.

Struckmeyer himself came to coaching with a distinctly heavyweight mentality. "Ken was a heavyweight at heart," remembers Bob Appleyard, who rowed on the lightweight boat during those years.[20] Wisconsin did not have a lightweight rowing program and the concept of a weight category in rowing was itself controversial. Lightweight rowing was not added to the World Championships until the 1970s and was not an Olympic sport until 1996, and even then only in a limited number of sculling events. The International Olympic Commission (IOC) was itself internally divided over lightweight rowing. In 2002, the IOC Programme Commission recommended that weight categories should not exist beyond combat sports and weightlifting, while the IOC Executive Board supported limited lightweight events. The main question was why should lightweight rowing exist in the first place? The answer given by the International Rowing Federation was that lightweight rowing was intended "to encourage more universality in the sport, especially among nations with less statuesque people."[21] And yet, there were not six-foot and under Olympic basketball competitions or lightweight American football leagues on the same premise. Nonetheless, lightweight rowing took off on the American college scene in the 1970s and 1980s at rowing powerhouses like UW, Cal Berkeley, Harvard, and Yale, but especially among the smaller schools with fewer resources, which found they could field competitive boats in the lightweight events even if they were overpowered in the varsity eight.

At WSU, Struckmeyer centered his recruiting on the heavyweight program. Ads in the *Daily Evergreen* called for rowers who were "over 160 pounds" and tall: "Wanted: 6' 2"–6' 4", 180 lb. & Up."[22] But there was a plain demographic logic to the fact that there were only so many tall athletes to go around—who weren't already on the basketball team—while the campus was littered with an abundance of energetic, high-strung, 5' 10" overachievers— former cross-country runners, wrestlers, and swimmers—who were eager to push themselves.

For those frustrated athletes not quite tall enough or fast enough for the basketball team, or big enough and strong enough for football, lightweight rowing gave them a sport. Yet they also realized they were second-class citizens. It was communicated to them in many ways, not least that Coach Struckmeyer referred to the varsity heavyweight boat as simply "the varsity eight" while he called the lightweight varsity boat the "lightweight eight." He changed this after a varsity lightweight rower complained that "they were varsity too!"[23] There were also the "chase" workouts where Struckmeyer sent out the freshman boat first, followed by the junior varsity, then the lightweights, and finally the heavyweight varsity eight. The boats had to row full pressure until the heavies caught everyone. Not only was the implication that the heavyweight boat was faster—which was usually true—but it also bothered the lightweights that Struckmeyer's launch followed the heavyweights closely from behind while the other boats were given less intensive coaching. The lightweights sometimes felt like no one was paying attention. That changed after Wisconsin.

As they prepared for their race in Madison, coxswain Kathy Figon (later Katz)—only one of a handful of women competing on men's rowing teams nationwide—realized something strange about her crew. They were usually loose and joking, but this morning they were wound up as tight as steel springs. As they prepared to launch, her rowers couldn't stop obsessing about their equipment—was this bolt tight, was this nut loose? She had never seen them so tense. The usually prim coxswain finally called them together and hollered, "Alright, has everyone now made sure their nuts are screwed?" Their jaws all dropped. Appleyard looked at her in disbelief. "I can't believe you said that!" But it worked. They smiled, relaxed, and rowed down the course to the starting line. As they prepared for the start, the coxswain of the boat next to WSU yelled, "I'm not going to lose to any goddamn woman!"[24]

They got off to a terrible start, but then they began to move. Figon called a "power ten"—defined as ten hard strokes of power—and the boat began to surge. The oarsmen could hear her hollering, "I've got their two seat, I've got their bow. We're in the lead!" It was not a call they were used to hearing. Although they had been "rowing well in practices," according to Struckmeyer, the lightweights "had not been able to put it together on race day."[25] That changed in Madison. Jim Rudd recalls that everyone in the boat was sort of dumbfounded as they took the lead, but once they got it, they weren't about to give it up. "We just dug in and powered it to the finish line," remembers Rudd. "We were all pretty jacked up."[26] There were lots of smiles after they crossed the line, but they were also in shock. This was uncharted territory. Appleyard couldn't believe it. It was "surreal" and "surprising" to have pulled away from the field. "Holy cow!" he thought to himself. "We won!"[27] Amidst the celebration, Jim Rudd wondered to himself, "What do we do now?"

What they did next was beat UW by open water the following Saturday on the Snake River.[28] They were aided by having the inside lane nearest the shore while the Husky eight wandered into the strong current at Boyer, and by the fact that UW did not send its top lightweight crew to Pullman. But a win over UW was a win over UW—and the Huskies never brought crews to Pullman that they expected would lose. The wins were piling up for the lightweights in the spring of 1974. The hard work was paying off. Rudd remembers their rising confidence. There was a sense of "we can do this" if we work together. "Collectively, we can make this happen."[29] Unfortunately, it did not happen that year. At the Western Sprints Regatta in Burnaby, British Columbia, they were in the mix at 1,500 meters, and then UW, University of California, Los Angeles (UCLA), Cal Berkeley, and OSU walked away from them. They finished fifth. But they wanted more.

The lightweight breakthrough began in earnest the following spring with the arrival of Vance Smith. A four-year MIT oarsman who was captain of the lightweight team his senior year, Smith came to Pullman, where his wife was doing graduate work, in the spring semester of 1975. He immediately began coaching and sometimes rowing with the team when they needed another oarsman.[30] He started working with the lightweights, teaching them how to get a quick, powerful catch without hesitating at the beginning of each stroke. He wanted them to maintain a little bend in their elbows on the recovery and then flick their wrists, straighten their elbows, and pop their blades in the water just as they reached the top of the slide.

If they did this correctly, they would achieve a swifter application of power and minimize "stern check," where the momentum of the boat slows or even stops between strokes. Smith was trying to teach them "swing," that magical phenomenon when a boat glides forward without slowing on the recovery. He was an impatient teacher, and they were impatient learners. They wanted to go fast, but they didn't always listen well—or perhaps the knowledge just didn't easily penetrate their hard heads. After Smith got frustrated trying to explain his method, he resorted to hands-on teaching: he climbed into the boat and, facing one rower at a time, had them slide towards him until they reached the top of their recovery. Then he pushed their hands upward, forcing their blades quickly into the water at the catch. A dim glow of recognition began to take shape in their minds.

Struckmeyer was delighted to have Smith working with the lightweights. To his credit, the head coach took help from all directions, and his ego did not insist that he know everything or control everything, as so many other head coaches tried to do. He left room for his rowers to learn and grow on their own, a method that is heralded by teaching experts but often under-appreciated by students themselves, who tend to want experts to teach them what they need to know. In Struckmeyer's case, his approach was not just about methodology. It was also about scarce resources. He needed all the help he could get. Moreover, his lightweights were a rowdy bunch of self-described "miscreants and troublemakers" who liked to drive fast cars, provoke their heavyweight teammates, and generally behave like rascals.[31] If Vance Smith wanted them, he could have them.

The lightweight crew of 1974–75 was a unique cast of characters. First, there was a core of veterans who had been with the crew since its founding— Bob Appleyard, Jim Rudd, and Doug Kee, a former heavyweight who sucked down nearly twenty pounds to join the lightweight squad. Appleyard was the calm, steady one—quiet and reliable. Kee was somewhat insane, known for having set the team record by running one hundred flights of Martin Stadium accompanied by his golden retriever, Jason the Wonder Dog, who, to his credit, began to simply wait at the bottom of each flight for his master during the record-setting exploit.[32] Jim Rudd was more conventionally wild. He had a motorcycle, and Appleyard remembers being on the back of it going 120 miles per hour along the river, thinking to himself, "I don't ever want to do this again."[33]

They were joined by newcomers who were even rowdier—Dave and Kenny Yorozu, Brad Sleeper, and Fred Darvill. Kenny Yorozu, their coxswain, had a souped-up Pinto with two single-barrel carburetors and a header; Sleeper had a Dodge Charger with a 383-horsepower engine, and Fred Darvill had a 1966 Barracuda with an Offenhauser manifold that he'd been gunning around the back roads of Mount Vernon, practicing how to fishtail around tight corners. They were a hard-driving bunch, both in their cars and on the water. Sleeper thought they were just "on the edge of being crazy." They liked to push the limits, whether it was driving, rowing, or "talking smack."[34] They called themselves "the Rude and the Crewed"—a reference to Harvard's famous "Rude and Smooth" varsity crew who went undefeated that same year of 1974–75— but some of the heavyweights started to refer to them more derisively as "the lightweight mafia."[35]

The leaders of the lightweight mafia were Fred Darvill and Brad Sleeper, whose antics and attitude led Doug Kee to believe they were both "lucky to have survived college."[36] Darvill's bad attitude might have been due to a chip on his shoulder or perhaps the fact that he spent the entire spring season half-starved. He had rowed junior varsity in 1973–74 as a heavyweight, but Struckmeyer approached him in the fall of 1974 and told him, "You're six-foot-one and not big enough for my varsity boat. You're either junior varsity or you're a lightweight." Darvill replied, "I guess I'm a lightweight!"

At that time, he weighed 180 pounds, so he had to lose 20 pounds. He took it upon himself to encourage his lightweight teammates to develop a distinctive identity beyond that of being hungry. He wanted to make them a "crew unto themselves." He and Dave Yorozu bought nine black welder caps because, as Yorozu said, "black cowboy hats would cause too much drag," and distributed them to the lightweight boat so they could call themselves "the black hats." They could be renegades, troublemakers, or loud mouths. It didn't really matter. It was all about cultivating a brazen attitude and bringing "a sense of character into the crew."[37]

Sleeper was a former cross-country runner from Bellevue who just wanted to go fast, whatever he was doing. He was known as the fastest runner on the team. During winter workouts, he took pride in always getting to the airport and back first. His speed was so highly respected among his teammates that when the train from Wisconsin stopped in Minot, North Dakota, for a ten-minute layover, Sleeper was designated to run to the market for beer. He barely made it back, although there might have been some heavyweights who would have preferred to leave Sleeper in Minot. His aggressive intensity rubbed some of his teammates the wrong way, but they could not doubt his total commitment to the club.

For Sleeper, rowing was everything. He had no interest in academics— he had not wanted to go to university in the first place, but his parents had enrolled him a few days before the semester began in 1973. The classroom was no fun for him. He was a self-described "terrible student" who might have quit except for rowing, which gave him something to look forward to each day. He couldn't wait to get out of class and go down to the river, where he discovered he had an affinity for "being able to apply power through the water." As someone who perhaps got tired of himself as much as his own teammates did, he appreciated that, when seated in an eight, his individual character dissolved into the collective identity of the team. "Who you are on the land doesn't matter when you're in the boat," he realized. Rowing freed him. Every day he "got a fresh slate."[38]

Sleeper and Darvill, and all the lightweights, became Vance Smith converts after a spring break practice in April when they finally got the hang of their mentor's "quick catch" drill. They went out that afternoon and beat the heavyweights in 500-meter pieces. Sleeper remembers that afterwards they "were springing off the foot boards and really driving together, and that made all the difference."[39] They came out of spring break hot. They traveled the next

The "Rude and the Crewed," the "Lightweight Mafia," or the "Black Hats," posing at Redwood Shores in the spring of 1976 in their distinctive black welder's caps that David Yorozu purchased at an Army surplus store because, as he said, "black cowboy hats would cause too much drag." Left to right: Rolan Rouss, Fred Darvill, Steve Norling, Steve Weed, Al Thiemens, Doug Kee, David Yorozu, Brad Sleeper, with coxswain Ken Yorozu in front. Photo courtesy of David Yorozu.

Thursday to Seattle, where they trained on Lake Washington for a warm-up before heading to Bellingham and the Western Invitational Rowing Regatta. They were doing pieces on the wind-protected side of the Evergreen Point Floating Bridge, and everything was working for them. They felt like they were flying. UW assistant coach Bob Ernst, who was accompanying Struckmeyer in the launch, took notice. He went back to the UW shell house and told head coach Dick Erickson that they had better take their top lightweight crew to Bellingham that weekend.[40]

Bob Ernst realized what the WSU lightweights had before they knew it themselves. Despite all their cockiness, they didn't really know yet if they were any good. They hadn't won many races, even if they were rowing well. Bellingham would be their first chance to test their newfound speed against UW's top lightweight boat. Their race plan called for them to go out at a relatively low stroke rate and pace themselves over the first 1,500 meters before sprinting. WSU rowers were used to UW being so far out of reach after 1,500 meters that the race usually centered around WWU and the other, smaller schools back in the main pack. But this time was different.

As they neared the 1,500-meter mark, they were alone with Washington as the two boats traded strokes and outdistanced the rest of the field. UW started their sprint early. According to the race plan, Kenny Yorozu was waiting to call for the sprint once they reached a previously agreed-upon point, but UW was now moving away. The Huskies had a boat length, and then open water, and Appleyard, the stroke, began hollering for Kenny to change the race plan. "We have to take it up now!" Kenny called them up to over forty strokes per minute and the boat began to surge back through UW. The Huskies came back into their peripheral vision. They were now moving past UW nearly a seat per stroke. Kenny was pounding on the gunnels and calling power tens. Their bow was on UW's two seat, and then it was over. They had come back through UW, but they started their sprint too late. Ron Neal, who was watching from the launch, told Appleyard, "You guys would have won the race if you had two or three more strokes."[41] Struckmeyer was disappointed but also impressed: "We scared the heck out of the Huskies."[42]

After the Western Invitational, WSU believed they were the fastest light-weight boat on the West Coast but couldn't prove it. They beat their own heavyweight varsity eight but lost to WWU's varsity eight in Clarkston the next weekend. Western's coach, Bob Diehl, didn't bring his lightweights on the trip after the pounding they had suffered at the hands of WSU in Bellingham. After the varsity race, Diehl made a point of congratulating the Cougar lightweights. He told them they were the best lightweight boat he'd seen, including UW's.[43]

They were just starting to believe it themselves, and then things fell apart. The week before the Western Sprints, they traveled to Seattle for the Steward's Cup, but instead of rowing 2,000 meters, as was usual for spring regattas, Dick Erickson changed the course to nearly three miles. That year the Huskies had received a special invitation to race Harvard over the four-mile course on which they annually raced Yale, in what college crew aficionados simply call "The Race." UW was now training for that distance, and so all the other crews at the Steward's Cup had to oblige, even though they had been training for the 2,000-meter sprint. The Cougar Lightweights had a sloppy, mediocre row, beating the small schools but finishing fourth behind two UW boats and OSU.[44]

At the Western Sprints Regatta the following week in Long Beach, they drew UW in their first heat and went all out trying to beat them, while the other boats in their heat rowed easily, far behind UW and WSU. They barely lost but were so exhausted for the afternoon heats that they failed to make the finals. Appleyard felt that "all the air had gone out." They had "just gone flat."[45] Struckmeyer was extremely disappointed for them. "I think this was one of the hardest things for us to accept in our lives," he lamented. "Some schools had not raced hard in the morning" and were livelier for the afternoon heats. "We keep learning, and next year this won't happen to us again," he promised.[46]

The "rude and crewed" WSU lightweight rowers failed to meet their own high expectations on the water, but they succeeded in bringing a competitive, unapologetic attitude to WSU crew that made high expectations possible in the first place. Certainly, they could be loud and mouthy. Steve Porter, one of the varsity heavyweights who the lightweight mafia had teasingly dubbed "Baby Huey," called them "assholes" one day, and they all just beamed. If they were assholes, then so be it. But there was a method to their madness. There was something more to it than just being mean or obnoxious: it was about creating an identity and a personality that said, "We're going to beat you." Even if they didn't win, they believed they could, which was something new for Cougar Crew. More than that, the act of creating an identity required a sense of shared experience. They realized that, as Fred Darvill said, "you have to be tight to form an identity." And while they might have lampooned the heavyweights with nicknames like "Baby Huey" and "Big Dummy" (their name for Paul Enquist), they sincerely wanted to bring the heavyweights along with them—to "get an attitude and roll with us."[47]

Their speed and attitude indeed pulled the heavyweight varsity eight along and made both crews faster. It added competitiveness to practices that had not been there before. Unlike UW, the heavyweight varsity did not have a second boat to push them. At WSU, the lightweights played that role. There was tension, but it was the kind of tension that pushed everyone to greater heights. The lightweights were always looking to take down the heavies, and for the heavyweights, "it was an absolute mantra: they could not lose to lightweights."[48] Doug Engle, a heavyweight from those years, remembered that "there was always a lot of kidding, ribbing, and competition between the heavy and light boats" but that the "daily competition fueled the successes we had in the early years."[49] In 1975, the heavyweight varsity eight was still waiting for a signature victory, but their time was soon to come.

Heaven Help the Foes of Washington

To be a heavyweight rower at WSU was to always be compared to the national powerhouse rowing program across the state with its giant oarsmen, described in the *Daily Evergreen* as "blond musclemen who shaved their heads" and "won almost every event in sight."[50] While the WSU lightweights had a chance at beating UW because the playing field was more level—every team had to average 155 pounds, with no rower greater than 160—in the heavyweight category, UW was a machine, regarded with awe for its Paul Bunyan-sized crews that tore through rowing regattas like lumberjacks through an old-growth forest.

If Cougar Crew wanted to claim an identity as a legitimate rowing program that deserved respect in its own right, they had to beat UW's heavyweight crew. How could an upstart DIY club program compete against one of the most storied teams in the country? It was like asking an intramural football squad to defeat Alabama. The University of Washington had history and tradition dating back to the 1890s and could boast numerous IRA national championships—most notably, the "boys in the boat" of 1936 Olympic gold medal fame. WSU did not attract high school rowers, while the Huskies recruited nationally, drawing top rowers from elite prep programs across the country, and they had a budget that dwarfed the self-funded WSU Rowing Club. "They (UW crew) are the big-budget program in the country," noted Struckmeyer. "They have tradition and a lot of money."[51]

For WSU heavyweight rowers, the playing field was certainly not level. Husky rowers didn't have to spend their time raising money to keep their club afloat. While WSU rowers were running car washes, selling buttons, cleaning up after sporting events, or donating their summer paychecks to purchase new boats and oars, Husky oarsmen could focus solely on training. While WSU commodore and varsity heavyweight Mike Kimbrell repaired his club's ancient shells with a flashlight in his mouth as he stood in a dark shell house that had no electricity, UW oarsmen enjoyed the sponsorship of famous boatbuilder George Pocock and always rowed with the latest, most advanced equipment. While WSU had one primitive first-generation ergometer (rowing machine), which was nearly always broken, UW crews had ergometers to spare, not to mention money for gear, travel, and even a lavish training table. These disparities were not an outright excuse for losing. Struckmeyer told his men that "money doesn't get in the boat and row." He believed that his club would "beat Washington in the next few years at the varsity [heavyweight] level" with or without adequate funding. "But the money sure would help," he added.[52]

To be a DIY start-up did afford Cougar Crew a sense of identity as embattled, underfunded outsiders. They were lean and hungry—always scratching and clawing—the poor team—the club team. Destitution bestowed WSU rowers with a certain moral purity. In contrast to UW, WSU oarsmen could claim an uncontaminated dedication to their sport, born of adversity and hardship. It was an identity that could easily be deployed as a shield to explain away their losses if they chose, but Cougar rowers wanted more than an excuse. They wanted respect, but that didn't come easy, especially from UW, with its elite tradition and well-heeled followers. UW saw WSU crew members at best as "smiley cowpokes and dairy farmers" who rowed in the remote desert "under the sagebrush and basalt cliffs," and at worst as "fucking hayseeds" who "might just start a barn dance right there on the riverbank."[53]

In those early years, WSU and Struckmeyer always felt slighted by the rowing establishment. When the Western Sprints program for 1975 referred to them as "Washington State—Pullman," Struckmeyer complained, "I guess we have to show people that Washington State are members of the PAC-8 and that we deserve even minimal recognition for our hard work and effort." When Struckmeyer tried to devise plans to have Randy Jablonic and his Wisconsin crew race in Pullman and then in Seattle on consecutive weekends in spring 1977, Dick Erickson "thought it would be great to bring Wisconsin out," but he balked at the suggestion that WSU be entered along with Wisconsin in the varsity race on Opening Day. "He apparently doesn't feel that his 'country cousins' are ready or capable of rowing over there in a big race," grumbled Struckmeyer. "I would hope that we would play a more prominent role in the racing and hosting of Wisconsin than just some 'farmers' getting in the way."[54]

Even though there were few wins to prove it, by 1976 things were looking up for the heavyweight varsity at WSU. The seeds of change had been planted in the fall of 1973 with the arrival of a particularly strong class of heavyweights—Jim Fischer, Paul Enquist, Steve Porter, Ray Wittmier, and Mitch Wainwright—joining veterans like Mike Kimbrell and Jim Austin to form the engine of some very fast boats. That group was the first and only class in WSU history to win Class Day three years in a row. By 1976, they were juniors and their heavyweight eight was showing promise. They began the season with a disappointing performance at the Western Invitational, where they managed a distant third behind OSU and UW. "This meet was to shake the cobwebs out," said Kimbrell, "but we were surprised to see we had so many cobwebs." Even so, Kimbrell was optimistic: "I think we're well on our way to being a power."[55]

The next weekend, UW traveled to Pullman and paid the price, according to the *Daily Evergreen*, "for leaving its number one heavyweight crew in Seattle."[56] Erickson never brought his first heavyweight boat to Pullman—not because he disrespected the Cougars but because he saw the trip to Pullman as a chance to test his third- and fourth-boat oarsmen in a race situation. No matter which oarsmen he chose, however, he expected them to win, and win handily. He was surprised for the first but not the last time in the spring of 1976.

1977 Class Day Winners. This was the entering class of 1973. By the time they graduated in 1977, they had won three straight Class Day regattas, and it would have been four had they not barely lost as freshmen. Back from left: Ray Wittmier, Jim Fischer, Paul Enquist, Steve Porter, Brad Sleeper, Mitch Wainwright. Front from left: Fred Darvill, David Yorozu, Tony Shapiro. Photo courtesy of David Yorozu.

It was the first ever victory by a WSU heavyweight varsity over a UW crew, and the Cougars were jubilant. According to one of the UW rowers, the crew that fell to WSU that day was a combination of third- and fourth-boat oarsmen. He called the race "the most embarrassing moment in our racing careers" and subsequently blamed the loss on the strong current in the outside lane and his hungover teammates.[57] It's true that Gene Dowers, coxswain of the WSU varsity eight, steered the "Great Circle Route" to perfection, keeping the Cougars close to shore to catch the back eddy in the last 500 meters while UW charged up the middle of the river.[58] But as they say, a win is a win, and UW is UW. The Cougar heavyweights had won their first set of UW shirts. "Even though Dick Erickson handicapped the boats, he never expected to lose the races," remembered Doug Engle. "There was hell to pay in the UW boathouse if you came back from Pullman with a loss."[59]

The victory over UW gave the WSU heavyweight crew confidence. As they traveled to Redwood Shores—the home of Cal Berkeley crew—for the Pac-8 Rowing Championships in 1976, they truly believed, in the words of Mitch Wainwright, "If we row a good race we can beat the U."[60] It was not to be. UW dominated the regatta. The *Daily Evergreen* reported that the Cougars were disappointed, but "realizing the inferiority of their program, especially in the financial sense, they were still satisfied."[61]

But they were not satisfied—they wanted more. And they got it in spring 1977, a season that showcased a growing club program that was increasingly able to compete with varsity programs on the West Coast. The team was getting larger than ever thanks in part to the recruiting efforts of Dave Emigh, one of the founding rowers, who had returned to Pullman in 1975 to coach the freshmen and conduct graduate work. Not only were Emigh's recruiting efforts attracting more students but his coaching with the freshmen was pushing stronger rowers up to Struckmeyer. By the 1976–77 school year, a rising tide seemed to be lifting all boats. Initial evidence of this was the "Buffalo Boat," the first truly fast, competitive junior varsity eight in WSU's history, composed of "an oddly-assorted, happy-go-lucky crew" of long-haired, bearded oarsmen, among them Steve Wells and Steve Ranten, who "asserted themselves with growing enthusiasm" against the varsity boat in practice.[62] Their speed, along with their irreverent, carefree shenanigans, "visibly annoyed" the heavyweight eight (which, of course, delighted them even more), but it also pushed the varsity boat to go faster. They weren't smooth, but they were competitive: after one "particularly drenching row," according to Steve Ranten, "Struckmeyer likened them to a herd of water buffaloes," and they were called the Buffalo Boat thereafter.[63]

The culmination of these factors—bigger numbers, more coaches, a fast junior varsity that pushed the varsity, and the freshman class of 1973 coming of age—led to a breakout year in 1977, beginning with their best finish ever in the Western Invitational, followed two weeks later by a dominating sweep of WWU in Pullman, where the "Cougs' varsity heavyweight boat cruised in nine seconds ahead of the nearest competition."[64] The next weekend was disappointing, as the varsity eight finished third in the Midwestern Sprints when they had expected second place behind Wisconsin, but that lackluster performance was forgotten when the heavyweights set a new course record of 6:08.3 while defeating UW in Pullman.[65] In that race, they rowed through UW in the last 500 meters after trailing by open water. "I could feel the power surge in the boat like never before," remembered Steve Porter, who sat at the stroke seat. When coxswain Jeannie Bohannon called for them to sprint, Porter felt like "everyone was just waiting for that moment to unleash all their frustra-

The 1977 heavyweight varsity pulls away from UCLA at Redwood Shores in a benchmark victory for Cougar Crew. Photo Credit: Dave Emigh.

tions, all their desires, all their dreams."[66] It was the highlight of a benchmark season that ended with the Cougar heavy eight pulling off "the biggest upset" of the Western Sprints, defeating a top-rated UCLA boat on the first day of competition and finishing fourth in the Pac-10.[67] Struckmeyer was euphoric. "With a win over UCLA, we gained a lot of respect."[68]

It is ironic that the narrative hook of the book *The Boys in the Boat* and the film documentary *The Boys of '36* is the contrast between the roughhewn kids from the Pacific Northwest and their elite competitors in a sport where the best crews hailed from schools like Harvard, Yale, Oxford, and Cambridge. "These kids were very representative of the Pacific Northwest, which was raw, newly shaped," explains writer Timothy Egan in the documentary. "These boys were the sons of loggers, the sons of fishermen. They did odd jobs for a buck a day. They used their hands as claws and their backs as levers, you know. They were grunts." When these "underprivileged outsiders" went to the East Coast to compete against "the sons of privilege who rowed for the Ivy League," Egan explains how that feeling of being outsiders could become a "real generator because it goes to that chip on their shoulder—that insecurity that you do not respect us or even understand us."[69]

The irony is that, by the 1970s, the University of Washington had become a bastion of blue-blooded rowing privilege and it was the upstart hicks from WSU who sported chips on their shoulders and were clawing for respect in a sport that seemed to sneer down at them. *They* were the outsiders now, not UW—farm kids, working-class kids who had never heard the word "regatta" before but were competing their asses off against the established programs. They were long-haired, plaid-shirted country boys from towns like Brewster and Ritzville who did not own sports jackets or ties or khakis, whose idea of winter formal wear was a lined denim jacket and a pair of leather work boots. They were bearded renegades from small towns like Mount Vernon, Port Orchard, Edmonds, Lacy, La Conner, and Ellensburg, all drawn together by the desire to push their bodies further than they thought possible.

For Doug Engle, who was in the engine room of the varsity heavyweight eight from 1977 to 1979, being a "Cougar team to the core" meant being "always discounted and ready to prove ourselves by taking a bite out of the big guys." Engle remembers that WSU "didn't have much equipment to train with" but "we were happy to be able to have the chance to put the work in and see how fast we could be."[70]

Engle rowed on the first Cougar freshman boat to beat UW, and he also rowed in the first two varsity heavyweight boats that defeated UW eights on the Snake River. Engle's crews were some of the first to push UW, and they were also the first to win a national championship during an era, in the late 1970s, that proved even a DIY club team less than a decade old could make their mark on the national level.

The Meatwagon

Getting a shell to "swing" is a mysterious thing. How and why some boats achieve it and most do not is a strange combination of factors that include body type, personality, training, technique, and other strange nuances that cannot be measured or even understood. Although everyone in a rowing shell appears to be doing the exact same thing, if they are not placed in precisely the right order, from bow to stern, a boat will flounder. Sometimes, simply switching the positions of two rowers in a shell can transform a boat from flailing to flying. At other times, a boat will move faster when an obviously weaker rower replaces someone stronger. Call it chemistry, alchemy, art, or religion, even the best college rowing coaches are hard-pressed to consistently assemble crews who mesh together well enough to pursue their collective potential.

Everything must come together just right. All the pieces must fall in place. At WSU, that happened in 1979 in a boat called the "Meatwagon," and the result was an IRA national championship.

The biggest chunk of the Meatwagon arrived on campus in the fall of 1975. Doug Engle was a 6' 7" basketball player from Lacy who planned to turn out for George Raveling's WSU squad but, until then, needed to stay in shape. The crew had sent out flyers to all incoming freshmen—part of new freshman coach Dave Emigh's more aggressive recruitment strategy—and rowing had been at the back of Engle's mind since he attended an invitation-only basketball camp run by Marv Harshman at the University of Washington that summer. The hundred or so athletes had been housed at the old Conibear Shellhouse on the banks of Lake Washington, and Engle had wandered through the trophy cases, admiring the rich history of rowing at UW. So, in August 1975, Engle showed up at the crew meeting spot, squeezed his tall frame into Struckmeyer's personal van, and rattled down to the Snake River for the first time.

After one week, Engle was hooked, and he never turned out for basketball. He loved the camaraderie of rowing. It was like a party that you attended daily. When classes were over, you headed to the meeting spot, greeted your buddies, and crammed into cars for thirty minutes of goofing around as you drove through the wheat fields. At the river, you got into boats to "work your ass off and boost up those endorphins," and then, relaxed from the effort, "you just kind of floated on back to campus." He also liked the athletic side. Engle had been a very good basketball player because of his size, hustle, and hand-eye coordination. But his primary strength had been his powerful legs, which seemed to get stronger as the game progressed. Engle realized he had a "diesel type engine" that wasn't fast but had a tremendous capacity for work. Later, he came to understand that he had predominantly slow-twitch muscles that were perfectly suited for rowing, an endurance sport that asked athletes to suffer at the edge of their aerobic threshold for long periods of time.[71]

Engle was joined at the river that fall by Chris Gulick from Bellevue, another tall, athletic kid with strong legs and a capacity for hard work. Dave Emigh, beginning his first season as freshman coach, could see their potential immediately. Engle had the body of a first team oarsman at any school in the country, and Gulick, while not as tall, was a lean and muscular 6' 3" with an easy temperament. Both were extremely competitive and coachable. Emigh liked Gulick's sunny, "jovial" personality, which kept everyone loose; at the same time, "when he was in the boat, he was all business."[72]

Fall 1976 marked the arrival of two more pieces of the complicated puzzle that, once completed, produced the Meatwagon. The first was Marty Michalson, who stroked Emigh's 1976–77 freshman boat. He was one of the few freshmen who arrived in Pullman already knowing how to row, and he immediately became the leader of the freshman squad, much admired for his prowess on the water and his elite rowing pedigree. Marty was no longer rowing for WSU in 1979 when the Meatwagon coalesced, but the connections and knowledge he brought to WSU rowing became an important ingredient in the Meatwagon's eventual success.

Marty's father, Vic Michalson, was the head rowing coach at Brown; when he visited Pullman, he befriended Struckmeyer and Emigh and offered himself as a resource for both coaches. Dave Emigh was drawn to Vic Michaelson, and the Brown coach became something of a mentor to Emigh, who was always looking for "that one drill that I could use to perfect technique and make boats go faster." Emigh called Michaelson frequently, and their friendship improved the technical proficiency of WSU rowers. Michaelson, for example, taught Emigh to have his teams row with their feet out of their boot stretchers, allowing the flow of the boat to carry them down their slides rather than pulling themselves with their feet. Far more importantly, Coach Michaelson and Brown University became an unofficial sponsor for the Meatwagon when they traveled to Syracuse for the IRA Regatta in 1979, providing them with the boat they used in their pursuit of a championship.

The other key arrival in the fall of 1976 was Rich Ray, a cerebral young man from Ellensburg who was just adjusting to his tall muscular frame. Ray had been "scrawny" throughout most of high school, but in his senior year his body "underwent a rapid metamorphosis" that brought him to Pullman with a 6' 4", 190-pound frame that seemed to be carved of solid muscle. He considered his new physique to be "the luck of DNA," but it was also the product of high school summers and weekends spent as a "hay buck," hauling alfalfa and timothy in the Kittitas Valley. On hot, summer days, Ray might stack sixty tons of hay, one bale at a time. "Not only did the endless lifting build a solid frame," he remembered, "it taught stamina through efficiency of movement." Ray grew up in a pious family that preached "no alcohol, no fun, and work, work, work!" He knew how to work hard, but he was also eager for new experiences. After emerging from WSU's Hollingbery Fieldhouse into the bright sunshine after registration, he saw something that would change his life: a "slender, gleaming, elegant eight-seat racing shell on a pair of slings." He stood there in awe, listening as "friendly guys in letter jackets" recruited him. The chance encounter "set the course" for his undergraduate years and, indeed, the rest of his life.[73]

All three rowers—Engle, Gulick, and Ray—were coached by Dave Emigh as freshmen and found themselves together on the varsity heavyweight boat in spring 1978. Along with rowing in the eight, they were having success that spring in a heavyweight four with Kelvin Eder, a wild, bearded architecture major known for pulling all-nighters at his drafting table with a bottle of whiskey on one side and a bottle of NoDoz on the other.[74]

On the flight back from Wisconsin in 1978, Emigh proposed that they seriously consider rowing together in a four and perhaps really do something with it. The idea took hold the following year when they found the fourth oarsman who completed the lineup. He was John Holtman, a workout maniac with a chiseled, powerful 6' 3" frame that in other years might have made him one of the bigger oars, but in the Meatwagon made him one of the shortest—perfect for the bow seat. Holtman rowed for Emigh's freshman boat in spring 1978 and broke onto the varsity eight as a sophomore in the 1978–79 school year. There was no one more committed to rowing than John Holtman, who liked to say that he majored in rowing at WSU. Holtman later coached the freshmen at WSU before becoming assistant coach at OSU under head coach Dave Emigh.

They all understood that, in Engle's words, "the idea of breaking into a four was kind of radical." If four rowers were singled out, it could potentially harm the cohesiveness of the varsity eight, especially if the four began to take precedence over the eight. For collegiate rowing programs, the premier race is the varsity eight. Every regatta includes many events—freshmen, novice, junior varsity, and lightweight rowers all race in both fours and eights. And yet, undeniably, the showcase is the varsity eight, or the "big boat." It is the prestige event by which all programs are ultimately judged. Put your top eight oarsmen—the biggest, the strongest, the most technically proficient—into one long, sleek shell, and have them row flat-out for 2,000 meters. The men's varsity eight is the fastest race in every regatta, with the best boats completing the race in under six minutes, rowing at maximum effort the entire way.

The eight is the fastest human-propelled rowing vessel in the world. When you ask, "Who won the Harvard-Yale race this year?" you are asking about the men's varsity eight. But for small schools and new programs, it is hard to field a competitive varsity heavyweight eight that matches up with the top schools, because rowing is a numbers game. You need a lot of recruits to end up with a competitive heavyweight eight, where each rower stands between 6' 3" and 6' 7" and has the wiry strength of a wrestler, the cardiovascular fitness of a marathoner, and the drive of an Olympian. The big programs, like UW and Harvard, can field two boats of oarsmen who match that profile. The small programs, like WSU or WWU, are lucky if they can fill one eight with experienced oarsmen of any size. For WSU crew, always scrambling to stitch together a volunteer band of oarsmen, the most important attribute for a recruit was not strength or height or athletic ability, but simply a willingness to persevere. Attrition was always a problem.

The dilemma of patching together an experienced, talented, and motivated heavyweight eight often tempts small programs to place their best rowers in a four. The varsity four is a less prestigious event than the eight, but it allows smaller programs to compete with the big schools. If UW's varsity boat was composed of giants from stern to bow, WSU's boats were far more uneven. There might be four true heavyweights joined by four undersized rowers with more heart than heft. It was always an enticing proposition: if you took those four true heavyweights, athletes who could compete at any school, could you match up with the majors?

Paul Enquist had tried to create a varsity four in 1977. Enquist himself was an impressive rower. He was 6' 6", powerful, and lean, with the competitive intensity and desire to take his team to the next level. But Enquist sometimes felt held back by rowers who were not as tall, strong, or driven as himself. By his senior year, there were enough large, powerful oarsmen on WSU's varsity boat squad that Enquist believed they could carve out a formidable four that could compete with anyone. He proposed to Struckmeyer that the four seniors in the varsity boat row primarily as a four. Struckmeyer was adamantly against it. He knew that "the pride of a relevant crew program is always in the eight."[75]

Dave Emigh approached his "project" gingerly. He didn't want to go behind Struckmeyer's back. They had an excellent working relationship that complemented each other's strengths. If Emigh's forte was the technical side of rowing, he realized that Struckmeyer's gift was "more inspirational"—"putting guys mentally at a place where they would work hard and be competitive."[76] Struckmeyer asked him one day, "Oh, are you taking some guys to the IRA?" Up until that moment, Emigh hadn't thought of the IRA Regatta. It had never occurred to him because he hadn't himself had an IRA experience, but for Struckmeyer, coming from Wisconsin, rowing in the IRAs was only natural. After discussing it, Emigh and Struckmeyer decided to work on the enterprise together, but only according to some strict ground rules. First, it had to be "done outside the regular team." They trained mainly on Sundays until the season ended. Second, the primary focus of the club had to be on the eights—the four could only be a "side project." Finally, the selection process would be based not only on who were the strongest oarsmen but also on who could afford the money and the time to take the trip back east. The club did not have the funding to support them.[77]

By spring 1979, the varsity boat was stocked with strong oarsmen who had experience and motivation. Struckmeyer was buoyant. "I think the attitude of the whole crew...is good, and our prospects are good too."[78] Indeed, it was destined to be one of the most successful seasons in WSU's short history. The varsity eight nearly beat UW's second boat in the Montlake Cut on Opening Day. They then went on to surprise the University of British Columbia (UBC) on the Snake River, winning five of six races against a team that was "considered one of the best in Canada," including an open water "rout" by the heavyweight eight. The performance was "definitely a shock, at least for me," an overjoyed Struckmeyer told the *Daily Evergreen*.[79] His heavyweights went on to place fourth at the Pac-10 Rowing Championships at Redwood Shores, once again defeating UCLA but losing to UW, Cal Berkeley, and OSU. The entire WSU team, including freshmen, junior varsity, and lightweights, placed third overall. Struckmeyer was "ecstatic" with the results,[80] but he predicted even greater things to come: "I'm more firmly convinced than ever that we can be first or second in the Pac-10."[81]

Midway through this successful season, the Meatwagon, joined by cox-swain Al Fisher, began to train on Sundays. Emigh had recruited Fisher to be a coxswain when he was visiting his sister in a campus dormitory and heard Fisher's booming voice bellowing down the hallway. He thought the oversize voice might be attached to a much larger man; when he saw Fisher's diminutive frame, he knew he had found himself a coxswain. Fisher was not a technical coxswain, which was fine—Emigh could work on technique—but he was very enthusiastic, "an inspirational type who could get the guys pumped up."[82] It's not that they needed any prodding—if there was one thing that united the four, it was their willingness to work hard on the water. They never had to be asked twice.

Their vow to not distract from the eight meant racing the four only "if the schedule allowed it not to conflict with the eights race."[83] They rarely raced it that season, but when they did, such as in early April at Lake Samish in Bellingham against a UW varsity four consisting of fifth-year seniors, they realized they had something special. In that race, they were slow off the line and fighting choppy water for the first seven hundred meters. The Meatwagon averaged 205 pounds—they were large and powerful—but with the waves hitting their riggers, they couldn't stabilize the boat and apply full pressure. They were a length of open water behind the Huskies when they hit smoother water. Fisher began to bark out power tens to focus his team on applying maximum force with each stroke. The boat began to jump. It took thirty strokes—three consecutive power tens—for them to move from a length down to a length up on UW. The boat was swinging. They rowed through a surprised UW team and won by open water. After the race, the coach's launch pulled up beside them and the laconic UW coach, Dick Erickson, said, "Nice race, boys." Struckmeyer "didn't say much of anything and didn't have to," remembers Engle: "He was just beaming."[84]

That victory over UW at Lake Samish was the moment when the Meatwagon began to believe in themselves "and the whole project of going to IRAs did not seem so crazy after all."[85] Later that month, WSU faced UW again in Pullman. The varsity eight lost, but the Meatwagon "trounced the Washington Husky shell by 31 seconds." By this time, the four was really coming together and Struckmeyer told the *Evergreen* that they would compete at the IRA national championships in Syracuse and likely be "one of the top six men's four shells in the nation."[86] Their confident coach was already predicting they would make the finals, which would itself be an impressive achievement. One month later, Struckmeyer was even more bullish on the prospects of his crew, calling their chance to win a national title "quite good."[87]

Struckmeyer and Emigh were coming to understand that the Meatwagon had a special combination of personalities that complemented one another. Holtman, who was the two seat in the eight but rowed bow in the four, had an intense, even manic personality. He was always working out and trying to push himself harder than anyone else. Rich Ray, who rowed seven seat in the varsity eight but rowed two seat in the German-rigged four, was more introspective but every bit Holtman's equal on the workout front.

Holtman thought Ray was a Clark Kent type, mild-mannered until you got him behind an oar or in the gym. They often competed, testing each other's will and fitness in everything from lifting weights to playing handball. During one extreme workout, Holtman recalled Ray had gone to the bathroom while they were doing a hellacious squatting exercise they called "Heiden Walks," named after gold-medal-winning speed skater Eric Heiden. When Ray returned, he was behind Holtman by sixty squats, so he did those, and a few more. Holtman did another set, and a few more; and then Ray did another set, and a few more. They kept trading the lead back and forth, neither willing to quit until, nearly exhausted, they finally agreed upon a truce.

Balancing out the zealous intensity of the bow pair, were Engle, who was long, solid, and steady as a rock at the three seat, and Gulick, the stroke, who was always lightening the mood with his never-ending comical repertoire. All of them had nicknames—Gulick was "Squishy" or just "Squish," Engle was "Doc," Ray was "Flip," Holtman was "Yumbo," and Al Fisher was "Shack" (from "Horshack" of the popular TV show *Welcome Back Kotter*). If more levity was needed, Struckmeyer provided that with the paddle in his launch, getting into splash fights with his oarsmen if they got too serious.

After Pac-10s that year, they squeezed in a few more practices on the Snake River with Struckmeyer and Emigh, and then they all flew to Syracuse, New York, where they challenged the best eastern crews on Lake Onondaga.

The two coaches and the oarsmen ate in Syracuse's dining hall and slept in the university's dorm rooms, sharing the spartan accommodations with rowers from Kansas State. It was one of those trips where everything fell into place. They had contacted Vic Michalson at Brown, and he lent them one of their boats—a fifteen-year-old Pocock shell that had once been an Olympic boat. Made in Seattle, it was just the right vessel for the Northwest crew. It was wide and perhaps a little slow, but Dave Emigh thought it was "the perfect boat" for his powerful squad, because they could just sit down and hammer.[88]

Practicing out of the Syracuse boathouse on the Erie Canal system, where the conditions were always sheltered and calm, the WSU four had some of their best workouts ever. They were a powerful foursome that rowed best in glassy conditions when they could settle into a rhythm; take long, smooth strokes; and apply full pressure. Engle never forgot those practices on the glassy water of the Erie Canal. The experience "of being fully extended at the catch, dropping your oar in the water and putting maximum effort into the stroke and not feel like you are working is awesome." In the *Amateurs*, David Halberstam says, "When most oarsmen talked about their perfect moments in a boat, they referred not so much to winning a race but to the feel of the boat." In those moments when everything in the boat was clicking, or "swinging"—the oarsmen locked into perfect synchronicity—"the boat seemed to lift right out of the water."[89]

There was another element to achieving swing that was perhaps even more important than the physical motion of the boat—it was the bond of trust that was formed when a boat achieved that moment of grace. According to John Biglow, the famous Yale oarsman and sculler featured in *The Amateurs*, swing "allowed you to trust the other men in the boat." Biglow, and all rowers, understood that "a boat did not have swing unless everyone was putting out in exact measure, and because of that, and only because of that, there was the possibility of true trust among oarsmen."[90] That's what was happening to the Meatwagon on the Erie Canal. A good boat was becoming a great boat. The four men and their coxswain were truly beginning to trust each other and to believe that, together, they could compete against the best crews in the country.

With each practice, they were rowing better than ever, but they also had no idea who they were up against. They hadn't raced the eastern crews before. Dave Emigh made some last-minute adjustments to their oars before the first heat. Although they had been rowing well, Emigh was worried that his rowers were pulling too heavy of a load through their stroke. To lighten the pressure, he moved the buttons on the oars and shortened the distance that the oars extended from the oarlocks to the water. It was the equivalent of shifting to a lower gear on a bicycle—each stroke would be slightly easier but also less powerful—and would require that his team row at a higher stroke rate to make up the difference. Having never practiced with this new configuration, the Meatwagon won their heat, but their stroke rating climbed from their usual 35 to nearly 40 during the race. It was an unusually high rating that raised eyebrows among the spectators. In a newspaper story about that day's races, the local paper said the WSU four was rowing the "Ratzeburg" style, referencing a German club that was known for their high stroke rates. Even so, their time of 7:03 was the fastest of the day, and they defeated crews from Coast Guard, Brown, and Boston University. Syracuse won the other heat in 7:08, defeating Penn, Purdue, and Marist College.[91]

The Meatwagon immediately buttoned their oars back to their original settings. In the final they would row as they always had—long and strong with a lower stroke rate. The boat felt good during the warm-up. The weather was perfect for them—a head wind, which would favor their powerful rowing style. In their prelims, Coast Guard had challenged them. Gulick told Fisher to let his boat know where Coast Guard was throughout the race—they didn't want to fall too far behind. It was never an issue. They battled Syracuse for the first 900 meters but established the lead by 1,000 meters and were decidedly in control of the race by 1,350 meters. By the 1,500-meter mark, they had two and a half lengths of open water on the eastern crews, who were now fighting for second place.[92]

"It was a great feeling to be in the biggest race of your life and cruising to an easy victory for the last 500 meters," relished Engle. Rich Ray could feel the "raging fire" of his lungs and legs, but in the midst of the pain, there was the elation of seeing the oar blades of their competitors fade to a "distant twinkle" behind them. As they brought up their cadence and pushed toward the finish line, the euphoria of near victory was sharpened by the fact that they were "friends, savoring together for the last time the headrush of a powerful swing."[93] For WSU rowers, it was a rare, intoxicating feeling. The *New York Times* reported that "the Washington State oarsmen were ecstatic after their shell crossed the finish line and the stroke, Chris Gulick, raised his arms in glee."[94]

Dave Emigh knew they could win, but he never dreamed it would be by open water over Syracuse, "a national power" rowing on their home course.[95] It really was like a dream. The four oarsmen collected more swag in that one race than most WSU rowers would ever win over a four-year career. They won fifteen shirts, handed over ceremoniously by the losing crews after the race, as well as medals, certificates, and photographs. They walked about the course the rest of the day, mingling with the festive crowd, their medals dangling over their

WSU tank tops, taking photographs and savoring the moment. Struckmeyer was especially proud—this was the kind of recognition WSU needed if they were to get more support.

And recognition they got. *Seattle Times* sports editor Georg N. Meyers touted the audacity and improbability of the Cougar victory: "As unlikely as a champion ice skater from Tahiti is a rowing champion from the Palouse."[96] The *Spokesman-Review* named them the amazing "Prairie Cougars" and voted them the "Inland Empire Team of the Week."[97] The headline in WSU's *Hilltopics* trumpeted, "Cougar Crew Claims National Rowing Title," dramatically describing how "the 50-mile-a-day commute to Lake Bryan and the long, hard, blister-producing workouts on the rough, windswept water of the Snake River Canyon" had "paid off in a national title."[98] When they returned to Pullman, it was summer break, but some rowers on campus made a cake and gathered a crowd to celebrate the Meatwagon's historic victory. Then there was a photo op with WSU's President Glenn Terrell. The four rowers, their coxswain, and their head coach, Struckmeyer—clad in sports coats and even a of couple ties—beamed as Terrell

The "Meatwagon" after their victory at the 1979 IRA National Championships, posing with WSU President Glenn Terrell. From Left: President Terrell, Rich "Flip" Ray, Doug "Doc" Engle, Chris "Squishy" Gulick, Ken Struckmeyer, and John "Yumbo" Holtman. Coxswain Al "Horshack" Fisher is front center. Photo courtesy of WSU Manuscripts, Archives, and Special Collections.

gushed about the team's unlikely victory. WSU rowing seemed to have suddenly come of age. It could not boast of the gold medal glories, like UW's "boys in the boat," but now the boys in the boat in the wheat fields had a national championship. They were no longer just the "best crew by a dam site!"

Conclusion

In the 1979 season—pronounced "the best ever" by Struckmeyer—the crew could point to "wins [against] Vancouver, B.C.; high finishes in Bellingham; the appearance of number one boats of UW in Pullman; participation of three boats in Opening Day Regatta in Seattle; a combined team finish of third in the Pac-10 and a National Championship."[99] All this from a club that was funded with $1,800 from the Associated Students of Washington State University (ASWSU), while UW received $95,000 from its athletic department; Cal Berkeley, $100,000; UCLA, $75,000; and OSU, $30,000. With such successes on so paltry a budget, it was time for WSU's athletic department to pony up.

This was the argument that Struckmeyer made in a memo written to WSU's athletic director, Sam Jankovich, on June 22, 1979. His appeal, which included a short history of the club's first ten years as well as a budget comparison of all the Pac-10 rowing programs, was "presented with the intent of using this information as a basis from which to begin discussions concerning the merger of the crew and the athletic department."[100] The time finally seemed right. In the wake of the Meatwagon's triumphant return to the Palouse and their ringing endorsement from President Terrell, the stars were finally aligned to move from club to varsity status, or so Struckmeyer thought.

Struckmeyer's seven-page memo contained a projected budget of just $25,700 for WSU men's crew, with no scholarships nor any paid coaching positions. The crew would travel on a shoestring budget and rely solely on volunteer coaches. Struckmeyer did include $4,000 for "administrative travel," which he explained in a handwritten note was for "my personal out-of-pocket expenses" based on a "yearly average for the past five years."[101]

His modest proposal was "turned down as excessive" by the athletic department.[102] According to the *Evergreen*, Jankovich countered that, while athletics might be able to find a campus job for the freshman coach and perhaps help pay the club's insurance bills, it was in no position to fully fund WSU rowing, even at such a cut rate. The *Evergreen* took a decidedly sympathetic position, cataloging the poor club's miseries: its beleaguered members spending their own money and begging for hand-outs, driving their own cars to and from daily practices, changing at the shell house in a facility "without running water or electricity," and even noting that, of all WSU's teams, "only the 1975 Cougar track team had previously captured a national title."[103] The newspaper's primary source was, of course, a frustrated Coach Struckmeyer, who explained his club's desperate need for funding: "We're trying to build a tradition and gain some respect in the conference."[104]

If the WSU rowers were to build a tradition and gain some respect, as Struckmeyer and his oarsmen hoped, they would have to do it themselves, as a club team—as they always had. The athletic department's rejection only meant that the noble struggle would continue. Cougar Crew would be driven by dedication rather than dollars. Rich Ray later lamented that "at Harvard there's a two-year waiting list of alumni who want to buy equipment [for the crew], but here we dig and scrape for every nickel."[105] It was true. Austerity itself had become, and would remain, central to Cougar Crew's tradition and identity. WSU crew was destined to remain a struggling club whose fortunes rested on the individual efforts of its underfunded athletes. A national championship did not change that.

Jim Rudd (1971–75)

Rowing is the ultimate team sport. There isn't anybody walking around being a showboat, saying, "Look at me, look at me!" Once you put your butt down on the seat you're in there with eight other people and you're busting your ass for them, for you not to let them down, to be a good oarsman. That's the biggest draw of rowing. It's by far and away the team aspect of it. Collectively, you really accomplished something and nobody had to score forty points. It's a group of people who say, "You know, we're as good as our weakest link." And nobody wants to be the weak link.... When we won in Wisconsin, we were in uncharted territory. What do we do now? We just won a race. We were all pretty jacked up. We all sacrificed together. We worked so hard together and then to actually have something come of it was really satisfying. There was a sense of "we can do this." It gave us confidence in ourselves. We thought, individually we might suck, but collectively we can make this happen!

Doug Engle (1975–79)

I just keep coming back to those Saturday practices. You're rowing downstream, and you keep rowing downstream, and you keep going and going. You've got essentially unlimited time. There's no set time you have to be back at the boathouse. So you're heading downstream, and something's not going right. Struckmeyer keeps lining the boats up for more pieces, going downstream, and you've never been that far downstream in your life. You're saying to yourself, I don't recognize any of these hills around here, and Struckmeyer says, "Line up and we're doing another 2,000-meter piece." You know you still have to turn around at some point and row the whole way back upstream against the current, and your butt is sore, and your hands are hamburger. But you make it back! You do it! You survive this huge physical challenge, and it just gives you confidence.

What separates crew from other types of sports like biking or running, where it's a solitary effort, is that you have to do it with seven other people in the boat to make it go right. You've got to physically lock your body, lock your center of mass, your momentum, in with other people to make it go right. When you do, you remember those days forever. It's a magical experience.

CHAPTER THREE

Êtes-vous prêts? Partez! Women's Rowing, 1974–1980

> We were women showing up to do a sport that had been a men's sport up until that time. Just the fact that we were there—that we thought we should be there—meant we were feminists, whether we thought about it or not. We were unspoken feminists.
>
> —Jean "Snake Action" Patterson (1975–78)

> Kristi Norelius was the perfect person to have on a new team when you were trying to develop a culture. She worked hard. She didn't say a word, but when she spoke, people listened to her. She had this great sense of humor. The other women on the team respected her. They would say, "If it's ok with Kristi, it's ok with me!'"
>
> —Bob Ernst, University of Washington women's crew head coach (1980–87)

When Kristi Norelius went to WSU in August 1975, she had no inkling of Title IX and the dramatic changes it would effect in women's sports and in her own life. She was not an athlete. In fact, she thought of herself as a "nonathlete." No matter that her older brother Mark had rowed at UW and was even then preparing to compete in the 1976 Summer Olympics, Kristi had not played sports at Issaquah High School, where there were few opportunities for girls. She was tall and gangly, but there was not yet basketball or volleyball for girls at Issaquah in the early 1970s. Instead of being an advantage, her height only made her feel awkward. When she went shopping with her friends, she could rarely find a pair of jeans or shoes that fit her. At size twelve in women's shoes, she sometimes resorted to wearing men's shoes. Being an adolescent girl was hard enough, but being a tall girl in the early 1970s, before sports made such physical attributes desirable, only made it harder to blend into the crowd.[1]

Tall, shy, and introverted, Kristi Norelius was not headed to Pullman to call attention to herself. She wanted to fit in. But in order to do that, she needed to find her people—a tribe with whom she could feel comfortable in her own skin. She saw a flyer in her dormitory for a meeting of the women's rowing club. Where did they row? She was familiar with the hallowed Conibear Shellhouse at the University of Washington, but she hadn't known that WSU even had a rowing facility. She had seen no indication of rowable water within the miles of rolling wheat fields that surrounded campus. She was curious, and the meeting also promised "snacks and a slideshow."[2]

When she arrived, she met Andrea "Andy" Moore and Roberta "Berta" Player, and she knew right then that she had found her people. They immediately made her feel welcome, and it had nothing to do with athletics, or that she was tall, or anything other than that she had walked through the door and was willing to contribute part of herself to the cause of building a women's rowing program at WSU. She learned that the women's club had just started in spring 1975. This was the beginning of something. They had little money and hardly any equipment. If she could help sell tickets for a gas raffle, she could contribute. It wasn't just about rowing—it was about her willingness to join this tight-knit community and make sacrifices for others that gave her an immediate sense of belonging. She was astounded by the beauty of the Snake River, but it was the camaraderie that pulled her into rowing at WSU and set her on a course that she could never have predicted.[3]

In 1975, there were changes swirling around the world of sports about which Norelius had no idea, but these changes later swept her up and made her part of them. She did not know that women's rowing was not yet an Olympic sport in 1975. Women's crew made its debut at the Olympic level the following summer in Montreal, when women were allowed to compete at the distance of 1,000 meters, while the men's events ran 2,000 meters. Norelius also had no notion that during the summer of 1975, as she prepared for her freshman year in Pullman, female rowers across the country were competing for seats on the national team boat, coached by Harvard's Harry Parker, who, it was rumored, would also be coaching the women's Olympic eight in 1976. Making the 1975 women's U.S. National Team boat coached by Parker would give them an inside track to break the gender barrier in Olympic rowing the following year in Montreal. That 1975 U.S. National Team boat, the famed "Red Rose Crew," won silver at the World Rowing Championships in England; and, the next summer, after her freshman year at WSU, Kristi watched the first American women's Olympic eight win bronze.

She could not have imagined then that she would later row with many of these same women on Olympic squads in 1980 and 1984, nor that she would row a double with one of them, Anne Warner, at the Lucerne International Regatta in 1980 (in lieu of the boycotted Moscow Olympics). Warner was famous, along with Chris Ernst, for leading the "strip protest" at Yale in spring 1976, where female rowers publicized unequal treatment by taking their shirts off in front of Yale's director of physical education to reveal naked chests and backs stamped with "Title IX."[4]

All of this was external to Norelius's existence during her freshman year at WSU as she figured out what it meant to be a rower, and maybe even an athlete. She began as a "social rower," but her mindset began to change during winter workouts that first year. As they met in the dingy confines of the gymnasium to do calisthenics, lift weights, and run, Norelius began to explore her physical limits for the first time. "Winter training stripped away the best of rowing and exposed its worst, magnifying the drudgery, monotony, and pain," writes Ginny Gilder, who would row on the Olympic teams with Kristi in 1980 and 1984. "There was no scenery to distract, weather to enjoy, boat to feel, or rhythm to seek."[5] This was doubly true during the icy Pullman winter. Norelius and her teammates sweated in the gymnasium, did sprints in the Fieldhouse, and then headed out to the airport for frigid runs, wearing old tennis shoes and baggy sweats that were seemingly designed to hold the moisture close to your skin until you froze.

Unlike on the river, where she was learning to row with eight other people in a boat, Norelius found that winter workouts provided her with direct feedback on her own efforts. If she ran harder, she could actually beat a few of her teammates. If she pushed herself more during exercises, she could feel her fitness improving. There was something addictive about it, something rising in her that she had never felt before. During those winter workouts, the women's crew often ran on the track under the stadium lights, sharing the oval with a number of gifted Kenyan runners, including Henry Rono, who would set the world record for 5,000 meters in 1978. Kristi was awestruck to be on the track with them. She thought it was a "privilege just to be breathing the same air." After she and her teammates finished a running workout one evening, one of the Kenyans complimented her on her speed. She was thrilled and surprised. She wondered, "Maybe I really am an athlete?"[6]

The thought hit home over her first winter break. She was trying to schedule a time to meet with an old friend, but every suggestion her friend made conflicted with her workout schedule. "No, tomorrow I'm running in the morning." "No, Wednesday afternoon won't work, I'm lifting weights." "Wait a minute," her friend finally said. "You're a jock now!" Norelius had to admit it was true. Even if she didn't own a pair of proper running shoes, and even if she had rowed at the Head of the Lake Regatta that fall wearing army pants and a ski parka, she was becoming a jock.

She spent part of her freshman winter break sewing her first sweat suit—light blue sweatpants and a matching hooded sweatshirt. She sewed in a zipper that was three inches too short, so she was self-conscious going back to Pullman because she figured her teammates would see that her new sweats were homemade. But at least she had sweats instead of army fatigues—and running shoes too, thanks to her teammate Peg Staeheli, who had showed off her own new running shoes to Kristi's mom while they were all staying at the Noreliuses' for the Green Lake Regatta that fall. "Kristi should have some of these, too!" she said. Mrs. Norelius took note. And Kristi returned to Pullman that winter ready to train.[7]

The 1976 season, the second for WSU women's crew, was a success in community and camaraderie, if not in competition. Kristi and her teammates grew as a team. They suffered disappointments together. They destroyed old equipment. They raised money for new equipment. They bought their own oars. They carpooled and slept on floors at their parents' houses when they went to regattas on the west side. But they did not have success in those regattas. Their primary objectives were minimal: as Kristi put it then to a *Daily Evergreen* reporter, "to make as little a fool out of ourselves as possible," or, as

The women's open varsity four in the spring of 1976 at Greenlake wearing their first uniforms, which they made themselves by hand-stenciling their tank-tops. From left to right, Laurie Michelson, Cyndi Johnson, Sharon McKendrick, Kristin Norelius, and Mo Carrick, with Andy Moore in the background. Photo courtesy of Mo Carrick Kelley.

her teammate Dawn Maguire added, "don't roll the boat!"[8] They rowed more for their curly-haired young coach Ron Neal than they did for themselves—they rowed to not disappoint Ron.

The 1977 campaign was different—perhaps a microcosm of a transformation, heralded by Title IX, that would see women's sports evolve from a social activity that emphasized exercise and participation to one that fostered more intense competition. Some believed this was unseemly, even in the 1970s. Rowing, as a sport, had emerged from the patriarchal order of the nineteenth century. Crew "built male character, muscle, and fraternal ties that might later prove important in the world of commerce, politics, and war. What use did a woman have for these?"[9] And yet, the times, as Bob Dylan had forecast, they were "a-changin'." More young women were starting to play competitive sports, and some of them, like Mo Carrick, who ran on the WSU track team, and Jean Patterson, who played on the WSU volleyball team, ended up joining the rowing club.

That spring, Kristi Norelius stroked the open four that would finish fifth on the West Coast, while Jean Patterson stroked the women's lightweight four that would miraculously finish second only to UW at the Pac-8 Conference Rowing Championships in 1977. "Up until last year, there was what you

The 1977 women's open four beat UW in Pullman, and then, with Kari Buringrud replacing an injured Cyndi Johnson in the bow seat, rowed to a respectable fifth-place finish in the Pac-8 Championships at Redwood Shores. This was Kristi Norelius' last race as a Cougar. She would go to Long Beach that summer with Dawn Maguire and learn how to scull. It was the beginning of her Olympic journey. From left to right: Dawn Maguire, Kristi Norelius, Mo Carrick (kneeling), Chris Carsten, and Kari Buringrud. Photo courtesy of Mo Carrick Kelley.

might call 'social rowing,'" explained Norelius, who, along with Jean Patterson, was now co-commodore of the team. "A more athletic type of girl started to turn out" this season, "so the decision was made to compete with other schools."[10] And compete they did.

Urged on by their coxswain Mo Carrick, who was "smart, decisive, and competitive,"[11] the WSU women's open four finished third at the Western Invitational and then beat UBC and UW in a race on the Snake River before ending their season at Redwood Shores, where they lost to Cal Berkeley in their first duel before handily beating both Oregon and Santa Clara. Kristi was unhappy that they had won two out of three races but had placed in the standings behind a boat that had lost two out of three. "But that's the way it is," she reasoned. It was still a success. If the previous season had been about not embarrassing themselves, "This year our goal was to be as competitive as possible in the Pac-8."[12]

That summer of 1977, Kristi and her teammate Dawn Maguire went to Long Beach to try their hand at sculling. They spent three months at the Long Beach Rowing Association before returning to the Pacific Northwest. Kristi decided not to return to college just yet. She wanted to get better at sculling, and she had been invited to train in Seattle with Bob Ernst, who was then the freshman coach at UW. She joined his "mosquito squad" of small-boat scullers who trained under his tutelage on Lake Washington. The group included another former Cougar—Paul Enquist—who was also just beginning his apprenticeship in sculling and whose path would also lead him to a gold medal in 1984. Norelius was horrible at first, finishing last in every piece. Ernst began to call her "everybody's doormat." He teasingly told Norelius and Ginger Cox, her doubles partner, "You two have a lot of potential. I just don't know if it is for rowing or roller derby."[13] But her efforts paid off. She qualified for an Olympic development sculling camp. One camp led to another, which in turn led to an opportunity to compete in the Olympic Sports Festival, which led to an invitation to the Olympic selection camp for sculling, and finally a place on the 1980 Olympic squad. She was the first WSU rower to make an Olympic team.

Kristi Norelius's journey would eventually take her back to school at the University of Washington in 1981, where Bob Ernst was now coach of the women's team. She won back-to-back NCAA championships in 1981 and 1982 while rowing both summers for the U.S. National Team. This led to a spot on the 1984 Olympic eight, also coached by Bob Ernst, where she sat at the six seat, in the engine room of a boat that included the legendary Carie Graves of Red Rose Crew fame. Graves had won bronze in the 1976 Olympics. With Kristi Norelius, she would row to gold in 1984, the last year before the IOC increased the distance of women's races from 1,000 to 2,000 meters.

Among the memories of her gold medal experience at the 1984 Olympics, one stood out. She was on the team bus heading for the opening ceremonies at the Los Angeles Coliseum. The rowing team manager was warning them they were entering a "dicey" neighborhood. South Central Los Angeles was dangerous, she said, and they would need to watch out for themselves. As the busses maneuvered through the largely African American neighborhoods near the stadium, Kris could see someone out of the corner of her eye running alongside the bus. She was trying to keep her eyes forward— she had long been trained to "keep her eyes in the boat." When she finally looked, she saw that "the streets were filled will cheering people from the local neighborhoods, waving homemade banners and signs." She saw an enormous cardboard replica of an Olympic gold medal dangling from the window of a tall apartment building. When they disembarked at the stadium, Kristi and her fellow Olympians were ushered into a secured area surrounded by chain-link fencing. People began pushing their hands through the fence. At first, Kris couldn't understand what was happening, until it dawned on her that they were holding pens and asking for autographs. They're probably looking for Carl Lewis or Mary Lou Retton, she thought. Why would they want *my* autograph?[14]

In 2010, Kris Norelius was invited to give a talk to Olympia Area Rowing (OAR) about her 1984 Olympic experience. The organizers of the event wanted her to narrate her gold medal race for attendees. In preparation for the talk, she watched the race again, sitting on the sofa with her cat. It is an amazing race to watch—a 1,000-meter sprint. Their strategy was simple: blast off the line fast at a high stroke rate, keep it high and fast, and hang on—"fly-and-die and hope your opponent cracks first."[15] The U.S. team was favored. They had beaten the East Germans twice that spring. There were no prelims in the women's eight that year. Only a final. No chance to work out the Olympic jitters. The U.S. boat had a decent start and moved out to a slight lead in the first 200 meters, but they had gone out too high and too fast and were beginning to spin their gears. One of them caught a partial "crab," where a person's oar gets stuck for a moment under water, slowing the entire boat. They lost momentum and the lead. Fortunately, their coxswain, Betsy Beard, had them take the stroke rating down and reestablish their composure. They began to move. The race was suspenseful, and as Kris watched it for the first time in many years, she wondered if they were really going to win. It all seemed so unlikely. They were still behind until the last twenty strokes of the race, when their boat surged and they powered through the Romanians for the victory.

When she had finished watching the race, she found herself weeping. And then she was talking out loud to herself. "How did that happen?" she wondered. And then, "But I'm so ordinary."[16] Her mind went back to the chain-link fence and the autographs. She thought: there was no difference between myself and the people on the other side of that chain-link fence. The only difference was that she had somehow been given that wonderful opportunity. She felt overwhelmed with a sense of gratitude. She had been so privileged to have the opportunity to achieve such a remarkable thing.

That opportunity had opened for her in 1976 at WSU when she was welcomed by Andy Moore, Berta Player, and the rest of the women's team. They had given a tall, shy "nonathlete" a welcome place where she could grow as a person and find herself as an athlete. She later wondered if she would have become an Olympic rower had she started at UW instead of WSU. She was timid. She had no athletic experience. "I might not have moved up through the ranks," she speculated.[17] She had proudly won championships as a member of UW's varsity eight in the early 1980s, but by then she was already an accomplished rower and a mature athlete. It was WSU's fledging rowing club that had first given her a sense of purpose and identity after having left the "nest of home." She found her people, and that community gave her confidence to inch toward her goals, step by step, on a journey that would eventually lead her to an Olympic gold medal. This was about life—not being an Olympian. And rowing at WSU had started her down the path, as it did for so many women who came after her.

The French Connection

Andy Moore grew up in an eastern Washington farming family, the thirteenth of fourteen children. On their one-hundred-acre farm near Sunnyside, Andy didn't have a choice of whether she wanted to be an active or outdoorsy girl— life on the farm simply required doing hard physical labor in the outdoors. When she was in high school, she was the oldest child left on the farm, and by then her father was battling emphysema. It was Andy's responsibility to take care of the cattle, drive the tractor, and do whatever else needed to be done. Fortunately, she liked being outside using her strength and capabilities, and she embraced challenges, both physical and mental. These characteristics made her a prime candidate for pioneering a women's rowing team at WSU, but, as a girl, she had never even played organized sports.

In her small town, Andy didn't know any girls who were "athletes." Girls playing sports was a novelty. It was quaint. She was raised in a community where girls certainly could be rough and tumble, but where they were not encouraged to play organized, competitive sports. There were no female sports teams at the school. The GAA—the Girls Athletic Association—provided exercise experiences for young girls, including all-girls basketball, bowling, and volleyball, but GAA girls did not compete with other schools. Games were intended to provide them with a sense of fun and camaraderie, but not to cultivate competition. Above all, it was about participation, cooperation, and healthy exercise. Even though she was physically strong, Andy did not think of herself as an athlete. When Andy got to WSU in fall 1974, she "discovered that girls from larger communities actually had competed and were quite adept at sports."[18]

That fall she saw a sign in the Duncan Dunn lobby: come to a meeting in the CUB if you're interested in starting a women's rowing team. She grabbed a few of her dorm mates, including Roberta Player, and headed off to find out what this was all about. Thirty people showed up to listen to a "crazy lady with a funny name" and a very thick French accent implore them to follow her to the Snake River and start a women's rowing club. She was Anne Marie Dousset, a French graduate student who rowed in France and had been going to the river that fall to row with the men's team. She was a fully emancipated woman, a type perhaps uncommon in Pullman in the early 1970s. Before workouts, she would walk right into the shell house and nonchalantly change her clothes in front of the young men who stood frozen with their jaws on the floor.[19]

Gene Dowers remembers seeing Anne Marie Dousset for the first time when he was a seventeen-year-old freshman. Ken Struckmeyer was lining up the crews when the young French graduate student began changing from her school clothes to her workout gear. "So we had Struckmeyer calling out 'ports on one side, starboards on the other,' and Anne Marie in the middle in her underwear," recalled Dowers. "I seriously did not know what to do, but it was something we got used to."[20]

When Anne Marie asked the men why there wasn't a women's team, they told her, "Well, we tried, but the girls, you know, they were worried about their hair, and being late for classes and what not, so they're not interested."[21] This was not a satisfactory answer for the strong-willed Anne Marie, who immediately set off to organize her own club. It was her last year in Pullman before returning to France, and she was determined that women at WSU, like Andy Moore, would have the chance to row.

In other times and places, someone like Andy Moore, a farm girl from eastern Washington, would not have been allowed within the elite, male confines of a shell house. The sport of rowing has always been embedded within the deep structures of class and gender. It emerged first as a modern sport among the professional watermen on the River Thames, promising cash prizes to its working-class participants. Upper-class oarsmen—realizing, in part, that they could not compete with professional boatsmen but also desiring to separate themselves from their social inferiors—created their own boat clubs within the elite boundaries of England's prep schools and universities. The British were the first to establish sharp distinctions between elite "amateur oarsmen" who competed for high-minded sporting ideals but never for profit and lower-class professionals who competed for money and prizes.

Although today we often romanticize "amateur athletics," imbuing them with inclusive, universal values, such as perseverance, discipline, character, and teamwork, toward which all humans can aspire, the classification of "amateur," as it was defined by the stewards of Great Britain's Henley Royal Regatta in the 1870s, was suffused with class prejudice: someone "who is not, among other things, by trade or employment a mechanic, artisan, or labourer."[22] That distinction prevented Jack Kelley Sr.—American sculling champion and future Olympic gold medalist—from racing in the Diamond Challenge Sculls at the Henley Regatta in 1920. He had worked as a "bricklayer."[23]

If "amateur" contained deeply classist roots, its origins were also fundamentally masculine. Amateur athletics and amateur rowing, as they evolved in the British and American school systems in the late nineteenth and early twentieth centuries, focused on cultivating Victorian notions of enlightened manhood. Rowing was part of an all-encompassing moral education that cultivated hard work, self-discipline, and sportsmanship.

One of the greatest proponents of rowing as manly preparation was Endicott Peabody, the head rector of Massachusetts's Groton School and its rowing coach. Peabody saw rowing as a path to cultivating "manly character" among his pupils. His students were drawn from the elite eastern establishment, and many of them—including Dean Acheson, W. Averell Harriman, and Franklin D. Roosevelt—went on to careers as prominent statesmen and business leaders in the mid-twentieth century. Rowing, which he placed among the "higher branches of athletics," figured centrally into Peabody's conception of a Groton School education. It promoted "self-denial and endurance of pain," "courage and determination," and the ability "to work for others, and not for oneself." It factored into a holistic education that developed "strong men." "If he is rowing on the eight," Peabody believed, "he is a worthy son."[24]

Rowing was a way "boys could develop essential strength and inner confidence that came with the mastery of physical skill,"[25] but what about women?

In the late nineteenth and early twentieth centuries, the qualities that rowing cultivated—strength, competition, endurance—"were considered transgressive" for proper women.[26] Not only was it unseemly to exert oneself and sweat, the very motion of rowing was hard to perform in dresses and harder still without exposing one's bare ankles to public spectacle. The development of muscles and strength, it was feared, would defeminize women, making them unattractive to men, and perhaps even threaten their ability to reproduce.[27]

These prejudices had their roots in the Victorian era, and yet they still existed in 1974 when women at WSU formed their rowing club. A 1973 article on women's rowing in the *New York Times* referenced the "Amazon syndrome," where female rowers were engaged in "weightlifting, ergometers, running the steps of the stadiums, and the flattening of the bosom."[28] It was quaint and becoming for women to paddle about in boats with their sweethearts, but was it appropriate for women to storm the patriarchal bastions of the oldest, and most hierarchical, sport in the United States? In the early 1970s, the male guardians of the rowing establishment were still barring women from full participation in their sport. Even though women had been allowed into international competition in 1954 at the distance of 1,000 meters (chosen for no other reason, apparently, than that it was half the distance men raced), women's rowing was not allowed in the Olympics until 1976, at the Henley Royal Regatta until 1981, and at the Leander Rowing Club, the oldest rowing institution in Britain, until 1999.[29] On the college scene in America, the heart of the rowing establishment was in the Ivy League, and at places like Yale, women were still battling for equal conditions in the mid-1970s.

Those women from Duncan Dunn did not realize it, but in asking to row, they were pushing against the weight of history. The women's movement was forcing change, but by the mid-1970s, it was also encountering a growing backlash from those who believed that the changes were coming too fast and going too far. The proposed Equal Rights Amendment, which simply promised that "equality of rights under the law shall not be denied or abridged by the United States or by any State on account of sex," was by 1974 becoming controversial among gender traditionalists.

Even if it was changing, the culture was still saturated with male sexism. On campus in 1974, men still gathered near Stimson Hall on the eighth of May to throw women into the Minerva fountain, while shouting "Hooray, hooray, for the 8th of May, it's outdoor intercourse day today, hooray!"[30] May 8, 1974, had in fact been a record-breaking year: nearly two hundred "unsuspecting females" were "sacrificed" to Minerva to the delight of cheering crowds of male students. The men bragged that they had only attacked women who were not wearing dresses, were not headed to class, and had no male escort. They proudly reported only one injury: "a mass of red scratches on the back of a Stimson resident received by one of the more unwilling recruits."

Despite complaints from female students and disapproval from WSU's president, Glenn Terrell, the Stimson "high priests" received "the okay" to proceed from the director of residence living on the condition that they "use some discretion." The WSU campus police received several calls from "irate women" asking them to do something, but they refused to intervene because they worried "that the situation might only intensify if the police attempted to control it directly."[31] In 1974, the balance of power on campus clearly rested in the hands of men.

Despite the changes promised by the passage of Title IX in 1972, WSU had not yet accommodated itself to the fact that women deserved the same academic and extracurricular opportunities as men. But the young women who gathered in the CUB that fall had a few things going for them. First, they were energetic and completely naive. They had no idea what they were signing up for—and not just because they understood only about half of what Anne Marie Dousset was telling them. Second, they had the feisty young French woman to lead them, and she was not naive. She was fully aware of the task ahead and determined that they would succeed. Finally, the men's rowing club at WSU had not been around as long as those at Yale, Harvard, Oxford, or Cambridge. They could not resist the entrance of woman into their arena on the grounds of tradition because they had no tradition. The same sexism existed in Pullman as in the rest of the country, but the forces of patriarchy were not centered in the shell house, as they were in New Haven or Cambridge, where traditional privileges needed to be protected at all costs. At WSU, when it came to rowing, nothing was yet ossified or set in stone. Things were still plastic, and there was enough flexibility there to allow for women to be added to the mold without breaking it.

That is not to say that there was no conflict when Anne Marie Dousset showed up with her rowers. The men still felt that their own existence was extremely tenuous. There were never enough shells, oars, or dollars to go around. They had worked hard to purchase two new shells, the *Cougar One* and the *Cougar Spirit*, and now, from their perspective, the women were showing up and demanding to use the equipment they had labored so hard to obtain. The men were all paying at least two hundred dollars a year from their own pockets to row, and they were scratching together whatever else they could from fundraisers and the ASWSU, where they had to bow and scrape for their annual line item, which amounted to only a small percentage of their costs. They felt they didn't have anything to spare for a women's team, which was now seeking to share their scarce resources. Besides, they weren't convinced that the women were serious and committed. There had been previous attempts to start a women's team, beginning in the spring of 1973, but those efforts had never taken hold—why would this attempt be any different?[32]

The men all claimed to welcome female rowers and disavowed any suggestion that they were male chauvinists. To them, the privileges of rowing had nothing to do with gender but rather a legitimate claim on the club's resources. It was simple: they had worked hard to build the club from scratch and the women hadn't. The women, therefore, had no legitimate claim on the team's shells and oars, or even the shell house itself. The women needed to raise their own money and purchase their own equipment, or settle for the leftovers and be grateful to have them. Moreover, the women would simply have to accommodate the men's schedule—the men's team would take their shells out first and return to the dock first after practice. As far as the men were concerned, if the women could find a boat to row in—like the heavy, antiquated *Titanic* or the warped *Stager*—and the daylight hours in which to row, they could have at it. The men weren't altogether too happy about it, namely because they believed that the women arrived with a sense of entitlement for what was not theirs. "It wasn't that they were women," explained Fred Darvill, "it was that they were coming in and trying to take something that you felt you had built."[33]

Those first women just wanted to row. To join the club like any other student and go out on the river. But they perceived immediately the possessiveness of the men toward "their" equipment. Peg Staeheli remembers, "There was a tone that you were using someone else's merchandise. You were borrowing." Jean Patterson recalled the men as helpful and respectful, but "from day one they made you understand that it was *their* program" and "you were an interloper." The women were "at the mercy of the men's boats and resources." After the men had launched their shells, the women rowed "what was left over." Some days Patterson and her teammates couldn't row at all, or had to go out in fours, or just went for a run and waited until the men came back. Andy Moore remembers that the women often got on the water so late that they left a person on shore to shine their headlights into the river so they could make it back to the dock in the darkness. The men were not hostile, but Jean Patterson recognized "there was still a kind of tacit hierarchy, and everyone understood that the women were second-class citizens." No one got "bent" about it because, back then, that was simply "the way it was."[34]

Both men and women recognized that the tensions at the shell house were primarily over scarce resources and not explicitly about their sex, and yet, given the context of the times, it was inevitable that their interactions would be freighted with the implications of sex and power. After all, what was the feminist movement, or Title IX, if not women asking to access resources equally with men? Although Title IX did not directly apply to the rowing team because it was a club rather than part of WSU's athletic department, both men and women on the team often viewed the tug-of-war over resources through its lens. Brad Sleeper's impression was that the women, because of Title IX, had arrived at the shell house and said, "We get half the boats in here."[35]

Indeed, some of the women did toss around Title IX as the basis of their claim on equipment. From their perspective, even if the law's strict provisions did not apply to the rowing club, its principles made sense: why shouldn't they have the same opportunity to row and the same equipment available to them as the men? The men's answer was always "because you didn't work for it like we did," but the women immediately saw through this argument, realizing that if they were not women but rather fifteen novice men, there would be no resistance to them using the equipment equally with everyone else. When one of the men told Mo Carrick, who joined the women's team in 1975, that "girls don't belong in the shell house because we worked to start this club and did all the fund-raising for these shells," she replied, "I know. But we will help raise more money, and we pay the same fees you pay for student clubs." He said, "Yeah, but you didn't fund-raise for these shells. You girls haven't earned this." She then asked him, "Did the new incoming freshmen boys help?" No answer. While most of the men remained silent, it was clear that some of them regarded the crew "as a kind of boys club that they didn't want to share" with women.[36]

For her part, Anne Marie Dousset navigated these tensions with poise and aplomb. She ignored pushback and simply proceeded forward as if it was self-evident that the women had every bit as much right to the equipment as the men. She could be pushy and determined, and sometimes wielded a sharp tongue, exhibiting a facility with English swear words that impressed Ken Struckmeyer—"lots of really good combinations that we weren't aware of before." Struckmeyer was surprised when Anne Marie showed up at the river one day with eight female rowers in tow. The men were standing outside as Anne Marie began barking orders to her rowers, who dutifully entered the shell house and commandeered an eight.[37] Struckmeyer's size could be intimidating, but Anne Marie was no wilting flower. She held her own, fought for access to equipment, and even managed to finagle his launch on occasion—without which she was either coaching from the coxswain's seat or running up and down the road alongside the river, screaming at her crew through a megaphone.

Eventually, the women would affectionately call Ken Struckmeyer "Uncle Ken" or "Father Crew," but Roberta Player remembered feeling intimidated by Struckmeyer and the men's team at first. She was impressed at how Anne Marie "stood up for us." Her rowers immediately developed a strong allegiance to her. She led them in fundraisers where they made crepes and sprinkled them with lemon and powdered sugar and sold them for a dollar. It was fun, but, remembers Player, "It was a challenge because we had to work around the men's schedule. We would row in the morning before the men, or we'd go in the afternoon after the men came off the water."[38] That first year was not easy. Their numbers dwindled from fifteen to ten. The women who stuck it out realized that they were being watched closely by the men, who wondered if this would be yet another fizzled attempt at founding a women's team.

Anne Marie Dousset was as demanding of her rowers as she was of Struckmeyer and the men. She worked them hard—Andy Moore thought she was "a little bit on the merciless side"—and she did not tolerate complaining. Although polite, cheerful, and charming when she was not coaching, once she stepped into her coaching persona, she was more overtly competitive than Ken Struckmeyer. "She pushed the women really hard," remembers Gene Dowers. Her coaching style was less focused on technique than effort and hard work.[39] "If you think there's a problem in the boat," she admonished them, "it's probably you!" She explained to them that rowing had a strictly hierarchical line of authority: "God, coach, coxswain, and then you." They all needed to understand their place. And, of course, she taught them the international command for starting crew races: "Êtes-vous prêts? Partez!" "Are you ready? Go!"

That first women's crew "had a few good athletes," remembered Andy Moore, "but most of us were just masochistic." Gene Dowers remembered that first women's crew as simply "tough"—"this was something they wanted to do and they didn't see any reason why they shouldn't be doing it."[40] They were willing to suffer enough to make it through an entire season, and finally, to row in two regattas in the spring of 1975. Their first race came in Pullman against UW. It was predictably dispiriting. The Huskies destroyed them. After that race, Roberta Player remembers, "We licked our wounds and set our sights on just being the best we could be."[41] Two weeks later, they rowed against UW again at the Steward's Cup Regatta in Seattle, and while they finished last among six crews, they showed a competitive spirit and finished much closer to UW than they had in Pullman. "The girls have really improved a lot," Anne Marie Dousset told the *Daily Evergreen*. "This was the first race they've really done well, despite the results. A lot of crews don't have any novices, while the rowers here have only been rowing for just two months."[42]

The women had completed their first season, but Struckmeyer and the men were still waiting to see what would happen next. *The Pull Hard* from September 1975 did not carry any reports from the women's team. Reading through its eight pages of detailed race results from the 1974–75 season, updates on budgets, fundraising, and the activities of a new booster club—the Friends of Cougar Rowing—a reader would be hard-pressed to recognize that a women's club existed at WSU, except for one reference in Struckmeyer's summary of the previous season: "Then on the last day of [spring break] practice, the women's crew was using my launch and it burned and subsequently sank at Boyer Park Marina."[43] Struckmeyer had received a call from Anne Marie late that evening: "Monsieur, your boat has sunk!"

Obviously, this was not welcome news, but it was made worse by the fact that Struckmeyer's previous launch had broken down earlier that spring, forc-

The first women's team photo in the *Chinook*, spring 1975. This is the only extant photo of the women's first head coach, Anne-Marie Dousset. Front row from left: Darth Dunbar, Nikki McConnell, Sharon McKendrick, Andy Moore, Roberta Player. Row Two: Anne-Marie Dousset, Suzanne Bonlie, Ann Marie Dahl, Kathy Curtice, Kim Sherman. Row Three: Shelley Timbers. Source: *The Chinook* (1975), 148, courtesy of WSU Manuscripts, Archives, and Special Collections.

ing him into a smaller fishing boat that could barely keep up with his eights. Now he was forced to coach from his van for two weeks while his student oarsmen engineering squad—he called them "Porter, Enquist, and Fisher Royal Engineers"—managed to rescue the sunken hull and bring it back to life.[44] It was only a footnote, but for some of the men, the story reinforced their belief that the women could not be trusted with their equipment.

Athletes, Renegades, and Unspoken Feminists

By fall 1975, relations were already improving between the men's and women's teams. For one thing, a new school year meant that a few of the territorial old guard had graduated, replaced by incoming freshmen who had no consciousness of life before a women's club. Also helpful was the fact that Anne Marie Dousset, who had returned to France, was replaced by Ron Neal, one of those old guard rowers who helped build the men's team. Neal had been with the team since 1972, rowing bow in the varsity eight for most of the 1973 and 1974 seasons. He was an older student, in his thirties, married with children, who was well-liked and highly respected among his teammates. His wife was affectionately called "Mother Crew."

Conflict with the men did not an end when Ron Neal took over as coach of the women's club; like his predecessor, he was not afraid to challenge the men. Fred Darvill was commodore of the men's club that year, and he and Neal occasionally exchanged heated words because Darvill, who greatly respected Neal, couldn't understand why his former teammate "wanted to take things away from his old crew and give it to the women" when the men's team "just didn't have anything to give." He told him, "Ron, we haven't got much for you, man!" But Neal was "adamant" that the women should have equal access to the equipment. Title IX was in the air, and Darvill told him, "Ron, we're a club sport. How do you expect us to do that?" It was an ongoing conversation that year, but Neal was not about to back down, and Darvill, for his part, wasn't about to take things too far because "nobody wanted to meet Neal in an alley if he was mad at you." Neal was a "rough and tumble guy" who was built like a "fireplug." Although only in his thirties, from the perspective of the young men on the crew, Neal was a "pretty old guy" and a "tough son of a gun."[45] From the perspective of the women, Neal was "kind," "gentle," "easygoing," and "gorgeous." He was a good teacher who got his point across without hollering, and, remembers Jean Patterson, he "didn't talk down to you like you were girls." He was also fun-loving. Patterson remembers him driving down to the river, singing, "You picked a fine time to leave me, Lucille," at the top of his lungs.[46]

The 1976-1977 women's crew with Ron Neal as coach. Back row from left: Mo Carrick, Cyndi Johnson, Marsha Lee, Sharon McKendrick, Kristi Norelius, Laurie Michelson, Peg Staeheli. Front row from left: Martha Sleeper, Roberta Player, Katie Berg, Chris Carsten, Carol "Panama" Baker, Jean Patterson, April Easter. Photo courtesy of Mo Carrick Kelley.

The most important thing that happened in fall 1975 was simply that the women showed up again, and they did so in even greater numbers. If the men were waiting for the women's team to wither away, it wasn't going to happen. Team leaders from that first season—Andy Moore, Sharon McKendrick, and Roberta Player—posted notices around campus during orientation and strong-armed their dorm mates. Their efforts paid off: in Player's words, "The fall of '75 brought a new batch of seriously athletic women" that included Kristi Norelius, Jean Patterson, Chris Carsten, Martha Witt, Peg Staeheli, and Mo Carrick, all of whom enriched the camaraderie and competition of the women's team. Peg Staeheli remembers that group as "really a mix of people and a mix of styles," who were "all over the place as far as our personalities, body types, and goals" but bound together by the "spirit of doing something different."[47] Growing up before the Title IX era, most of them had not played on competitive sports teams, but they were interested in pushing their limits and doing something that was, in Jean Patterson's words, "pioneer-ish." They were an "independent-minded bunch," and rowing offered them a "socially acceptable format to be on the fringe." Patterson felt they were "renegades and free spirits" who "didn't want to be defined by a predetermined narrative."[48]

For Mo Carrick, the predetermined narrative that she wanted to smash was that women weren't suited to be competitive athletes. She had been fighting that fight since she was in high school. First, she was told she couldn't take auto shop because she was a girl and would "be a distraction" to the boys. She joined the cheerleading squad, and she liked the athleticism and the team dynamic, but she wanted to be out in the elements doing competitive sports, and the only sport offered for girls at her school was tennis—everything else was Girls Athletic Association (GAA) intramurals, which to Mo meant no coaches and no competition. She started running on her own. It was the early 1970s, and "men and boys would hoot and jeer, shout rude comments, and do double takes." Even though she was logging the miles, she was told she couldn't run on the high school cross-country team "because girls couldn't safely run more than a mile—it would be too taxing." So, she followed behind the boys on their runs, "occasionally overtaking some of them." This was a time when women were still not allowed to run in marathons, and she was told by one man that if she kept running, she would ruin the shape of her "lovely legs" with too much muscle.[49]

Her high school finally started a girls' track team, and Carrick, although not fast, became the school's top hurdler because of her technical proficiency—her ability to master technique helped her later in rowing. When she went to WSU, she ran on the women's varsity track team in spring 1974. The experience only deepened her belief in the inequities that existed in sports between boys and girls, men and women. While the WSU men's team drove team vans and received ample per diem and nice lodgings when they traveled away for meets, the women drove their own cars, had an inadequate per meal allowance, and were crammed four or five together into hotel rooms. They even had to make their own uniforms, purchasing tank tops and cutting felt and stenciling WSU on them.

Her own experience strengthened her desire to become a girl's athletic coach—so that she could mentor young women in a way that she never experienced herself. She became part of the first class of women at WSU to earn a coaching minor—a program that was created in the wake of Title IX to prepare coaches for the future wave of high schools girls' teams. When Andy Moore approached her at Duncan Dunn about joining crew in the fall of 1975, Carrick joined to row—and did row, in the stroke seat, at a fall regatta against UW—but she soon found that, at 5' 1" and 110 pounds, becoming a coxswain would allow her to transition from athlete to coach.[50]

When Mo Carrick turned out for crew, she was perhaps more ready than some of her teammates to see sexism, take offense, and push back. The women's team wasn't in the habit of talking politics or debating women's rights, and they certainly weren't aligned on anything except their desire to row. They ran the gamut from those like Jean Patterson, who considered herself, at the time, basically apolitical, to Mo Carrick and Peg Staeheli, who were becoming more politicized on women's issues and were eager to push the envelope. But even Jean recognized that they were all, in their own way, "unspoken feminists," simply by doing what they were doing, and what they were doing was asking for the opportunity and resources to row.

Whatever their political inclinations, they all understood the problem as one of resources, and they set about getting more. That goal found them in the office of the assistant athletic director late that year, appealing to get more gym time for winter training. Peg Staeheli remembers the interview with Sam Jankovich as "tough" and intimidating. She had never encountered entrenched male authority, but upon entering his office, she immediately felt as if they had stepped into a realm of male power where he held all the cards. It made her feel smaller than she already was. He was polite, of course, and they made their case, and he gave them more gym time, but Staeheli remembered the entire ordeal as incredibly condescending. As the women were leaving, Jankovich patted Staeheli on her head—a patronizing experience that petite women in the 1970s well understood.[51]

The women's team appealed to the principles of Title IX if they felt it was a useful tool to gain more gym time or squeeze resources from the university, but Title IX did not give them new boats or oars. They still had to work for those things themselves, just as the men had, and they set about doing just that. They each bought oars for themselves that year, and they also began a series of fundraisers to purchase a new boat. The main event in their $10,000 fundraising campaign was a twenty-mile "Celebrity Row-A-Thon" they planned for Saturday, November 15, 1975. They collected pledges per mile, gathered news coverage, and managed to lure WSU's head football coach, Jim Sweeney, and the head basketball coach, George Raveling, as well Sam Jankovich and Ken Struckmeyer, to the Snake River at six in the morning on a cold, windy, November morning to kick off the event. Their goal was to "raise enough money to buy equipment of their own," as they were "completely dependent on the generosity of the men's crew team and the availability of their equipment."[52] Unfortunately, the wind was so bad that they could not complete the entire twenty-mile row that day, but they did complete the distance after racing in the Frostbite Regatta on Green Lake the following Saturday.

The proceeds from that event, along with pledges they collected for a sixty-mile row to Lewiston and back the following spring, plus a ten-mile run to Moscow, Idaho, allowed them to purchase the first women's-only shell—the *Tomanawass*. In its prime, the boat was a championship vessel rowed by UW. By the mid-1970s, the three-part sectional eight was a heavy, ancient hulk of a shell, but it was theirs. Andy Moore, Ron Neal, and Gene Dowers, a men's coxswain who later became the head women's coach, drove to Seattle to pick it up from legendary coach Frank Cunningham at the Lake Washington Rowing Club (LWRC). They brought it back to campus and placed it in one of the stock pavilions on Farm Way, where they lovingly sanded it down, then patched, resurfaced, and varnished it in preparation for its launching.

President Glenn Terrell on the Boyer dock at the christening of the first women's shell, the *Tomanawass*, in 1976, which was purchased with monies from fundraising, including their first row-a-thon. The shell made it to Boyer only after much hardship and effort. In the foreground on left is Mo Carrick and on the right is Sharon McKendrick. In the background you can see the rest of the women's team, including Cyndi Johnson, Kris Norelius, Peg Staeheli, Kari Buringrud, and Robin Young, holding the *Tomanawass*. Photo courtesy of Mo Carrick Kelley.

When the shell was finally ready, the entire team gathered and loaded it onto Andy Moore's old farm truck to take it to Boyer Park for its baptism in the Snake River. Not far outside Pullman, a strong gust of wind blew the middle section clear off the rack, and it crashed into the wheat fields like Dorothy's house in the *Wizard of Oz*. The shell they had labored so hard to purchase, that they reconditioned themselves and were now prepared to row, lay in the field in shards. Sharon McKendrick was devastated—she sat crying by the side of the road as others pulled up. Kristi Norelius was in one of the cars that followed. She couldn't believe it. It was so painful. They were so proud of the shell, and now they had destroyed it. It was almost too much. "We just leaned against the side of the truck and started laughing," she remembered. Otherwise, they would have cried. Along with Ron, they stooped in the field to pick up all the pieces, some of which were very small.

After the wreck of the *Tomanawass*, "they were disappointed but defiant."[53] They called up Frank Cunningham, who said, "Bring it back over and I'll fix it." Andy Moore and Roberta Player drove back over to Seattle with the fragmented remains and delivered them to Cunningham at his house. He fed them sandwiches and they all chatted, and he told them, "Sure, I can fix it." They were incredulous. The shell was torn into pieces. But they left it there, and Frank Cunningham repaired it in his garage. Kristi Norelius called him a "magician." It came back to them later that spring, and they were able to bolt it together and take it out on the river. It was even heavier now—and less responsive—but it was still theirs, and from now on they would affectionately call it the "Tomato Sauce."

In the short term, the story of the *Tomanawass* was a tragedy: they lost money and training time, and it further confirmed the stereotypes of those who thought they were incompetent "girls." No matter how many boats the men had wrecked by then, Martha Witt remembered that it "took a long time for them to live that down."[54] But for every guy who "thought they were stupid because it had fallen off the truck," Peg Staeheli realized there were more who took note of the women's grit and resolve. They were serious about rowing, and even a shattered shell or two wasn't going to stop them. The guys began to recognize that the women were behaving like WSU rowers. The women were earning their respect.

The men's team also began to take note of the successes of the women's crew on the water. By the 1976–77 school year, the women's club was adding more rowers—including Felly Bergano, who had been on the WSU gymnastics team, and Kari Buringrud, whose great-uncle rowed and won national championships for UW in the 1920s. They had enough rowers to field lightweight, junior varsity, and open fours, and they were beginning to have some success against credible competition, such as UBC and UW. The open four, with Mo Carrick, Kristi Norelius, Dawn Maguire, Chris Carsten, and Cyndi Johnson, beat UW in Pullman and then, with Kari Buringrud replacing an injured Johnson in the bow seat, rowed to a respectable fifth-place finish in the 1977 Pac-8 Championships at Redwood Shores. Even more surprising was the lightweight four, made up of coxswain Peg Staeheli, Jean Patterson, Robin Young, Martha Witt, and Felly Bergano, which ended up taking second place behind UW.

The women's lightweight four that rowed to second place on the West Coast in 1977. From Left to right: Martha Witt, Robin Young, Felly Bergano, Jean "Snake Action" Patterson, and coxswain Peg Staeheli. Photo courtesy of Mo Carrick Kelley.

Stroking the lightweight boat was Jean Patterson, who came to be known as "Snake Action"—"Snake" because she was long and thin like a snake, six feet tall and only 125 pounds, and "Action" because if there was something going on Jean was usually in the middle of it. On the surface, she shared many similarities with Kristi Norelius: both were tall and competitive; both stroked their respective boats—Kristi in the open boat and Snake in the light-weight boat—and both shared leadership responsibilities as co-commodores during the 1976–77 season. But unlike Kristi, Jean was not quiet, calm, or unassuming. She drew attention wherever she went. She could be loud and temperamental. She wasn't shy about letting people around her know how she felt, whether it was her coxswain, teammates, or the guys.

Growing up, Jean Patterson loved playing team sports, but schools did not have competitive teams for girls. So she participated in the GAA intramural program for girls and bided her time. When she got to Pullman, she was thrilled at the sporting opportunities for women. She played volleyball as a freshman in 1974–75, but in the fall of 1975, during her sports physical, the doctor detected an irregular heartbeat and told her she couldn't play on the WSU volleyball team. She had heard about crew from guys in her dormitory and was a little nervous about joining because she thought rowing was an "elitist sport" that only "rich people did." But she wanted to be part of a team, and she knew the rowing club did not require a physical to compete—that was all it took.

Patterson immediately fell in love with the sport as well as the daily ritual of going to the river. She loved the excitement of leaving campus, "the aesthetics of the wheat fields" they traveled through to reach the Snake River, and the "liquid meditation" of rowing itself.[55] Now she was stroking the lightweight boat that, although not seeded at the Pac-8 Championships, surprised "the fans and competition" when it "breezed past Oregon and OSU to reach the finals" and "gave top-seeded Washington a strong challenge."[56]

If at first the men thought "the girls" lacked seriousness, were a nuisance, or patronizingly thought they were "quaint" or "cute" for trying, by the end of 1977 there was no question that the women, through their earned efforts, now commanded their respect. The tensions that had existed in the first year of the program had fallen away, largely because the men could no longer doubt their dedication. Peg Staeheli recognized that "once the men started to respect the women's commitment to the sport," some of their resistance "was broken down." In a few short years, the women had made a place for themselves in the club, and increasingly the two teams were inseparable. As Ken Abbey liked to say, "One program, two teams."[57] To those who came after 1977, the crew often felt like one club, women and men, together.

One Club, Women and Men

The Pull Hard that was published in January 1978 contained a first. Since its inception in 1973 as a "somewhat irregularly" published newsletter of Cougar Crew, it had never yet carried a report from the women's team. With Commodore Kari Buringrud's column in 1978, the women were now fully part of the club. Her report was important not only for its inclusion but for three other reasons as well.

First, she announced a new coach, Steve Porter, the fourth in four years of women's crew, in what had become a revolving door of former WSU oarsmen—Ron Neal, Doug Kee, and now Porter—taking the job on a temporary, one-year term. The women's team had yet to find its Ken Struckmeyer; and, in fact, it never did. In the sixteen seasons from 1974 to 1990, when the women transitioned to a varsity program, the team had ten different coaches, all of them men, except for Anne Marie Dousset, and eight of them were former WSU rowers.

Secondly, Buringrud's report heralded the arrival "a brand new four as yet unnamed" that became the *Ron Neal*. The women's team, which looked to be, according to the commodore, the "biggest and best women's crew" ever at WSU, was adding more equipment. It was never enough, of course, but the fundraising efforts of the women were easing some of the pressure on the club's scarce resources.

Finally, at the bottom of Buringrud's column, an editor's note stated that "the women have requested that they be referred to as 'oarsmen.'"[58] It was not an important political statement, per se. The women's team had not debated if they should be "oarswomen" or "oarspersons." But the simple statement seemed to sum up an important reality by the late 1970s: the women were simply a part of the crew, and they did not need to be separated from the rest of the club. They belonged. They were oarsmen like everyone else. Enough said.

A lot had changed since Anne Marie Dousset and her band of pioneers came down to the shell house in fall 1974. For one thing, the women were no longer a novelty. The 1977–78 school year contained the first senior class of men who had never experienced Cougar Crew without a women's team. Also, women joining the club in the late 1970s no longer asked themselves, "Do we belong here?" It was a self-evident truth that women were an integral part of the club—and of college rowing generally.

The WSU rowing club took its third—and final—trip to Wisconsin in the spring of 1978. For the first time, a women's crew accompanied the men to Madison. One woman from WSU had competed before in Madison. Kathy Figon was the first female coxswain for the men's team in 1972 and was very likely the first female ever to compete in a men's rowing race in Madison because, in 1974, Wisconsin's Coach Jablonic still did not approve of women coxing men's boats. "I don't believe in that," he told Struckmeyer, "but go ahead and do whatever the hell you want!"[59]

Now Struckmeyer was bringing three boats of women to Wisconsin; and for the first time, they would be rowing the same distance as the men, which in Madison was 1,850 meters. Up until that 1978 race, women's crews had raced 1,000 meters at the Midwestern Sprints, but 1978 became the first year men and women competed at the same distance in a college regatta, in large part because Jay Mimier, coach of the Wisconsin women, had pushed for the change. Mimier had coached the Badger women since 1973 and also served as assistant to the women's U.S. National Rowing Team. He had coached some of the greatest female rowers of the decade, including Wisconsin's own Carie Graves, a legend for her power, endurance, and grit. The conventional wisdom that a woman like Graves, or any female competitor, could not row the same distance as men was increasingly hard to justify.[60]

By participating in the Midwestern Sprints in 1978 and rowing the same distance as men, WSU women, whether they recognized it or not, were part of the broader struggle for equity between male and female athletes that was playing out on numerous fronts throughout the decade. The longer race "calls for a completely different race strategy than we are used to," Buringrud told the *Daily Evergreen*, "but we are in shape for it."[61] Indeed, the WSU women, used to racing only 1,000 meters, had been preparing for the longer distance in the spring of 1978, even while the men had been ribbing them. "The men were giving us a hard time that we weren't going to be able to do it," Buringrud recalled. "But, of course, we did." Buringrud's open boat made the finals, while the lightweight boat had a commanding lead in the final before it was disqualified for veering into another lane. It was not a spectacular showing, but the women, as Kari wrote in a letter to her parents, "proved we can row 1,850 meters and row it well."[62]

Kari Buringrud had not come to Pullman thinking she was going to participate in competitive athletics. She had been an active girl at Bellevue's Newport High School, competing on the tennis and badminton teams. Growing up on the shores of Lake Washington, she also loved swimming and being around the water. Her great-uncle, Harry John Dutton, had rowed on championship crews for UW in the 1920s and was enshrined in the UW athletics Hall of Fame, but Kari did not think of herself as an "athlete." That changed in the fall of 1976. She saw a sign, attended a meeting, met some "wonderful people" who convinced her that never having rowed was not a liability, and soon found herself running stadiums and doing calisthenics during two weeks of grueling land workouts that "almost killed her."

The suffering was worth it. When the team finally took the novices to the Snake River for the first time, she was hooked. Rowing practice became the favorite part of her day—a daily respite that allowed the hyper-organized Buringrud to "leave campus and classwork behind." Not only was the Snake River Canyon "so very beautiful and different" from Pullman, but even as a novice, she could tell that "moving a shell together and gliding over the surface of the water was amazing." She had always loved the feeling of being on the water—the beauty and peace of it. Now she experienced those moments of grace when everyone in the boat worked together in perfect synchronicity.

The experienced rowers welcomed Kari and the other novices. Kari remembers Mo Carrick and Chris Carsten teaching her the basic elements of the stroke. Although she was in a sorority, Kari began to feel an even closer connection to her crew family. As commodore of the women's team for two consecutive years, from fall 1977 to spring 1979, Kari became a central hub of the crew, immersing herself in club fundraising, communications, scheduling, hosting regattas, arranging trips, ordering uniforms, organizing team dinners, and generally "keeping everybody going in the same direction." She found herself skipping sorority functions to attend to crew events. Rowing gave her a reason to avoid some of the drama of the sorority, and it also fostered the most important and durable relationships from her time at WSU. She had found her true community.

Not only was Buringrud a tireless organizer, but as a journalism major, she was also an articulate spokesperson for the entire crew, women and men. When she wasn't herself writing pieces on the crew, she made sure that the women and men received equal coverage.[63] In the first years of women's crew, their exploits, if they were covered at all by the *Evergreen*, often appeared in separate articles.[64] In 1977–78, for the first time, the *Evergreen* covered the men and women not only in the same article but as the same team. After Class Day 1978, the paper quoted Struckmeyer himself treating the teams as one and the same: "I think the attitude of the whole crew team, men and women, is good, and our prospects are good too."[65] After both the men and women decisively defeated SPU in late April on the Snake, Struckmeyer told the paper, "It was a good warm-up to Madison for both the men's and women's crews."[66] Increasingly, the two teams were merging together as one united club.

Kari Buringrud was the ideal student leader to usher in a new era of Cougar Crew, where men and women worked together to realize Ken Abbey's vision of two teams inhabiting one program. For one, she made friends easily with the men and felt comfortable with them. She held them to account, but she didn't take offense easily. When the men, led by her future husband, Steve Ranten, secretly installed the seats backwards in the women's new shell, the *Ron Neal*, Kari might not have found it as hilarious as they did, but she also saw it for what it was: immature hijinks by "the boys." When Doug Engle and Chris Gulick found it amusing to throw Kari in the hotel swimming pool at Pac-8s, she made them give her quarters for the laundry and gamely added "Aqua-Bear" to her ever-growing list of nicknames (to go along with Kari-Bear, Sugar Bear, etc.), but she didn't see it as a malign expression of male power. Kari believed that in her era, "there was no concerted effort to try to make life miserable for any particular group."[67]

This did not mean that there were no longer conflicts over resources or that the women never yielded to the priority of the men's team. It was still true that the men always got on the water first at practice, but Kari and her teammates did not see this as second-class citizenship as much as a reasonable accommodation out of respect for Struckmeyer himself who, for his part, was willing to cooperate with the women to resolve conflicts to everyone's satisfaction. The women liked and respected Struckmeyer, who was good-natured and gracious toward them. Sheri Van Cleef remembered the women affectionately calling him "Crew Dad" and his wife Marjorie "Crew Mom."[68] The women's officers worked closely with the men's officers, and both groups looked to Struckmeyer for guidance and leadership, which he offered to both teams. Whether it was fundraising, organizing, traveling, sharing boats, or just driving to the river for practice, by the late 1970s, the men and women were "in it together."[69] Kathleen Randall, who followed Kari Buringrud as commodore in 1979–80, felt that, by then, the men were no longer as fixated on protecting their own resources. Agreements on everything from gas money to sharing boats to loading the shell trailer were made in good faith—and often on the spot—and both resources and responsibilities were divvied up in a climate of cooperation.[70]

For women who arrived in the late 1970s, the integration between the two clubs was part of the attraction of rowing. Susan Ernsdorff, who began rowing in 1977 and was predictably dubbed "Sue Crew," remembered piling into Kelvin Eder's old Cadillac convertible—the "Eder beater"— bouncing down to the river with the music cranked, and then returning later in the evening to the dining hall, where the crew, men and women, ate together like a family.[71] Kerin McKellar, who joined the women's team in 1978, remembers the men and women as a tightly bonded community—they ran stadiums together, lifted weights together, cleaned up after concerts together, sold programs together, and always cheered each other on. There was competition between the men and women, like carrying each other up the stadium steps or doing wall-sits during winter workouts—no one wanted to be the first to break. But everything was done in a spirit of camaraderie and fun.[72] It was no wonder that those late 1970s crews produced a number of couples who later married—Kari Buringrud and Steve Ranten; Rich Ray and Kathleen Randall; John Holtman and Eve Boe; and Sandy Schively and Mike Buckley.

The Battle of the Sexes was over, as far as Cougar Crew was concerned. In fact, some of the most apparently sexist slogans from that era of women's crew, ones that make us wince today, like "Strokin' it Long and Hard on the Snake!" and "Fast Hands and a Slow Slide makes for a Good Piece!" emanated from the women themselves, who could be intentionally irreverent in choosing a motto for Class Day t-shirts, which, in the words of Kathleen Randall, "were often sexually suggestive or just downright crude."[73] Rich Ray, who later coached the women, viewed their "salacious plays on words" as an expression of "funny, self-confident, and assertive individuals" who sought to "startle, if not offend, the conventionally minded."[74]

Mostly, times were good, and when they became hard, the women and men of Cougar Crew endured them together. Whether it was the nightmare of finding a way home from Wisconsin in 1978 during a Northwest Airlines pilot strike, or the shared suffering of the foolhardy rowathons of the late 1970s, or simply the inevitable broken down car on a road trip, women and men shared these life lessons together, seemingly over and over again. Unfortunately, not all of these shared hardships were easily overcome: one of them amounted to the greatest tragedy in the history of Cougar Crew.

Cristy Cay Cook

Deb Julian had been an athletic girl in high school. She was 5' 10" and competitive. During her senior year at Kennewick High School, she participated in basketball, volleyball, and track—all varsity programs. Girls her age now had opportunities beyond the GAA intramural leagues. When she went off to Pullman in the fall of 1977, she no longer had time for sports. If she wasn't in lectures or science labs or the library, she was cleaning cages and surgery rooms at the WSU vet clinic. It was great experience, and she also needed the money to put herself through school. But she missed athletics and longed for the competition and camaraderie. By the start of her junior year at WSU, fall 1979, she had, remarkably, made enough money at the vet clinic that she didn't have to work. She began to look for another activity. Like so many other students over the years, Julian was lured in by the beautiful wooden Pocock racing shell that the rowing club strategically positioned to catch the eye of students as they emerged from Bohler Gymnasium during fall registration. Well, she was also lured by the tall, cute guys milling around beside the boat. She had never even heard of crew, but they told her they were looking for tall girls, and she fit the bill. She liked it from the start: it was a challenge, which she welcomed, and rowing was so aesthetically pleasing, especially on the Snake River. But what really drew her in was the immediate connection she felt with the other novice women who were turning out that fall: Sandy Schively, Kathy Schaaf, Kathy Murphy, Karla Karshner, Jennifer Dore, Kellie Williams, Arlette Ward, Heidi Falk, and Cristy Cay Cook.

She was especially drawn to Cook. They were both juniors among the mostly freshmen novice women. Cristy Cook was smart, beautiful, and fun-loving. She liked to drive her 1977 Chevy Camaro to the river. Julian often rode with her, sitting in the front seat, just talking. There was so much to discuss. Cristy Cook had ideas and opinions. Originally, she was a pre-med major, but she had changed to pre-vet because she was already thinking she wanted to have more time with her future family than a career as a doctor could give her. Along with a strong domestic side—she loved cooking meals for friends and family—Cook was complex and mature, possessing the talents and experiences of someone much older than twenty. She had a pilot's license—in fact, she'd been flying since she was seventeen—and was an outstanding student and an accomplished pianist who had won awards for her skills. Despite her accomplishments, there was no hint of arrogance in Cristy Cook's manner—she was down to earth, honest, and open. Her style was genuine and disarming. She was the kind of person who liked to help, and she didn't wait around for an invitation—if she saw a way to be useful, she was already doing it. She surprised Deb Julian and Kathy Murphy that fall by immediately introducing herself and offering to drive them to the river. She had heard they both worked at the vet clinic, and neither of them owned a car. There were no team vans at that time, no designated drivers, no certification tests. If you had a car and could drive, it was welcomed—all hands on deck.

That fall, the women's team was splitting their practices between mornings and afternoons because there weren't enough boats to go around. Morning practices were brutal: you had to drive to the river in the predawn hours so that you had time to put the boats away and make the thirty-minute trek back to campus in time for eight o'clock classes, hopefully leaving enough time to change out of wet clothes and grab breakfast, but this was unlikely. On Wednesday, November 7, the team was training for two late fall races in Seattle. The novice women were just starting to click, and Gene Dowers, a former WSU coxswain now entering his second year as women's coach, was hopeful. Earlier that fall, he had told the *Daily Evergreen* that the women's team possessed "twice as much depth" and "a better training program this season."[75] Dowers had reason for optimism—his team had a good balance of experience and exuberance, and it was also the first time in its short history that the women's crew had the same coach for consecutive seasons.

Dowers was young—too young, probably. He had taken over the team at age twenty-one and was just finding his own voice as a coach and a person, even as he was placed in charge of mentoring women who were nearly the same age as himself, and sometimes older. He had made plenty of mistakes his first season. He had felt overmatched and "completely intimidated" by some of the veteran varsity women.[76] They were older than he, tough as hell, and they did what they wanted—it was a power struggle. But this fall, Dowers was more secure in his position, and he was eager to take the women's program to the next level. He had a coxswain's eye for technique and innovative ideas about everything from training to nutrition. That morning, November 7, the weather was clear as he packed a load of rowers into his giant old Cadillac—the "cattle car"—eager to squeeze in another training session before his crews raced for the first time that year.

That morning, Cook picked up her own crew—Deb Julian, Kathy Murphy, Kelli Williams, and Heidi Falk—and headed down to the river. They drove through the wheat fields in the predawn darkness, everyone in the backseat napping. Cook played music, talked with Julian, and tried to wake up. They saw the sunrise while rowing and felt the rush of adrenaline from sweating and working together on the water, surrounded by the silent, sublime canyon that climbed up around them. At the end of practice, four of them were waiting for Kathy Murphy, but the swirling currents were challenging that morning, and Murphy, a coxswain, missed the landing on her first try and had to take her boat to the back of the queue. She told them to leave without her.

Arlette Ward took Murphy's spot in the back seat. It was nearly half past seven, and they were trying to make it back in time for eight o'clock classes. Cook's Camaro was the first car away from the shell house. It was still clear as they wound their way up the grade, but when they passed over the Snake River breaks, they dropped into a thick fog. Ward was sitting immediately behind Cristy Cook. Kelli Williams was behind Deb Julian, who sat sideways in the passenger seat so that she could look at Cook while they talked.

By now, Cook had driven this route dozens of times. The fog was so thick, they didn't even notice as they passed the farmhouse on the west of the highway just about a half mile before the road became a T, with a yellow blinking light followed by a stop sign. They were listening to music on the radio, talking and laughing. All the sudden, for a brief moment, the fog was gone, replaced by a rock-and-earth embankment. Time stopped. Deb Julian took a big breath and waited for the impact.[77]

As the caravan of cars behind them came upon the scene, it was not clear at first that the crash was catastrophic. Kerin McKellar was in the car behind Cook's, and at first she thought the Camaro had just run off the road into the field. When she reached the car, it was clear that this was serious. McKellar, who later became a nurse, stayed with the vehicle and tried to help rescue her teammates. Kathy Murphy, Gene Dowers, and many more ran to the Camaro to help. Others were dispatched to the farmhouse to fetch blankets and call 911. Still others tried to keep more cars from piling into the crash scene. They began to move the girls out of the car. They had all sustained severe injuries—none more so than Cristy Cook, who took the full impact of the steering wheel. She died at the scene in what seemed like a fifteen-minute eternity as they waited for emergency transport to arrive from Colfax. Among those waiting was Tammy Jane Cook, Cristy's sister, who was a coxswain for the novice crew.[78]

The four survivors were taken first to Colfax and then to Spokane—except for Arlette, who *only* sustained a broken leg, cuts on her face in need of stitches, and bad bruising. She stayed in Colfax General Hospital. Deb Julian was headed for the intensive care unit at Deaconess in Spokane. She sustained major damage to her face—broken upper and lower jaws on both sides as well as the cheek bone and orbital on her right side. She also suffered a collapsed lung, a broken arm, and a broken collarbone—the latter injury so "minor" compared to the others that doctors did not discover it until a week later. Kelli Williams, who also suffered severe facial damage, and Heidi Falk were sent to Sacred Heart Hospital. Falk was released after a week, but Williams, like Julian, spent a couple weeks recovering in the hospital.[79]

The accident cast a dark shadow over the crew. The horrid event seemed "unreal" to Sandy Schively, one of Deb Julian's best friends. If Cristy's car had been two feet farther to the left, Sandy thought, they would have just driven into a field. How could this happen? Kathleen Randall was commodore of the women's team that year. She was to row that afternoon, so she hadn't been with the team that morning. Ken Struckmeyer called her. It was hard to fathom what he was telling her. She lived on Observatory Court with a bunch of crew people. As she went from trailer to trailer bearing the sad news, there was disbelief and sorrow. She and Gene Dowers informed the rest of the women's team while Commodore Tim "Haole" Richards told the men. Richards had been friends with Cristy. As a team leader, he liked reaching out to everyone, and he'd had an immediate fondness for Cook, who, like him, was a pre-vet major. He liked to be around her. She didn't "put on airs." She was steady and level-headed, and also exceedingly positive and warm, with a gentle smile for everyone.[80] When Randall told Richards that Cristy "didn't make it," he couldn't understand at first. "You mean, she didn't make it home?" he asked. "Tim," she said, "Cristy died." Richards, like everyone else, was shocked. Crew members made the trek to Spokane to visit Deb, Kelli, and Heidi. The extent of their injuries, especially those of Deb Julian, who, at one point, was read her last rites, made the accident real for those who weren't at the scene.[81]

As the team gathered to memorialize Cristy Cay Cook at Kimbrough Hall, there was deep sadness for having lost a teammate, but there was also anxiety about the program. Would the university shut them down? The answer to that question depended in part on how the Cook family reacted to the tragic accident. Their response was nothing less than remarkable. Despite their own pain, they were unflinchingly kind and generous toward the crew—a type of selfless magnanimity and consideration for others that is almost beyond words. Gene Dowers remembered that the Cooks "were much more concerned about how we were feeling than in their own grief." In fact, just weeks earlier, Cristy had been at home and could not stop talking about the crew, how much she loved rowing and her teammates. The Cooks chose to honor their daughter's memory by taking the high road—they didn't sue the university or demand anything. In fact, in their time of suffering, they chose to help the crew, buying a new women's eight-oared shell for the team, which they christened *Cristy Cay Cook* at a half-time ceremony during a WSU basketball game that winter. They asked Gene Dowers and the women's team to sprinkle Cristy's ashes off the dock at Boyer Park—a testament to her family's understanding of how much WSU rowing meant to her.[82]

The event changed the crew. The wild times of the 1970s gave way to a more regulated approach—now drivers were chosen and designated, and when financing became available, team vans replaced personal cars. Morning practices were out. But the changes were more than just procedural. The team had lost one of its own, and in response, they rallied around each other and became even closer. The tight-knit community of crew was bound even more tightly by the disaster. Sandy Schively remembers that they "all got a lot closer" after the accident. Sheri Van Cleef thought it "drew people together." Tim Richards called it "a galvanizing moment." Kerin McKellar recalls that they all responded to the shock of the incident like a family would, drawing on each other for support. In the wake of the catastrophe, McKellar thought "there was nothing else to do but go back to the river." It was what they had to do—healing would only come by rowing again. In fact, all the women who

survived the crash came back to row, and even Cristy's sister Tammy finished
out the year on the team. Deb Julian was not able to row again until the next
fall, and when she did, she was a different person—not as carefree and outgo-
ing, more cautious. Ever after, she refused to ride in the passenger seat of any
vehicle if she could help it. Going back to the river in the fall of 1980, she was
forced to bear the anxiety of two thirty-minute car rides a day, each passing
by the site of the tragedy. Despite her fears, she did it, with a stoic forbearance
that is hard to fathom.[83]

Conclusion

It was a strange and momentous year for Cougar Crew's men and women. The
WSU yearbook, *Chinook*, carried no photo of the crew for the first and only time
since the rowing club began. Instead, there was a feature on Cristy Cay Cook,
with a picture of her smiling, one foot propped on the tire of the small airplane
she flew, her elbow resting on her knee as she turned to face the camera with a
brilliant smile, looking every bit like Amelia Earhart.[84] Posted in the women's
workout room that year, penned by an anonymous poet, were the lines: "When,
because of fate, one no longer can participate, we as individuals and as a team
must dig deeper, try harder, and give that last ounce, that final push for those of
us who are sidelined." With every stroke, Cristy would live on in their memories. Later, the crew named its primary operating fund after Cristy Cay Cook so
that she is remembered with every deposit and withdrawal.[85]

The momentous events continued. On May 18, as the team was driving
up Interstate 5 in Northern California on their way home from the Pac-10
Rowing Championships, they learned that Mount St. Helens had erupted
in what was the largest, most devastating volcanic event in the history of the
United States. At first there was excitement. When Ken Struckmeyer stood
at the front of the bus and announced the news, Hollywood images of molten
lava and visions of Hawaii flashed before their eyes. Then there was disbelief—what do you mean most of the roadways in Washington are closed?
Then the realization hit home that this would be yet another Cougar Crew
ordeal—one they would endure together as a team, women and men.

Unable to make it back to Pullman, they were diverted to Seattle and the
University of Washington shell house. There they were picked up and parceled
out among Seattle-area families until they could return to Pullman, where
they were supposed to be taking final exams. A few days later, when the roads
finally reopened, they crowded back onto the bus, loaded with face masks to
take to the citizens of Pullman. They traveled the long way around—down to

Portland, up the Columbia River Gorge, and then to Lewiston, Idaho. When they ascended the grade to the top of the Snake River breaks, the landscape was moon-like, the land covered in heavy, cement-like ash. They could not see more than a few feet in front of them. The bus inched into Pullman at twenty miles per hour. By the time they arrived, the university was already making final exams optional, and students were deserting the ash-strewn campus. It was a strange but perhaps appropriate way for the year to end.

While the Cougars were struggling with the fallout from Mount St. Helens, Kristi Norelius was interrupted on her own journey. By 1980, two years of hard work sculling under the tutelage of Bob Ernst and numerous Olympic Development camps had put her in an elite class of American rowers. In June 1980, the *Daily Evergreen* announced her inclusion among the top rowers in the country: "A former WSU student and member of the women's crew team has been selected to row for the 1980 USA Olympic women's rowing team."[86] By that time, however, President Carter and the United States Olympic Committee (USOC) had already determined that the United States would boycott the Olympic Games in Moscow, protesting the Soviet Union's invasion of Afghanistan the previous year. Even so, WSU rowing had its first Olympian, and it was one more indication of just how far the women's team had come since 1974. In five short years, women rowers had gone from outliers to full participants in the club. They had produced boats that made the finals at Pac-10s on several occasions, and their lightweight four raced in women's nationals in 1978. Now, they could claim an Olympic rower as one of their own. Norelius would go on to even greater heights in 1984—and she would be joined there by another WSU rower, Paul Enquist.

Andy Moore (1974–77)

I started at WSU in June 1974, and that winter there was a crazy lady with a funny name trying to get a women's crew started…and the girls from Duncan Dunn thought we would go to the meeting and check it out. It turned out to be Anne Marie Dousset, the first women's coach. She was a WSU graduate student who had been going down to the river with the men's crew and wondering why there wasn't a women's crew. The guys told her, "Well, we tried, but the girls, you know, they were worried about their hair, and being late for classes and what not, so they're not interested." Well, Ann Marie thought she'd give it a try anyway. And so we did. And it was a hoot. We did fundraisers for our crew because it was just a club sport then. One of the fundraisers was making French crepes with lime juice and powdered sugar. We were using Stevenson Tower because they had a little kitchen downstairs, and we were selling them faster than we could make them for a dollar a piece. It was hilarious. We made enough money to go to regattas at Green Lake and the Montlake Cut.

Hardly any of us even knew what crew was. The guys gave us the older boats to work out in because they thought it was "kind of cute" that we were trying to do this. They thought it would never last. But we hung in there, and we got a little bigger and little stronger and little more viable each year. When Anne Marie Dousset went back to France, Ron Neal was our next official coach—a curly-headed guy. He discovered you couldn't motivate women the same way you motivated men. You could yell at men and shame them, and they would do stuff, but the girls would just say, "Fuck you, I quit." So he had to modify his approach. But he was adorable and gorgeous to look at, so everybody wanted to turn out for crew, and it continued to grow.

Roberta "Berta" Player (1974–77)

What did women's crew mean to me? Crew helped me to develop confidence in myself as a woman. There were limited opportunities for me to engage in sports during my high school years, so I hadn't had the chance to challenge my abilities. Even though the role of women in society was starting to change with the women's movement, there were still many people at the time who didn't believe that we had the physical and emotional stamina to be competitive athletes. But Anne Marie Dousset did. As our first coach, she helped us stretch and grow to reach our capabilities. We were not women's libbers—we were just developing a sense of our "selves," not limited by society's expectations at the time. Rowing was giving us confidence. We weren't just the gals in the kitchen anymore. We were becoming more independent. I remember one time we had to take an eight out of the water with six of us. We were a mixed boat, and some of us were kind of puny. To encourage one another, we said, "We are women. We can do this!" It was not easy to get that eight up and over our heads, but darned if we didn't feel good after we got that boat in the shell house! I think it was Anne Marie's ability to instill confidence in us that made it so important to me to ensure that WSU Women's Crew remained alive after Anne Marie returned to France. She had embedded in our minds, "We are women. We can do this!" and we couldn't let her down.

CHAPTER FOUR

―――――――

Rowing Pilgrim: The Journey of Paul Enquist, 1973–1984

I can't believe that Paul and Brad were ever cut, but that is what all good club athletes feed on. Tell them they are "nothing special," and they will find a secret lake or river and become *very* special.

—Ted Nash, head rowing coach, University of Pennsylvania

On August 5, 1984, in the finals of the Olympic Doubles Competition, the puzzle came together for Lewis and Enquist in a performance that flirted with perfection. In these precious moments of peak performance, Lewis and Enquist's years of practice found expression as a unified whole that was vastly greater than the sum of its parts. And then these magical, almost religious moments of near perfect wholeness were gone.

—Michael Livingston, 1972 Olympic silver medalist

In all his years of rowing, the most incredible moment Paul Enquist experienced on the water was not his gold medal victory at Lake Casitas in Los Angeles in 1984. It was not winning the U.S. Olympic Trials. It was not the lightning fast semifinal race in Duisburg, Germany, that launched his double into the finals of the 1983 World Championships. It was not his first victory—it was not even a race. It was just a practice, with a crew that felt rough and only rowed together once and never again. A fleeting experience that nonetheless stayed with him forever as perhaps the most special, surprising moment of his rowing career.

It took place in Hanover, New Hampshire, in July 1984 at the Olympic training camp. The Olympic trials were over. The boats were set. Harry Parker was coaching the eight Olympic scullers while Polish émigré Kris Korzeniowski trained the sweep oarsmen. To break up the monotony of the daily workouts, Parker decided to throw his scullers in two quads and race against Korzeniowski's sweep boats. In one quad was the crew that won the Olympic trials and would represent the United States in Los Angeles. Stroking the other quad was single sculler John Biglow, who won bronze at the World Championships in 1981 and 1982 and would soon row to a fourth-place finish in the Olympics; rowing in the seats behind him were Paul Enquist and Brad Lewis, the Olympic double, and in the bow, the Olympic spare, Tiff Wood, one of the towering figures of U.S. rowing over the previous decade, who won bronze in the single at the 1983 World Rowing Championships and had been on three consecutive Olympic teams.

These men had all rowed in numerous camps together and competed with and against each other in dozens of races in previous years, but they had never rowed in this configuration. Their rowing styles did not necessarily match, nor did their personalities. On the long row to the start of the racecourse at Dartmouth, the boat felt terrible. They stopped their warm-up. No one was particularly happy, but Brad Lewis was never one to suffer quietly. "John, if you're gonna row like that, I can't do this!" he hollered. Biglow turned around and yelled back, "Well, I can't change how I row now, Brad!" The argument was heated and loud, and Enquist was seated directly between the combatants with his head down, thinking to himself, this is going to be a long, miserable practice. Finally, the elder statesman, Tiff Wood, spoke up. "Look, let's just make the best of this and get through the workout." They pointed their boat toward the starting line and finished their warm-up. As they pulled to the line, none of them had high expectations—their primary goal was to endure the workout and make it back to the boathouse without killing each other.[1]

Four boats paddled up to the line: Parker's two quads, Korzeniowski's eight, and a straight four—four oarsmen with no coxswain. The start would be staggered, with the straight four beginning first, followed by the two quads, and finally the eight. "If all four crews were of equal ability," Brad Lewis reasoned, they would all "finish in a four-way tie." Lewis wanted badly to beat the Olympic eight, which was stroked by his longtime nemesis Bruce Ibbetson, who had been one year his senior at UC Irvine. Lewis had nicknamed Ibbetson "Golden Boy" because of Ibbetson's blond hair and tanned, muscular physique. Ibbetson was perhaps the rower that Lewis always secretly longed to be—confident, powerful, fierce, and highly respected—the kind of guy you voted for to be team captain. Lewis was many things but *not* that. He was moody, inconsistent, hard to get along with, and quick to perceive any slight directed his way, especially from Ibbetson, whom he overheard at camp telling a teammate that Lewis and Enquist "had somehow cheated to win the trials."[2] Lewis wanted to hammer Ibbetson now, but he thought it was unlikely, given how fractious the quad felt. Enquist, on the other hand, had no feuds with anyone. His rowing was not fueled by animosity or anger. He was quiet and hard-working. He got along with everyone. In the quad that morning, as always, Paul Enquist was the calm, steady engine, chugging forward despite the chaos around him.

On Parker's command, the boats took off down the racecourse. The quad was "really rough." They were "just trying to survive and keep going," remembered Enquist, but after the start, "we looked around and we are open water up on the other quad."[3] By the end of that first 2,000 meter race, Enquist's quad, rowing together for the first time, had opened up a ten boat-length lead on the Olympic quad that had been rowing together for months. Moreover, they fought valiantly to hold off the sprinting eight, finishing nearly even with the boat that would soon claim the silver medal in the Olympics.

That first race was an eye opener. Their thrown-together quad, despite infighting and rocky rowing, was exceptionally fast. But it was the final 2,000-meter race that morning that stood out to Enquist as something very special. During the fierce competition with the eight, the four scullers were no longer at odds with each other. Their entire focus was on defeating the Olympic eight. As they neared the 1,500-meter mark, the eight was inching up their stern, and they could hear Bob Jaugstetter, the coxswain, hollering at the top of his lungs, "We have the quad!" Then, Tiff Wood was hollering back at him like a madman, "Oh, no you haven't, you little bastard!"[4] Enquist, in the three seat, his legs burning as they neared the finish, could hear Jaugstetter unleash a "string of profanity aimed at us" while Tiff Wood, behind him, was screaming back "at the top of his lungs with the kind of language that would make any longshoreman blush."[5] Lewis was amazed at how "Tiff possessed the rare ability to scream at the top of his lungs in the very heat of battle."[6] It was more intense than any race Enquist had ever experienced. With Tiff and Jaugstetter screaming the entire way, his quad managed to hold off the eight through the finish line.

As they rowed in silence back to the boathouse, Enquist was thinking, "What just happened? What's going on here?" It was the most extraordinary and surprising practice he had ever experienced. Harry Parker was thrilled at their performance. Back at the boathouse, he was all smiles. He just beamed, knowing he also had witnessed something special. Parker's great gift as a coach was putting his athletes in competitive situations where he could draw out their best performance. "Even for people who are motivated," Parker realized "there's a pretty natural built-in resistance in the body to working hard," and the "coach has to help the oarsman overcome that."[7] Parker loved to see his rowers push beyond their limits, as this makeshift quad had just done. But it was a onetime experience. They put the quad away and everyone went back to their own boats that afternoon: Biglow and Wood to their singles, Enquist and Lewis to their double. Enquist wrote in his logbook that he was exceptionally tired that afternoon and the next day—he had given everything he had, and the others felt the same way.

Enquist called it "one of the most incredible things I've ever experienced out on the water."[8] To him, the workout was memorable because it was so surprising and unexpected—to be so rough but so fast was thrilling. To hold off the eight was thrilling. To take four oarsmen who hadn't rowed together and perform on such a level was thrilling. To do so in a practice rather than a race elevated the experience to a level of intrinsic purity that epitomized the amateur rowing ethos—no glory, no fame, just uncontaminated pain. Rowers lived for those moments of unexpected grace, when the power of four flawed individuals is channeled into one flawless, fleeting moment. Then, just like that, the workout ended, and the boat never reassembled again. But the memory of that practice stayed with him.

The quad was surprising and remarkable in many other ways, not the least of which was how a rower from Washington State University—a program that Brad Lewis speculated was, of all the college rowing teams in the United States, "perhaps the furthest from being termed a rowing power"—ended up sharing a boat with the greatest scullers of his era, guided by the greatest American rowing coach ever, Harry Parker.[9] In the quad, he was sandwiched between three of the main characters in David Halberstam's book, *The Amateurs: The Story of Four Young Men and Their Quest for an Olympic Gold Medal*: John Biglow, the storied stroke oar of Yale's famed championship boats of 1978–79; Tiff Wood, one of the most powerful oars ever to row at Harvard, who anchored the renowned "Rude and Smooth" championship crews of 1974–75; and, finally, Brad Lewis, the brooding Southern Californian who fashioned himself as the idiosyncratic outsider intent on "crashing the party at the Harvard boathouse."[10]

To Enquist, they weren't legends, they were just Tiff, John, and Brad, his best friends—people with whom he had shared numerous camps, suffered through countless practices, eaten countless cheap meals. He wasn't in awe of anyone, even the legendary Harry Parker. He was just trying to make it through another day of practice and row his best. On that day in Hanover, Enquist was quietly doing what he did throughout his entire rowing career: exhibiting unflappable consistency even as the maelstrom swirled around him.

The Amateurs contains a photo of that miraculous quad, even though David Halberstam never mentions it in his narrative. Halberstam was one of the greatest journalists of his generation—perhaps the greatest. His book *The Best and the Brightest* was a story of how hubris and political calculation led to tragedy in Vietnam, and *The Amateurs* was, in one sense, the "best and the brightest" for rowing, exploring the ambitions, flaws, and failures of four scullers pursuing the right to represent the United States in the single sculls at the Los Angeles Olympics. Halberstam did not choose Enquist to be one of his central characters—he was not one of the "four young men" in the subtitle. He appears throughout the book but never in the spotlight, even though he and Brad Lewis—not Tiff Wood or John Biglow or Joe Bouscaren, the Ivy Leaguers featured in the book—won gold in Los Angeles. The lack of attention did not bother Enquist in the least. He liked to tell the story of Halberstam calling him up after the Olympics. They only spoke for a few minutes before the famous writer unexpectedly said, "Hey, I have to go. I'll call you back!" Halberstam never called him back, and Enquist's role in the book's narrative, to the extent that it was told at all, was gathered from others. Enquist joked that his story was "probably too boring" for Halberstam, who had more material than he needed without Paul's input anyway. He didn't take it personally. In keeping with his low-key personality, he was happy to avoid the limelight.[11]

Perhaps, on first blush, Enquist's story lacked the necessary drama that Halberstam needed to fuel his bestselling books. Enquist was the guy everyone liked: the quiet workhorse, the laconic fisherman from the Pacific Northwest who didn't complain, didn't rage against his coaches, didn't come from either squalor or wealth, didn't attend Harvard or Yale, didn't seek to stand apart, but rather sought to fit in, get along with others, lend a hand, be useful and constructive. After he was cut by Parker from the 1984 sculling camp, he stuck around, went rowing every day by himself, and then drove the Harvard boat trailer back to Cambridge because he was one of the few rowers Parker trusted to navigate the rig safely through the crowded streets of Boston.[12] Other rowers called him "Zenquist" for his calm demeanor even amid turmoil. He was universally well-liked. On the day he was cut from camp, one of the rowers selected over him for the Olympic double, Charlie Altekruse, who had rowed for Parker at Harvard, taped a four-leaf clover to a card and gave it to Enquist as a sign of his appreciation and respect. There were no hard feelings on Paul's side either. "Good luck," Altekruse told him, "I'm sure I'm going to see you down the road."[13]

Halberstam might have missed the boat: Enquist's story, like the story of WSU rowing itself, contained inescapable drama because it was the most improbable of all the stories Halberstam tells in *The Amateurs*. Four years before that quad practice, Enquist had quit rowing and was working in a sail-making loft in Ballard. Three years before that, in 1977, he had graduated from WSU, where, as Halberstam writes, "the program was new, the coach was inexperienced, and the team always lost."[14] How did Paul Enquist ascend from one to the other? How did the son of a fisherman, a working-class kid from a Scandinavian immigrant enclave in Seattle, rise from the fledgling club team at WSU to the very top of the sporting world?

Enquist's Dilemma

George Raveling might have had a champion basketball player in Paul Enquist, but he never had the chance to find out. Enquist had played at Ballard High School, but he was thin and gangly—just seventeen when he graduated, only 170 pounds but still filling out. He spent the summer before his freshman year on his father's fishing boat, working hard and eating well, thanks to the Norwegian cook. By the time he arrived on campus in fall 1973, he was 6' 6"and weighed 210 pounds; Enquist was ready to recognize his true talents on the basketball court. His dorm mates in Rogers Hall told him he would need the basketball coach to sign a class block to keep his academic schedule from interfering with team practices, so off he went to the basketball office.

It was George Raveling's second year as head coach. He had a strong recruiting class from out of state, and the assistant coach that Enquist spoke with did not seem too interested in this walk-on from Ballard, even if he was 6' 6" and clearly motivated. "We practice in the afternoons," he told Enquist. "Just sign up for classes that don't meet in the afternoons."

Enquist went back to his dorm and figured it all out. When he took his schedule back to the basketball office, the assistant coach took a quick glance and said, "Looks great." But on Sunday, when Enquist received his schedule, he saw that his science classes had labs in the afternoons. "What the hell?" Enquist realized immediately that the assistant basketball coach didn't care whether he turned out for basketball or not. If he had wanted Enquist on the team, he would have given him a computer card that would restrict his class times to the morning. To hell with him, Enquist thought. That day, the WSU basketball team potentially lost a hard-working, extremely competitive second team forward who would have played defense and rebounded with more enthusiasm than anyone else on the court, while the WSU crew gained their best rower ever and U.S. rowing gained a future gold medalist.

On the first day of classes, Enquist had a technical drawing class for mechanical engineering majors at one in the afternoon. Before the class began, the professor wrote "Crew" on the board and then invited those who were interested in rowing to see him after class. When Enquist, alongside two other tall engineering students—Steve Porter and Jim Fischer—lumbered up to talk to him after class, the professor looked them up and down and said, "Go see Professor Pratt on the second floor. He will be very happy to see you!"

The three walked upstairs to see Dave Pratt—former UW oarsman and Navy rowing coach—who told them where to meet for the ride down to the Snake River. That Wednesday, Enquist packed a bag of clothes and walked from his two o'clock class in Todd Hall to the meeting spot near Cleveland Hall, and he never looked back.

The fall of 1973 was Ken Struckmeyer's first year as head coach. The team was lucky to cobble together three eights for each practice, and everyone was needed. With Enquist, Struckmeyer wasted no time. There would be no long apprenticeship among a large group of novices, as most first-time rowers experienced in large programs. No rowing machines or tanks or barges to soften the learning curve. They needed tall rowers like Enquist (as well as Porter and Fischer) on the varsity boat immediately, and that first practice, having never been in a shell before, he found himself sitting in the five seat of an eight with experienced oarsmen rowing a 2,000-meter piece from the grain elevator at Almota back to the shell house. Enquist watched the stroke intently and tried to drop his oar in the water at the same time, but he missed a lot of strokes that day. "I'd say to myself, okay, I'm going to get in on this next stroke, and I tried my darnedest, and then I would take a breath, and think, okay, so I missed that one, but I'll try to get in on this next one," remembered Enquist, of his inelegant initiation into the sport.[15] He ended up with blisters on his feathering hand from gripping his oar too tight, as all new oarsmen do, so when he showed up at the next practice, he switched to the port side, and suffered through another 2,000-meter piece. Now both his hands were torn up. On Saturday morning he arrived with tape over both hands, but it was drizzling, and before long the tape had balled up into a wet, sticky wad, not to mention that his gray sweats were soggy and dripping wet both from the rain and their thrashing oars. Rowing at WSU was not for the faint of heart, but Enquist was a fisherman's son—he loved it from the very beginning.

Paul Enquist and Jim Fischer rowed together for four years on the WSU varsity eight, but Fischer missed one regatta his senior year, so Enquist liked to say that he was the only rower in WSU's history to row in every varsity race over a four-year span, and therefore, he joked, he also lost more shirts in varsity races than any other oarsman in WSU's history. He was probably right. After a victory over UPS and PLU in Pullman in spring 1974—the first victory ever for WSU men's crew—Enquist's boat lost every race they entered that spring. Even so, his freshman season was a revelation, introducing him to the larger world of college rowing beyond Pullman, to which he felt immediately connected. The team traveled to Madison for the Midwestern Sprints, where Enquist saw firsthand how one of the great programs in the country operated. He also spied in the boathouse a shell named after Norm Sonju, the former Wisconsin head coach, who used to work summers on his grand-father's salmon-fishing boat in Alaska. Rowing, Enquist would soon discover, was a small universe whose doors were open to all seekers. When UW came to Pullman the next weekend, Enquist hosted some of the Husky rowers on his floor in Rogers Hall, and there began rowing friendships that Enquist was already cultivating beyond WSU.

Enquist's first season at WSU in 1974 culminated with two memorable regattas that would shape his future in ways he could not yet imagine. First, at the Western Sprints in Burnaby, British Columbia, Enquist witnessed an epic final in the varsity eight, where UW, Cal Berkeley, and UC Irvine bat-tled their way down the course, passing the lead back and forth. The Huskies won, but it was a surprising performance from an upstart UC Irvine program, giving hope to small programs like WSU that, with the right ingredients, UW could be challenged. More to the point for Enquist's story was that the young Irvine coach, Bob Ernst, was immediately offered a coaching job at UW. Dick Erickson had the resources to co-opt the competition, if necessary, and he was not about to get beat by Ernst if he could hire him instead. The very next summer, Ernst, now UW's freshman coach, organized a summer sculling program in Seattle that attracted Paul Enquist and Ray Wittmier—it was Enquist's introduction to both single sculling and Bob Ernst, who would become Enquist's first sculling coach after he graduated from WSU.

The other memorable regatta occurred after the season was over, in summer 1974, after everyone had left for summer break. Harvard's famous, undefeated "Rude and Smooth" crew was coming to Seattle to race the Hus-kies on the Montlake Cut, and Dick Erickson told Struckmeyer he had a spot in the junior varsity event if Ken could patch together an eight. Enquist rowed in that boat, and after their race finished, they sat floating with the rest of the shells in Portage Bay and watched Harvard and UW race through the cut as the crowds cheered on both sides and from atop the Montlake Bridge.

This was the most famous of all Harry Parker's Harvard crews, with big personalities like Tiff "The Hammer" Wood, Dick Cashin, and the stroke, Al Shealy, who used to announce Harvard's final sprint by hollering, "See you later, Yalies!" or, in this case, "See you later, Huskies!" as Harvard pulled away toward inevitable victory. They were arrogant and obnoxious, perhaps, but so captivating that you could not look away, especially in a sport where collective anonymity usually obliterated individual glamour. Enquist certainly could not look away, and he watched in amazement as Harvard lengthened their lead, while coxswain Mike Klier, with his mathematical mind, narrated: "Harvard is rowing at a 34, and Washington is at 38 strokes a minute, and Harvard is walking away!" Enquist had no idea that ten years from that moment, he himself would be coached by Harry Parker and rowing with Tiff Wood in the Olympic sculling camp, but he was hooked.

When Enquist returned to WSU as a sophomore in fall 1974, no one could yet predict his potential. He was tall, but he didn't strike anyone as an Olympic specimen. Brad Sleeper rowed on the team with Enquist for four years—he entered in that same strong class of 1973–77, a group that nearly won Class Day as freshmen and then dominated the next three years. Sleeper was a lightweight, and his boat was having success already in 1974, with wins in the Midwestern Sprints and against UW, while Enquist's heavyweight varsity boat still floundered. "Paul was nothing special when he was at Washington State," remembered Sleeper. "He was a solid rower, but he didn't stand out." Sleeper could see that Enquist was tall, but he was also "narrow-shouldered and gawky looking." Sleeper thought that other rowers on the team, including Paul's friend Ray Wittmier, were more physically impressive.[16] Even Mike Klier, Enquist's coxswain for his first two years, did not see his potential at the time since he "had no real personal experience, no real perspective of what an Olympic-caliber oarsman would look like."[17]

It was perhaps easy for his teammates to underestimate Enquist. Sure, he was tall and, according to Mike Kimbrell, had "abnormally long arms," physical gifts that suited him well to rowing (and required his mom to make his shirts; otherwise, his sleeves ended midway down his forearms), but Enquist was so genial, so quick to laugh, and so good-natured that at first glance one might overlook his competitive, self-driven nature. Kimbrell liked Enquist from the moment he met him. As a freshman, he found Enquist sort of goofy, gullible, and easily excitable. Later, Enquist would often be described as quiet and calm, but Kimbrell remembered that the young Enquist "couldn't stop talking" when they were on the shore before a row. What struck Kimbrell even then was that once Enquist got in a boat and they pulled away from the dock, it was as if a switch had turned, and Enquist became all seriousness with an "absolutely clear, single-mined focus" on rowing. This struck coxswain Mike Klier as well: "When he was in the boat and you were underway, there was nobody more devoted to what was happening than Paul."[18]

By his junior year, Enquist's competitive nature was more visible to everyone. He directed winter workouts that year in the old boxing room of Bohler Gym. He demanded much of his teammates and even more of himself. Doug Engle thought that Enquist led by "example and coercion." You had to put "your best effort into a workout or boat that he was in," remembered Engle.

"He had a drive that was contagious."[19] On sweat-drenched mats, surrounded by photographs of Pacific Coast League boxing champions, Enquist guided his teammates through an excruciating routine of calisthenics followed by stairs in Martin Stadium or runs out "Pig Road" toward the airport and back. Enquist wasn't the fastest runner, but he started analyzing the fast guys— former cross-country runners like Sleeper—and trying to emulate them. He would stay with them as long as he could and usually lose them on the hills coming back into town, but he stayed closer to them each time, and he could feel his endurance improving.

For Enquist, it was all about paying attention to the details, whether it was on the water or during winter workouts. If he analyzed what he was doing, Enquist believed he could improve, and he tried to apply this principle to those around him as well. As a freshman, in the winter of 1976, Rich Ray was surprised when Enquist, by this time an imposing senior, pulled him aside and told him he could run faster if he changed his technique. Ray had never even spoken with Enquist before, and he figured that the upperclassman would not

Paul Enquist stroking the senior boat at Class Day, 1977. His class won three straight Class Day events, from 1974 to 1977. Photo Credit: Dave Emigh.

have even the slightest interest in a freshman like himself; and yet, here he was, asking the young man to "shorten his stride" if he wanted to "improve his time."[20] According to his best friend Ray Wittmier, Enquist's analytical mind was "always trying to figure out what would make them go faster."[21] Engle remembers Enquist continuously talking about "rowing theory, boat design, rigging engineering, and workout strategies."[22]

Rowing was, in one sense, a physics problem that involved angles, fulcrums, leverage, force application, and displacement. But Enquist realized the physics of rowing also depended upon humans and their individual willingness to commit themselves to hard work and vigilant self-improvement. Enquist was willing to devote himself entirely to this project, but he was surrounded by others who weren't always as dedicated. He had no patience for those who saw the crew as more of a "social club" than a rowing team.[23] Although mostly easygoing, he could be critical of teammates who weren't giving full effort, and he could also be disapproving of Struckmeyer if he felt his coach was allowing it to happen. He never forgot how Struckmeyer placed "a guy in jeans" into Enquist's freshman Class Day boat, which then lost by only two seats, thereby preventing the Class of 1977 from winning four straight Class Day titles. To Enquist, anybody wearing jeans to the river wasn't prepared to row and didn't deserve to be in a boat.

He felt the same way when Struckmeyer placed a hungover athlete in the stroke seat during a hard Saturday workout. For Struckmeyer, it was an effective way to punish the reprobate, and also get him to work hard—there was no hiding in the stroke seat. "Yeah, but what about the rest of us?" Enquist asked Struckmeyer. It made for a "shit practice," and it incensed him even more to be rowing behind "some guy who has been out partying" when Enquist himself was rarely placed in the stroke seat. It was something that he never let Struckmeyer forget. "I wasn't good enough to stroke for Washington State," Enquist teased Struckmeyer later, "but I was good enough to stroke the double that won a gold medal!"[24] Enquist considered Ken Struckmeyer a "close friend and mentor" during his time at WSU, but even years later, when Ken was retiring from teaching, Enquist still remembered. After praising Struckmeyer for producing a gold medal-winning oarsmen, Enquist joked that his coach's "method of achieving genius" was that "he only once allowed me to sit in the stroke seat in four years. It was always somebody else. It didn't matter that they might be hung over, out of shape, or missed practices."[25]

It made for a good punchline years later, but during his senior year, in spring 1977, Enquist was tired of rowing with guys who were "hung over, out of shape, or missed practices." By then, the varsity had a strong core, but

A sign of things to come. Paul Enquist takes Dave Emigh's single for a spin on the Snake River during Class Day, 1977. The next year, Enquist would bring his own single to Boyer. By then, he was embarking on his Olympic journey. Photo Credit: Dave Emigh.

unless all eight oarsmen on the varsity boat were equally devoted, in Enquist's mind, you had nothing. When someone didn't show up because they had tests or labs, Enquist thought, "Come on guys, we all have tests and labs." If someone did not run stadiums because it was freezing or didn't come to the river because it was windy or raining, they dragged everyone else down with them. Such was the nature of crew. Enquist's solution was that he, Mitch Wainright, Ray Wittmier, and Jim Fischer—all seniors who had rowed together for four long years—should race a four instead of the eight at Pac-8s. The previous year, they had watched a UW four composed of third boat oarsmen—rowers they had raced against and beaten—win the Pac-8 Championships at Redwood Shores. Why couldn't they do the same?

The seniors presented the idea to Struckmeyer, and he was not happy. He was unwilling to sacrifice the eight. At a team meeting, Struckmeyer told the seniors if they wanted to row a four, they'd have to do it on their own time, and not during regular crew practices. The seniors backed off, but Struckmeyer knew they would not be satisfied without giving it a shot. With the tension growing, the coach finally conceded that he would allow them to race it out. On a Saturday morning practice, he split the varsity eight into two fours: the four seniors in one boat and the remainder of the varsity boat in the other. They would row a 2,000-meter race—if Enquist's crew was substantially superior, Struckmeyer would consider breaking up the varsity eight. The coach did not have to worry: the underclassmen won, and, after the boats were put away, Enquist and the other seniors never talked again of splitting the eight.[26] Privately, Enquist believed the race was a joke—the team only had one legitimate four, the *Spirit of '73*, which the underclassmen rowed, while the seniors had to row a "four" made from the salvaged pieces of the *Loyal Shoudy*, one of the eights destroyed on Black Thursday. "Struckmeyer knew the race was rigged by making us use that four," Enquist said later, "but we were so frustrated with some of the guys, we agreed to try it." In the end, Enquist and the seniors achieved what they had wanted all along: after the controversy, the eight oarsmen came together, and everyone began showing up for practice. The result was one of the best seasons for any varsity eight in WSU history. They beat UW in Pullman and defeated UCLA at Redwood Shores to take fourth place at the Pac-8 championships. "If we had broken off into our four," Enquist said later, "the win over UCLA might not have happened."[27]

In his years at WSU, perhaps Enquist's greatest virtue—even more than his size, strength, and total devotion to his oarsmanship—was his remarkable capacity for allowing personality conflicts and verbal taunts to simply wash down his back like a rough, wet row—you simply dried them off and moved on to the next practice. Not only did he have a singular focus that prevented him from dwelling on anything other than rowing harder and better, but he also had enough self-confidence and depth of character that he could take ribbing from his teammates without letting it get under his skin. In short, Enquist took rowing very seriously, but he didn't take himself so seriously, a trait that would serve him well as he moved up the competitive rungs of elite rowing. The most telling example of this was Enquist's nickname. During those years, everyone had a nickname, some more complimentary than others. Enquist ended up with the moniker, "Dummy," shortened from "Big Dummy," abbreviated from "Big Dumb Swede," which came from an inside ethnic joke between him and Struckmeyer, born of their common Scandinavian ancestry. The stereotype of the "Big Dumb Swede" was a common trope in Scandinavian communities. The character of John Johnson—a dense, cloddish, drunk who spoke too loudly with a thick Swedish accent—was used to poke fun at and by Scandinavian immigrants, as were a series of jokes about "Ole and Lena" or "Sven and Ole" that were often self-referential.

Upon hearing Struckmeyer jokingly mutter "Big Dumb Swede" during Enquist's freshman year, the lightweights—like merciless sharks—were quick to strike, immediately shortening the nickname to simply "Dummy." It seemed to them the perfect bait to taunt the tall, gangly, good-natured Enquist, who refused to bite. He had thick skin—conditioned by many years of working the back deck of fishing boats with his father and uncles, where Swedes and Norwegians worked together and ribbed each other constantly. Trying to goad Enquist further, one of the lightweights named a particular calisthenic exercise "Enquist's Dilemma" because Paul allegedly could not master a series of jumping jack-like moves that had to be performed in rapid sequence.[28] It still didn't bother Enquist. He just laughed. In fact, Enquist liked the lightweights—he appreciated their verve and competitiveness. They had created a culture where everyone was committed to working hard and going fast. If they wanted to fling arrows, it was fine. Enquist and the heavies could fling them right back.

However, sometimes the arrows did have barbs. After Enquist famously turned off his engine and tried to coast his Volkswagen down the steep Snake River grade, locking up his steering wheel and nearly plunging himself and three passengers Evel Knievel-style into the Snake River Canyon, he had to suffer a more concentrated barrage of "Big Dummy" for a while. It was, according to Brad Sleeper, the *only* truly dumb thing Paul had ever done. But that didn't keep Sleeper from tormenting Enquist afterwards. It didn't matter. "Paul had this generous, overwhelming sense of humor," said Mike Klier. "Even if he was the object of the joke, he took it good-naturedly." He was impervious to outside noise that would distract him from his sole purpose of rowing better—a characteristic that made Enquist, in the words of Brad Lewis, his future rowing partner, "steady" and "virtually unflappable."[29]

Enquist's personality and experience at WSU prepared him well for the next phase of his life, where he had to navigate a labyrinth of personalities at national team selection camps, and where the "joking" might be performed with sharpened blades. Handling criticism, deflecting taunts, or managing oversized but fragile egos were never among Paul Enquist's dilemmas. He was well equipped by temperament to deal with those things. His real dilemma was what to do after graduation. He could pursue a career in engineering and sit in an office all day long—a thought he liked less than catapulting his Volkswagen across the Snake River Canyon. He could follow in the footsteps of his father, grandfather, and uncles, and take up the life of a fisherman—it was in his blood, after all. But what Enquist really wanted to do was keep rowing. His dilemma: how could he do that?

Rowing Pilgrim

From 1977 to 1984, Paul Enquist embarked upon an arduous rowing odyssey, traveling to the sacred sites of rowing, like Philadelphia's Boathouse Row and Harvard's Newell Boathouse on the Charles River, and seeking out the guidance of rowing gurus like Harvard's Harry Parker and the University of Pennsylvania's Ted Nash. Enquist's would be an extended pilgrimage that took eight years and thousands of hours of training, during which time he experienced precious few moments of enlightenment. Nothing clicked immediately; no lightbulbs went off; the sky did not open to reveal to him the secrets of the universe. As he described it later, his was a "long path" and a "slow progression" that, at times, became so "humbling" he nearly quit. But Enquist did that one thing that separated himself from others—he "just stayed with it and every year got a little bit better."[30] Kathleen Randall once described WSU rowers as being, fundamentally, "non-quitters." It wasn't a glamorous title, but it was the truth, and Enquist's DNA carried this hallmark feature very strongly—he was, at his very core, a non-quitter.

Enquist's quest for enlightenment began at home, in Seattle, at the University of Washington's Conibear Shellhouse—the West Coast's largest temple of rowing. After graduation, he showed up at Conibear and told Dick Erickson and Bob Ernst that he wanted to keep rowing and become a national team oarsman. Erickson had watched Enquist row at WSU for the last four years, and Ernst, now UW's freshman coach, had run summer sculling programs in which Enquist and Ray Wittmier had participated. Erickson told him, "Show up here tomorrow morning at six o'clock and we'll have something for you."

Erickson had two boats that were training for the Royal Henley Regatta that summer, and he was looking for oarsmen to fill out a third boat to compete with his crews. The next morning, Enquist found himself in a makeshift eight composed of current and former Huskies as well as Bruce Ibbetson, a former Irvine rower who, in a few years, would be stroking the U.S. National Team eight. It was a revelation for Enquist. His thrown-together eight was consistently beating Erickson's junior varsity boat and was competitive with UW's top boat, which went on to win Henley later that summer. With each practice, his confidence grew. "I can row with these guys," he thought. Rowing at WSU, there was always a mystique when it came to UW. The Huskies were somehow different, by nature superior. It took only a few practices for Enquist to demystify the magic of mighty UW. There was no magic. "These guys do the same thing we do!" he realized. Yes, the Huskies were big, but so was Enquist. Yes, the Huskies worked hard, but so could Enquist. Rowing was rowing, whether it was on Lake Washington or the Snake River.

In September, after fishing with his dad for the summer, Enquist participated in an Olympic development camp for sweep rowers in Squaw Valley, California. Every day, the young oarsmen went out for two practices under the watchful eyes of Harry Parker. Parker didn't say much, but Enquist could see something special in Parker's taciturn, quiet demeanor. Here was someone who had a gift for pulling the most out of his rowers and making crews go fast. Enquist wanted to be one of those oarsmen. But he never even spoke to Parker during the camp, and when it was over, it was back to Seattle and a sail-making loft in Ballard. Enquist's rowing journey had just begun, but it already felt stalled. He was unsure of the next step.

He visited Bob Ernst. "I want to keep rowing," he told Ernst. "What should I do?" Ernst looked Enquist over and thought to himself, "Do I need this big of a project?" He had seen Enquist row in a single before, and he was "pounding holes in the water." He also knew that Enquist was diligent and could make boats go fast. Ernst remembered back to the spring of 1975, when he had gone out on Lake Washington in a launch with Ken Struckmeyer while WSU was preparing for the Western Invitational. Sitting in the six seat, the long, lanky Enquist had caught Ernst's eye even then. He also liked Enquist's laconic, dry, fisherman's sensibility. Ernst was always looking to learn new things, and Enquist could teach him about commercial fishing while he taught Enquist about sculling. "Paul, if you really want to keep rowing, you need to buy your own single," Ernst told him. "I'll give you a place in the boathouse to store it, and you can row with my scullers in the mornings."[31]

Ernst was a believer in the power of using small boats to make better rowers. That was how he had taken UC Irvine from an also-ran to a West Coast contender. At UC Irvine, he didn't have enough rowers to field two eights, and it was hard to build a fast varsity without competition. Ernst's strategy was to send his oarsmen out in pairs and singles: they would learn better oarsmanship and compete against each other. It worked. Irvine got fast quickly, and several very good oarsmen, including Ibbetson and Brad Lewis, emerged from Ernst's program. He began to host summer sculling programs every year at Irvine, and they attracted young rowers from Harvard, UCLA, and all over the country. When he was hired by Erickson in 1974, he saw a young woman out sculling on Lake Washington. She was rough but determined. She told him, "I want to make the world championship team and the Olympics!" Ernst said, "Well, if you need any help, let me know." Her name was Liz Seneer. She became Ernst's first sculling student in Seattle, and she did indeed make the U.S. World Championship squad the next summer. Many more scullers followed Seneer, including Carol Brown, the Princeton graduate who rowed on

Harry Parker's "Red Rose Crew," Kristi Norelius from WSU, some of Ernst's former Irvine rowers, and a diverse flotilla of local rowers, old and young, men and women, slow and fast. It was a "real mob" of scullers who assembled to row with Ernst at six in the morning every Monday, Wednesday, and Friday at the UW shell house. Dick Erickson was amazed. He thought all the small boats looked like a bunch of mosquitos, and he dubbed them the "Mosquito Squadron"; the name stuck.[32]

Immediately after his conversation with Bob Ernst, Enquist went to see Stan Pocock, son of legendary boatbuilder George Yeoman Pocock. Stan pointed to a cedar single in the racks and said, "That one's available. It's a heavyweight single and the guy who ordered it never picked it up." Enquist said, "I'll take it." Minutes later, he was loading it on his car, and minutes after that he was back at the UW shell house asking Ernst where he could store it. Enquist joined the Mosquito Squadron and began his sculling career in winter 1977, rowing in the mornings before he went to work at a sail-making and rigging loft in Ballard, where his mom also worked.

When Enquist got up that first morning for sculling practice, his mother asked, "Where are you going?" Paul answered, "I'm going to rowing practice and coming in an hour late to work. I hope that won't be a problem." Felix and Doris Enquist were Depression-era people—hard stock Scandinavian fisherfolk who didn't easily understand why a young man would spend his mornings rowing when he should be at work. But Paul knew they would adjust, and he wasn't worried about losing his job at the sail-making loft—everyone there was like family, and no one was going to fire him for coming in late.

His father sometimes muttered about Paul continuing to row. "Boy, you can't eat those oars," he said.[33] He once asked his son, "Paul, why are you still rowing—you're not beating anybody?" But Felix Enquist knew that Paul was strong-willed. If Paul wanted to row, he was going to row. Best to leave him alone about it. When Paul finally did beat a few people and won the gold medal, Felix never said much to his son about it, but down at the docks, the usually quiet fisherman was telling everyone who would listen, "My son won the gold!"[34] In the end, Paul's family stood behind him while he pursued a dream that promised neither fame nor fortune. Even if Felix "had little interest in rowing," Doris "gave him unbridled support."[35] Most of all, they provided him food to eat and a place to live during those thin years when Paul and his fellow sculling monks lived a hand-to-mouth existence.

In spring 1978, Ernst encouraged Enquist, and anyone who had rowing ambitions, to go east for the summer. In the nineteenth century, Horace Greely said, "Go west, young man!" But for young West Coast rowers in the

1970s, the opposite was true: if you wanted to make the national team, you had to spend your summers in Philadelphia or Boston, or you might as well be rowing in Timbuktu. As a young West Coast coach just out of the military, Ernst himself had gone east, showing up unannounced at Harvard's boathouse in 1968 and undertaking an impromptu apprenticeship with the master himself, Harry Parker. It was just what you did back then if you were serious about rowing: you put your shell on your car and you went east, found a boathouse where you could lay your head and store your single, then you relied on the generosity and patronage of coaches like Parker and Ted Nash, who were remarkably accommodating to these seasonal pilgrims. In the 1970s, there were no permanent training centers for the U.S. National Rowing Team, so the clubs and boathouses of Philadelphia and Boston served as way stations for Olympic hopefuls. Enquist, just one year out of WSU, was still rough, but he was getting faster, and Ernst knew he needed more consistent competition to become an elite sculler. In going east, Ernst figured Enquist would either get faster or not, gain inspiration or quit, but either way it was a necessary next step in his development.[36]

When he wasn't rowing with the Mosquito Squadron, Enquist rowed with another group of young scullers who were themselves making plans to go to Philadelphia for the summer. Dr. John Sack, a Seattle hand surgeon, rowed a single out of the UW canoe house every morning, and he had come to know all the young scullers in Enquist's group. A Philadelphia native, Sack had a lifetime membership with the Undine Barge Club. Founded in 1856, Undine was one of the oldest rowing clubs in the United States, a castle-like structure situated along the Schuylkill River on Boathouse Row. Jim Barker, Undine's coach and a friend of Sack's, arranged for Enquist and his group to stay at the Undine boathouse that summer. In a world that lacked money or notoriety, such personal connections were as good as gold for young scullers. Later, in 1983, Sack would allow Enquist and John Biglow to train in his Swiss-made Stämpfli double—but that was six years and a world away from 1978, Enquist's first summer of competitive sculling.

Enquist and Jim Schultz loaded their singles on Jim's van and headed east. They were joined by another young sculler from Southern California, Brad Lewis, who had also come to Seattle to train under Bob Ernst. Enquist didn't know Lewis well and had hardly spoken to him. He had seen Lewis in a few practices, but there were many boats in the Mosquito Squadron. Though they hadn't socialized outside of those few morning practices, Enquist and Schultz were happy to have Lewis, and his single, along for the trip: he was one more person with whom to share the driving and expenses. When they arrived at

Boathouse Row, Lewis grabbed his single from the van and wandered off down Boathouse Row; that was the last Enquist saw of him all summer. As it turns out, Lewis made the national sculling team and competed at the World Championships that summer. He had been serving his sculling apprenticeship in Philadelphia for three summers, while Enquist's initiation into the world of East Coast rowing was just beginning.

At Undine, Enquist and his Seattle buddies slept on the floor of the balcony overlooking the Schuylkill River. There was a small alcove off the locker room with a sink and an old gas stove where they could cook food. It was a Spartan-like existence: up at five in the morning to row before the heat of the day, and then cereal and sandwiches—or whatever they could scrounge—to fuel themselves for their afternoon practice. For a West Coast rower and fisherman familiar with the crystalline waters of the Pacific Northwest, rowing in Philadelphia was a culture shock. Philadelphia itself was crowded, noisy, hot, and humid. The Schuylkill River, so famous for its rowing, was dirty and smelly. To Enquist, it was like rowing in a "cesspool." When they drove across the river to row at Nationals in Camden, New Jersey, the temperature was ninety-eight degrees, with 99 percent humidity, and Enquist's oars disappeared in the heavy green muck. Enquist found the environment horrifying, but the rowing was exceptional. After three weeks of two-a-day practices at Undine, with Jim Barker coaching him in the afternoons, his boat speed was improving dramatically. He rowed the Independence Day Regatta—the biggest rowing event in Philadelphia each summer—as well as Nationals at Camden. At each, he made the finals while competing in the "Intermediate" category, which was beneath both the "Elite" and "Senior" classifications but still plenty competitive.

After Nationals, Enquist heard that Ted Nash, the Penn coach, was putting together boats to row at the Olympic Sports Festival in Colorado Springs. He walked down Boathouse Row and introduced himself to the loquacious Nash. If Harry Parker was the taciturn and enigmatic dean of U.S. rowing, Ted Nash was his opposite twin. Both were medal-winning Olympic rowers who became the helmsmen of the best college crews in the nation, Parker at Harvard and Nash at the University of Pennsylvania. Their personalities could not have been more different: Parker was "flinty and unsentimental" while Nash was inspirational and engaging, a flamboyant personality. But they both were pulling in the same direction—supporting and developing prospective national team oarsmen.[37] When Enquist introduced himself to Nash, he already had a strong connection with the coach—Enquist was then rowing for the Lake Washington Rowing Club, the same team Nash represented when he became an Olympian and won the gold medal in the 1960 games in Rome. Nash was always eager to support and accommodate LWRC rowers like Enquist. In fact, Bob Ernst called him the "biggest accommodator on the face of the earth."[38] If a poor, wayfaring rower needed some food, Nash would give him money for a sandwich and a place to store his boat. He knew that rowers from Seattle like Enquist needed help finding their way. Nash was a benefactor of the transient rowing class.

Nash immediately put Enquist into his lineups, and he "became a Penn guy for a couple weeks." The result was that Enquist found himself on a plane headed for Colorado Springs, where he stayed for a week at the Air Force Academy. After the heat, humidity, noise, and pollution of Philadelphia, Enquist thought he had "gone to heaven right then." He enjoyed three solid meals a day at the dining hall, an air-conditioned room, and the fresh, crisp Colorado air. Enquist realized that the Sports Festival itself was somewhat "phony." His boat had qualified as the "West Coast four" in trials that involved no other boats, and then, in Colorado Springs, they rowed 500-meter sprints on a little pond where Enquist won "some gaudy medals that didn't mean anything" and "a big bag of sweatshirts."[39] Ted Nash saw Enquist as a "quiet, yet friendly giant," so he was surprised that Paul was so "ecstatic at the Sports Festival." Nash believed that Enquist "cherished the USA uniforms and the large gathering of all sports," which was certainly true, but what Enquist cherished most was the chance to get out of Philadelphia for a week and receive the support of Ted Nash, who would later, during the pivotal summer of 1981, let Enquist keep his single in the Penn boathouse.[40]

For Enquist, the summer of 1978 had been a whirlwind introduction into the world of East Coast rowing, and it ended, as did most of the summers that followed, with the Royal Canadian Henley Regatta at St. Catharines, Ontario. Enquist made the finals in the intermediate singles event, and when he looked across the starting line, he realized that five of the six scullers had raced each other three months earlier at the Elk Lake Memorial Day regatta in British Columbia. Rowing, and especially sculling, consisted of a small community of true believers, those who were dedicated enough to put off careers and family in order to follow their ascetic journey. When the races were over, they loaded up Schultz's van with their singles and headed back home to Seattle. On the way, Enquist rode with his buddy, Tom Hazeltine, a lightweight hopeful from Seattle. As he sat in Hazeltine's Pinto, he reflected upon his dizzying first summer back east. He had rowed hard, learned a lot, raced well, and made a bunch of friends. And yet, he was still an "intermediate" sculler with a long road ahead of him.

If 1978 had been the summer of Ted Nash and Philadelphia, 1979 was the summer of Harry Parker and Boston for Paul Enquist. For his first weeks in Boston, he lived in the Harvard boathouse. The Harvard coach didn't go out of his way to make Enquist feel welcome, but at least, in Enquist's words, "He didn't kick me out." Parker supported all the itinerant rowers who were seeking spots on the national team. "All the boathouses did," remembered Enquist. There was no money in rowing, and "if you weren't a trust fund baby, they had to help you out."[41]

Around mid-May, Parker approached him. "I need a rower. Can you fill in for practice this morning?" Enquist would be rowing in the Harvard junior varsity boat for a team practice. Hell yes, I can row, thought Enquist. It was the first, but not the last, time he would fill in for one of Parker's college rowers during a Harvard practice. They rowed hard and fast. Enquist could tell they knew what they were doing. Not long after that, Parker told him that Pete Gardner, Dartmouth's head coach, needed oarsmen for a national team training camp. Enquist wasn't going to make the national team in sculling that year, so he jumped at the opportunity to compete as a sweep oarsman. The Pan American Games would be taking place that summer, and Harry Parker himself would be selecting the men who would row on the U.S. eight. Enquist grabbed his duffel bag, boarded a greyhound bus, and headed for Hanover, New Hampshire, where he would be housed in an old ski lodge in the mountains with a bunch of other national team rowing hopefuls.

Even if his sculling dreams were on hold for the moment, Enquist was happy to row in Dartmouth, train for a berth on the national team, and eat three square meals a day in the university cafeteria. For now, he would focus on making the national team in any capacity. And there were promising signs. Later that summer, when Parker convened the sweep camp in Dartmouth, Enquist was among the eighty rowers from across the nation invited to compete for a spot on the team that would row in the Pan Am Games. Enquist rowed for two weeks and survived several cuts, but when Parker winnowed the team from thirty-two to twenty-four, Enquist's name was not among the list of survivors. One of the rowers to make the U.S. national eight that year was Bruce Ibbetson from UC Irvine, whom Enquist had rowed with in Seattle in 1977 in the makeshift eight that practiced with the Henley-bound UW squad. Another was John Biglow, the stroke of Yale's 1979 championship crew—a Seattle native whose path would cross and mingle with Enquist's a few times in the coming years. But for now, Enquist was simply another guy who did not make the U.S. National Rowing Team.

Enquist went back to Seattle to fish with his dad and consider his next step. He was on a journey toward a goal that was still not entirely clear even to himself, and he began to have doubts. That December, Harry Parker came to Seattle for the U.S. Rowing Convention. Enquist and some other Seattle-based national team aspirants practiced for Parker, who would be the head coach for the Olympic team in 1980. Parker ignored Enquist during those sessions—didn't say one word to him. Enquist came out of the experience thinking the "handwriting was on the wall." He would not be among the chosen for 1980.

Why am I doing this, he wondered? Two and a half years out from WSU and all Enquist had to show for his efforts was, frankly, nothing: he had not yet won a major sculling event, even at the intermediate level, and he had not yet made a national team. It was winter in Seattle. Getting up every morning in the damp darkness to punish himself on the water in pursuit of a formless dream that seemed to be vanishing before him was becoming more difficult by the day. If you were rowing on a team boat, you had to show up—the others were depending on you. But the sculler was accountable only to himself. He gave in to the darkness of his thoughts. He stayed in bed one morning and then the next. He was twenty-three years old and going nowhere. It was winter 1980, and Paul Enquist decided to quit rowing.

Enquist went back to working full-time at the sail-making loft in Ballard. He didn't row at all for the first four months of 1980. He could stay up late. He could sleep in on weekends. He didn't have that constant bone-weary fatigue. He felt rested and even energetic, but not entirely happy. Something was missing. As spring came to Seattle and the weather warmed and the days grew longer, Enquist wanted to row again. At first, he would just go out on the weekends with friends, have fun, and enjoy the feeling of being on the water on a warm spring day. But he quickly realized something surprising: he was just as fast as he had been when he stopped rowing the previous winter. His skills had not atrophied, and his body felt stronger than ever. He realized something else: all his friends were rowers. And he was still young, relatively speaking. He was only twenty-three. He wouldn't be missing anything that summer—President Carter and the USOC had already issued the Olympic boycott for 1980. What about 1984? He would give himself four more years to see what he could do, at which point he would still only be twenty-eight—plenty of time to pursue a career and build a family. His goals were not sky-high. He was not intent on achieving something unrealistic, like winning a gold medal. He simply wanted to "do better" than he'd already done. If he had to nail it down, his specific objective was to become a national team rower. He didn't need to be the best rower in the country, but he wanted to be considered among the best, and he already knew that was possible. He had said as much in a letter to

Ken Struckmeyer in the fall of 1979: "Having spent the last two years rowing with and against the best oarsmen in the United States and Canada," Enquist told his former coach, "I realized that they were no different than the people that turnout for crew at WSU."[42]

And then, serendipity: as soon as Enquist made the decision to continue rowing for four more years, he saw a Flymo single for sale in Seattle. Designed like the expensive German-built Empachers, it sold at a fraction of the cost. An English boatbuilder had brought two to Seattle for the rowing convention in December 1979, and there was still one available; it happened to fit Enquist perfectly. Stan Pocock had already told Enquist that the shell he currently rowed was too small for his tall, 215-pound frame. Enquist purchased the boat and began rowing again with determination. He stayed in Seattle that summer—the only summer between 1977 and 1984 that Enquist did not go east. Instead, he rowed in the Green Lake Regatta and won lots of blue ribbons. He was first in five events: single, double, mixed double, four, and eight. His competition in the single was mostly older men—Frank Cunningham and John Sack—so Enquist, as he explained in a letter to Dave Emigh, "tried to row a good, strong 1,000-meter piece and ignore the competition because they were miles back." His time was fast—a 3:39 on flat water with no wind.[43] Enquist had a new boat and a new attitude, and his boat speed was improving. Now all he needed was a breakthrough—at the very least a sign of tangible progress that would validate his decision to keep rowing.

Breakthrough Years, 1981–83

The summer of 1981 was the beginning of Paul Enquist's emergence as an elite sculler. He won the intermediate single in Philadelphia's Independence Day Regatta; and then, two weeks later at the National Championship Regatta in Tennessee, Enquist finally won a "big" race, taking the senior singles event. "It was really satisfying," he wrote to Dave and Jill Emigh, "But the most exciting race of the weekend was the elite single." Indeed, it was the first time that Enquist made the finals in an "elite" singles race; and even better, he was only 0.4 seconds away from medaling, barely losing to third-place finisher Brad Lewis. "By the time we got to the last twenty, Lewis had about three-quarter length on me, and so I started driving the rate up, and I just ran out of racecourse," he told the Emighs. "It was really fun being 'in the race' with the 'big boys.'"[44]

Enquist's success at the National Championship was followed by an even greater benchmark of his progress: in August 1981, he made the finals in the

World Rowing Championship trials, which determined who would represent the United States in the single sculls at the World competition later that summer in Munich, Germany. Now he really was running with the "big boys." When he looked down the starting line, he saw the five best scullers in the country, the same ones who would be competing to represent the United States in the Olympics three years later: Tiff Wood, John Biglow, Joe Bouscaren, Jim Dietz, and Brad Lewis. And now, Paul Enquist. What struck him at the time was not that he had arrived but just how quiet it was while they were warming up. There were no coxswains barking commands—just six elegant singles gliding up and down the lanes like graceful birds skimming across the water on a quiet morning.[45] In most sports, "having arrived" is usually greeted with loud cheering. In the world of sculling, arriving at the top was like entering the monastery with your fellow monks.

Enquist was now in the conversation, and he was determined to remain there until he made the national team. He was so close. He was now at the top of the invitation list for national team sculling camps, but his number had yet to be called. The next summer, 1982, he rowed in a double that finished second by only a half-length at the World trials. But 1983 would be the true turning point in Enquist's journey. He went to Boston in April to train out of the Harvard boathouse, where Harry Parker was overseeing the scullers who would likely represent the United States at both the Pan American Games in Caracas, Venezuela, and the World Rowing Championships in Duisburg, Germany. Parker paired Enquist with the oversized Ridgely Johnson for a race at Princeton. They made a giant double, but they were very fast—surprisingly so—just barely losing to a double that Parker thought would race at the World Championships.

When the scullers retreated to the doubles camp at Dartmouth, it seemed like Enquist's boat went fast no matter who he was paired with—Johnson, Biglow, Tony Hornvath, and, finally, Brad Lewis. The speed of Enquist's doubles, paired with the lackluster performances of other team boats, had Parker switching around his boatings at the last minute. First, he had Enquist and Hornvath designated as the Pan Am double and John Biglow and Joe Bouscaren as the World Championship double, but then Parker put Enquist and Lewis together in a double and they changed his mind. They were rowing four-minute pieces and the Enquist-Lewis double was getting clobbered. Enquist, rowing in the stroke seat, had the rating too low. Parker had been watching quietly, but he'd had enough. He drove his launch over to Enquist and Lewis and hollered angrily at them. "How can I tell what you're capable of when you're rowing four beats a minute lower than everybody else?" As

Parker's boat motored away, Enquist turned to Lewis and said, "Look, I have to sit up taller and shorten up a little bit if the stroke rate is going to come up." The next piece, instead of rowing at twenty-eight, Enquist took them out at thirty-two, and everything clicked. They went from getting drubbed to winning the next piece by open water. Lewis got excited. They both could feel the speed. It was a "lightbulb moment" for all of them. Harry was as thrilled as they were—he drove his launch over to them after the piece and yelled excitedly, "Yeah, yeah, that's what I want to see!"[46]

Parker designated Enquist and Lewis as the double that would represent the United States at the World Championships and put Biglow and Bouscaren in the quad. At the World trials in Princeton, the Enquist-Lewis double won by twenty-five seconds and punched their ticket to the World Championships. Paul Enquist had realized his dream: he was now a member of the U.S. National Rowing Team. In Duisburg, Germany, Enquist and Lewis showed glimpses of what would make them gold medalists the following year. In the semifinals, they needed to finish third to make the finals, and in the last 500 meters they "rumbled past the Soviets, and then, on the last stroke," they sneaked past the Canadians. They had rowed a lightning fast 6:17 and finished second to the East Germans. It was an exceptionally strong showing. They had made the finals, which was unusual in world competition for an American double. It was, according to Lewis, "dramatic, gutsy rowing."[47]

Unfortunately, the finals did not go so well: with 750 meters to go, they got caught in the chop of boat wakes, couldn't steer, and finished only sixth in the world.[48] For Enquist, it was thrilling to simply be on the U.S. team competing in the World Championships. Doris Enquist flew to Germany to watch Paul, and afterwards they drove up to Sweden to visit Enklobb, the Enquist family farm on the tiny Island of Enklinge. He and his mother were the first relatives from their side of the family to visit since his grandfather left the homeland in 1903.[49]

Writing about that 1983 double in *The Amateurs*, David Halberstam said that "sustaining the friendship" with Lewis was "one of the hardest things" that Enquist had ever done. "There had been long periods when Lewis barely spoke to Enquist, and sometimes Brad treated him as if he were an opponent, not a teammate."[50] Halberstam, casting Lewis as an antisocial individualist who couldn't function well as part of a team, perhaps overplayed how hard it was on Enquist to row with Brad Lewis. "It wasn't easy, but it was okay," recalled Enquist. "Brad was Brad, and we had to get along, and we did."[51] For Enquist, simply being on the U.S. National Team and competing in Europe for the first time was heady stuff—it was all brand new, and there was so much to process. Brad was the least of his worries. And they complemented each other well in the boat—Enquist stroked at a steady rhythm, and Lewis, in the bow, liked to steer and call the cadence.

But if the Enquist-Lewis double was functional and even fast in Europe, upon returning to the States, fissures were starting to open that would drive the pair apart by the end of 1983. At a Pre-Olympics race on Lake Casitas in the fall, they led the field at 1,200 meters and then things fell apart. "First the Norwegians passed us, then the East Germans, followed by the Finnish double. Paul and I would have needed an extra set of lungs and legs to stay ahead. By the time we limped across the finish line, every boat except the Italians, two lightweight scullers, had passed us."[52] After the race, Lewis vowed that that he would "never row the double scull again—not with Paul Enquist, not with anyone." Lewis determined then that his rowing future "would be decided in the single scull, the one-man boat." He did not want to rely on anyone else: "You make your own success in the single scull. You win or lose by your own toughness. You alone are responsible for the outcome of the race."[53]

It had been clear even before the race, however, that Lewis was striking out on his own. He did not stay with his teammates at the hotel. John Biglow remembered Lewis showing up every day in a luxurious rental car. He was "showy and ostentatious" thought Biglow, and clearly "not interested in being part of the team."[54] Meanwhile, Enquist was simply enjoying his time among his teammates and the coterie of international rowers that gathered around the hotel pool and hot tub in the evenings. He spent most of his time trying to converse with the East Germans. There was plenty of good food, and Enquist was having a wonderful experience. It was clear that Brad Lewis was moving on from their double and would be pursuing the single in 1984, but that wasn't the end of the world. Enquist was now considered a top candidate for the double in 1984, and there were plenty of scullers who might be willing to pair with him, including fellow Seattleite John Biglow. In fact, at Lake Casitas, the two of them were hatching plans to train together in the double during the winter.

The Shell Game

If you were a rower in the mid-1980s, you knew of John Biglow. He was the idiosyncratic but brilliant oarsman featured in Stephen Kiesling's book *The Shell Game* (1982), and then again in David Halberstam's *The Amateurs* (1985). Although he grew up in Enquist's hometown of Seattle, Biglow was as close to a blue blood as you could get 3,000 miles west of Boston. He came from a storied family of Yalies. His grandfather had rowed on the 1907 Yale crew that defeated Harvard.[55] Biglow rowed at the private Lakeside School in Seattle for the venerable sculling coach Frank Cunningham, himself a sixth-generation Harvard man who had stroked the Crimson varsity boat in the 1940s.[56] Biglow went on to stroke the highest achieving Yale boats in the modern period and was considered by some, like his teammate Stephen Kiesling, to be perhaps the greatest Yale oarsman of any era. His Yale crews had won the Eastern Sprints twice. Although they had never defeated Harry Parker's Harvard crews in "The Race," Biglow stroked the Yale eight in 1979 when they had lost by only four seconds over four miles in what was considered by many as the "greatest race in the two schools' history." As Halberstam described it, "Time and again when Harvard had made its move and threatened to row through Yale, Biglow had refused to concede and had brought Yale back."[57]

Given John Biglow's pedigree, then, it is ironic that when he called Paul Enquist in May 1981 to ask if he could practice with him in Seattle, it was Biglow who thought Enquist was "arrogant," not the other way around. "I don't know," Enquist answered. "Have you gotten any faster?"[58] Enquist had seen Biglow row a single the previous summer and hadn't been impressed. Enquist, by then, was a serious sculler, the fastest in Seattle, and Biglow was just beginning his transition from sweep oarsmen to sculler. But during winter 1980, Biglow had trained with some of his former Yale teammates, rowing long pieces up and down the Housatonic. Then he had gone to Boston in the early spring and begun training with Tiff Wood and other top scullers. Biglow didn't want to brag, but he knew he was faster since Enquist had seen him last.

They went out on Lake Washington with Bob Ernst, and Biglow was beating Enquist in piece after piece. Biglow "didn't want to be rude about it," so he was staying pretty close to Enquist, and if the workout had continued along those lines, the outcome might have been more agreeable. Instead, when they turned their shells around at Leschi Point, three miles from Conibear Shellhouse, Ernst called for one full-pressure piece back to the boathouse. Biglow didn't think it was a good idea—there was no use for it. He had been winning the pieces already. At full power he would win by an even greater margin, Enquist's confidence would take a hit, and neither rower would get any coaching on the way back to the shell house. But full pressure was full pressure, and the integrity of John Biglow would not allow him to back off even one degree. He pulled away from Enquist and won by a horizon of open water.[59] Enquist was impressed. "John beat me good," he remembered. "He had gotten a lot faster." Ernst was also impressed. "You might want to keep your eye on him," he warned Enquist.[60]

Biglow "felt bad" for Enquist after the workout.[61] He was worried that he had embarrassed Enquist, but there was nothing to be embarrassed about in losing to John Biglow. He was one of the few rowers Brad Lewis acknowledged to be tougher than anyone, including Lewis himself. Joe Bouscaren, a Yale teammate, called Biglow "an aerobic machine."[62] As it turns out, a few months after that workout, Enquist and Biglow would line up for the finals of the World singles trials in Princeton. Biglow would say hello to Enquist while they were warming up, and then he would go on to win the right to represent the United States at the World Championships in Munich, where he took the bronze medal and became the third best sculler in the world, a feat he would repeat in 1982. That workout with Enquist in May 1981 was a turning point for Biglow, a "good sign" that he was successfully making the transition from one of the best sweep oarsmen in the country to one of the best scullers—in fact, *the* best sculler. There was no shame in losing a practice piece to John Biglow.

That workout in May 1981 was also the beginning of a strong friendship between Paul Enquist and John Biglow, one that flourished especially during the winter of 1983–84 in Seattle, when Enquist and Biglow trained together in a double—a boat that both men thought might be their best bet for the 1984 Olympics. Biglow knew he was not always easy to row with. The summer after high school he had competed in a pair with his friend from Lakeside, Peter Most. They had gone back east to try their luck at the nationals. Once, while working out near the UW boathouse, Most turned to Biglow and said, "John Biglow, you're the hardest person to get along with in the world!" When he started rowing with Enquist, Biglow asked him, "Paul, don't you have trouble with me?" Enquist shook his head and said, simply and honestly, "No." They had to tailor their workouts that winter to accommodate Biglow's back injury, which was aggravated during long pieces, so they rowed shorter, high-intensity pieces. It was fine with Enquist. Biglow thought it was remarkable that Enquist was so agreeable and easygoing. They never had any arguments.[63]

Biglow's quirky personality had confounded his Yale teammates, who couldn't figure out if he "was a hick pretending to be a sophisticate" or a "sophisticate pretending to be a hick."[64] When it came to Enquist, however, Biglow was completely at ease. Enquist carried none of those eastern prep school pretensions. He was genuine and honest. He was quiet and sincere. He wasn't vain, didn't call attention to himself, didn't deflect blame. He worked hard, and he was constructive. Biglow thought that Enquist was a natural-born gentleman with an innate sense of appropriate behavior. Biglow had high standards for his friends, and Enquist lived up to the Biglovian code of ethics, which above all mandated a proper sense of humility. When Biglow had won the bronze medal at the World Rowing Championships in 1981, the German papers had described him using the word, "unterlächelnd," which means "quietly smiling, kind of humble."[65] He was proud of that assessment, and he thought of that moment again at the Olympics in 1984 as he watched Enquist's expression on the trophy dock while accepting his gold medal—Enquist was solemn, humble, barely smiling, not calling attention to himself. Biglow thought they shared the same inherent code of conduct—"you did not boast of what you would do or had done, nor did you embarrass a loser."[66]

For his part, Enquist was thrilled to be training with Biglow that winter. He had never seen anyone row or work out with such intensity and single-minded focus. One of their signature workouts was running steps on their "secret flight of stairs" near Biglow's parents' house. It was the perfect instrument for inflicting maximum suffering and dramatically increasing their strength and fitness. The stairs reminded Biglow of the saying they had for the Rotsee, a natural lake in Lucerne that was perfect for rowing: "When God made the Rotsee, he had rowing in mind." When God made these stairs, thought Biglow, he had Paul and him in mind. Biglow could run ten flights. The first time Enquist tried them, he was only able to run one flight, but finished ten flights by "walking, and then crawling to the top." Afterwards, he was so sore he "couldn't walk for a week." By mid-April, just before leaving for Boston to train at Harvard, they both could run up twenty flights.[67] Sometimes, after their workouts, they would go to Enquist's house and experiment with different pancake recipes, most of which involved large stacks of pancakes with various combinations of toppings—peanut butter, yogurt, apple sauce—layered between each one. Biglow loved going to the Enquist home, which was loud and informal compared to his parent's quiet, staid household.[68]

On the water, they trained under the watchful eyes of Dick Erickson, Stan Pocock, Charlie McIntyre, and, especially, legendary Seattle sculling coach Frank Cunningham, who placed beauty and grace above all else when it came to rowing. Cunningham was a rowing purist who still taught the fundamentals of the old Thames waterman stroke, as passed down through George Yeoman Pocock. He was critical of eastern coaches, including Harry Parker, who Cunningham believed privileged power and endurance above technical perfection. Every time Biglow would go east and row under Parker, Cunningham noticed a deterioration in his style. "With John, he'd be rowing pretty well, and then he'd go back and row for Harry and lose it all."[69]

Cunningham preached to Enquist and Biglow the need for a relaxed catch, a smooth application of power, and an effortless release. Each stroke needed to be smooth and elegant. He criticized Biglow for grimacing "every time he set his sculls." Cunningham was convinced that it was "energy wasted" and set out to "eliminate every extraneous gesture" in Biglow's technique. For Enquist, Cunningham focused on shortening his slide and making his stroke more economical, as well as getting him to loosen up his back and give himself "a moment of relaxation before the catch."[70] It was nearly impossible to meet Cunningham's exacting standards. Enquist and Biglow liked to joke that if Frank ran the regattas, the winning boat would not be the fastest but the one that looked the prettiest. They accepted his technical advice with gratitude, though, and wedded it together with their own rigorous physical training regime. Their boat speed began to take off.

In the days before they left for Boston in April 1984, Enquist and Biglow went to British Columbia and raced against the Canadian double that had competed at the 1983 World Championships. They won handily. Enquist was hoping their performance "would be enough to keep John away from the single," but "no such luck." When they returned to Boston, Enquist and Biglow were the fastest double on the water, and it especially surprised Biglow. The previous year, with his back ailing, he had been slow. On Easter Sunday, Biglow decided to test himself in a singles race against Joe Bouscaren and Tiff Wood. To his great surprise, Biglow beat them both. "It blew my mind. I had no idea. Where did this come from? How could I have gotten fast again?"

It didn't surprise Enquist at all. He knew the quality of work they'd been doing on the water and on the stairs.[71] Halberstam writes that after Biglow won the race on Easter Sunday, Enquist "had not said anything, but there was a sad look on his face. Later, Enquist had shaken his head and made a downward circling motion with his right hand. The meaning was perfectly clear. Their double was down the drain."[72] Enquist knew that if Biglow raced the single at the Olympic trials, he would win, and the Enquist-Biglow double would be gone forever. And that's how it happened. Biglow won the trials and would represent the United States in the single sculls at the Olympics. Enquist went to Harry Parker's sculling camp and tried to make the Olympic team with another partner. He was joined there by the forlorn Brad Lewis, who bet everything on the singles trials but narrowly lost to Biglow in the last twenty-five strokes.

Assault on Lake Casitas

Brad Lewis's first assault on Lake Casitas was with Paul Enquist in the double at the pre-Olympics in the fall of 1983. It did not go well. His second was in the middle of the night later that winter, sneaking through the fence with his single to row a midnight piece and visualize his eventual Olympic victory. His third assault was supposed to be the fulfillment of that visualization, with Lewis representing the United States as its single sculler. But his dream to be the U.S. single sculler had vanished in the final strokes of the Olympic trials when Biglow rowed through him. Now, instead of being the solitary individual against the world, he had to go to camp with everyone else—scullers he had defeated at the trials!—and bow and scrape before Harry Parker for a spot on the team boats.

In *The Amateurs*, Halberstam depicts Lewis as complicated, moody, difficult, and largely estranged from "the other oarsmen, who were eastern in shape, form, and manner."[73] Lewis thought that Halberstam's characterizations of him as a brooding outsider were superficial. Perhaps the journalist had the contours of the story correct, but it was far more nuanced than what Halberstam had gleaned from his short time among the scullers. Lewis liked to say that Halberstam didn't spend enough time with the oarsmen to really understand their subculture—it was as if Herman Melville had spent only a long weekend on the *Pequod* before writing *Moby Dick*.[74] Lewis liked to point out that he had, in fact, been on the U.S. National Rowing Team since 1977, competing in team boats, and that he was friends with most of the other scullers.[75]

But Halberstam was nothing if not intuitive. Whatever may have happened in the past, in 1984 Lewis had deliberately framed an identity that was individualist and contrarian. Sure, he was friends with many of the scullers, but he had not trained with them in Boston. He had developed his own training regimen in Newport, and he felt increasingly alienated from the sycophantic Ivy Leaguers who trained out of the Harvard boathouse and worshiped at the feet of Harry Parker. He respected Parker, and he acknowledged Parker's evident success as a coach, but Lewis thought there was something cult-like about the oarsmen who rowed for the mysterious Harry Parker. They hung on his every word and gesture as if he were God himself. While Parker's record as a championship-winning coach spoke for itself, Lewis concluded that the magic of Harry Parker, like any religion, only worked if you believed in it. And Lewis was not a true believer. In his experience, nothing Parker had ever said or done made him row faster.

In fact, Lewis had a low opinion of rowing coaches generally. All he needed from them, but rarely got, in his opinion, was technical advice and perhaps some useful drills that would improve his stroke. He could take care of the rest. As the Olympic trials had proved, he was quite capable of preparing himself for elite competition. But now, that playbook—*his playbook*—was down the drain. Lewis was no longer in charge of himself. At Parker's camp, he tossed his training diary aside and sunk into himself. Call it an "attitude problem," a "funk," or a full-on depression—at camp, Lewis became uncommunicative. On May 20, Enquist reported in his training journal simply that Lewis "isn't talking."[76]

While Lewis was nursing a wounded psyche, Enquist was nursing a strained left forearm. On the second day of camp, Parker paired Enquist with Tiff Wood and the boat was tilted to port the entire row. Enquist struggled to keep his starboard oar in the water. His journal for that practice read: "Really rough, unbalanced. Strained left forearm!!!" The injury bothered him for the entire camp. He had no strength in his left arm and could barely grip his oar. Some practices, he rowed "trying to protect his left arm from going numb." In "keeping with the rower's ethos," Lewis later noted that Enquist did not tell anyone about the injury.[77] Enquist continued rowing without complaint, but he was not having a good camp. Like Lewis, Enquist was also beginning to doubt Parker's approach to choosing the team boats, which amounted, essentially, to daily 2,000-meter races with different combinations in doubles. This Darwinian approach put everyone on edge and did not allow time for certain combinations to gel together.[78]

Parker's method lent credibility to the complaints of Lewis and others that the camp's structure favored the scullers who had been training out of the Harvard boathouse all winter. For the double, that meant Charlie Altekruse, one of Harry's boys from Harvard, and Joe Bouscaren, Biglow's teammate from Yale. This was perhaps an oversimplification, but Parker allowed the hard feelings and misunderstandings to fester. His style was to focus solely on training his athletes, not monitoring their "feelings" or involving himself in their interpersonal affairs. This approach created fast boats at Harvard, where his young athletes revered him without question, but it fell short in the context of coaching experienced national team athletes who had ideas of their own and wanted to be heard.

On Wednesday, June 6, after four long weeks of a camp that Halberstam described as "filled with anxiety and tension and paranoia," Enquist's workout journal recorded the following: "2 x 5 minutes, quads; Charle A—me—Bill—Sean vs. Bracken—Brad—Jack—Tiff. Brad and me switch; he won by 2 seats. Ridgely and me cut after practice."[79] Enquist was out—the ninth man on an eight-man team. His Olympic dream was seemingly over. Lewis visited him in his room. Enquist was quietly knitting a stocking cap, like a "sad fisherman." He didn't complain. "I knew it was coming," he told Lewis, resignedly. "My Mom is really going to be unhappy." His words at that moment struck

Lewis as revealing "the true Paul." His primary concern "was for his mother's feelings and not his own."[80] Lewis had not been cut, but he was number eight of eight, designated as a spare—or, as he called it, the "spare's spare," since his role would be to row with the real Olympic spare in a double at a pre-Olympic regatta in Lucerne, Switzerland. He left the team. "I decided to cut myself loose from Harry's clutches," he wrote later. "Fuck being a spare. I hadn't rowed for thirteen years just to be spare. No fucking way."[81]

Enquist and Lewis were decisive: emboldened by Bob Ernst, who reassured them that the rowing shells on the team trailer did not belong to Parker but rather the U.S. Men's Olympic Rowing Committee, they "stole" a Carbocraft double without Parker's permission and embarked on a journey that would take them first to Squam Lake, in New Hampshire, and then to Ithaca, New York, where Yale's head coach, Tony Johnson, and Cornell's coach, Fin Meislahn, were conducting a training camp for college rowers who would be competing at the Olympic trials. Johnson and Meislahn were happy to host the Enquist-Lewis challenge double, which would be good competition for their four-oared sweep boats.

Ithaca was the perfect environment for their mission. They had food and lodging, excellent water, good comradery, helpful coaching, and weeks to train and sharpen their strategies for defeating Parker's designated Olympic double, which was now competing in Lucerne. Enquist knew that Altekruse and Bouscaren were beatable—he and Lewis had almost pulled through them at camp one practice, even with Lewis's wounded ego and Enquist's injured arm. Parker knew it too—which was why he had offered Enquist a spot as a spare on the U.S. team going to Lucerne after he heard that Enquist would be joining Lewis to challenge his select double.

"Harry was worried because he knew that Brad and I were going to be waiting for him at the trials, and he was trying to avoid that," said Enquist. Now, after a little rest, Enquist's forearm was healing; when he rowed with Lewis, the boat was "rock-solid steady, balanced, and level," which helped his arm even more. Rowing with Lewis was so solid, thought Enquist, it was like rowing on an ergometer. He didn't need to worry about anything except how hard he could pull on the oars.[82] He knew they could be fast—they were, after all, the double that had represented the United States at the World Championships just a year earlier.

After all the disappointments of the summer, Brad Lewis realized that rowing with Paul Enquist in the double was the best thing that could have happened to him. If he had won the trials, he would have been racing for third place at the Olympics, because international competition was dominated then by Finland's Pertti Karppinen and Germany's Peter-Michael Kolbe, who were the Magic Johnson and Larry Bird of 1980s single sculling. Now, he and Enquist had the chance to do something brilliant; and as he looked at Paul, he saw a rower who was "relentless," a "monster" who could "really crank on the oars."[83] Enquist was not only super steady and reliable, someone who would not choke in a big race, but he was also willing to buy into Lewis's self-styled training regime that went beyond rowing to include weightlifting, massage, aura-balancing, visualization, and listening to a tape by Lewis's philosophical rowing guru, Mike Livingston, which began, "Good day. We are privileged to live another day in this magnificent world. Today you will be tested."[84]

Most observers, and even Lewis himself, at times, figured that Enquist merely tolerated Lewis's "gimmicks," and yet Enquist bought into Lewis's program enthusiastically. For one, he realized that none of it would hurt them or make them slower. He was also smart enough to see that Lewis's methods made sense. Although Halberstam and others would later portray Lewis's tactics as unorthodox at best and verging on New Age shamanism at worst, Enquist could see that—boiled down to its essence—Lewis's regime involved nothing more than hard work, core strength training, and hyper-focused mental discipline. For the time, Lewis's methods were innovative, foreshadowing techniques embraced by modern sports psychologists, who today use visualization and mindfulness to get athletes to "be in the zone" and tap into "flow states."

Enquist also bought into Lewis's theory that a myriad of things had to go perfectly to make a championship crew—there were so many moving parts, from training, nutrition, and technique to rigging boats and race strategies. But nobody could do *everything* perfectly. If there were fifty things that had to go right to win Olympic gold, even the best crews in the world were probably doing only forty of them. Maybe some of Lewis's ideas, thought Enquist, could push them over the top.[85] Enquist could also see with his own eyes that every day they spent in Ithaca, they were getting faster. Lewis could be a little testy, for sure, but Lewis could be managed, and Enquist had plenty of experience managing cantankerous teammates—if Enquist could handle Brad Sleeper and the WSU lightweights, he could handle Brad Lewis.

Ted Nash was surprised that Enquist and Lewis did not make the U.S. Olympic team in the first place, but he realized it could work out to their advantage in the end—"that is what all good club athletes feed on. Tell them they are 'nothing special' and they will find a secret lake or river and become *very* special."[86] That is what happened at the U.S. Olympic Trials. When they pulled up to the line, they were supremely focused on the task at hand—all their training, all their visualizations, had prepared them for this moment.

Charlie Altekruse, in the lane next to them, said, "Good luck, guys." Neither Lewis nor Enquist responded. They channeled all their energies into the race, and, as it turns out, they did not need any luck: they defeated the second-place boat of Tiff Wood and Jim Dietz by open water and destroyed Parker's team double of Altekruse and Bouscaren. They were now the U.S. Olympic double. When the U.S. team quad also lost, Parker, according to Lewis, "let out a soft cry and seemed to cave in."[87] For Parker, the trials were a disaster: his select boats had all lost to the challenge boats; and his oarsmen, who had won their place on the U.S. team in a grueling selection camp and then performed admirably at Lucerne, now had to give their uniforms to the very people who had been cut from Parker's camp or were never invited in the first place. It was a bitter pill.

After having won the trials, Enquist and Lewis needed to decide two things: where would they train and who would be their coach? These decisions almost tore the new Olympic double apart. For Lewis, the answers were clear: They would train in Southern California, where they would be racing, and get Mike Livingston to coach them. Enquist was not having it. For him, the answer was just as clear in the opposite direction: Harry Parker should be their coach and, since they were now on the Olympic team, they should train under Parker at the designated Olympic training facility at Dartmouth. Was there any argument that could stand up to good food, uniforms, accommodations, and training with your best friends and teammates, all fellow Olympians, under the guidance of the greatest rowing coach in the country?

Enquist was willing to concede that Parker might have botched the selection camp. But selection was over now, and Parker was better, *way better*, Enquist believed, at coaching rowers than he was at selecting rowers. In Enquist's experience, there was no coach in the United States that did a better job of preparing his crews to race. Enquist had been around a lot of coaches by then. Parker, above all, knew how to win. His crews were always ready to race. Why would they not want someone like Parker helping them prepare for what would be the biggest race of their lives?[88] But Lewis was not convinced. The sculling team voted for Parker, and Lewis left for California.

Over the next tension-filled days, Lewis tried to convince Enquist to leave the Olympic camp and join him in California. They had long, heated arguments on the phone. Only days before, they were warriors who together "had conquered the world" and now they "were becoming adversaries."[89] Enquist wasn't about to yield. All the years of sacrifice since 1977 had led him to this moment. Whether they would lead to gold or not was immaterial: what was important now was that they were Olympians. He had made the Olym-

Paul Enquist (left) and Brad Lewis receive their gold medals after rowing through the field in the final at the 1984 Olympics on Lake Casitas, California. Photo courtesy of Paul Enquist.

pic team! Now he wanted to train with the Olympic team. "We are on the Goddamned Olympic team, Brad! We made it! We did it!" Enquist argued. "Now we get to train at the Olympic rowing camp and be fed and housed and coached. Why would you want to throw that all away?"[90]

Bob Ernst thought that rowing in the double with Enquist was as close as Brad Lewis could get to rowing in a single.[91] The assumption was that Enquist was so easygoing that Lewis could call the shots. In this case, however, that wasn't remotely true. Enquist was stubborn and determined, and he refused to yield. He finally prevailed on both questions. Lewis came back to Dartmouth, and they trained under Harry Parker. Using both Lewis's and Parker's methods, they won the gold medal at the 1984 Olympics in a race that was textbook perfect. They had been assigned lane six, on the outside, with Belgium, Canada, Germany, Italy, and Yugoslavia lined up between them and the shore. When the gun went off, they executed their race plan without reference to the other teams. It was the strategy of a supremely confident crew. While Belgium and Canada dueled for the early lead and the other crews struggled to maintain contact, Enquist and Lewis rowed at a steady, controlled rate, crossing the 1000-meter mark in fifth place, open water separating them from the leaders. With 500 meters to go, they were in fourth place but surging. They rowed down the Belgians in the last 200 meters, their cadence ticking upward but still as even as a metronome. They crossed the finish line one-half length ahead of the Belgians, becoming the first U.S. rowers to win Olympic gold since 1964, and the first U.S. crew to medal in the double sculls since 1932. Later, Lewis was not only grateful for Paul Enquist as a teammate but also for Enquist's wisdom and steadfast commitment to training at Dartmouth under Parker.

Later that winter, Harry Parker sat down in his small office in Harvard's Newell Boathouse and handwrote a letter to Paul Enquist, apologizing for the events of the previous summer: "It was obviously a mistake on my part not to have included you in the group going to Lucerne and I felt badly then and still do about that decision," Parker explained. "On the other hand, I was pleased for you personally that you won the trials and I enjoyed working with you from that point forward, very, very much. And I thought you rowed a great race in the finals at Casitas."[92] It was heartfelt praise from the restrained Harry Parker. But Enquist didn't need an apology—he blamed Parker for nothing and always held him in the highest regard. He also realized that having *not* been selected for the team before Lucerne was probably the best thing that happened to him and Brad. Between travel, jet lag, and racing in Europe, the Lucerne boats had lost weeks of hard training while Enquist and Lewis had employed the time to focus entirely on increasing their boat speed. It was ironic, but being cut from the Olympic team was one of the myriad things that needed to happen to complete their gold medal journey. Somehow it had all worked to perfection.

Conclusion

Paul Enquist, the young rower from WSU, had persevered. It was an archetypical WSU story: hailing from the provinces—a cow school with no rowing tradition—Enquist worked hard in anonymity and ascended to the very top of the rowing world. If Cougar Crew was about improbability and perseverance, Enquist became the poster boy for both. Enquist's story did not end in fame or fortune. "It's not like I won the hundred-yard dash," Enquist later said. "Outside of the rowing community and my family, not many people realize what we accomplished. There's not a lot of money in rowing, and there's no pot of gold at the end of that rainbow."[93] Enquist went back to fishing, and later became a longshoreman. There was *one* pot of gold at the end of the rainbow, however. Enquist met his wife Lisa at a celebration of his Olympic victory in Ballard. He hung up his oars, settled down, and built a family.

Paul Enquist's victory seemed to validate something essential about Cougar Crew: that individuals could persevere in anonymity until they reached greatness, at which time they could continue to persevere in anonymity. Enquist's story, and the story of Cougar Crew, resembled the Buddhist saying, "Before Enlightenment, chop wood and carry water; after Enlightenment, chop wood and carry water." For generations of WSU oarsmen, endurance, dedication, adversity, and perseverance would not lead to gold medals, fame, or fortune but rather to hard-earned modest successes that would invariably be followed by more hardship, more adversity, and more perseverance. That was the story of Cougar Crew in the 1970s and 1980s, as it is today.

Jim Austin (1972–75)

Paul was very strong. I wanted seven more Paul's behind me! I mean, I used to think, can we just duplicate him, does he have cousins or brothers? He was a very good oar but was he the best oar? Yeah, he was probably the best rower we had just because of his physical makeup, but was he that much better back then? No. But he stuck with it. He was also just the nicest guy. Paul was unassuming, you know, just a really nice guy. He had no ego at all, right? Even after winning an Olympic gold medal, it didn't change him a bit.

Harry Parker, Coach, Harvard and Olympic Team, Letter to Paul Enquist (1985)

Paul,

Hope this makes some sense to you. I've not ever expressed out loud to you my feelings about last summer. It was obviously a mistake on my part not to have included you in the group going to Lucerne and I felt badly then and still do about that decision. On the other hand, I was very pleased for you personally that you won the trials and enjoyed working with you from that point forward very, very much. And I thought you rowed a great race in the finals at Casitas. I hope life is quieting down a little by now and that things are going well for you.

Sincerely,

Harry

CHAPTER FIVE

Rowing on the Edge, 1979–1989

This is going to be a good—great—year. There is more interest and support for crew than ever before. Let's exceed our expectations and move up to even more wins and a higher finish in the Pac-10 for all boats. I have some new ideas to make the boats go faster. All you have to do is get in shape and continue to work on your academic work. I would like to continue the academic reputation of the crew, which is a good one, as well as its athletic reputation, which is one of a winner. Have fun, see you this fall. Let's have a GREAT YEAR.

—Ken Struckmeyer to the "Oarsmen of
Washington State University," 1980

You can talk about Struckmeyer all day. He works for nothing and gives all his own time and money. He stresses we have a good time and overcome our problems, like lack of money.

—Michael Riley (1984–88) in *Chinook* '87

The year was 1979, and it promised to be a good one for Coach Ken Struckmeyer and the Cougar Crew. Sixty-seven men and twenty-four women were training with the club, which was not only growing but becoming more competitive and successful every year. Struckmeyer himself was now tenured and happily married to a woman who shared his same basic values, especially the understanding that his coaching was a labor of love, measured not in salary—for there was none—but in friendships, family, and shared experience. Marj was every bit as much a part of the crew family as Ken Struckmeyer, and their married life flowed with the current of the rowing club's annual migrations to Seattle for fall regattas, and then to Bellingham, Seattle, Spokane, and Redwood Shores for spring races. Marj and Ken never had children, but they counted every year's growing class of rowers as their own.

For a life so dedicated to internal rewards, Struckmeyer was overwhelmed by the announcement in December 1978 that he was Pac-8 Coach of the Year. Dick Erickson, Washington's head rowing coach, had nominated Struckmeyer and argued on his behalf that, of all the Pac-8 crews, "WSU has done the most

Ken Struckmeyer gives instructions from the launch as his crew rows upriver toward the shell house. Increasing numbers of rowers and increasing boat speeds augured well for Cougar Crew as they entered their second decade. Photo courtesy of WSU Manuscripts, Archives, and Special Collections.

with the least." Struckmeyer was grateful and extremely proud, but his focus was on his oarsmen. "It's the guys' hard work. They are taking part in building a tradition," Struckmeyer said. He believed his rowers "work harder than any other team" at WSU.[1]

Struckmeyer's joy at receiving the award was tempered by his growing dissatisfaction with the lack of resources his club received from the university. Besides calling attention to the efforts of his oarsmen, he made sure the *Daily Evergreen* reporter understood that he and all the coaches were volunteers while the team itself received only a pittance from the ASWSU and nothing from the athletic department. "The only school that doesn't recognize us is the one we represent," he asserted.

As if to validate Erickson's nomination, in 1979 WSU had one of its most successful years on the water, with another win over UCLA, another fourth-place finish in the Pac-10, and an IRA National Championship to top it off. Throughout, Struckmeyer never missed an opportunity to publicize that his club was operating with an austere budget and volunteer coaches, even while competing against university-funded athletic programs. He knew that Erickson was right: they were doing the most with the least. It was nice for someone to recognize that fact, and yet it wasn't what Struckmeyer wanted for his oarsmen. Just once, he wanted to try it the other way around and see what they could do *with* some funding. He wondered what they could do if they didn't have rowers quitting because they couldn't afford the travel costs, or if the club could pay and maintain a professional coaching staff. He was tired of his team wearing poverty as a badge of honor. That's why he submitted a $28,000 proposal for varsity status to the athletic department in the summer of 1979, and that's why, when Sam Jankovich, the athletic director, turned him down, he became increasingly frustrated that his crew was forced to do so much with so little.

Adversity and grit were good words to describe the history of Cougar Crew, but Ken Struckmeyer kept coming back to two words: "fragile" and "vulnerable."[2] No matter how hard its members worked, the club's fortunes could shift on a dime. He knew from experience that shells, and even an entire boathouse, could be destroyed in a moment. Boat trailers could fail. Trucks and vans could break down. Funding could vanish. Fundraisers could flop. Rules and regulations from the WSU administration could hamper their activities. Injuries, sickness, and academic ineligibility could destroy the fortunes of promising crews. Volunteer assistant coaches could—and must—quit and move on. Volunteer head coaches—like Struckmeyer himself—could be undermined by disgruntled rowers or be forced to quit because of financial, personal, or professional pressures. It seemed to Struckmeyer that even during good times, Cougar Crew was forever rowing on the edge of instability.

———————————————

Yet somehow, remarkably, despite the continued fragility and vulnerability of the perennially underfunded club, the team's second decade yielded some of the greatest successes in the history of Cougar Crew. If the club was continuously on the edge of instability, it was also on the edge of a breakthrough. The 1980s saw the emergence of a strong alumni organization—the Cougar Rowing Association—that spearheaded serious fundraising campaigns, including the expansion of the club endowment fund, and perhaps more significantly, conducted significant alumni outreach efforts using *The Pull Hard* as well as a direct-mail campaign to draw former rowers back to the program. The result was increased financial support from alumni as well as the first truly big Class Day weekends. The 1980s also witnessed record turnouts for Cougar Crew, new carbon fiber shells and oars for both men and women, two gold medalists from its alumni, Pac-10 championships for the lightweight men and women, and, finally, a brand new, two-bay boathouse with electricity, two sheltered docks, and access to better rowing water than the crew ever experienced at Boyer Park. To top it off, toward the end of the decade, WSU rowed in Istanbul, Turkey, an experience that Struckmeyer cherished as one of the highlights of his career. It was a decade of institution building for the organization and unparalleled successes both on and off the water, but one that also bred greater, and perhaps unrealistic, expectations for future successes. It was a decade that, for all its achievements, deposited the crew on the edge of momentous changes and turbulence.

Garcrewco: Building the Institution of Cougar Crew

In September 1979, Ken Struckmeyer received a letter from Paul Enquist, exhorting his former coach that it was "time for WSU crew to take the step to the top." Enquist believed that step "was not impossible, but small and very achievable in the *near future*." He believed that WSU already had the necessary "conditions to develop top crews," namely "equipment, training facilities, leadership, and most important, the knowledge of what it takes to win." The only difference between WSU and other crews, Enquist argued, was money, but "money doesn't make boats go fast, people do." Enquist quoted Stan Pocock—"no fast wagons, only fast horses"—and ended his letter encouraging Struckmeyer "to start reaping the benefits of past knowledge and experience. WSU can win, believe it."[3]

Struckmeyer was pleased with the letter and read it aloud to his crew. It was an inspirational message. Paul was right. Money did not make boats go fast. But Struckmeyer also knew that money lubricated the gears of the entire operation, and without it, the club was dead in the water. Moreover, their situation made it inevitable that more energy had to be devoted to fundraising, necessarily leaving less time and energy for both athletics and academics, the latter of which Struckmeyer valued above all. The month before receiving Paul's letter, Struckmeyer himself had drafted his annual letter to his "Oarsmen and Oarsladies," updating them on the coming year. The balance of his message described the various fundraising activities arranged for the crew that year. After basketball games and concerts, they would clean Beasley Coliseum; they would work twelve-hour shifts transporting computers to a new computer science building during the first weekend of Thanksgiving break; they would sell "souvenirs" at football games on a commission basis. "We need the money," he stated, flatly. It was not lost on Struckmeyer or his rowers that they were reduced to cleaning up after the university-funded teams. Only the last lines of his letter alluded to their athletic goals: "Keep running. Keep working. It is going to Happen!!! BEAT WASHINGTON."[4]

Struckmeyer put on a good face for his oarsmen, but his exasperation over the lack of funding and resources from the university—which to the coach also conveyed a lack of respect for his club—reached new heights in winter 1979 when the crew, the same one that had won a national championship that summer, lost exclusive access to the Olympic weight room during closed hours and was also barred by its club status from the weight room used by varsity athletes. This left the team working out in Pullman's National Guard Academy—"a lonely gymnasium without windows and proper ventilation" that also lacked proper weight equipment—where each crew member paid one dollar per night out of his own pocket for the privilege of doing "isokinet-ics." Struckmeyer's defiance could hardly be contained. "We are going to try and have another good season and show the athletic department we still have a quality team," he said. "Struckmeyer's squad must be dedicated to having another championship year to go through the times and trials they have so far," the *Evergreen* reporter chimed in, picking up Struckmeyer's messaging. "Even with a drastically reduced budget and minimal practice facilities, the squad endures and continues its quest for success."[5]

In nearly every *Daily Evergreen* feature about Cougar Crew in the early 1980s, Struckmeyer used the platform to remind everyone who would listen that his crew received nothing from WSU itself, that the coaches were volunteers, that the shell house had no running water or electricity, that his rowers raised their own monies and relied on donations from alumni and parents, and yet, their goal was still to win a Pac-10 title and defeat the Huskies, whose budget was more than six digits and growing. "We're trying to build a tradition and gain some respect in the conference," he repeated, again and again, in an increasingly futile quest to boost the club's funding.[6] In 1983, the *Evergreen*, taking the hint, began referring to them as the ASWSU Crew rather than the WSU Crew, underscoring that the club received funding from the student body but not the university itself.

In the early 1980s, a revolution in glass fiber, carbon fiber, and Kevlar was widening the gap between the haves and have-nots of the rowing world. This was a frustrating reality for the ever-competitive Struckmeyer. His crews needed carbon fiber Dreissigacker oars and composite boats if they wanted to compete with UW and Cal Berkeley, who were not only upping their games with sophisticated, expensive technology but were also recruiting foreign ath-letes to row on their teams. In spring 1983, a very fast WSU freshman crew

The shell trailer in the early 1980s, loaded and ready to travel. This was an iconic image for rowers in the 1980s—Ken Struckmeyer's old green Chevrolet truck pulling a trailer stacked with wooden Pocock eights. Photo Credit: Gene Dowers.

coached by John Holtman placed second at the Pac-10 Championships, losing to a crew that was rowing in a 270-pound composite shell while they rowed in the 326-pound *Cougar One*. Struckmeyer admitted that they lost the race because their competitors were "very good," but WSU was *also* very good, which begged the question, "What difference did the equipment make"?[7] Struckmeyer knew, like Stan Pocock, that it was the horses and not the wagon, but he couldn't help wondering if a lighter boat might have made a difference in the quest for a Pac-10 championship. How could they compete with other varsity programs without more funding from WSU?

When Dick Young became athletic director in 1983, there was another short flirtation with the idea that rowing might become a varsity sport, but it amounted to little more than a hollow gesture. Meanwhile, WSU budgets were being slashed in response to a national recession, and Struckmeyer himself was forced to take a 20 percent pay cut. This, combined with the fact that he was floating the team thousands of dollars a year for gas and expenses, not to mention his time, made the lack of funding from the university smart even more. He was worn down. "Sometimes I don't do a very good job of teaching or coaching," he lamented.[8]

To make matters worse, Struckmeyer's department was nagging him to publish more and coach less. "I am under pressure from the 'university' to do other things," he explained to his oarsmen.[9] In the early 1970s, the Department of Landscape Architecture had encouraged Struckmeyer's coaching, wisely considering it a form of teaching and mentoring that benefited WSU students. His tenure committee was very supportive, believing that coaching the crew was a valuable form of service to the larger university. But the 1970s were the last years of innocence at WSU. In the 1980s, the pressure was mounting from all academic departments to increase their emphasis on research and deemphasize teaching as part of WSU's quest to become a bona fide research institution. Administrators still paid lip service to the holy triumvirate of research, teaching, and service, and Struckmeyer had two of the three covered, but not the *one* that counted. One of the associate deans for the College of Agriculture—a person he had counted as a friend—told Struckmeyer that if he wanted to be a *teacher* he should go to a junior college.

Struckmeyer still refused to give up a teaching-focused approach to his profession, much to the benefit of thousands of landscape architecture students who were influenced and inspired by his pedagogy and mentoring; nor did he give up coaching the crew, much to the benefit of thousands of rowers, who enjoyed the relative stability that Struckmeyer's volunteer efforts afforded the club over two decades. He also steadfastly refused to give up the club's focus on academic achievement. If varsity sports teams had their athletes working out three times a day, or switching their majors to accommodate their workout schedule, Struckmeyer could boast a program that upheld the ideal of the student athlete. "We work hard on the athletic side, and we do the best that we can," he maintained, "But we try not to let athletics overpower academics." In 1983, WSU's athletic department conducted a workshop for their athletes called "Life after Athletics," but Struckmeyer insisted that Cougar Crew's concept was instead, "Athletics after life, and rightly so."[10] Unfortunately, taking the moral high ground did not translate into more funding from WSU or more victories on the water against varsity programs. The responsibility of funding Cougar Crew from year to year, as well as building a durable institution that could withstand the vicissitudes of funding cuts, coaching changes, and myriad other challenges, would ultimately fall to the club itself, and, in particular, its alumni.

In the early 1980s, one of those alumni was Rich "Flip" Ray, who had graduated in 1980 but stayed in Pullman to pursue a master's degree in American studies. Ray had won a national championship rowing in the Meatwagon in 1979, and the following year he was voted All-Pac-10. "A team not funded by the WSU athletic department placed one man on the Pacific-10 All-Conference rowing team," noted the *Daily Evergreen*,[11] ever sympathetic to the plight of the perennially underfunded crew. That same summer, Ray, John "Yumbo" Holtman, and Kerin McKellar won another IRA national championship in the pair with coxswain, after which Struckmeyer quipped, "That's not bad for a sport that's lost all recognition by the university."[12]

Even before he graduated, Ray had become an articulate advocate for increasing the crew's funding from the university. In his senior year, he argued stridently in the *Evergreen* that "if the Cougar Crew is to continue the phenomenal growth it has shown since its birth," it would require "paid coaches (all are presently voluntary), new equipment and facilities, and an alternative to automotive transportation." He concluded that "club members simply cannot be expected to bear this burden," and he was confident "our needs are legitimate and that what we offer this school is significant."[13] But Ray's pleas were no more effective than Struckmeyer's—the athletic department not only rejected the club's request for funding, it denied them further access to training facilities under the logic that any concession made to the crew would have to be extended to every WSU club, including, as Struckmeyer liked to say, the "tiddlywinks" club.[14]

The financial obligations of Cougar Crew would continue to be borne by student athletes, their families, and their overburdened coaches. Generations of rowers would fund their masochistic pursuit of excellence despite little help from ASWSU, no help from the athletics department, and with all the glory and recognition of an unknown order of monks. Like monks, they embraced their voluntary poverty and used it to spread their unique doctrine of physical hardship and sacrifice. Sometimes they had fun doing so, like in the late 1970s, when the team's true believers conjured up the mother of all fundraisers: a 370-mile rowathon down the Snake River from Lewiston to Portland in the summer of 1977, an event they imagined would not only set a world record but raise thousands of dollars for the crew. It did neither, but it was a stunt that Ray, one of the head instigators, called the "zaniest, most foolhardy, and most enjoyable fundraising project that any of us have ever been involved in."[15] Doug Engle remembered the rowathons as exercises that "were not very efficient" as fundraising events but "built team camaraderie" and "were a lot of fun."[16]

For Engle, Ray, and the other swashbuckling participants, both men and women, rowing to the point of physical exhaustion and braving the elements was a "fun" and rewarding way to spend a summer week. When UW coach

Dick Erickson heard about their madcap expedition, he doubted they could do it—and he pledged a fiberglass four-man shell if they could. They managed it, and they took home the hardware from UW along with about $1,000. And everyone survived. In what might have served as a slogan for the WSU crew generally, Rich Ray described the entire adventure as "one of partial successes."[17] They tried it again the following summer, making it to the Tri-Cities this time before their gunwales cracked in heavy whitecaps and the boat began taking on water. They patched the seams with duct tape and made it to shore near Wallula Gap, where they walked barefoot for miles on hot rocks along the railroad tracks in search of help. "Rather than getting anybody hurt and losing the shell completely, we called it quits," explained Struckmeyer. Nonetheless, they brought in $700 and raised awareness of Cougar Crew.[18] These were vintage Cougar Crew experiences that created memories of hardship, camaraderie, and adventure; but as Engle noted, they were not efficient means of fundraising.

By 1981, Ray and Engle, another Meatwagoner who was also still in Pullman working on a graduate degree, were convinced that the WSU rowing club needed to make an organizational leap to become sustainable and self-sufficient for the long term. They had loads of ideas for how to make Cougar Crew faster, stronger, and bigger, but most of them spiraled down the drain with other late-night ramblings that no one ever pursued. At bottom, Ray and Engle were convinced that the club needed to professionalize its governance, formalize its fundraising efforts, and transition from its wild and wooly pioneer days—where a good idea for raising money was to brave giant barges and whitecaps during daredevil rowathons—to an era they hoped would be defined by effective self-government, financial stability, formalized traditions, and increased responsibility all around. What was needed now, ten years after the club's formation, was for the alumni to take a leading role in financially supporting the club and guiding it from infancy to stability. If the institution of the club was stable, then victories on the water would follow.

The drive began with a bold manifesto to all Cougar Crew members, decrying "the advanced state of entropy into which our club has fallen," and calling on everyone to take a greater share of responsibility for the crew's operation, so as to unburden Struckmeyer from having to carry the team on his shoulders. "What in the name of Harry Parker are we waiting for?" they asked. Their open letter was a call to action, intended to translate griping and bitching into tangible progress by making the club into a "vital, responsive political unit which absorbs and utilizes good ideas, instead of simply swallowing them forever."

Ray and Engle proposed a specific plan for increasing the club's capacity for self-governance, including a regular news bulletin with officer reports, a club to-do list, and a "conditioning status report" that listed each rower's scores on fitness tests devised by the commodore, vice commodore, and freshman coach, who would govern team workouts as the so-called "Tri-Lateral Commission." This step would increase each athlete's accountability and "also take some of the pressure off Ken" to run workouts. Ray and Engle also detailed new responsibilities of the club's officers and insisted that the club operate with a strict chain of command that would eliminate "telephone-bombing" the Struckmeyer residence for help when club members could instead solve their own problems. "Ken and Marj are not running an answering service," Ray and Engle admonished club members, "so let's cease treating them as if they were." Their manifesto ended with this conclusion: "We have reached the stage where we must either mature into an autonomous and vital democracy capable of responsibly, sensibly, and efficiently governing our political, financial and athletic interests, or else die a slow and painful death."[19]

It was the beginning of an ambitious effort to organize current club members and alumni around common goals, and Ray printed their letter using a word processor in the WSU English department. On the cover page, he typed COUGARCREW and then used the word processor's formula to randomly repeat those letters in different patterns and shapes. When he printed out the shape of an oar, its narrow handle coincidentally repeated the word GARCREWCO, and there was something about the neologism, according to Ray, "which sounded to my ear both humorous and appropriate." He took to ending long alumni organizing sessions with the phrase, "Garcrewco, Goodnight!"

Engle also liked zany wordplay, but he believed the phrase came to inhabit something more than just a silly reformulation of "Cougar Crew." To him, "Garcrewco" embodied the "spirit of the crew"—it was "the drive that took hold in Rich Stager's brain in 1969 and has been infecting those that hear the siren call of rowing and pushing for the development of Cougar Crew ever since."[20] Many other alumni would heed that siren call in the early 1980s, including Dave Emigh, Bob Appleyard, Steve Wells, Dave Yorozu, Jim Rudd, Craig Illman, Steve and Kari Ranten, Kathleen Randall, John DeLong, John Lafer, Tim Malkow, Brett Purtzer, Kim Heggerness, and Tammy and Roger Crawford. All of them desired to build a powerful alumni presence that would not only support the club financially—since clearly WSU's athletic department would not—but also constitute a powerful bond between current and former rowers whereby institutional knowledge, history, and the team's legacies could be transmitted from one generation to the next.

The first step was to strengthen the Cougar Rowing Association (CRA), bolstering it with a new constitution and bylaws that would better allow it to expand fundraising and connect with alumni. This was not a novel idea. The CRA had its roots in the "Cougar Crew Booster Club," also known as the "Friends of Cougar Rowing," which was founded in 1974 to take the burden of fundraising off Struckmeyer and the rowers themselves, although nearly half of the founding members of the "Oar Club," who donated $85 and received an oar, were named Struckmeyer, including Fred and Helen, Donald and Barbara, and Coach Struckmeyer himself. Struckmeyer pushed for the creation of a board of directors to oversee raising and managing funds for the fledgling club. With no help coming from university athletics, the coach early on realized that the club needed "firm and long-range planning to ensure its continued and lasting existence." Struckmeyer saw a strong alumni association as vitally important to "relieve the coaches and student oarsmen" from the burdens of sustaining the crew so that the athletes "can study and the coaches might retain their teaching and research appointments at the University."[21]

In 1976, the Friends of Cougar Rowing was rebranded as the Cougar Rowing Association, steered by an unwieldy seven directors and an even larger "advisory group." In spring 1981, under the leadership of Ray, Engle, Bob Appleyard, Steve and Kari Ranten, Dave Yorozu, John DeLong, and others, the new CRA constitution established a three-person board of directors as well as a president, vice president, and secretary-treasurer, all dedicated to, as Appleyard explained in *The Pull Hard*, raising funds for the purpose of "maintaining a quality rowing program at WSU." The new CRA recognized that the crew's success was ultimately dependent on the "students themselves" but that "the alumni can provide their experience, time, and resources to guide and assist the program in many different ways, to keep interest in competitive rowing alive for years and years to come."[22]

The revivified booster club embarked on a major drive to raise money for the Cougar Crew Endowment Fund, which first began in the mid-1970s with a $3,000 gift from Jim Austin's dad. By 1980, the fund was barely over $8,000. The new effort began by developing an alumni database and promoting the CRA as a dues-paying organization where former rowers could show their gratitude "for the years and miles and friends that rowing gave us."[23] The CRA advertised Class Day as a weekend journey back in time to the good old days and pushed hard to get former rowers back to the Palouse, one year even offering a "travel package" that included a Greyhound charter from the west side, accommodations at the University Inn at Moscow, and an itinerary consisting of a "fun row," alumni meeting, cocktail hour with childcare, and, of course, the Class Day Banquet.[24] The results were record turnouts for Class Day by the end of the decade, such as in 1988 when over forty alumni returned to Pullman from distant points—Tim Richards from Hawaii, Mary Farrell from New York, Mike Noble from Corpus Christi, and Mitch Wainwright from Denver.[25]

Communicating all these achievements to a growing alumni base was *The Pull Hard*, which was not new—it was first published in 1973 by Bob Orr— but would be published consistently and professionally for the first time in the 1980s under the guidance of Kari Ranten, Kathleen Randall, and Rich Ray. Looking at the twenty editions of *The Pull Hard* published during the decade, it is impossible to see Cougar Crew as just another student club at WSU—it was a growing, thriving, evolving organization where current rowers, coaches, and alumni pursued common goals on many fronts.

In the 1980s, the grand aspirations of the CRA—Ray and Engle in particular—were never more apparent than the effort to develop small Liberty Lake near Spokane as a world-class buoyed six-lane racecourse modeled after the IRA national championship course in Syracuse. The idea emerged from Engle's graduate work in environmental science, where he was studying water quality and conducting environmental mitigation work on Liberty Lake for an Environmental Protection Agency grant. The small lake was surrounded by houses, and runoff from sewage and lawns was creating algae blooms.

While working there, Engle couldn't stop thinking about how perfect the lake would be for rowing—it was just long enough for a 2,000-meter course; there were no crosswinds or currents; and it had a quaint beach resort at one end with plenty of room for boats, trailers, and spectators. After millions were spent cleaning the lake, its residents were enthusiastic about the prospect of a "colorful brand of watersport to advertise the success of the restoration," and Ray and Engle proposed an annual rowing regatta.[26] The homeowners not only accepted but donated thousands of dollars as well as launches, stake boats, and manpower to develop the Albano-style racecourse—with lines of buoys marking the lanes—that Ray and Engle hoped would bring a first-class regatta to eastern Washington.[27]

Ray, still living in Pullman while doing graduate work and coaching the women's crew, worked nearly 2,000 hours constructing the buoyed course. Dozens of other alumni, such as Steve Wells and Bob Appleyard, stepped up to organize and officiate at the Liberty Lake regattas, which began in 1982 and continued for three years, culminating with WSU hosting the Pacific Northwest Regional Championships at Liberty Lake in 1984.[28]

Hosting regionals and drawing the University of Washington as well as crews from the entire region to Cougar country for a major regatta was a signal achievement for the CRA and for WSU crew generally; and yet, the effort also underscored just how hard it was to build lasting institutions in the hinterlands of eastern Washington. As long as former rowers like Ray and Engle were in Pullman and willing to dedicate thousands of hours to the cause (shades of Struckmeyer), the crew could expand and grow its reach, but when enthusiasm waned, when former rowers moved away to take jobs and start families, who would pick up the slack for major initiatives like Liberty Lake that required teams of organizers to carry off? The Liberty Lake experiment showed the ambitiousness of the CRA but also suggested its limitations. A few devoted people could do only so much, and when they moved on, their efforts proved impossible to sustain.

While the CRA sowed seeds among the alumni, Ken Abbey, Cougar Crew's man on the inside, pulled the necessary levers within the French Administration Building to convince two university committees as well as WSU President Glenn Terrell to allocate $75,000 to fund construction of a new shell house. The initial plan was to place the new building across from the existing boathouse at Boyer Park, using the old one for storage and repairs, but that idea was scrapped in favor of building above the dam at Wawawai.[29] The new boathouse was scheduled to be ready in the fall of 1984, but a suspicious fire swept through the nearly completed building only ten days before completion, forcing the contractors—two of whom were at odds—to begin all over again. Remarkably, the fire occurred on August 5, 1984, the same day that Paul Enquist and Brad Lewis won the Olympic gold medal in the double sculls race. "While everyone in Pullman was discouraged with the fire," Abbey joked, "maybe we just have to build every shell house twice."[30]

Although the building wasn't quite ready for Class Day in 1985, alumni were able to tour the grounds, see the docks, and gaze with wonder at the impressive new structure. It was a heady Class Day in 1985, with Paul Enquist and Kristi Norelius returning triumphantly to Pullman, gold medals in tow, but Enquist said the highlight of the weekend was peeking into the new facility. The large two-bay boathouse, the two docks protected from current and wind, and the water conditions were, in his view, "more than any early alums or supporters would have dreamt."[31] "The twentieth century has at last arrived at the Cougar shell house," proclaimed *The Pull Hard*. "The facility is now well-lit with fluorescent tubes, and on the west wall near the side door is mounted an honest-to-God GTE touchtone. Best of all, utility and telephone bills will be picked up by the University Physical Plant. Touché!"[32]

By the end of the decade, Kim Heggerness, one of the CRA directors, could boast of the phone drive that pushed the Cougar Crew Endowment to nearly $32,000, a fourfold increase in nine years, despite stock market shocks. She could point to the regular publication of *The Pull Hard*, with its readership of nearly six hundred households, and a dues-paying CRA membership of 113. Heggerness and the CRA understood that the success of Cougar Crew was not just measured in wins on the water but also "what occurs behind the scenes." The CRA, according to Heggerness, "has found its stride and is progressing nicely."[33] The crew was creating traditions and institutions that have since become a permanent facet of club rowing at WSU. These successes "behind the scenes" were establishing Cougar Crew as a permanent institution in collegiate rowing, while WSU's performance on the water in the 1980s was also yielding unprecedented successes.

Brand New Heavies

When Mike McQuaid arrived in Pullman from Mercer Island in fall 1982, he was prepared to make his mark, though he didn't know exactly where or how. As he explored the campus during registration week, he made a point of visiting the different club booths, examining the literature, listening to the recruiting pitches. At Mercer Island High School, he hadn't been a star athlete, but he was ready now to throw himself into something that would develop both his body and his mind. Mike McQuaid, as anyone who knew him could attest, was serious about making the most of his college experience. As he looked around, one poster kept catching his eye. It seemed to be stapled up everywhere he looked: "Strong and healthy. Keep Growing with Rowing!" The message called to him, as if it was written for him personally. He knew he wasn't done with sports yet—in fact, he hadn't even begun to explore his potential. He figured himself to be a late-blooming athlete, and he certainly wanted to grow himself as a person in college. He arrived at WSU ready to embrace all the clichés about the transformative powers of a college education, but there was also something deeper that was tugging him toward crew.

When he was six years old, McQuaid's grandfather had taken him out on Lake Washington in his little runabout. They motored out toward the Lake Washington Floating Bridge, where they watched the University of Washington race from the bridge down to Seward Park—likely they were watching the Head of the Lake Regatta. The experience struck Mike profoundly. In his first-grade class the next week, he drew a colorful picture of that regatta on Lake Washington. It was one of those precious innocent creations that mothers save, and Mike's mother not only kept his piece of primitive art, but she had it framed and presented to him for Christmas many years later. Mike McQuaid was always fond of a good quotation, and one of his favorites, attributed to Louis Pasteur, was, "Chance favors the prepared mind." As he looked at the recruiting poster for WSU crew in the fall of 1982, he felt as if chance had prepared his mind for that very moment, and he was ready to seize the opportunity. He attended the orientation meeting, went down to the Snake River, and never looked back.[34]

McQuaid's freshman year was as successful as any in WSU history. His freshman boat won Class Day and became the only class in WSU rowing history to win four straight Class Day regattas. Freshman coach John "Yumbo" Holtman, another former Meatwagoner, called them a "cocky bunch," and they had reason to be: they beat WWU at Lake Samish and UPS at home, edged OSU in the Tri-Cities, and then defeated UCLA at Redwood Shores in the semifinals before losing to UW and taking second place in the Pac-10 Championships. It was the kind of success that UW and Cal Berkeley freshman were accustomed to but had not been the usual standard at WSU, and it suggested that the program was on the edge of a great breakthrough.[35]

McQuaid and his teammates—Randy Hoff, Pete Ramels, Steve Vassey, Joe Eastwood, Randy Kurosky, Scott Nowak, Simon Nash, and coxswain Scott Fisher—were themselves tall, strong, and athletic, but they were also

The 1983 frosh boat coached by John "Yumbo" Holtman placed second at Pac-10s behind UW. Left to right: Simon J.C. Nash, Mike McQuaid, Scott Nowak, Randy Kurosky, Coxswain Scott Fisher, Joe Eastwood, Steve Vassey, Pete Ramels, and Randy Hoff. Photo courtesy of Mike McQuaid.

benefiting from an emergent history, tradition, and culture of rowing at WSU. By the early 1980s, with the crew now over ten years old, McQuaid's class was one of the first arriving into a program where, despite continued financial hardships, everything seemed within reach.

Even if Struckmeyer himself worried about the club's fragility, the traditions he had imported from Wisconsin and Bob Orr had brought from UW seemed firmly established. Especially to 18-year-old recruits like McQuaid, it appeared that the program had existed for decades. There were stories of past and recent glories, even national championships, that set the bar high but also conveyed a sense of possibility, that these kinds of successes were attainable for all WSU rowers. Paul Enquist was not only "out there" somewhere, rowing on the edge of an Olympic gold medal, but he was also occasionally showing up at Boyer Park, racing his Flymo single against McQuaid and his teammates. The famed Meatwagon national championship crew was not only mythic lore, but Rich "Flip" Ray and John "Yumbo" Holtman were both living in Pullman and rowing their pair to another IRA championship in the summer of 1981. After that, Flip stayed on to coach the WSU women and Yumbo took up the WSU freshman from 1981 to 1983 before relocating to Corvallis and coaching the novice crew at OSU under former Cougar rower and now OSU head coach Dave Emigh.

As WSU's freshman coach, Holtman instilled in his rowers a sense of discipline as well as a "no excuses" attitude that demanded they take responsibility to train themselves hard and master their technique. He didn't care if they were a club. His own experience showed them that any hardworking WSU rower could, like him, win a national championship—even two national championships. Holtman was a workout maniac who had befriended the strength and conditioning coach for the WSU track team, Tony Tenici, and convinced him to run training sessions for the crew. Tenici was one of a kind—a charismatic personality whose off-color running commentary would have made him a YouTube viral sensation forty years later. His demanding, take-no prisoners workout routines helped elevate the WSU crew's physicality.

Holtman was also committed to getting his crew as much water time as possible. His philosophy was that the freshman would be first on but last off the water. He also imbued his crew with a sense of rowing's historical and cultural cachet, encouraging them to do what he had done: go to Philadelphia and row for the summer on the historic Schuylkill River. His approach opened up for them possibilities beyond Pullman and also within themselves.

McQuaid thrived in this environment of heightened expectations. He was growing as a rower—just as the WSU crew recruiting poster had promised—and he was eager to push his boundaries even further and witness for himself what rowing looked like at the national level. After their wildly successful freshman season, McQuaid and three of his teammates—Randy Hoff, Pete Ramels, and Joe Eastwood—spent the summer in Philadelphia rowing for the storied Vesper Boat Club, the rowing home of Jack Kelly Sr. (who won the gold medal in sculling at the 1920 Olympics and was also Grace Kelly's father). To McQuaid, Vesper was like rowing in a museum, and he eagerly assimilated the traditions and values of rowing. He also achieved immediate success on the water beyond his wildest imagination. He earned a seat in a Vesper eight that won a national championship that year, and he also stroked a pair that finished sixth at nationals. He arrived back in Pullman in the fall of 1983 as a sophomore who was already a national champion rower, eager to build on his successes and take WSU rowing to an even higher level.

What Mike McQuaid had learned his freshman year was that everything was possible for WSU crew; and yet, when they returned to Pullman, Hoff, Ramels, and Eastwood drew very different conclusions. After seeing the larger world of rowing on Philadelphia's Boathouse Row, the three sophomores felt as if they were somehow lowering themselves by returning to WSU's modest program. Holtman's wager had not paid off for the three of them: instead of desiring to lift Cougar Crew up to their level of aspiration, as McQuaid intended to do, the "Vesper Three" wrote off rowing at WSU, convinced it was a program destined for failure.

It was a bitter parting that created tension within the varsity heavyweight crew. Hoff and Ramels had been the stroke pair on the successful freshman boat, and the tall, powerful Eastwood had rowed in the engine room at five seat. All three were slated to row on the varsity eight that year, joining their freshman teammates Vassey, Nowak, and Nash with the powerful Paul Hensel, a novice the previous year who had nonetheless rowed on the varsity eight, in hope of producing one of the fastest WSU varsity boats ever. Instead, the departure of the Vesper Three created a vacuum that had to be filled with novice oarsmen. It also contributed to a sense of unease among the heavyweights, as some wondered if the critiques of the Vesper Three were valid.

Was WSU crew an exercise in futility? Was there some magic formula that existed in Philadelphia, Boston, or Seattle that could not be replicated in the Palouse? For his part, McQuaid was incredibly disappointed. He was the only Vesperite who continued on with the program. He kept rowing every summer at Vesper, but he was committed to using his experience to improve the club at WSU, bringing his technical knowledge and his floppy white boating hats back to Pullman every fall. He felt duty bound to stick it out, believing he had made a "commitment to a four-year experience" of rowing at WSU.[36]

The next three years were frustrating ones for McQuaid, as his ambitions for WSU crew were never fully realized. After a magical freshman season, the rest of his rowing experience at WSU was not what he had imagined for himself and his teammates, which was to compete with UW's first boat and become a legitimate contender on the West Coast. By any objective measure, however, the mid-1980s yielded very fast heavyweight crews at WSU—boats that dominated regional competition, set course records, defeated varsity program boats from OSU and many California schools.

Despite losing the Vesper Three, the heavyweight crews of the mid-1980s still had McQuaid, Scott Nowak, and Steve Vassey from that fast 1983 freshman boat to go along with several other talented rowers, such as Paul Hensel, Doug Wordell, Dave Curran, Randy Bell, Ernie Iseminger, and later, Erron Williams and Bob Barton. They might not have been dominant, but they had their moments, such as their impressive victories over OSU in the Tri-Cities in both 1985 and 1986.[37] But those victories did not erase the overwhelming sense that they were underachieving. "It was kind of a disappointing season for the varsity," McQuaid said of his 1986 boat. "We were the fastest varsity boat that Washington State has had. We were always fast during practice, but when we got in some of the bigger races, we couldn't put it together."[38]

Whether it was objectively true or not, the heavyweights in the 1980s believed they were failing, and their mindset often caused turmoil amongst themselves and with their coach, who they believed should be doing more to ensure their success. Some of them felt Struckmeyer should be intervening more technically. Some believed he should be a more "hands-on" coach, barking at them from the launch and offering motivational speeches, like a rowing Vince Lombardi. It made sense. Many of the heavyweights were former football and basketball players who were accustomed to their coaches intervening more intrusively to shape the culture of their teams, but Struckmeyer was not cut from that cloth.

Struckmeyer was more like Harry Parker than his heavyweights would care to admit—he designed hard workouts, and he quietly expected his rowers to work out the rest themselves, including interpersonal matters. He was not known as a technical coach, but he had a good eye.[39] In practices, Struckmeyer told his rowers when they were hanging at the catch or shooting their butt, or rushing up the slide. With his droll Wisconsin accent, he would say, "Two, slow your slide." Next stroke. "Two, slow your slide." Nothing happens. "Two, can you do *something* different so that I know you're hearing me?"[40] But otherwise, he gave his oarsmen the flexibility to reach their own level. If they wanted to run up the Snake River grade as a team after practice, Struckmeyer beamed, but he never required such extra effort. If rowers needed to miss practice because of labs or tests, that was also fine. It was a club, after all, and Struckmeyer realized he needed to leave the level of dedication and effort up to the rowers themselves or risk driving rowers from the club. He also understood that sometimes effective coaching required staying out of the way.

Occasionally, Struckmeyer used passive-aggressive humor to poke his heavyweights—when, for example, he gave the entire varsity boat baby pacifiers in the spring of 1984 and told them to "suck it up." He occasionally publicized his frustrations, as in fall 1985, when he told the *Daily Evergreen* that his heavyweights had talent, experience, and ability, but that their lack of self-confidence was "a real problem." Struckmeyer compared them unfavorably to his lightweights, who were "confident and ready to go," while the heavies were "almost afraid to have that real confidence that the lights have." Struckmeyer admitted that he had no answers. "You can try joking with them, and you can try bitching at them or blasting them," he said of his heavyweight crews. "Or you can just remain quiet and hope they work it out for themselves."[41] Struckmeyer took the latter course—he largely remained quiet and waited for them to work it out themselves, but the process was often painful for the heavyweights during those years, especially in contrast to the successes of the WSU lightweight boats, which only seemed to magnify their frustrations and their critique of Struckmeyer's methods.

There is perhaps no other sport where the coach holds so much mystique as in rowing. In part, this is because everyone in the boat is doing the same thing and the coach does not share credit or blame with standout athletes who are scoring forty points or dropping touchdown passes. David Halberstam concluded that "in rowing, where everything was so subtle, where it was so difficult to calibrate the differences among oarsmen, all of whom looked powerful, the coach's views were even more crucial." Halberstam was trying to understand the mysterious power and authority of Harvard head coach Harry Parker, who "was as much myth as man."[42]

Parker was mythic because his Harvard crews dominated collegiate rowing for twenty years—and they did so *not* because Parker was a technical genius but because he was an innovator. He was the first U.S. coach to start importing European shells and oars, the first to put his crews on ergometers, the first to practice "seat racing," and the first to transform the sport of rowing from a seasonal hobby to a year-round training regime that included lifting weights and running stadiums. All of these innovations, plus the fact that Parker worked with exceptionally motivated young rowers who hailed from the nation's top prep rowing programs, led to two decades of Harvard domination.[43] As for imparting special technical skills to his rowers, Parker was more concerned that they rowed together, pushed their limits, and believed in themselves—which was easy since they were usually winning.

Even if the boat speed of Harvard, UW, or Wisconsin was not solely the result of any specific rowing technique, the nature of rowing—with its many esoteric technical facets—always created the creeping suspicion that fast crews harbored special technical knowledge. Losing crews often wondered if there was some particular mechanical adjustment that would push them to the next level. Was it slower hands out of bow or faster hands out of bow? A more powerful catch or a more finessed catch? Reaching out farther or shortening their reach? Leaning farther back at the release, or less? John Holtman, when he left WSU and began observing other coaches and their technical styles, realized that rowing, more than most sports, was given to fads. Losing crews immediately began copying the technical style of each year's winning crews.[44]

This copycat thinking was common at WSU from the beginning. The first crews under Bob Orr changed their style nearly every week based on what they saw from the crew that beat them. Later WSU crews also believed they were lacking some important technical element that was keeping them from going fast. In the mid-1970s, Enquist sometimes questioned whether he and his teammates were as technically proficient as their opponents, but when he graduated from WSU, he immediately realized he could row with oarsmen from UW and the Ivy League schools.

Those rowers, he learned, fundamentally did the same thing as WSU rowers. Somehow Enquist and hundreds of other WSU oarsmen *had* learned how to row in Pullman, despite the nagging fear that their rowing education was limited. Although they thought they were inferior, WSU oarsmen who continued to row after college—and there were many of them—often experienced the same thing: upon being dropped into a boat with former UW or Cal Berkeley or Yale rowers, they realized they were no different. The *only* difference was that these other rowers were confident and used to winning because they had come out of large programs that fielded at least three competitive varsity boats, whereas WSU was usually scraping to pull together eight dedicated heavyweight oarsmen.

It was always a numbers game, determined more by the strength of the lineup than by specific technical differences. As if to underscore how important it was to have dedicated athletes at each seat, Paul Enquist remembered rowing at the U.S. National Team sweep camp in 1979. He had made the cut down to thirty-two oarsmen, and he was feeling confident when Harry Parker seat-raced him against an oarsman who had made the national team the previous summer. In a five-minute piece, Enquist lost by two lengths of open water. His first thought was, "Well, I guess I'm about to get cut." His second thought, was, "Wow, look how much difference one oarsman can make in just five minutes of racing!"[45] The lesson was telling if you applied it to Cougar Crew. For WSU heavyweights, just one weak link could make the difference between competing with UW and losing by three boat lengths of open water in a 2,000-meter race.

When John Holtman rowed in a national team camp under Randy Jablonic, Wisconsin's head coach, he realized that Jablonic's style and approach was "exactly the same as Ken Struckmeyer's." And yet, Jablonic's crews at Wisconsin were competitive on a national level every single year while Struckmeyer's heavyweights struggled. It was the math more than the coaching that made the difference. The equation was clear: twenty-four rowers at 6' 5" and 200 pounds equals championships. Holtman was surprised at first because he figured that coaches at the national level would be "so profound." He was ready to learn from Jablonic the mysterious secrets that Struckmeyer had been hiding from him or did not know. What Holtman concluded instead was that coaching alone did not prevent you from achieving your goals, nor did it ensure that you would succeed—those questions could only be answered by the rowers themselves.[46]

Certainly, the 1979 national championship Meatwagon crew that Holtman was part of must have concluded they had not been held back by rowing at WSU under Struckmeyer, but that was not how the WSU heavyweights of the mid-1980s interpreted things. They felt they needed something more from Struckmeyer. He was "too nice" to be a good coach; he wasn't a "good technical coach"; he lacked the skills to effectively deal with interpersonal conflict within the varsity boat.

Eric Weseman was a coxswain for both the lightweights and heavyweights during those years. On the Pac-10 championship lightweight boat in 1985, he saw how brilliantly Struckmeyer's methods worked with them. For example, after that lightweight boat lost to UW in Pullman, Struckmeyer let his oarsmen figure out what was wrong and fix it. The results spoke for themselves—they beat UW on their way to a championship. Weseman saw Struckmeyer's approach as a deliberate methodology—not merely a lack of attention—and it clearly worked for the lightweights. But the following spring, in 1986, Weseman was coxing the heavyweight boat when they lost their dual to UW on the Montlake Cut after leading at the 1,000-meter mark. They had fallen apart in the race; afterwards, Weseman couldn't help but wonder if the heavies needed a more forcible coaching intervention to pull them back together and get them on the right track.

Whether they needed a motivational speech or some cutting-edge technical assistance to help them generate boat speed and confidence, Weseman didn't know, but he suspected that the heavies required something more.[47] Harry Parker could afford to take a hands-off approach at Harvard because he was working with elite young rowers who arrived in Cambridge with years of technical training behind them. On the Palouse, Struckmeyer was working with raw materials that needed refining, but his coaching style was more like a cool breeze than a Bessemer furnace.

Struckmeyer, unlike Bob Ernst when he coached at UC Irvine, could not take his rowers out in pairs or singles to refine their technique. Nor was he going to rip into them, tell them to straighten up their act, or give them an emotional speech that would spur them to great heights—even if they needed it. It was just not Struckmeyer's style. His only regret, as he looked back on it, was that he truly believed that his heavyweights could compete with UW, and this belief had perhaps created unreasonable expectations among his oarsmen. Despite the structural inequalities between the two programs—ones that only widened in the 1980s with carbon boats, increased scholarships for rowing, and the influx of foreign recruits—Struckmeyer and his rowers were unwilling to accept second-class status, and this contributed to even greater frustrations among his crews, who could not always see the big picture.[48]

For all the whispers of training regimens or technical secrets that other crews had and WSU lacked, as Dave Emigh liked to say, it was "all about the numbers" for heavyweights at WSU.[49] UW could cast its net and drag in four boats' worth of 6' 3" to 6' 7" oarsmen every single year, guaranteeing that its top two boats were filled with ultracompetitive, fit, and athletically gifted rowers. When WSU's club cast out its net, it pulled in three boats full of hungry and determined 5' 10" rowers, making the lightweight program competitive. But when you shook the net, you were lucky if you caught six dedicated rowers who were above 6' 2". As much as they hated to admit it—because to admit it would be an admission of futility—WSU heavyweights were continuously rowing up against the edge of a structural barrier that had nothing to do with their talent, determination, fitness, or technique. Unfortunately, many of them interpreted their inability to reach their lofty goals as their own failure, internalizing their inferiority—or conversely, as the failure of Struckmeyer for not giving them whatever magic formula Bob Ernst or Randy Jablonic or Harry Parker were apparently giving their oarsmen.

Aurora Borealis

If the coaching, or lack of coaching, was holding the heavyweights back, Struckmeyer's light-handed approach succeeded brilliantly with his light-weights in the 1980s. It was true that the lights did not face the same structural barriers as the heavies. In the mid to late 1980s, WSU crew could always recruit enough lightweight-sized rowers to ensure necessary competition for the top boat. "I have 16 to 20 people trying for the boat," said Struckmeyer of his lightweights in 1987. "When you have the competition, you have the ability to put people in there who are working well."[50] Those lightweights could also throw their full effort into conditioning their bodies and improving their technique, knowing that they would be competing on a level playing field. Whether it was UW or Yale, every boat averaged 155 pounds with a maximum weight of 160. This is why small programs can challenge the dominant schools when it comes to lightweights—the numerical advantage those large programs have with heavyweights disappears in the lightweight classification. However, there are still fast lightweight boats and slow ones. If the technical deficiencies and lack of coaching that allegedly plagued the heavyweights was negatively impacting the lightweights, it did not show in the 1980s. They somehow learned to row well and win under Struckmeyer's calm, equable oversight.

Mike Noble, one of the pillars of the varsity lightweight boat from 1977 to 1981, appreciated Struckmeyer's "easygoing" approach, giving his rowers the basics but not micromanaging them. Struckmeyer left a lot of discretion for oarsmen to determine for themselves the extent of their own commitment as well as their own success. Noble was the only lightweight on the freshman boat in spring 1978, but his studies were suffering. He went to Struckmeyer and told his coach he would be quitting the team. Struckmeyer calmly told Noble, "Take whatever time you need to catch up, and then you can come back whenever you want." Noble thanked Struckmeyer, and as he walked away, he truly believed that he was done with Cougar Crew. He immediately threw himself into his studies and, remarkably, two days later was all caught up: he had written papers and completed all his homework. He never realized how much time he had when he wasn't rowing. But it was too much time. He went back to practice on the third day, and he stayed with it for four years.[51]

If Struckmeyer was somewhat laid back, Noble also thought he was very observant and incredibly perceptive in choosing his lineups. He knew his rowers' strengths and weaknesses and shuffled them accordingly into the boat. In Noble's junior year, for example, Struckmeyer replaced him at stroke with

Keith Kesselring since Kesselring was calmer than the excitable Noble. The opposite occurred the following year, in 1981, when Struckmeyer put Noble back in the stroke seat, replacing John Neal, a former UW and high school prep rower, and the boat took off that spring, notching impressive second-place performances at the San Diego Crew Classic and the Pac-10 Championships in Redwood Shores, where the lights, like the heavyweights of 1977 and 1979, defeated UCLA in the first round of the dual race format.[52]

The lightweights of the early 1980s did not have to look far for inspiration. Like all WSU rowers, they were inspired by the Meatwagon's IRA victory to believe that, if they worked hard, they also could achieve great things. The 1980 lightweight crew that included Noble, Tim Richards, Tom Anderson, Tom Caudill, Andy Kirk, Tim Malkow, John DeLong, Keith Kesselring, and coxswain Lisa Coble, reaped the rewards of their hard work: they defeated UW's second boat in Pullman and also won the Midwestern Sprints in Madison, pulling away from the field with 250 meters to go as Tom Caudill, rowing in the bow, screamed with surprise, "We're going to win!"

In 1981, they worked even harder, and the results were even better on the water. Tony Tenici was by then conducting strength and conditioning workouts for the crew, and he helped Noble and his teammates get stronger without gaining unnecessary muscle mass. Tenici also introduced them to a nutritional program that helped fuel their workouts while keeping their weight down. Noble had never heard anyone talk about nutrition before. It was just one of many revelations during a season where they defeated the Cal Berkeley lightweights in Pullman and where three of them—Noble, Andy Kirk, and Tim Malkow—rowed in the IRAs and then competed for a spot on the lightweight national team boat.[53]

From 1982 to 1984, the lightweights had tough years. Struckmeyer's coaching was the same, but the number of rowers and the level of competition for the first lightweight boat slumped—and the results showed it. Then something happened in the mid-1980s. After dismal performances in the Pac-10 Championships for three straight seasons, the lightweights of 1985 and 1986, according to coxswain Eric Weseman, somehow trapped lightning in a bottle. In the midst of record turnouts, a group of dedicated lightweight oarsmen converged to form boats that would, for the first and only time in WSU rowing history, beat UW's top lightweight varsity boat not just once but *four* times in two seasons and then go on to win consecutive Pac-10 championships in 1985 and 1986.

The core pieces of those successful lightweight boats coalesced during the down years between 1982 and 1984. There was Jim Gressard from Santa

Ana, a tanned Southern California kid whom Struckmeyer, in his obsession for nicknaming, immediately dubbed "Valley Jim," or "VJ." There was Don Ernsdorff, whose sister Sue also rowed at WSU. Ernsdorff was arguably the most formidable lightweight to ever row at WSU. He was a lean, powerful 6' 2" with an impressive aerobic capacity and a clean stroke. His erg scores— under 6:20 for 2,000 meters—were not only the best on the lightweight boat but among the best on the entire squad. There was John Sanders, thick and powerful, built like a wall of solid muscle, who could take as much punishment as anyone. There was Bob Nehring, a former state champion wrestler who liked to pin his teammates to the mats in the old boxing room during winter workouts and make them beg for mercy, and who was also a perennial champion at the WSU "smokers"—rowdy amateur boxing matches that have now gone the way of politically incorrect wet T-shirt contests. Nehring was as tough as they come, a gut puncher in the ring and in the boat, who wore old-school baggy gray sweat suits even as his teammates were transitioning to Lycra tights. Then there was Jess O'Dell, a salt-of-the earth farm boy from Omak, a former cross-country runner who was as gritty and competitive as anyone, despite the fact that he was certainly the nicest of all the lightweights as well as their moral compass. The five of them rowed together on a boat in 1984 that finished tenth on the West Coast, beating only USC and WWU at the Pacific Coast Rowing Championships, which was in a way a success for them since they had lost to WWU during the regular season.

Those five were joined by four sophomores in spring 1985 to form WSU's first Pac-10 championship eight: Dave Reeder, Thad O'Dell, Aaron Sharp, and Eric Weseman. Reeder, at 6' 2", was the only other lightweight on the 1985 boat besides Ernsdorff who was six feet tall. He was also the only novice on the boat and the only varsity lightweight who hadn't played sports in high school, unless you count marching band. He was cerebral and quirky but preternaturally calm and ready to explore his untapped athletic potential. Reeder epitomized the benefits and possibilities of the club ethos—he never would have rowed had crew at WSU been a varsity sport—but in turning out for the club, he found something in himself he had never imagined. Also joining the boat that year was Thad O'Dell, Jess O'Dell's younger brother, who had just as much heart and grit as his older brother but even more hair. He was the boat's Paul McCartney, the cute heartthrob with a dimpled smile. Aaron Sharp was a former competitive swimmer and self-acknowledged goofball; though consistently underestimated by his teammates, he was perhaps the grittiest of them all. And finally, there was coxswain Eric Weseman, who lacked neither a booming voice nor self-confidence.

The take-off moment for this crew was the Husky dual at Wawawai in April 1985—the first time UW had visited the new shell house and the first time the Cougar lightweights raced their new carbon fiber racing shell, the *Cougar Lights*. "We're preparing for this as any other regatta," Eric Weseman told the *Daily Evergreen*. "There's no cause for getting butterflies in your stomach in practice two days before the race. We're confident in our racing strategies." And yet, Weseman acknowledged that this was no ordinary regatta. The UW lightweights of 1985 hadn't lost a race in two years. "They're so strong nationally, they can't help but have one of the best lightweight crews in the country," Weseman acknowledged.[54]

The WSU lights figured they were fast—they had been practicing well, and they had obliterated UPS the previous weekend. But this was UW. Before the race, Ernsdorff called the team together and gave them an inspirational speech. Jess O'Dell remembered Ernsdorff's talk as one of those cliché locker room exhortations: "We can beat these guys! They're only human! They put their pants on one leg at a time!" It was a good speech, but O'Dell knew that none of them really believed it. This was UW, after all, and "the Huskies didn't lose back then." Yes, WSU had beaten second, third, and fourth boats from UW, but never a varsity UW eight. For all they knew, maybe the Huskies "*didn't* put their pants on one leg at a time."[55]

At the start of the race, one of the WSU lightweights "jumped his seat" and knocked it off the tracks. The chaos and panic that ensued led to UW gaining more than two boat lengths of open water on the Cougars. Now the chase was on. For the rest of the race, the WSU boat closed the gap steadily, gaining seats on every stroke. When the finish line came, they were still five seats behind the Huskies. They had lost to UW, as they always had, but this time it felt different. Every rower on that boat knew that they had just rowed the 2,000-meter course at least two boat-lengths faster than UW. After they put their shell away, Ernsdorff gave a post-race speech that was, as far as Jess O'Dell could tell, "the same speech almost word for word" that he had given beforehand, but with one big difference: this time, everyone believed what he was saying.[56] That loss to UW was a turning point. Unlike every other loss to the Huskies, this one did not reinforce WSU's inferiority. Just the opposite. Later that morning, the WSU lightweight eight broke up into fours and destroyed UW's fours, and then they went on to defeat UW every time they competed over the next three years.

At the Pac-10s in 1985, WSU drew UW in their heat and beat them handily—that prelim was the first defeat of a UW varsity eight at the hands of WSU. The next day, they beat UW again in the finals, along with Cal Berkeley, UCLA, and OSU, thereby becoming the top lightweight boat in the Pac-

10. Winning the Pac-10 championship in the mid-1980s was a meaningful accomplishment. All the big schools still had lightweight programs, and they still awarded medals to the Pac-10 champions, even though the larger competition at Lake Natoma—now officially called the Pacific Coast Rowing Championships—encompassed many universities that were not members of the Pac-10. This included UC Irvine, UC Santa Barbara, Long Beach State, and SDSU. As fate would have it, an emergent lightweight crew from SDSU, who also had the best performances in their entire history in 1985 and 1986, won the Pacific Coast championship that day, denying WSU the ability to claim West Coast superiority. And yet, it was more than the Cougar lightweights had expected, and the victory was heralded by Struckmeyer as a great achievement. "We've arrived," he said simply. "And it's kind of nice."[57]

At the beginning of that year, when they had gathered as a team to set their goals for the season, Jim Gressard was skeptical that they could win a Pac-10 championship. He had rowed on two losing crews in the previous years and thought their goals should be more realistic. Yet, no one was more crucial to that championship and the one that followed the next year than "Valley Jim" Gressard. A strong cross-country runner, Gressard was supposed to run at UC Davis, but he wanted to leave California and attend a university with a top veterinary program. WSU fit the bill. Later, he realized that he was following in the footsteps of another WSU lightweight, Tim Richards, who had rowed on the varsity lightweight boat a few years before him and also attended vet school at WSU before taking up practice in Hawaii. After Gressard graduated, Richards hired him to work at his veterinary clinic, and the two WSU lightweights, who had never rowed together, became veterinary teammates for decades—one more example of Cougar Crew serendipity.

Gressard was 5' 10" on a good day, but he had an impressively long stroke for his size, and curiously, in one of those intuitive decisions that didn't make sense on the surface, Struckmeyer placed Gressard in the seven seat, matching him up with strokes who were far taller—Ernsdorff in 1985 and Dave Reeder in 1986. Somehow it worked, to the tune of two championships and the winningest boats in WSU's history. Not only was Gressard an anchor in the stroke pair during those years, he was a team leader off the water as well, serving as both commodore and vice commodore in 1985 and 1986. He was particularly well-suited to the latter role, leading team workouts. No other rowers pushed themselves harder than Gressard. He had been mentored by Tim Gattenby, a tanned, ripped, workout maniac of the first order who was on the 1983–84 lightweight boats. Gattenby and Gressard started running the Snake River grade after practice when the team was still at Boyer Park—they would set off after the boats were stowed and see how far they could make it before they were picked up. In 1985, the team moved to Wawawai, but Gressard kept running the grade. Soon he was joined by nearly all his lightweight teammates, including Nehring who, refusing to lose to his faster teammates, grunted and sprinted erratically throughout his runs like a horse with a bee in his ear.

Those grade runs created the camaraderie that formed the basis of winning lightweight crews in 1985 and 1986. They trusted each other, and they liked each other. They were also extremely competitive with one another—especially the heavyweights—turning every activity into a competition, whether it was throwing rocks in the river before practice or rolling boulders down the banks of the Snake River Canyon. Gressard could not remember them arguing on the water or off. They all worked hard, played hard, and supported each other— there was no "I" in this crew. It was corny, but Gressard could not explain the success of those boats without resorting to clichés about trust, teamwork, commitment, common goals, selflessness, and taking personal responsibility. Those lightweight boats had what sports analysts often call "chemistry."[58]

The 1986 boat was even faster, returning six oarsmen from the previous year's championship crew. They were more confident, knew from the beginning that they could beat UW and win Pac-10s again. They also knew they could be the fastest lightweight crew on the West Coast if they performed their best. In what Mike McQuaid, the crew spokesman that year, called "the best season [the lightweights] have ever had," the 1986 campaign began with dominant victories over Gonzaga, UPS, WWU, and OSU. Then came the dual race against UW on the Montlake Cut. UW and WSU traded leads down the course amidst the noise and pandemonium of the narrow channel. WSU's victory required a fierce sprint in the final 300 meters. "To the cheers of the hearty band of Cougar supporters," *The Pull Hard* reported, "the lights won by a scant three seats, which was the biggest lead of the race."[59] After the race was over, Gressard turned around from the seven seat and told his boatmates they needed to work out even harder because he never wanted to suffer that much to win a race again. "We're going to run up the grade every day!"

They had beat UW's first varsity lightweight eight on the Montlake Cut. It was a giddy row back to the UW shell house, where the proud crew hoisted their boat on their shoulders and walked past the quiet onlookers. This was the first and only time that a WSU crew defeated a UW varsity eight in Seattle. They posed standing beside the lake with UW jerseys tucked into their waistbands—it was a good day to be a Cougar lightweight.

At the Pacific Coast Rowing Championships in 1986, there were three heats of lightweight eights, and the winners were WSU, UW, and SDSU.

The 1986 lightweight 8 after defeating UW on the Montlake Cut. This boat would go on to win the Pac-10 championship, placing second on the West Coast behind SDSU. From left to right: Aaron Sharp, David Arnold, Thad O'Dell, Craig Maitlin, Bob Nehring, Jess O'Dell, Jim Gressard, Dave Reeder, and coxswain Scott MacClear. Photo courtesy of David Arnold.

For the finals the next day, the Cougars drew lane five, on the outside, while SDSU had lane two, near the shore. The Cougars lights that year were known for a fast start, and by 500 meters they had six seats on the field. By 1,000 meters they had a full boat length on SDSU. It was surreal. It seemed too easy. They were pulling away. And then, their concentration began to break. SDSU started its sprint along the shoreline. They began to take back seats, but they were too far away for WSU to see or feel. Coxswain Scott McAlear called for his crew to sprint but they could not seem to respond. It was as if they were rowing in a bad dream where they could not move and could only watch in horror as they witnessed their worst nightmare. For the second straight year, they had defeated UW, OSU, UCLA, and Cal Berkeley in the final and won the Pac-10 championship, only to lose to SDSU for the West Coast title.

They were shell-shocked. They had been leading by a full boat length. What had happened? Wind? Lack of concentration? Lane assignment? It was the same result as the previous year, but this time it brought disappointment instead of jubilation. The team that defeated them was good: the SDSU light-weights went to nationals that year and finished second to Princeton, ahead of Harvard and Yale. They had a good coach—Doug Perez—and three oarsmen who ended up rowing on lightweight national teams.[60] There was nothing shameful about losing to that San Diego State crew, but everyone on the WSU lightweight boat knew in their heart that they had not rowed their best race. They had a very mediocre final 500 meters. Their sprint did not snap to, as it had against UW. It was a sign of their high expectations that even while "winning" the Pac-10 championship, it felt like losing—which it was.

After the 1986 season, Mike McQuaid told the *Chinook*, "It looks like there is no end to lightweight rowing at Washington State."[61] He was partially right; 1986 was followed by more good years and continued high expectations by WSU lightweight crews—years that saw strong finishes at the San Diego Crew Classic and the Pacific Coast Championships, victories over Cal Berkeley at home, and domination of Northwest regional competition. But the lightweight varsity eight was never again as successful as it had been in 1985 and 1986. In fact, in the late 1980s, it was the lightweight junior varsity that won a Pacific Coast championship and carried on the strong tradition of lightweight rowing at WSU, underscoring how important sheer numbers were for the success of those lightweight crews in the 1980s.

By the end of the decade, the golden age of lightweight rowing had waned. UW dropped its lightweight program in 1987. Bob Ernst took over as head coach for Dick Erickson, and because of Title IX, he needed to reduce the number of male rowers at UW. Unsurprisingly, lightweights—the UW team that had lost to WSU—were first on the chopping block. There would be no more victories over UW for WSU lightweight boats. And in the mid-1990s, Cougar Crew deemphasized lightweight rowing in favor of building more competitive heavyweight crews.

The WSU lightweight crews of the mid-1980s—the "northern lights," if you will—showed that eight strong, competitive oarsmen who were committed to each other and willing to hold each other accountable could compete with anyone. They also revealed that the "club ethos" was not in conflict with winning—each crew had the ability to write their own story, based on their own goals and willingness to pursue them. Finally, they showed that, while he was no technical genius, Ken Struckmeyer was not holding anyone back.

Women's Rowing on the Edge

If the men's team was rowing on the edge of a great breakthrough while simultaneously skirting the edge of conflict and precarity, the same was true of the women's team in the 1980s, except for one major difference: the men had stability at the head coach level while the women's team had seven head coaching changes over the course of the decade. Otherwise, the storyline for the women during the 1980s was remarkably similar to that of the men. Their lightweights, when they fielded them, competed for West Coast supremacy, even winning gold in 1989. Their novices sometimes shone and exceeded all expectations. Their open weight varsity boats were undersized, overmatched, sometimes riven with internal conflicts, but always gritty and competitive. By the end of the decade, the women were also rowing on the edge of a great transition that would forever change Cougar Crew—in 1990 the women's club gave way to an athletic department program, and club rowing for women at WSU would not be revived again for two decades.

The history of women's club rowing at WSU in the 1980s can nearly be told through the story of one person: Tammy (Boggs) Crawford. As a rower, Tammy represented the heart and soul of the women's club from 1980 to 1984, stroking the novice boat her first year and then stroking the varsity eight for three straight years while also serving as commodore for three years. She returned to coach the WSU novice women in 1985–86, guiding them to a win over UW and to the finals at the Pac-10s, and then, after a stint coaching at the University of Washington, she returned to Pullman in 1990 to become head coach of the new varsity women's program.

Tammy Boggs arrived on campus in fall 1980 intending, like Paul Enquist and Doug Engle, to play basketball for WSU, but practices didn't start until October and she needed to stay in shape. Like so many others, she saw those beautiful cedar shells displayed on Rogers Field during registration week and decided to give rowing a try. She was already somewhat familiar with the sport because legendary UW coach Dick Erickson lived in the Marysville neighborhood where she grew up. She knew Erickson's kids, who were always wearing UW rowing gear, and she followed the exploits of the Huskies from afar, hearing of trips to Henley and national championships.

Her first trip down to Boyer Park was a revelation. Like many western Washington transplants to Pullman, Boggs had been searching for signs of trees and water in the Palouse. She didn't see many trees, but she felt euphoric leaving campus and driving her little Datsun pickup truck to the Snake River Canyon, where she found water, open spaces, boats, and kindred spirits. She was hooked immediately. There was something deeply satisfying about that daily trip to the river. She loved the water, the canyon, and the work. It quickly became the favorite part of her day, and she never missed a practice in four years. What began as a means of staying fit for basketball became an all-consuming passion for Boggs, one that defined her education, her career, and even her family life. She married Roger Crawford, a rower she met at WSU, and spent the balance of her professional life coaching rowing before pursuing a PhD in education, writing her dissertation on "Intercollegiate Athletic Participation and Undergraduate Student Engagement," and becoming a professor of sport management at WSU.[62]

For Boggs, the most important part of rowing was the camaraderie. She was devoted to her teammates, who became her closest friends. At stroke, she sat between her two best friends in the world: coxswain Kim Heggerness and seven seat Sara Bolson. Heggerness, Boggs, and Bolson formed the core of the women's varsity in the early 1980s. Rich Ray, Boggs's coach during her junior and senior years, called her and Bolson—the stroke pair for three years—"the heart and the core of the team."[63] Those crews, like all WSU women's varsity boats, were perennially undersized compared to their opponents, but they were always gritty, competitive, and self-motivated. As a rower, there was no one more competitive and driven than Tammy Boggs. Her teammates and coaches saw an athlete who was as demanding of herself as she was of her teammates. Intense and plainspoken, she let people know if they weren't pulling their weight.[64] Ray was deeply impressed with Boggs's work ethic and complete devotion to the crew—he had never coached an athlete who was so singularly focused. Her competitive instincts were off the charts.[65]

For her first two seasons, Boggs thrived under Gene Dowers, who by 1981–82 was coming into his own as a coach. He was attentive, organized, and innovative. He had finally realized that coaching, for him, was more than a lark or a hobby. He began college in the mid-1970s as an engineering student, then moved on to business administration. But by the early 1980s, he had settled on exercise physiology as a major, with a minor in coaching. He was now more than a graduate student just helping out but rather a coach in training, eager to experiment with new, cutting-edge training methods. He began incorporating his growing knowledge of exercise physiology into his team's workouts while also experimenting with the latest theories of sports psychology. While this did not lead to immediate victories for WSU, it did lead to increasingly competitive crews. Boggs's boats did not have profound success during those years, but they competed hard. As Dowers acknowledged, "a crew averaging 5' 6" and 135 pounds (us) is only going to get so close to crews going 6' 0" and 160 pounds (Huskies and [Cal Berkeley] Bears)."[66]

If Dowers offered Boggs a role model of an organized and innovative coach, her second coach, Rich Ray, brought the example of a former Cougar rower who had succeeded on a national stage, showing that it could be done in Pullman. Unlike Dowers, Ray was not destined to make coaching his career, but he was every bit an advocate of women's rowing. As a coach, he gave rowers a certain amount of volition—he was not interested in micromanaging

The 1983 women's varsity eight, stroked by Tammy (Boggs) Crawford, rowing at Redwood Shores. From stern to bow: Coxswain Kim Heggerness, Tammy Boggs, Sara Bolson, Susan Howe, Susan Van Leuven, Natalie Delbrecht, Cindy Van de Ven, Lisa Stivers, Brenda Fredrick. Photo courtesy of Tammy Crawford.

his crew. Boggs's competitiveness and Ray's willingness to allow his rowers to make their own decisions led to one of the more tense—and ironic—circumstances in Ray's coaching career.

In 1984, Boggs wanted to scrap the varsity eight at Pac-10s to field a more competitive open four. Like so many other determined Cougars before her, Boggs desired to compete at the highest level. It was clear to her that the eight could not make the finals, so she pushed for a four that would include herself, Bolson, Heggerness, and two undersized but strong rowers—Lisa Stivers and Brenda Frederick. Ray was conflicted. He absolutely understood Boggs's motivations as well as her frustrations—he had been there himself. In Cougar Crew, there was always friction between ambitious rowers who wanted everyone to come up to their level and the broader reality that it was a club sport where everyone could choose their own level of commitment. Club rowing could be frustrating for rowers like Paul Enquist and Tammy Boggs.

On the men's side, Struckmeyer had determinedly opposed breaking up the varsity eight, even if it meant fielding a four that could have more success.

In the case of the Meatwagon, he had allowed them to train but insisted they do so outside the framework of regular team practices. Now Boggs was asking Ray for permission to do what Struckmeyer had always resisted—break up the eight in order to field a more competitive four. In the end, Ray left the decision up to his athletes, and Boggs, by this time a senior who had been commodore for three years, got her wish. At Pac-10s, their open four was the only WSU boat to advance through the heats and qualify for the grand final at Lake Natoma. They didn't medal, but according to Frederick, they rowed their hearts out, were happy with their race, and finished the season with "no regrets."[67] It was the last race Tammy Boggs rowed as a Cougar.

After graduation in spring 1984, Boggs left Pullman for student teaching. She returned the following fall, in 1985, to serve as a novice coach for Gene Dowers, who was head women's coach again. In the short time that Boggs was absent from Pullman, the reins of the women's team had been passed from Ray to Bob Appleyard and now back to Dowers. This was the plight of the Cougar women during those years: one coach followed another in rapid succession—a new style and a new technique introduced each time—only to be replaced the following year by another style and a different technique. In keeping with this mode, Tammy and Gene would only coach together one year, to be replaced the next season by Piotr Rylski, who coached for only one year before he was replaced by Thad O'Dell, who was replaced the following year by Jess O'Dell, and two years after that by Tammy.

Tammy's crew in 1985–86 was undersized, scrappy, and overachieving. The stroke of that crew, Stacy Jenkins, was the only rower on the boat who stood six feet tall. Behind her, Tracy Vadset and Pam Ware were 5' 10". After that, the height dropped off dramatically, but not the competitiveness or the grit. Jodi Rutter was only 5' 5", but she rowed like she was 5' 10". Stacey Gosney was 5' 4"; three years later, she would win a West Coast championship as a lightweight rower. Brenda Riche, Shari Schneider, and Mo Flurry were even shorter, but they were all gifted athletes and supremely competitive. Riche was a distance runner who had been recruited to run at WSU, and Schneider and Flurry were both competitive swimmers.

By the mid-1980s, Title IX had trickled down to girls' sports at the K–12 level. These 1985 novices were very different from their female predecessors of the mid-1970s. With one exception, they arrived in Pullman already identifying as athletes, having cut their teeth in competitive sports programs that looked nothing like the earlier GAA (Girls Athletic Association) teams, where girls were taught to cooperate and play nice.

On Cougar Crew, Tracy Vadset was an emblematic model of the new, competitive female athlete in the post-Title IX landscape. At Shorecrest High School, she competed in swimming, basketball, and track. Voted "most athletic" in her class, Vadset went to Maui after graduation. There she took community college courses and raced outrigger canoes, swam, and ran triathlons. When she arrived in Pullman, she was determined to make the swim team, and she was good enough. Her father had been an NCAA All-American point guard for WSU's basketball team during the Marv Harshman era—in fact, he was a three-sport athlete who also played on the WSU baseball and golf teams— and Vadset was ready to carry on the family tradition. Instead, she ended up on the rowing team because, like so many others, someone handed her a flyer during registration week that changed her entire direction. She'd had no idea there was a body of water near Pullman. A self-described "water woman," Vadset had spent more time in the ocean than on dry land when she lived in Maui; and now, in landlocked Pullman, she had been headed toward the swimming pool, the only local body of water she knew of. She was thrilled to learn that she could row a boat every day on the Snake River and threw herself wholeheartedly into the program.[68]

Amidst the prep athletes on the novice boat that year, there was one exception. Remarkably, their stroke, Stacy Jenkins, had never played any sports in her life. As a high school student, her focus had been entirely academic: she was salutatorian, had the second-highest SAT scores in her entire class, and played the violin. She planned to apply to Harvard but never completed the application. The lead Shorecrest counselor approached her in April to ask which school she had chosen and was shocked to learn Stacy hadn't even applied. "If you're willing to go to WSU," he told her, "we can arrange a full-ride academic scholarship." That was all it took. She headed off to Pullman and began to work toward a degree in architecture. In the fall of her sophomore year, however, she was gaining weight and knew she needed to change her lifestyle. At the urging of one of her McCroskey Hall roommates, she turned out for crew in fall 1985 simply to get some exercise. Surprisingly, she found herself in the stroke seat of a very fast novice boat that season and sat in the engine room of a high-achieving varsity eight the following year.

It was a classic WSU crew club story. Much like Dave Reeder, who also came to WSU never having played sports but found himself stroking the varsity lightweight eight, Jenkins tapped into a part of herself she never knew existed, and it changed her identity and her life forever. There were moments that year that struck her profoundly as she came into her own as an athlete. The first was running back to Pullman after practice with Tracy Vadset, who she considered athletically superior to herself. The vans had dropped them off six miles from Pullman, and as they ran, Jenkins could see her silhou-ette alongside Vadset's. She thought, "Oh my God, I'm an athlete!" It was a "life-changing revelation" that gave her more confidence in herself. The fol-lowing year, she was rowing on an ergometer next to Donna Kloster, who she considered a "rowing goddess," and pushed herself to keep up with Kloster's demanding pace. She did it, and it made her feel like she could do anything—a feeling that has stayed with her ever since.[69] The crew club, because it was a club, attracted athletes as well as students like Jenkins and Reeder, who had never before competed, and it changed them while also enriching the club.

Boggs's novice crew looked to the WSU lightweight men for a model of how to succeed. Like the men's lights, their crew had a special "magic alchemy." Their personalities jelled, and they committed themselves to work as hard as they could, running the grade, lifting weights, and doing whatever Boggs asked of them on the water. They believed that if they worked hard enough, they could achieve anything. They trusted each other, and they also trusted Boggs, who threw her heart and soul into coaching them.

Stacy Jenkins thought Boggs was everything you wanted a coach to be: "She was hard on us, she wanted to make us better, but we could tell she cared about us." As a coach, Boggs was enthusiastic, supportive, competitive, and single-minded. According to Pam Ware, she gave them her "total focus and total support." The results were good. That spring, they defeated UW on the Montlake Cut—a first for the WSU women's crew, equaled only by the men's lightweight victory that very same day. It's true that they had raced UW's second boat, but they demolished them by open water. It was something that just did not happen, and as her crew arrived back at the UW shell house after the race, Tammy was already fielding job offers from Jan Harville, the head women's coach at UW. Much like Erickson had done with Bob Ernst in 1974, UW's philosophy remained, "If you can't beat them, hire them." Indeed, Tammy Boggs headed off to UW the next fall as a novice intern coach with the Huskies.[70]

At the Pacific Coast Rowing Championships on Lake Natoma that spring, Boggs's novices duplicated the feat of Gene Dowers's groundbreaking novice crew of the previous season, making the finals and finishing fourth. In fact, 1986 was a banner year for the WSU women, with four boats making the finals at Lake Natoma. It was the first time the women's varsity open boat had ever made the finals. That crew contained some very strong second-year rowers—including Carlene Anders, Lori Haugen, Donna Kloster, Marion Jones, and Loresa Soviskov—whose novice boat the previous year was the first women's eight in WSU history to make the finals. In 1986, their varsity open boat had overcome turmoil and tensions that divided and nearly destroyed them, but they managed to pull themselves together and make the finals at Pac-10s. The junior varsity eight also made the finals and finished fifth, while the lightweight four took second. "Our performance was pretty outrageous if you consider the fact that we have never had more than one boat in the finals at any one time before," Dowers said.[71]

Building on two strong novice classes, Dowers believed that the women's 1986 performance was perhaps the beginning of something sustainable. "I think we are at the point now where we can expect to put all of our boats in the championship heats on an every-year basis," he predicted.[72] However, Dowers left WSU after that 1986 season. The next year, Boggs's novices joined returning rowers from the 1986 varsity squad—Kloster, Haugen, and Annie Calvin—to form an eight that would once again make the finals, finishing fifth on the West Coast. Their coach, Piotr Rylski, brought years of international experience to Pullman and refashioned their stroke to mimic the style of East German crews—the "Easties"—who dominated international competition in the 1970s and 1980s.[73]

Compared to Boggs, Rylski had "zero warmth," according to Stacy Jenkins, but they were in awe of his rowing achievements and embraced his new technique as well as his rigorous physical training regime. Rowing for Rylski was not as "emotionally satisfying" as rowing for Boggs, but he had a clear vision for them and was a quiet, calming presence in the launch.[74] Vadset loved Rylski's professional, uncompromising approach, which demanded much from his rowers. She wanted to push herself, train harder, and master the superior East German technique. But Rylski's approach was challenging for everyone, including those, like Vadset, who embraced it. "It has been a trying experience for the varsity boats to learn a totally new style and coach," Patty Culleeny, Rylski's assistant coach, told the *Daily Evergreen*. "We will row very fast this year," Rylski predicted. "The question is how fast we are going to row and how fast the other teams are going to row."[75] The answer was that they made the finals and finished fifth on the coast, their highest finish ever to that point, eight seconds behind fourth place Cal Berkeley, but still a distant thirty-five seconds behind UW.

Rylski's short, one-year tenure was a success in terms of the standings, but his unyielding workouts and demanding methods drove rowers away—by spring 1987, just eight varsity rowers remained on the women's team, and only three of them returned the following year.[76] Rylski had worked them hard, transformed their technique, and then moved on to another coaching position and left the WSU women's team depleted and without direction.

Struckmeyer took over the women in the fall of 1987 and then Thad O'Dell stepped in during the spring of 1988, assisted by his brother, Jess O'Dell, who coached the novices. With Rylski gone, rowers like Vadset felt that the team was moving backward—the technique she had worked so hard to master was now discarded for the more familiar WSU West Coast style that the O'Dell brothers had learned rowing for Struckmeyer. For the varsity, 1988 was a transition year, but Jess O'Dell's novice eight formed the backbone of another resurgence in 1989 and 1990.

Jess O'Dell took over as head women's coach in fall 1988 and remained there for two seasons. Although he had none of the international experience or technical expertise of Piotr Rylski, the women's club had the greatest successes of its entire history in his short, two-year tenure. In 1989, his lightweight varsity eight won the Pacific Coast Championships—the only WSU women's eight ever to do so. The 1981 women's lightweight eight had won Pac-10s under Gene Dowers, but there was a large asterisk: there were only two boats competing that year, so it was essentially a dual race between WSU and OSU. This time, however, there was a full field of women's lightweight eights, and WSU's boat took gold. The next year, in 1990, O'Dell's open varsity eight not only beat UW's second boat on the Montlake Cut—a first—but it also made the finals and placed fifth at the Pacific Coast Championships, equaling Piotr Rylski's 1987 varsity boat and rowing the course at Lake Natoma faster than any WSU women's crew had ever done. That year, O'Dell's crews also won every single race in the Tri-Cities for the first time ever, trouncing OSU and WWU on their way to a dominant overall team victory. "The highlight of the weekend was the women's crew team sweeping every race," the men's commodore, Kent McCleary, told the *Evergreen*.[77] O'Dell's rowers, like every other successful boat in WSU history, bought into his program, committed themselves fully, and trusted each other. O'Dell, for his part, allowed his rowers room to take responsibility for the results. They did, and they thrived.

The women's crew of 1989 and 1990 proved, once again, that winning on the Palouse didn't require esoteric technique imported from elsewhere. It took belief and commitment from at least eight devoted rowers. Gene Dowers got that from his 1985 novices; Tammy Boggs got that from her 1986 novices; Rylski got that from his 1987 varsity boat; and Jess O'Dell got that from his 1989 lightweights as well as his 1990 varsity boat. It didn't matter if you were rowing the East German style or the Hiram Conibear stroke, what mattered was that you had eight committed athletes who trusted each other and trusted their coach.

O'Dell's 1990 women's varsity boat was the third in a decade to make the finals at Pac-10s. All of those boats were undersized compared to their competition. They faced the same structural barriers that WSU's heavyweight men faced. Yet, competing against and sometimes beating varsity-funded crews gave them a feeling of pride, ownership, and achievement. Many of them—undersized fighters like Brenda Frederick, Jodi Rutter, Brenda Riche, Shari Schneider, Mo Flurry, and Stacy Gosney—might have been rejected from varsity programs for their size alone. Cougar Crew gave them an opportunity that they did not waste. That was about to change.

It was ironic that the women's club would cease to exist after experiencing its greatest successes. In 1990, the WSU women's club—its boats and rowers—were swallowed by a shiny new varsity program under the command of Tammy (Boggs) Crawford. The club would never be the same, and Ken Abbey's old concept of "one program, two teams" no longer held. After 1990, there were two programs at WSU, one club and one varsity, and the WSU women's club, after fifteen years of grit and perseverance, ended.

Istanbul (Not Constantinople)

It seems inconceivable to me now that my own rowing career at WSU ended in 1988 with a trip to Istanbul, Turkey, where we rowed across the Bosporus Strait from Asia to Europe and raced on the Golden Horn in front of thousands of spectators, with the ancient city as a backdrop. The logistics alone seem so daunting that I can't imagine myself, in a similar advisory role, even attempting such a complicated journey. Struckmeyer arranged for us to take a bus from the Pacific Coast Championships in Sacramento directly to the San Francisco Airport, fly to Chicago, board a Yugoslav Airlines flight to Belgrade, tour Belgrade on a long layover, and board another flight for Istanbul. Then he shepherded twenty-five guileless American college students on a week-long tour of one of the most byzantine cities in the world (no pun intended).

I still can't believe it happened—that Struckmeyer pulled it off; that *we* pulled it off. And yet, I am so glad it happened because I cannot imagine my life without that trip, just as I cannot imagine my life without having rowed crew at WSU. As I wrote in my journal then, the trip "helped me to close up some wounds I suffered in my last couple years of crew," but, more importantly, that trip marked out a direction that my life would take.

As someone who had never before left the North American continent, that week in Istanbul bought clarity to my life. I knew what I had to do upon returning home: I would work the salmon season in Bristol Bay, sell my car, buy a backpack and a pair of boots at REI, purchase a Eurail Pass and a roundtrip ticket to Europe, change the rest of my money into travelers' checks, and tramp across Europe until I reached Istanbul again. That three-month solitary journey, a month of which was spent in Turkey, solidified the transformation in myself that had begun with our trip to Istanbul in May 1988. It not only changed me into a brie-and-artisan-bread-eating liberal, but it set me on a path toward graduate school in history (a good career choice for brie-and-artisan-bread-eating liberals). In fact, my application to graduate school at UCLA contained an essay that referenced our Istanbul trip and my subsequent journey back to Turkey as a transformative moment in my young intellectual development. Who knows, maybe the essay nearly disqualified me as a candidate for graduate work, but I'd like to think that at least one sympathetic reader discerned the truth of my hackneyed story—travel opened my mind to possibilities that I had never imagined.

At WSU, I rowed on the successful lightweight boats of the mid-1980s. I was a member of the 1986 Pac-10 championship crew that had suffered the thrill of victory and the agony of defeat simultaneously. After that year, our performances never matched our abilities or our sky-high expectations for ourselves. In our minds, no matter that we still had tremendous successes, we were always underachieving. Beating WWU and OSU and placing fourth on the West Coast was no longer fun. Anything less than a West Coast championship would not suffice. The most frustrating thing was that we *knew* we could achieve our goals, but we lacked some intangible element that kept us from doing so—complete faith in each other and ourselves, perhaps? I can't even remember my last race in the finals at the Pacific Coast Championships. Did we place fourth or fifth? It didn't matter. I was tired and ready to be done. What kept me going was the knowledge that after we loaded the shell trailer, I would be heading for Istanbul, Turkey, for one final race as a Cougar.

The origins of that trip trace back to the arrival of Recep Akıcı in Pullman in fall 1985. Akıcı had rowed on and coached for the Turkish National Rowing Team and was, by 1985, also head rowing coach for Boğaziçi University in Istanbul. He came to Pullman to study and immediately became a regular in the launch beside Ken Struckmeyer. For that year, 1985–86, Akıcı was essentially an assistant coach whom we welcomed for his technical expertise. It was through him that WSU received an invitation to row in Istanbul that summer, in a regatta that would include Oxford, Cambridge, Boğaziçi, and WSU. The offer came with room and board for ten days and the use of an Empacher shell and oars. "You bet your sweet bippy we're going," said Struckmeyer. "We're gonna try very, very hard to get there."[78] It did not happen that year. Actually, it required two years of planning and fundraising, but the epic journey finally did occur in May 1988.

I cannot imagine the process by which Struckmeyer managed to choose Yugoslav Airlines for our trans-Atlantic flight, but I'm sure it involved several middlemen on the take who required, in return for our dirt-cheap fares, that we spend a day in Belgrade, where we would take a bus tour and eat a large meal in a fancy "authentic" tourist restaurant, complete with traditional Serbian folk music. I would not have had it any other way. As soon as we stepped on that plane in Chicago, we entered another world, with Catholic nuns on pilgrimage to Međugorje and stern stewardesses who seemed to take cruel pleasure in denying whiny Americans their necessary hydration as we waited for hours on the hot tarmac with no air-conditioning. We already felt as if we had entered the Eastern Bloc, where the values of American consumerism ("the customer is always right!") no longer ruled.

By the time we arrived in Istanbul, we were all dead tired but full of wonder at our surroundings. The Kennedy Lodge, where the men were housed, was a lovely old colonial guest residence with burnished wood floors and bathrooms that had foot pads and drop holes rather than toilets. The lodge was situated amidst the trees on the steep hillside overlooking the Bosporus Strait. When I gazed out the bathroom window, I saw a breathtaking view of the strait and the distant city beyond, with its modern suspension bridges and ancient minarets. Surrounded by unfamiliar smells and sounds, we were all Orientalists—Westerners whose cultural preconceptions framed our every experience. I wrote in my journal of "the teeming streets, the air full of spice and mud and mystical Eastern music." My journal reads like one long cliché—a young American in the exotic Middle East.

Everything was new to us, from the food in the university cafeteria and the candy bars sold in the small shops to the carts, taxis, and mopeds that crammed the streets. I had never eaten Middle Eastern cuisine—this was the 1980s, before every American town had a kebab stand and before extra virgin olive oil was a middle-class necessity, like sliced bread.

We had never rowed in Empachers before; we had never tied into foot stretchers with athletic shoes rather than crude leather straps fixed to wooden foot plates. We carried our foot stretchers and seats down the hill to our shells, which were stored in the little waterfront community of Bebek, where we launched amidst the wooden Turkish yachts bobbing along the seawall. We practiced on the Bosporus, the historic and strategically important strait that connects the Mediterranean Sea—via the Sea of Marmara—to the Black Sea. Large Soviet tankers plied the waterway, and each row seemed like a new universe of risk, adventure, and experience.

Between practices, there were trips to the famous tourist sites of Istanbul—

the Hagia Sophia, the Blue Mosque, the Grand Bazaar. There was a boat cruise up the Bosporus to the Black Sea. However, the most memorable experiences were the simple interactions we had with fishermen, shopkeepers, and our hosts, who treated us with kindness and forbearance. We had six young guides from Boğaziçi University: Zeynep Ulner, Esra Özsoy, Hakan Gürocak, Çan Ding, Okay Egdirici, and Defne Koror. They took us to their dorm rooms and homes. They showed us the city. They tried to teach us some of the language and cultural nuances, to little avail.

The rowing was the least important part of the entire trip. It was mostly exhibitionistic, especially for the women—they were told not to embarrass their Turkish female competitors, who clearly had not rowed for long. The men raced a 500-meter sprint, which was longer than 500 meters, and a 3,000-meter race, which was shorter than 3,000 meters, and we lost both of them to the boat from Boğaziçi University, which we later found out was stacked with ringers from the Turkish National Team. It was like playing a little league game against opponents who had beards. But it didn't matter, not when you

Turkish rowers don Washington State tanks after racing, and beating, WSU on the Golden Horn. Recep Akıcı is squatting front right. Photo Credit: Kent McCleary.

were rowing on the Golden Horn and exchanging jerseys with your Turkish competitors. After rowing, we were free to enter other events during the university sports festival in which we were participating (Spor Bayramı '88). I ran the 3,000-meter race on an irregular dirt track that required us to do something like twenty laps. I won the race, tracking down and passing some guy in track spikes who had probably been smoking a cigarette before the start. He had gone out at a sub-five-minute-per-mile pace, and by the time I passed him on the last lap, he was probably running ten-minute miles. But a win is a win, and I still have my certificate of victory, signed by the head rector, the general secretary, and the president of the sports board of Boğaziçi University.

When I returned to Istanbul in November 1988, I was a more seasoned traveler. By then, I had seen some impressive and beautiful cities—Rome, Paris, Madrid, Florence—but I didn't think any of them rivaled Istanbul. I checked into the youth hostel and called my friends at Boğaziçi. When I met Çan, Hakan, Okay, Esra, and Defne for lunch in Bebek, I told them they didn't need to act as my hosts again—I was self-sufficient and could find my way around. But Okay insisted that I stay in his dormitory room at Boğaziçi, and of course, they arranged to take me everywhere, including to Recep's office, where he invited me to work out with his team and proudly showed me the fall 1988 issue of *Pull Hard* with Jess O'Dell's piece on our "Anatolian Adventure."[79]

I wrote Jess a long letter from Istanbul, filled with purple prose about my trip back to Turkey and the adventures I was having. I felt a great sentimentality for Cougar Crew and for our trip to Istanbul in May, which had opened up new possibilities for me and made me realize that rowing at WSU had prepared me for the challenges and adventures of life. I told Jess that I wanted him to remember Istanbul "as vividly as I'm experiencing it now. Just try to remember that view from the bathroom of the Kennedy Lodge, or the smiles of Okay or Hakan or Esra or Çan or Defne or Zeynep. It's important to remember, and to possibly return because what we did here was something special. It will never be duplicated. It doesn't have to be. But there is something that remains—a friendship, an affinity with the place and the people that should survive."

Conclusion

The 1980s proved that a club sport could compete with varsity programs and sometimes even win. Lightening could be trapped in a bottle, but it was more likely to happen when the number of rowers was large enough to ensure competition for the first boat. Given their fluctuating membership and the revolving door of coaches, it's remarkable that the women's club was so successful during that decade. Even though they faced the same structural barriers, the varsity women achieved far greater successes than the heavyweight men, making the finals at the Pacific Coast Championships three times in the 1980s. The heavyweight men had good rowers and fast boats, but they always battled attrition as well as a lack of faith in themselves and also, perhaps, too great a willingness to look elsewhere for blame. Lightweights on both the men's and women's sides had an easier time competing and winning because the playing field was always level. It is ironic that the most successful boats on the club team during the 1980s, the lightweights, turned out to be the first casualties of the 1990s, as the women's varsity eliminated lightweight rowing altogether and the men's crew focused on the heavyweights.

The most important events of the 1980s happened off the water. The institution building of Ken Abbey and the CRA yielded new boats, more alumni support, a larger endowment, and a new shell house. These accomplishments created a more concrete, stable foundation for Cougar Crew that could not be blown away by the Big Bad Wolf of budget cuts, coaching changes, or club reorganizations. Without the strengthening of Cougar Crew as an institution in the 1980s, it might not have made it through the 1990s, a decade that would prove to be the most challenging in its history.

Brenda Frederick (1982–86)

One of my most memorable races was a varsity four at the Pac-10 Championships in 1984. Road-tripping down to California for the big competition was the most exciting event of the season. That year, I had the honor of rowing with coxswain Kim Heggerness, a dynamo of a gal with a booming voice; stroke Tammy Boggs, who later coached the women's team as it became a varsity sport and was much beloved by her charges; Sara Bolson, a lovely force, all in all; and Lisa Stivers, my bow partner, with whom I had weathered many grueling workouts and powered through all the thick and thin of what would be four years of rowing together. Our coach Flip had worked with us the past two years, bringing out our potential and pushing us to reach beyond our limitations. That year we were ecstatic to advance through two heats and qualify for the grand finals. We were the only WSU boat to advance that far for that particular year. We rowed our hearts out in the finals, and though we didn't medal, we were completely happy with our race. We had done our best, with no regrets. And that is what life is all about—throwing your heart into it and giving it your best shot.

Ole Jorgenson (1985–88)

Thirty years later, the WSU Crew racing memories have begun to fade, but I will always remember my first fall ergometer test as a novice. I asked to go first, eager and wanting to show everyone my moxie, and in retrospect, I was absolutely unprepared for what I was about to undertake. As I recall, the rule then was that the commodore went first, so I was slated second behind Jess O'Dell. Even after just a few months in Pullman, I knew enough about Jess to appreciate his stature on the crew; his athleticism, humility, and fierce competitive spirit were already legendary among the lightweights. So I stood outside the erg room door, stretching and deep breathing and, eyes closed, visualizing my successful, impressive first erg pull.

After an interminable wait, the door opened and I walked into the stuffy, stark erg room, which back then was just a storage closet the university allowed us to use. Whatever illusions I had about emerging from that closet with a victory over the ergometer evaporated with the vision before me: I held my breath while two varsity lightweights gently helped lift Jess off the erg as his lungs surged and he moaned, eyes closed, having spent himself so fully that he was unable to stand by himself. I just stared as his buddies each took an arm over their shoulders and half walked, half dragged him out of the room, his chin bobbing on his chest. Welcome to WSU Crew!

Friendships among members of the Classes of 1986–89 were of a sort I'd not experienced before, never having participated on a team, much less in an endurance sport—our bonds were built on trust and hope and forged in endless hours of shared voluntary suffering. We relied on one another because we held the same goals and fears and faced obstacles that could not be achieved or overcome individually. We laughed, we believed, and we worked our asses off together, and it was apparent pretty quickly that we were special among the throngs of students on campus, but we were the only ones who understood that.

The biggest impact of WSU Crew on my life was Coach Struckmeyer. He was so central to the whole crew experience—his humor, his patience, his silent watching from the launch. That otherworldly look he often seemed to have, out on the river, surrounded by the majesty of the canyon. Day in and day out, Struck was there for us, as each year a new combination of boats and rowers lived out their hopes and trust and suffering on the water. And laughter—Struck always made us laugh!

I often wonder how Struck did it all—finding support for a rowing team, building and sustaining a vision even though the program faced (and faces) tremendous odds, keeping us all motivated and engaged through years when we struggled to achieve results. And he did this, all the while navigating what must have been tremendous professional resistance from the university bureaucracy and pressures brought by the expectations of his day job that surely was compromised by his devotion to his volunteer coaching life.

As it turned out, in my own professional trajectory, I've come to struggle in a bureaucracy, to repeatedly strive to convince people to stay focused and believe in a shared goal despite persistently falling short, and to move an organization against great odds toward an unlikely positive outcome. So, in the decades since I left Pullman, I view Ken Struckmeyer's stewardship of the rowing program with far richer understanding of his legacy to WSU Crew and of his powerful influence on me as a leader.

I could not have known in 1988 that my future professional life would sometimes reflect the glimpses I saw of Struck's world. I know now that when confronted with similar challenges, I have tried to address them with the sort of courage, humor, grace, and resolve that Coach did. I will always be grateful.

CHAPTER SIX

Turbulent Waters, 1989–2002

I am now supporting women's crew going into athletics. I know several are disappointed in my switch, some have questioned my sanity, and most alums are asking serious questions. An explanation is due. First, the women's team has never had the continuity that Coach Struckmeyer has given the men. If we have been lucky, a coach has stayed for a second year, occasionally a third.... The move to athletics offers the promise of developing this needed missing factor that has held the women back.

—Ken Abbey, *Pull Hard*, 1989

We're still developing our program, but we're past the club team stage. We only compete against varsity crews, and we are beating some of them. In a couple years, we may be beating all of them.

—Ernie Iseminger, *Daily Evergreen*, 1995

So it is fated that all things run to the worse and fall dropping backward; even as one who with strain of oarage urges a skiff up stream, if once he slacken his arms, the prone river current sweeps him headlong down.

—Virgil, *The Aeneid*

Marietta "Ed" Hall had one of the most successful rowing careers in the history of WSU. In 1990, she rowed on a varsity eight that handily defeated UW's second boat at Opening Day, that demolished OSU in the Tri-Cities, and placed fifth in the grand final at the Pacific Coast Championships. The following year, the first year of the women's varsity program, WSU did not field an eight, so Ed rowed in the varsity open four that won the Pac-10 championship. She also managed something that no one will ever duplicate: she served as the last commodore of the women's club team in 1989–90 and then as the first commodore of the women's varsity team in 1990–91. She was also elected captain of that first varsity squad by her teammates. After she left WSU in the spring of 1991, she achieved perhaps the most unlikely of all rowing feats: she returned to Alaska and became the prime mover in the development of club rowing in the forty-ninth state. She helped build the Kenai Crewsers Rowing Club as well as the Anchorage Rowing Association and went on to coach and row—and medal—in numerous World Rowing Masters championships.

Ed owed her life in rowing to another Alaskan rower—gold medalist Kris Thorsness, who had rowed on the same Olympic-winning U.S. eight as had WSU's Kristi Norelius. Thorsness had graduated from Anchorage's West High School in 1978, rowed at the University of Wisconsin, and, despite her size— only 5' 9" and 150 pounds—became an All-Big Ten rower and a member of the U.S. National Rowing Team. In 1984, when Ed Hall was a freshman in high school, Thorsness became the first Alaskan to win an Olympic medal in any sport. It was cause for celebration, and there was a large parade in Anchorage in Thorsness's honor. Ed was at that parade, and she found a new hero and role model in this fellow Alaskan. She determined right then, as a freshman in high school, that she would become a rower. She stayed true to her pledge, which was no surprise to anyone who knew the willful young Marietta Hall.

In the 1980s, there was no rowing whatsoever in Alaska, so her dreams had to wait until college. Meanwhile, she ran distance and cross-country skied. When the time came for her to go to college, she made sure every school to which she applied had a crew. When she arrived in Pullman in fall 1987, she was undoubtedly one of the rare WSU freshmen who was actively looking for the crew's recruiting posters. Before she had even met any rowers, she was already telling her dorm mates that she would be rowing on the WSU crew. She finally found a crew poster (in fact, she pilfered one, and it hangs today in her Anchorage home), attended that first orientation meeting, and watched Ken Struckmeyer preside over a large gathering of potential rowers in the amphitheater of the Landscape Architecture Building. She hadn't even been to the river yet, but she already knew that she had found her place. There was no women's coach—Piotr Rylski had left after the 1987 racing season—but this did not deter Ed Hall. She had been committed to this moment since 1984. She was a gritty and determined 5' 8"—an inch shy of her hero, Kris Thorsness—and ready to apply herself entirely to this sport she had yet to try.

By a quirk of fate, in April 1991, Ed's senior year, her sister married Kris Thorsness's brother, making Ed Hall and Kris Thorsness not quite in-laws but, as they liked to say, at least "outlaws." Ed was to be a bridesmaid at her sister's spring wedding, meaning that she would miss one regatta. She was conflicted; she had never missed a race her entire rowing career at WSU. She consulted her former coach, Jess O'Dell. "What would you do if one of your brothers was getting married?" she asked him. "Ed, none of my brothers would schedule their weddings during crew season," he replied. She couldn't argue with that logic, nor could she skip her sister's wedding. She missed the race that weekend but gained a new family that included her hero.[1]

Not only had Kris Thorsness inspired Ed Hall's rowing career at WSU, but the serendipitous fact that her sister was now a Thorsness kickstarted her Alaska rowing career as well. It began when a group of intrepid women from two small towns on the Kenai Peninsula purchased a pair of rowing shells from Gonzaga and started searching for a rowing coach in Alaska. Someone suggested they call up "that Thorsness gal" from Anchorage who won the gold medal in rowing. A quick scan of the phone book led them to Ed's sister, who informed them that Kris Thorsness lived in California but there was another rower in Anchorage who might be willing to coach them. Ed did not hesitate. With no coaching salary, she drove three hundred miles roundtrip twice a week from Anchorage to Seward to coach two boats of novice women—"nearly the entire female population of Cooper Landing and Moose Pass," she joked. In November 1998, she took two boats of novice masters women to the Frostbite Regatta at Green Lake, where Hall's "Kenai Crewsers" won their first race. *USRowing* magazine snapped photos and featured the unlikely crew in its next edition. The coverage they received thrust Hall's upstart Alaska club into the rowing limelight.[2]

Ed Hall was becoming Alaska's Ken Struckmeyer, coaching club rowers for nothing, pulling a shell trailer around Alaska behind an old, beat-up truck, accompanied by an overweight golden lab. By 2020, rowing had taken root for good in the Alaska permafrost: there were 150 members of the Anchorage Rowing Association, and the Kenai Crewsers were still going strong. Ed was competing in regattas around the world, as were her husband and son. There were many highlights: a gold medal in the pair at the World Rowing Masters Regatta in Edmonton; a bronze in the quad at Sydney; a silver in the single at the U.S. Masters Nationals; a silver in the masters single at the Head of the Lake Regatta. One of her fondest achievements was in 2013, when the Alaska Rowing Association fielded a women's eight that won silver at the World Masters Games in Torino, Italy—the entire boat was filled with women who had learned to row in Alaska, with the exception of Ed, who was the only college rower in the lineup. Traveling the world to regattas from Alaska had become a way of life—one that began her novice year at WSU, when she rowed in Istanbul, Turkey.

When 2020 came, Ed Hall was divided. It was the thirtieth year of the varsity women's team and the fiftieth anniversary of the club team. She felt like a child whose parents had divorced. She loved them both. She had spent three years as a club rower, been commodore of that team, and savored their fifth-place finish in the grand final her junior year as her greatest rowing achievement at WSU. She had also been a founding member of the varsity squad, a commodore and captain of that team, and a Pac-10 champion in the open four. She took pride in the ongoing accomplishments of the WSU varsity women's crew, but when it came down to it, she realized she was really more a product of the club team, where men and women had shared their burdens collectively, where the rowers themselves had exercised ownership from the bottom up rather than being in the top-down athletic department structure where athletes were part of the "system." She had to admit that her own identity, as well that of the Alaskan rowing clubs she helped build, reflected what she called the "build-it-from-nothing, make-your-own-support, pay-your-own-way" mentality.[3]

At WSU, Ed had always taken pride in the DIY nature of club rowing, where nothing was handed to them. She remembered her year on the varsity team, when they were literally handed their practice shorts, T-shirts, and underwear. "Seriously?" she thought to herself, "Underwear?" It was a different world. Although club rowers always imagined how money would liberate them from their hardships, the reality was that more money and more resources had not made the experience of rowing at WSU more rewarding for Ed Hall—in fact, just the opposite. It was as if her mother had married up and become rich, at the expense of a controlling, materialistic stepfather, while her real father remained poor but true to his values. When she went back to Pullman, she was drawn to her poor father rather than her rich mother. And she wasn't the only former club rower who felt that way: generations of female rowers on the club side felt alienated from the rich new varsity program that emerged in 1991. It was so professional and well-funded that it did not resemble the crew they had been part of. Some of the undersized rowers wondered if they would even have made the varsity squad—and they knew the likely answer: probably not. Ed Hall, having rowed on both teams, realized that her rowing career, even her identity as a WSU rower, was caught at the interstices of a major schism in the history of Cougar Crew.

The men watched the creation of the women's program from across the boathouse. Since the founding of the women's crew in 1974, the two teams had been part of one club. They had raised funds together in collective activities, like Ken Abbey's beloved casino nights during the 1980s, where the proceeds were divided between the two teams. They had shared rides to the river, boats, launches, coxswains, a common racing schedule, the shell trailer, the shell house and, of course, a common identity as hardscrabble club rowers. Now their intermingled history, their equipment, and even their identity needed to be disentangled and separated. Cougar Crew would never be the same.

Some of the men resented the new varsity program; others envied it, hoping to emulate it. The emergence of an athletic department-funded varsity crew in one half of the shell house created friction that affected everyone. That friction spread into the men's bay, where long-simmering tensions and frustrations rose to the surface, ending Ken Struckmeyer's tenure as head coach in February 1993. After twenty years under Struckmeyer's guidance, Cougar Crew would enter its third decade in uncharted and turbulent waters, as fragile and vulnerable as it had ever been. Yet, through the efforts of many unheralded club rowers who kept the old learning alive like monks during the Dark Ages, the club ethos and the club itself survived the turbulence of the 1990s and came out on the other side primed for a resurgence.

The Blair Decision and the Rise of Varsity Rowing at WSU

There had been numerous attempts before 1990 to make the women's crew club into a varsity sport. The first was in 1979, when Ken Struckmeyer presented a proposal to the athletic department that involved both the men's and the women's teams. Struckmeyer tried again in the early 1980s, hoping to emulate the University of Washington, which in 1980 had combined the men's and women's rowing teams together under one umbrella. But by the mid-1980s, it was becoming clear that if any rowing team was going varsity at WSU, it would be the women alone, under the guise of gender equalization. In 1986, rowers Tracy Vadset and Shari Schneider presented a proposal to the athletic department to make the women's club a varsity sport. Their arguments presaged those that were used successfully in the coming years—that women's crew was an existing, competitive program that could be quickly transformed into a varsity sport with minimal complications.[4] In 1986, however, WSU's athletic department was not ready to move. That would change shortly due to a momentous court decision handed down in 1987, one that compelled WSU to add three varsity women's teams between 1989 and 1991.

The forces that pushed the women's crew toward varsity status began in 1972 with the passage of Title IX of the Equal Education Act, which promised that no one would be "excluded from participation in, be denied the benefits of, or be subjected to discrimination under any educational program or activity" on the basis of sex.[5] Title IX increased WSU's commitment to women's sports over the course of the 1970s, but in the view of many female athletes and coaches, the university was not moving fast enough.

Tammy (Boggs) Crawford and Ken Struckmeyer pose together at the conclusion of the 1986 Pacific Coast Rowing Championships, where Tammy's novices made the grand final and Struckmeyer's lightweights won the Pac-10 championship. Photo courtesy of Tammy Crawford.

By the end of the decade, gender equality in sports at WSU was still a distant dream; and so, in 1979, forty current and former WSU female athletes and their coaches filed a class action suit against WSU on the basis of Washington State's Equal Rights Amendment as well as its Law Against Discrimination—a strategic decision to test state law rather than federal law under Title IX. The case, *Blair v. Washington State University,* was decided in favor of the female athletes and coaches in 1982, but Superior Court Judge Philip H. Faris problematically allowed WSU to exclude football—a large all-male sport—from its calculations when determining gender equity. It was a weak, symbolic victory, and the plaintiffs appealed to the Washington State Supreme Court. In August 1987, the state high court reversed the crucial part of Faris's ruling that allowed WSU to exempt football from its equity calculations, ruling that "the exclusion of football would prevent sex equity from ever being achieved since men would always be guaranteed many more opportunities than women."[6] The Blair decision was cataclysmic. WSU was now forced by state law to move much more rapidly toward equality in its athletic programs, meaning that new women's teams and more scholarships for female athletes were needed immediately.

After Blair, the athletic department moved quickly. The plan was to add a sport per year, beginning with women's soccer in fall 1989.[7] Crew and softball seemed the odds-on favorites to go online next, but, during the 1989–90 school year, it looked like Athletic Director Jim Livengood's ambitious schedule would be put on hold for at least a year.[8] Then, in another turnabout, the Washington State Legislature passed a bill to help WSU achieve the gender equity demanded by the Blair decision, appropriating $300,000 to the university for the 1990–91 academic year.[9]

Livengood knew that WSU had to act immediately to secure those funds, but time was running out. In late April 1990, a decision still had not been made, but by then it was so late in the year that women's crew had a decided advantage over softball—it was the only sport being considered that already existed at WSU and required no new facilities in order to move from club to varsity status. The university announced in May 1990 that women's crew would be joining the athletic department. The search was on for an interim coach.[10]

Fortunately for athletics, they did not have to search long for a new head coach. In fact, Tammy (Boggs) Crawford came "knocking at their door." She had been in communication with Ken Abbey, with whom she worked closely when she was a commodore at WSU in the early 1980s. She knew what was

Felicia Beluche, Stacy Fox, and Ed Hall (from left to right) anchored the last women's club varsity eight in the spring of 1990 before the transition to varsity status occurred that same fall. The varsity boat, coached by Jess O'Dell, made the finals and finished fifth at PCRCs, tying the best performance in the history of the women's team. Source: The *Chinook* (1990), 179, courtesy of WSU Manuscripts, Archives, and Special Collections.

afoot and had been monitoring the situation from Seattle, where she was in her third year as assistant coach for the UW women's crew. When Abbey told Crawford that a decision had been made to go varsity, she contacted Livengood and applied for the interim position immediately. "I pretty much came to them," Crawford said.[11]

Livengood and Marcia Saneholtz, the associate athletic director, were thrilled. Crawford came with the imprimatur of the top rowing program in the entire country. She was an assistant to the U.S. National Rowing Team coach, Bob Ernst, who was also UW's head coach, but she was also a Cougar at heart, having rowed for four years in Pullman, serving as commodore for three of them, and coaching the WSU novice women to one of their most successful seasons in 1985–86. "University of Washington has one of the best crew teams in the country, and we are fortunate to have her," Saneholtz beamed.[12]

At the University of Washington, Crawford had taken her coaching to a new level, recognizing things about the sport that she never considered at WSU, where she had rowed under different coaches and never developed a cohesive understanding of rowing technique. Now, instead of just telling her rowers to slow their slides and pull hard—the main advice she remembered receiving in Pullman—she was paying attention to the nuances of their blades and bodies, calculating the ratio of drive to recovery, watching their spacing, and monitoring their stern check, all the while exhorting them to suspend their body weight against the oar, using it as a lever to propel the boat through the water.[13] Rich Ray witnessed Crawford's coaching at UW first hand, riding with her in the launch as she coached her Husky novices in the spring of 1988. He was impressed with her technical prowess and the unique vocabulary she had developed for communicating with her athletes—a "crew language." Sporting a purple baseball hat emblazoned with a gold "W," she used a large bullhorn to give her crews "a steady stream of instruction and feedback":

> I want to keep the ratio on the slides now when we take this next power piece. Push it back and let it run. Don't be in a hurry, Carolyn, matching coming out of bow right with Shannon. Shannon, you've got good circles going here today. Good job of holding your mark. No tapping on the recovery now. Keep the weight on the hands, Shannon, coming over the knees. Not so stiff now—relax, relax—follow your hands out. Loosen up the inside hand—not so tight—it's pushing your inside shoulder up. Matching on the paddle now— matching! Carolyn, you're opening up before Shannon. Swing the bodies together, in and out of bow....[14]

Tammy was happy at UW; she was fulfilling a dream. But she also realized that she was just a cog in the machine of UW rowing. There was already a system in place, and she knew that it would operate with or without her. The system determined the daily regime: if the team had rowed 2,000-meter pieces along the bridge the previous year on this day, then they were headed to the bridge. You followed the system, and it resulted in championships. It was a winning formula, but it left very little room for individual creativity. She also didn't like "the emotional distance between coaches and athletes resulting from the size of the [UW] program."[15] She longed for the more intimate environment of WSU rowing.

While her UW experience had been crucial in developing her coaching skills, it also underscored what she had really loved and missed about Cougar Crew, which was the sense of community and companionship. At UW, for example, there were so many novice rowers that they came to practice in cohorts of sixteen throughout the day. They had little opportunity to meet other rowers outside their cohort and might see people on campus wearing crew sweatshirts whom they would never meet or know.[16] At WSU, all the rowers, men and women, knew each other, and the crew formed a tightly bonded community. Tammy Crawford had a coaching resumé from UW, but she still carried the mindset of a WSU rower. The WSU Athletic Department, if they could have built their prototype head coach, would have constructed Tammy Crawford.

Everything seemed aligned for a "Kumbaya" moment—the return of a prodigal daughter to the Palouse. Instead, that first year was dominated by a number of conflicts, the first of which emanated from returning club rowers who opposed the transition from club to varsity status. Before the decision was made to take women's rowing varsity, and long before hiring Crawford, a vocal resistance to the prospect of joining the athletic department as a varsity team had already emerged among the women's team's leadership. They questioned how the new varsity program would be operated: Would the team still be open to all comers? Would women be cut from the crew? Who would get scholarships? What would the relationship be like between the men's and women's teams? What reimbursement would the club receive from the athletic department for essentially confiscating its hard-won equipment? In the view of the club's officers, especially Ed Hall, its commodore, their concerns were not being sufficiently addressed by the athletic department, which was not consulting or communicating directly with the student leadership of the club. In April 1990, Hall was quoted on the front page of the *Daily Evergreen* in open opposition to the move, arguing that the athletic department's offer "was not suited to crew." Without the help of the athletic department, Hall's coach, Jess O'Dell, had brought stability and success to the team. Hall was worried that a national coaching search would attract someone to WSU with no respect for the club history of Cougar Crew. She was also worried about the fair distribution of scholarships and equity in recruiting, and she "did not want to see the men's and women's crew teams split up."[17]

When the decision to make women's crew a varsity sport was finally made in May 1990, Jim Livengood, Marcia Saneholtz, and Ken Abbey invited the women's club team to a meeting where they unveiled their plan. The three administrators were caught off guard when Hall and others voiced their opposition to the change. But by this time, the hay had already been baled and stored in the barn. Livengood told them that WSU's athletic department already owned the shell house *and* the boats, so if any women *wanted* to row, they would row on the varsity team or not at all. The athletic director was perplexed and frustrated with the resistance: instead of being thrilled at the prospect of not having to pay to row, Ed Hall and some other club rowers believed that the athletic department was essentially hijacking the club team.[18] Ken Abbey was not pleased with their position either, but at least he understood their perspective. "One of the benefits of being a club sport is that you're relatively independent," he explained to the *Evergreen*. "They (the players) had a great deal [of independence] in running the program."[19] Abby was correct. Hall and the other club officers were certainly not used to taking orders from the athletic department.

Tammy Crawford, still in Seattle, wondered why any rower would oppose what she was setting out to do, which was simply to make fast crews on the Palouse. To be clear, the protests of club rowers like Ed Hall had nothing to do with Tammy Crawford. In fact, at the meeting in May, Hall told Livengood that the transition to varsity status could only be successful if the athletic department hired former WSU club rower and novice coach Tammy Crawford, whose candidacy was supported by Hall's coach, Jess O'Dell. Hall had worried that Livengood's national search would yield a newcomer who did not understand Cougar Crew's unique co-ed club history. Later, when she learned that Crawford had been hired, Hall felt relieved that her new coach was coming from the WSU club tradition. But there was no getting around the fact that Crawford was now the face of the new varsity program, not the old club, and it was understandable that she interpreted the resistance of the former club rowers, and especially their commodore, as primarily directed at her. As Hall later said, "Tammy arrived in Pullman loaded for bear."[20]

Crawford was young—only 27—and she was fierce, competitive, and blunt. Now in charge of building a Pac-10 varsity rowing program, she returned to Pullman singularly focused on that goal. Anything or anyone who distracted her from that mission was unworthy of her time or attention.[21] While she was a Cougar at heart, she had also been conditioned by the top-down UW model more than she probably realized. At UW, Bob Ernst's word was law. There were no negotiations between athletes and coaches. Athletes did what they were told. They got *with* the program or they got *out* of the program.

Ed Hall, the second-year commodore, refused to get with the program, and she immediately fell out with her new head coach. The conflict began when Crawford put the varsity rowers alongside the novices that fall and began teaching everyone her rowing style from scratch, as if they were all novices. The tensions worsened when Crawford relegated Hall's former head coach, Jess O'Dell, to the crew office in the athletic department. "In the spring, I was sitting at the starting line of the West Coast Conference grand final in the varsity eight, and now I was a novice again and the coach that got us there was stuck doing office work," Hall lamented.

The relationship between Hall and Crawford quickly deteriorated. "I made Tammy's life a living hell that year," Hall admitted. "I defied her in every way."[22] Tammy reciprocated, even asking Hall to quit at one point, seat racing her endlessly, and attempting to diminish her status as commodore by introducing the new designation of "captain" in the hope that Hall would be voted out by her teammates. She wasn't. She also doggedly held on to her seat in the varsity boat. Hall held her ground and Crawford held hers.

It wasn't a fun year for either of them, despite the fact that it ended with a Pac-10 championship in the open four. Even that was a battle, as Hall believed that Crawford was insulting her rowers by refusing to race an eight. Hall never cherished that Pac-10 championship because she believed the four was "everyone's third boat." Ed Hall wanted to race against the best from other schools, not their third boats. But she also came to respect Tammy Crawford's integrity. She realized that Crawford could simply have changed the votes in the secret-ballot election for team captain, but she didn't. Nor did she force Hall out of the varsity boat, as much as she might have wanted to. Later, when Ed Hall was building her rowing club in Alaska, she called up Tammy Crawford and purchased a number of boats from her, including a four named the *Jess Stuart O'Dell*. Crawford put them on the shell trailer and drove them to Seattle, where they were loaded onto a barge for Alaska.[23] By the late 1990s, two fierce competitors were putting their conflicts behind them.

The relationship between the men's and women's teams also deteriorated that first tumultuous year, as Crawford came into a situation where the men's side was expecting things that she could not deliver. After the *Blair* decision, no one had advocated for the women gaining varsity status more than Struckmeyer. In talks with WSU President Sam Smith, Athletic Director Jim

Livengood, and Vice President of University Relations Stan Schmid, Struck-meyer made the case that, while other women's sports—like softball—would have to begin from scratch, women's crew was an existing competitive pro-gram with facilities already in place. His advocacy was not entirely altruistic. He realized the women would benefit, but he also hoped there would be a trickle-down effect on the men's side.

At the outset, Ken Abbey was skeptical, but he shared Struckmeyer's hope that the longstanding mutualism of the two clubs might continue in some altered form. Under his philosophy of "one program, two teams," Abbey had long resisted any move that would separate the men's and women's teams. He was truly inspired by the way both teams supported each other. Witnessing "a member of the men's crew hugging one of the women after the women swept at Tri-Cities, or one team helping the other get their shell out of the water, or the women's officers worried that the men are getting their fair share of the funds after a joint fund-raiser," convinced him of the benefits of a co-ed club. Until the late 1980s, Abbey steadfastly opposed moving the women to ath-letics without the men. "You must take both teams or none," he insisted. Then he had a change of heart based on his concern for the long-term financial sustainability of both teams as well as his own weariness at having struggled so long to keep the rowing club in the black.

While he was still convinced that "keeping the two teams together is the optimum solution," Abbey finally concluded in 1989 that the move to varsity status would safeguard women's crew while allowing fundraising on the club side to be directed solely toward the men.[24] The move would stabilize the women, finally closing the revolving door of temporary coaches, and Abby also hoped it would benefit the men by allowing some of the annual fixed costs of the crew program to be subsidized by the women's varsity team.

Before Crawford arrived in Pullman, Struckmeyer believed there was an agreement in place, negotiated with a handshake between Ken Abbey and Jim Livengood, for the women's varsity team to cover certain shared costs, like insurance, the boat trailer, maintenance of the launches, and gasoline, thus alleviating those annual financial burdens on the men's club.[25] But there was no written agreement stipulating these terms, and Tammy Crawford was caught in a bind. She wanted to help, and she did help that first year; but when she showed her budget numbers to the athletic department, it did not fly: monies designated for X could not be diverted to Y.[26] There was some sharing of the shell trailer at the beginning, but that fell apart quickly as the athletic department purchased a new trailer for the varsity women who began to attend different regattas than the men's club.[27]

The shared dream of an integrated men's and women's crew died in 1990 for reasons that made sense but were no less hard to take. Crawford could not subsidize the men's team. She was in charge of an athletic department program, and she had one responsibility: to build a winning crew. That was all. Her contract did not involve relations with the men's team or any such accommodations. She drew strict lines between her team and the men's club. It was a new day. Jess O'Dell, Crawford's novice coach, shared Struckmeyer's hope that both teams could be lifted by the infusion of new wealth into WSU rowing, but in retrospect, he realized that he and Struckmeyer were wearing rose-colored glasses: "How could we think that a Title IX initiative designed to benefit the women would work to benefit the men?"[28]

The separation made sense, but it also hurt. Struckmeyer felt diminished by the new relationship between the teams. He was Cougar Crew's perennial Rodney Dangerfield, never getting the respect he believed his crew deserved. Crawford was just as dumbfounded. She remembered back to when she was club commodore in the early 1980s and she and Struckmeyer had driven to Seattle together to pick up a new shell. They drove through the night and arrived back in Pullman just as the sun was coming up. It was a fond memory and, when she thought back on that trip, she wondered how her relationship with Struckmeyer had deteriorated so badly. A perfect storm of miscommunication and misunderstanding had created conflict between two strong-willed, competitive personalities. In later years, Crawford reached out to the men's club team, inviting them to row pieces against her varsity women. In 2010, at the dedication of the Ken Abbey Shell House, she and Struckmeyer both gave speeches in commemoration of Ken Abbey, who died in 1995; in that moment, Crawford felt the self-inflicted wounds from those years finally beginning to heal.[29]

Crawford's novice coach, Jess O'Dell, watched the conflict that first year with disappointment and sadness. He believed that he could have been a good faith bridge between the men and the women, but instead he watched with a feeling of helplessness as the relationship between the crews spiraled downward. As head women's coach the previous two years, he had an inside track on the interim head coach position for the varsity women, but instead became a champion for bringing Tammy Crawford back to WSU.

O'Dell truly believed that Crawford was more qualified than he, that he could learn from her, and that her history as a WSU club rower who had also coached in a varsity program made her the perfect candidate to both build the varsity and work harmoniously with the men's club. Instead, O'Dell's status as novice coach was immediately diminished as Crawford, eager to work directly with her first batch of novice rowers, dispatched O'Dell to their athletic department office, where he worked on recruiting. After one year manning the crew office, he packed his bags and returned to Omak to take over the family farm.[30]

That first year was a rocky one for everyone, but the situation quickly normalized for Tammy Crawford and her crew. The former club rowers graduated, and she began to build a competitive varsity program in Pullman that was soon among the best in the country. The irony of *Blair* and Title IX as it related to crew at WSU was that the transition from an inclusive women's club to an exclusive varsity rowing program did not create *more* athletic opportunities for women at the university. It simply created more opportunities for *some* rowers while eliminating opportunities for others. There was no longer a lightweight team, as a premium was placed on size. Going forward, there were fewer opportunities for undersized but gritty rowers to secure a spot on the squad, not to mention there being no place for social rowers who were not fully committed to the new regime, which demanded more hours of workouts each week. Previously, women could choose their level of devotion, but now it was all or nothing.

Lisa Stivers, one of those undersized but gritty club rowers from the early 1980s who had rowed with Tammy (Boggs) Crawford, could not imagine herself making the WSU women's varsity crew. At a sturdy 5' 6", she was not a lightweight, nor did she fit into the mold of tall former basketball and volleyball players who would be recruited by the new varsity program. "It was no longer a club of people who desired to row for self-improvement," she said. "I don't think I would have been given the experience if it had been a school-sponsored sport."[31] Many other former WSU women's club rowers felt the same way. They believed the new varsity crew no longer represented the team on which they had rowed, where men and women rowed together as part of the same club and shared their experiences collectively, like one big family. Generations of former WSU women rowers now felt disinherited from their own program, and when they came back to Pullman for Class Day, it was to participate in the festivities with the men's club, to which they now felt more affinity.[32]

Finally, the emergence of a women's varsity program on one side of the shell house created unforeseen tensions on the other side. Thom Eldridge, commodore of the men's club during the transition, imagined that the women's varsity team would be essentially the same as the club team but with money, which would also help the men's side. "We naively thought there would be an equal sharing of all the benefits," Eldridge remembered. He anticipated that

Tammy Crawford would somehow help tow the men's club along in her wake, pulling both teams to another level. However, when he arrived back in Pullman that fall to see the women riding to the river in shiny new team vans, he realized that the varsity team was not like the old club team with money but rather something altogether new and separate.

Crawford was setting a new tone and drawing a clear line of demarcation between her team and the men's club. Eldridge later realized this was exactly what she needed to do, but at the time "it felt like betrayal."[33] Eldridge was not enamored with Crawford's approach, but others on the men's side—including novice coach Ernie Iseminger and his rowers—saw the varsity women as a model to emulate. The coming of the women's varsity program unleashed longstanding tensions between the club ethos and athletic team approach that would come to a head in the years that followed, culminating with the departure of longtime men's head coach Ken Struckmeyer.

Uncharted Waters: The End of the Struckmeyer Era

For the men's club, the existence of a varsity-funded women's team brought into relief their own shortcomings. The women now had all the things the men did not—an adequately paid coaching staff, a budget for equipment and travel, athletes with the full array of athletic department resources at their disposal, including study tables, tutors, scholarships, nutritionists, trainers, uniforms, and paid travel expenses. All of it came without one bit of fundraising from the students themselves, whose only responsibilities were to study and train, and not necessarily in that order. The contrast had the effect of magnifying what the men were *missing* rather than what they *had* and increasing discontent among some oarsmen who wanted everything the women had. This discontent became strongly rooted among Ernie Iseminger's novice rowers as they matriculated up to Struckmeyer's varsity team in the early 1990s. Influenced by some alumni who were eager for a coaching change and encouraged by their fiercely competitive novice coach to believe they were superior to the upperclassmen, a certain vocal faction began to see Struckmeyer himself as the primary obstacle to their success. The upshot was a controversial vote of nonconfidence in February 1993, which resulted in the dismissal of the longtime face of Cougar Crew, most of the varsity team quitting, and many alumni walking away from the program for a time. Although he was not the prime mover in these events, Ernie Iseminger, who succeeded Ken Struckmeyer as head coach, stood at the center of Cougar Crew's tumultuous decade, and like Struckmeyer, he would become a lightning rod for both criticism and praise.

When he entered WSU in fall 1984, Ernie Iseminger had never seen a rowing shell and barely knew anything about crew. He had no inkling that Cougar Crew would play such an oversize role in his life for the next thirty-five years. Before it was all said and done, he had rowed for four years, served as club commodore, coached the men's novice team for three years, served as head coach for five, played a significant role in the rise of the Cougar Crew Alumni Association (CCAA) in the 2000s, purchased a number of shells for the crew, and become the first alumni in Cougar Crew history to donate more than $100,000 to the club. Few people have had more impact on the history of Cougar Crew than Ernie Iseminger, and few people's lives have been more impacted by Cougar Crew.

If it weren't for Cougar Crew, Ernie Iseminger never would have graduated from WSU. If it weren't for Cougar Crew, he never would have had a successful career in higher education development. That is saying a lot, because Iseminger was not only the first in his family to graduate from college, he was also the first to graduate from high school. His parents had both dropped out of high school; they had Ernie, the oldest of five children, when they were still teenagers. He grew up in a working-class household that struggled to make ends meet, and college was out of the question. When he was twelve, his father—a teamster—asked him what union he was going to join when he grew up; Ernie, who was enamored with George Raveling's WSU basketball team during the mid-1970s, told him he was going to college. It was not the right answer. "Do you think you're better than me, son?" his father asked. Later, Len Iseminger became one of Ernie's biggest fans, traveling to every Cougar Crew regatta with Ernie's stepmom Elna on their Honda Gold Wing touring bike. But Ernie was on his own when it came to college, a fact that he later came to appreciate because it forced him to forge his own path in life. "I always knew that my life was my life," he said. That path included getting on a plane to King Salmon, Alaska, the day after he graduated from high school to take a job in a salmon plant in Naknek, Alaska, on Bristol Bay, one of the greatest wild sockeye salmon fisheries in the world. Working in Alaska during the summers and picking up odd jobs on campus—like making sandwiches in the CUB—allowed Ernie to study in Pullman and row on the Snake River, which became the most important and meaningful experience of his entire life.[34]

Iseminger's first trip to the Snake River was memorable. At the urging of varsity coxswain Eric Weseman, who had been one year his senior at Thomas Jefferson High School in Federal Way, Iseminger found himself squished into Ken Struckmeyer's van with his high school buddy, Bob Barton, and at least a dozen others. As Struckmeyer turned left to head down the Snake River grade

As commodore, stroke of the varsity eight, freshman coach, head coach, super donor, and alumni association stalwart, Ernie Iseminger poured his heart into Cougar Crew since he arrived at WSU in 1984. Source: *The Chinook* (1987), 178, courtesy of WSU Manuscripts, Archives, and Special Collections.

to Boyer Park, Iseminger watched in amazement as Doug Wordell, a sophomore in the varsity eight, tucked his road bike into the van's draft at forty miles per hour. Wordell was perhaps the fittest of all WSU rowers in those years—a cross-country runner and road bike fanatic who was inspired by Olympic speed-skater-turned-cyclist Eric Heiden. On this first day of practice in fall 1984, Wordell was wearing a rainbow tie-dye unibody triathlon suit that accentuated his Heiden-esque physique.[35] It was a formidable display of verve and physicality that impressed Iseminger and all the other young novices in the van. When the van pulled into the shell house, the water was flat glass—it was one of those magical autumn days on the Snake River. Iseminger got in a boat, took one stroke, and knew that rowing would be his sport.

Iseminger liked the camaraderie of the crew and the environment of the Snake River Canyon, but for him rowing was fundamentally a vehicle to maximize his individual potential. He realized that no sport rewarded hard work more than rowing—a central truth that guided his career as both a rower and coach. "So much of crew is hard work," Iseminger said, "If you want to put the time in, you'll get something out of it."[36] No one worked harder than Ernie Iseminger to transform himself from a high school football, basketball, and track athlete into a collegiate rower. He and Doug Wordell, his companion in the varsity eight in 1986 and 1987, worked out five times a day on their "hard days," which consisted of weight circuits in the early morning, running at noon, cycling to the river, running up the grade, and rowing.[37]

By the time Iseminger was a senior, he felt as if he had maximized his physical potential. Unfortunately, as he grew stronger, the varsity eight grew slower and slower; 1986 turned out to be a high point. They defeated OSU and dominated the small schools in the Pacific Northwest, but most of the strong rowers from that boat—McQuaid, Hensel, Nowak, Curran, Vassey—graduated in 1986. By his senior year, 1988, the varsity eight just didn't have the horsepower. They possessed a core of strong rowers—Iseminger, Bob Barton, and Erron Williams—but they were also racing with novices in the varsity boat. They lost to Gonzaga for the first time in WSU history. By the end of that spring racing season, Iseminger felt burned out and used up. He had thrown everything he could into rowing, but his expectations—that the varsity eight would "jump into the top four" on the West Coast by 1988, were never met.[38] He watched WSU's strong lightweight boats excel during those years, as the heavies sank further into mediocrity. For someone who had worked so hard, it was not the way he wanted to end his career.

After graduation, Iseminger was invited to row with some of his former teammates—Hensel, McQuaid, Nowak, and Weseman—at the Seattle Rowing Club. They were putting together an eight to race at the Head of the Charles Regatta in Cambridge, Massachusetts. The experience was an epiphany for Iseminger, and it helped shape the worldview that he would take back to Pullman as a coach. Rowing in an eight with a handful of former Huskies, he realized, to his surprise, that he could compete with them. The UW oarsmen were also surprised. "We can't believe we used to beat you guys so badly!" they told him. "Look at all the talent!"[39]

Iseminger had left WSU with an inferiority complex. "We always thought there was something wrong with us," he remembered. Now he was rowing with and against former heavyweights from top programs. He was also getting good technical advice from Pocock's Bill Tytus and the legendary Frank Cunningham, and the boat was moving fast. Iseminger was excited. They were learning how to row well instead of just "throwing water around," as his teammate Dave Curran once called it back at WSU. One day, Tytus stopped the launch, pulled Iseminger from the two seat, and placed him at stroke. The boat took off. Iseminger was beaming. He belonged; he could compete. The sense of inferiority that he had absorbed at WSU dissipated. They placed a respectable tenth out of thirty-two crews in the club eight category at the Head of the Charles.

For Iseminger, stroking that Seattle Rowing Club eight was life-changing. The primary conclusion he drew—one that was greatly influenced by Paul Hensel, perhaps the strongest of all the WSU heavyweights of the 1980s and a person he greatly admired—was that they had not received adequate coaching at WSU. It was not only that the technical training from Tytus and Cunningham revealed for Iseminger the gaps in his rowing education, but it was also the high expectations Tytus set contrasted with his experience at WSU. It needn't have been that way, he lamented, but "We didn't know what we didn't know."[40]

In 1990, Iseminger returned to Pullman to finish his BA and become the freshman/novice coach at WSU. He threw himself into the job with a fervor, determined to take WSU crew to the next level by instilling in his novices the same lessons he had learned at the Seattle Rowing Club: with hard work, high expectations, confidence, and some technical training, they could row with anyone. He appreciated how much Struckmeyer had given of himself for WSU crew, but Iseminger had an entirely different approach that stemmed from his own athletic upbringing in football and basketball, his days as a "dock boss" in Alaska, as well as his hard-driving and self-confident personality. While Struckmeyer was calm, good-natured, and laconic, Iseminger hectored and cajoled his athletes, driving them hard, building them up and breaking them down. He told them they should be faster than the varsity, but if they gloated after winning a piece in practice, he hollered at them, "You haven't done anything yet! Do not compare yourself to those losers! You need to be thinking about Washington and Cal!" He believed they could compete with anyone if they pushed themselves hard enough, and he wanted his rowers to believe it too. He didn't want his crews to absorb the same inferiority complex he had imbibed while rowing at WSU.[41]

Iseminger was possessed during those years. He arrived at the boathouse at six in the morning and ran three practices a day while squeezing in stints as a substitute teacher. He was recruiting hard, and the number of rowers was rising. Sometimes he and Struckmeyer had ten eights on the water on a given day, and he remembered them working late into the night to fix broken equipment. The result was that Iseminger's novice boats began to have success on the water. His 1992–93 novice boat was stacked with large competitive rowers like 6' 6" Tadas Petrys, a Lithuanian who rowed at the six seat and transferred to Cal Berkeley after 1993, later rowing on the U.S. National Team; 6' 7" Tim White at the five seat; and 6' 6" Jeff Earl at seven. That boat was stroked by a junior transfer student, Geoff Owen, a track and cross-country runner from Ellensburg, who was relatively short at only 6' 3".

"Our goals are higher than ever this year," Iseminger pronounced in fall 1992. He predicted that UW was "going to have to start racing their number one against us," which would be a "huge accomplishment" because "they usually don't race their number one boat against anybody but Cal Berkley and in big championship races."[42] He believed that WSU was "good enough to be number three on the West Coast."[43] Indeed, Iseminger's 1993 novices won the Husky Invitation on the Montlake Cut that April, defeating OSU, WWU, and Gonzaga, and their win forced UW to bring their number one frosh boat to Pullman the following week.[44] UW won that race by nine seconds, but Iseminger was thrilled. "This race was an awesome performance for us," he told the *Evergreen*. "This was the first time ever that Washington sent their first novice eight boat to compete against WSU. We're really proud of this race. This shows our program a lot of respect."[45] His novices defeated OSU in Corvallis and went on to place second at the Pacific Coast Rowing Championships in 1993, where UW and Cal Berkeley did not race in the novice event.

It was a good year for the WSU novices, but it was a turbulent year for the crew.[46] Iseminger's hard-driving approach was yielding faster novice crews, but it was also beginning to sow divisions within the team. Rowers in the men's club could already see a contrast between their club and the women's varsity team. Now they witnessed the difference between Iseminger's ambitious, hands-on, energy-charged approach and Ken Struckmeyer's subtle stewardship of the club. Iseminger expected his rowers to attend every practice, and he had the entire crew run up the Snake River grade for every unexcused absence. His expectations resembled the athletic department culture of the women's team more than they did the club approach that had dominated the men's crew for decades. Many of the upperclassmen, especially the lightweights, resented Iseminger's forceful tactics, such as in 1991 when he insisted that his novices be allowed to row in the *Cougar Lights*, the newest, fastest shell designed specifically for lightweights. They also resented the way Iseminger disparaged the varsity to motivate his novices.[47] But many of his former novices, as they moved into the ranks of the varsity, remained loyal to him and became discontented with Struckmeyer's approach, which was so different from Iseminger's. Struckmeyer's quiet approach, his lack of barking, hollering, and motivating, convinced some of them that he was not coaching them enough, or even at all.

Struckmeyer no doubt gave his oarsmen plenty of discretion. If they wanted to do extra work, like lifting weights or running the grade, that was up to them. He guided the crew with an invisible hand, letting his boats work out their problems and come up—or down—to their own level. His club-centric approach was still yielding some successes in the early 1990s. Iseminger himself had gushed when Struckmeyer's varsity eight clobbered Gonzaga at the Head of the Spokane Regatta in 1991. "They beat them by one minute," he said, "That's unheard of in this sport." Iseminger told the *Evergreen* that "there were tears in the eyes of some of our rowers" as they carried their boat through the crowd of five hundred spectators who "gave them a standing ovation."[48] The next fall, in 1992, with Struckmeyer still at the helm, Iseminger declared that "our heavyweight boat has the potential to be the best that we've ever had in 22 years of rowing at this school."[49]

The weight of these rising expectations, however, was boiling over into discontent among a vocal faction of varsity rowers who were also being led to believe that a new coach, and a new approach, was waiting in the wings. By fall 1992, the varsity women, under Tammy Crawford, were already competing with UW as near equals. Iseminger wanted the WSU men to be doing the same, but he acknowledged that "we're still going to have to raise it up a level to compete with UW."[50] His former novices, now on the varsity, wanted to get to that next level sooner rather than later.

That fall of 1992, Tony Hensel, the younger brother of Paul Hensel, transferred from San Diego State to row at WSU. Conversations intensified among the club leadership around the idea that SDSU crew coach Del Hayes, who had rowed on the exceptional SDSU lightweight boats of the mid-1980s and had coached Tony Hensel, would be willing to come to Pullman to take the reins of the men's club if they wanted him. Paul Hensel had long been pushing the idea among the alumni that it was time for a coaching change; and now, with his brother in Pullman, the time seemed right. Club officers agreed.

In late winter 1993, it fell on Commodore Mike Williams to convey to Struckmeyer that many rowers had become dissatisfied with his coaching and were seeking a change. Emboldened by University Recreation (UREC), which emphasized that students had the ultimate say in determining their coach, the club leadership asked Struckmeyer to step down.[51] Struckmeyer did not fight back. He'd been working hard to keep the club afloat for two decades, and he'd been fending off factions within the crew who wanted his departure for at least a decade. He received Williams's final call on Sunday night and simply did not return to the shell house the next week, nor for the remainder of the season, nor for the next ten years after that.

In February 1993, the Ken Struckmeyer era of Cougar Crew ended abruptly. It was a painful blow for Struckmeyer. After twenty years at the helm, coaching crew at WSU had become his identity. It had been a struggle sometimes, but it also had been a great joy. For better or worse, it had been his life. He and Marj considered the many generations of WSU rowers, men and women, as their grown children. And while his coaching had taken him away from research and professional advancement within his department, it had opened other doors for him at the university. Without it, he never would have been on a first-name basis with a series of presidents, vice presidents, and chancellors at WSU who knew him as Ken Struckmeyer, head coach of Cougar Crew. His status as head coach of perhaps the university's most highly respected club afforded him tremendous respect on campus. As with so many other great college coaches, the end of the ride was sudden and jolting.

When families splinter, everyone is forced to take a side. It is nearly impossible to remain neutral. With Struckmeyer's departure, the Cougar Crew family was thrown into shock. For many alumni who had tracked Cougar Crew from a distance, it was as if Mom and Dad, whose bond seemed unshakable, had just filed for divorce and no one saw it coming. Many of the children of Cougar Crew, especially those from the 1970s, could not imagine a crew family without Struckmeyer seated at the head of the table. He was Cougar Crew's benevolent patriarch. The club's paterfamilias. "Ken Struckmeyer was not just a coach. He *was* Cougar Crew, in my book," said Kathleen Randall, who had rowed in the late 1970s and had remained active with the CRA and *The Pull Hard* in the 1980s. "Ken held the crew together. He was the glue between the alumni and

An iconic image: the oversized, sweater-wearing Ken Struckmeyer sits in the coxswain seat of a boat rowed by coxswains at Class Day, 1985. In 1993, the Struckmeyer era came to an abrupt ending. Photo Credit: Gene Dowers.

the current team."[52] Jim Rudd, who had rowed under Struckmeyer in his first year as head coach and remained a loyal supporter of the club and an active CRA member in the decades since, "took a big step back" from the team immediately after the coaching change. "Wait a minute, you want me to support you after asking Struckmeyer to leave?" A lot of other alumni from Rudd's era felt the same way. Many of them cancelled plans to return to Pullman for Class Day. "There were a lot of us who just stayed away for quite a while," Rudd remembered.[53] Alumni donations dropped off. Class Day was diminished. *The Pull Hard* was not circulated for an entire decade.[54] The institutions that had been built up in previous decades to sustain the crew hung in the balance.

There was also chaos among the varsity rowers in the wake of Struckmeyer's departure. They had asked their coach to leave, but there was no succession plan in place. The SDSU coach did not arrive in Pullman to save the day, although he did visit Pullman and met with Paul Hensel about the position.[55] The leadership approached Iseminger about taking over head coaching duties for the spring of 1993, but he needed promises and was not willing to leave his novices for an interim position, especially when some of the seniors resisted hiring him as a permanent coach. Most of the oarsmen quit the team—including those who had led the movement to oust Struckmeyer in the first place. Only nine rowers and two coxswains stayed on the varsity team for spring 1993. They had no coach. They approached Gene Dowers, the former WSU women's coach (and by this time also the former coach of the Gonzaga women), who was back in Pullman for the year to complete his graduate work. Dowers agreed to take them through the spring, and it was an oddly magical season for the WSU men's team. The oarsmen who remained were classic WSU club rowers: they were "non-quitters" who simply wanted to row for the joy of it, and they made the best of their strange season. They rowed a lightweight four and a heavyweight four, and then combined to make a varsity eight. The lightweight four was the only WSU boat in history to go undefeated throughout the entire season, even beating a UW heavyweight four at the dual in Pullman, and finally winning gold at the Pacific Coast Rowing Championships. They were earnest, hard-working, and fun. Dowers, who had never coached a men's crew before, had one of the most rewarding seasons of his entire coaching career.[56]

Anyone who followed Struckmeyer was going to have a heavy lift, that was clear. But Ernie Iseminger took over a team in the fall of 1993 that was teetering on the edge of an abyss. He had almost no returning oarsmen, and he lacked alumni support. It was the beginning of a mercurial five-year tenure as head coach, with highs and lows that reflected Iseminger's ambition and boundless

1993 varsity men's crew after Ken Struckmeyer's departure. A heavyweight four with coxswain, a lightweight four with coxswain, and a spare. They combined together to field a varsity eight and then rowed independently in fours. The lightweight four was undefeated, including victories against UW and at the PAC-10 Championships. Seated, left to right: Phil Demeray, Jon Walston (lightweight), Brent McGill, Chris Kuranko (lightweight), Coach Gene Dowers. Standing, left to right: coxswain Rachel Dechenne, Jason Doten, Steve "Ivan" Kettel, Jay Miller (lightweight), Howard Kwong (lightweight), coxswain Kelly Cannon. Photo courtesy of Gene Dowers.

energy. He recruited big, strong athletes like Mike Slotemaker, Drew Osborne, Thad Smith, Dan Warren, Jesse Wolfe, and Bryan Smith. He trained them hard and told them, "If we row to our potential, we can compete with anyone."[57]

Iseminger not only built them up, but he gave them experiences that previous WSU rowers never had—racing UW's first boat on Lake Chelan; winter rowing camps in Hawaii, where they trained with and raced against Harvard; dual races against Stanford and Cal Berkeley at Redwood Shores; and even a visit to Pullman in 1995 by Stanford's varsity. "When Stanford brings their men's varsity team to compete against our team, that shows a lot of respect," Iseminger said.[58] He predicted his crews would soon be competing with, and perhaps beating, the top programs on the West Coast. Unfortunately, they never reached those lofty heights—perhaps the high point was a second-place finish behind Columbia in the 1996 Cal Cup at the San Diego Crew Classic.

Nonetheless, like all the strong WSU crews of previous eras, they put in the work; rowed hard for each other; built camaraderie; and according to Thad Smith, club commodore in 1996–97 and one of the strongest oars of that period, developed a "mutual suffering society" unto themselves.[59]

The mid-1990s Cougar Crew under Iseminger had large teams with strong, fast boats that dominated regional small-school competition, as they did in 1997 when they swept the Daffodil Regatta in Tacoma.[60] But it felt as if all their achievements were taking place in a vacuum. With the exception of one photograph in 1993, the men's crew was absent from the *Chinook* during the 1990s. *The Pull Hard* was not published and circulated to alumni between 1990 and 2000. Class Day was no longer a gala event; the alumni were nowhere to be seen. To Commodore Thad Smith, "it seemed like there was a hole there."[61]

Iseminger tried to fill the hole with incessant fundraising, which yielded new club vans, carbon fiber eights, and even a shiny new Chevy Suburban for the head coach. He began working with the WSU Foundation office and picking up tips from some of the best fundraisers in the country, like Vice President for University Advancement Connie Kravas, and her assistant Greg Sheridan. Iseminger also went to Kravas's husband Gus, WSU's vice provost for student affairs, and finagled a fully funded teaching assistantship for the frosh/novice coach, a position that was filled from 1994 to 1997 by Glenn Putyrae, a former Husky oarsmen and assistant coach at UW who built fast novice crews at WSU during the middle three years of Iseminger's tenure.[62] There is no doubt that Ernie Iseminger was making things happen. He was indefatigable in his efforts to take the crew to greater heights, but the model was ultimately not sustainable.

Iseminger believed that with better recruiting, harder training, and more successful fundraising, he could build a self-perpetuating machine at WSU that would begin to fuel itself. Instead, Iseminger could not sustain the pace required to feed the machine, and it began to devour him and his rowers. He was working from dawn to dusk and drawing a modest salary of just over $20,000, but that was still more than the crew could afford. His rowers were also suffering from burnout. He had them working out three times a day because that's what UW was doing and if you wanted to be the best you had to train like the best. But his oarsmen, like WSU rowers throughout the ages, were also working "tables and chairs" in the Fieldhouse at football games and concessions at Beasley Coliseum, not to mention trying to keep up their grades. The pace was too much. He was losing rowers—few oarsmen were making it to a fourth year during the Iseminger era. Also, by 1997–98, the club's finances were falling further into the red. The club commodore that year,

Shawn Bagnall, had to cut Iseminger's salary by half.[63] Iseminger's dream of taking the WSU men's crew to the top was becoming a nightmare. In August 1998, he left WSU for a college development position at Oberlin College.

Ernie Iseminger was Cougar Crew's Icarus—he tried to take the club higher than ever, but he flew too high and crashed headlong into the reality that his dreams for the club exceeded the resources he needed to achieve them. He had tried to impose an athletic department mentality upon a club culture. While he achieved some notable successes, his rigorous regime required more effort than he and his men could maintain on their own. He truly believed that WSU could row with UW and Cal Berkeley; and yet, by 1998, they were losing ground. Instead of reevaluating and readjusting his goals and expectations, he pressed forward and drove himself and his rowers even harder. There are a thousand different ways to make fast crews, but Iseminger learned through experience the truth of Cougar Crew: without enough rowers and alumni support, it was impossible to sustain a healthy rowing club on the Palouse. By 1998, he had neither of those ingredients, and he realized it was time to move on, at least temporarily.

Fortunately for Iseminger, and for Cougar Crew, his years coaching in Pullman were an apprenticeship for a career in college development that would give him the resources to become the biggest alumni donor in Cougar Crew history. It was in this capacity that Iseminger would make his lasting contribution to Cougar Crew. While coaching, Iseminger began an internship at the WSU Foundation, where he worked closely with Greg Sheridan, then senior vice president of the WSU Foundation, who became his mentor during those years. This apprenticeship not only gave Iseminger the experience that helped him earn the job at Oberlin's development office in 1998, but it was the beginning of a highly successful career in university development that eventually wound him back to the crew he loved in the 2000s. Iseminger and his wife Alice donated money, racing shells, and time, all of which contributed significantly to the club's organizational "reawakening" in the first two decades of the twenty-first century. Before Iseminger, the WSU Foundation did not prioritize raising money for club sports—it simply wasn't on their radar. Iseminger's pivotal work brought Cougar Crew into a closer relationship with the WSU Foundation that continued after he left and continues to this day.[64]

The Boy with His Finger in the Dike

The most man-to-man conversation that Shawn Bagnall ever had as commodore of the men's club in 1997–98 occurred in the Cougar Crew club office in the CUB. He sat across from Ernie Iseminger and told his coach—who he knew was trying to raise a family and make ends meet by coaching and substitute teaching—that the crew needed to reduce his salary to $10,000 a year. Iseminger took the news in stride—it was not a surprise to him—but it was a hard conversation for a college student to have with his coach. Bagnall, who had been voted commodore the previous spring as a sophomore, took his duties as the student representative of the crew club very seriously, and when he realized that the team's finances were in the red, he did what he had to do. The irony of Bagnall's role in reducing his head coach's salary was that, three years later, he would become the head coach at WSU, earning the miserly salary that he himself had engineered. How Bagnall went from a college junior to novice coach to head coach at WSU in just three years provides insight into the fortunes of Cougar Crew in the late 1990s after Iseminger's departure as well as into the scrappiness of Bagnall himself, who sacrificed his senior rowing season to coach the WSU freshman and would later coach at Gonzaga, Syracuse, and Navy, where he built the Middies into a national lightweight rowing power.[65]

Bagnall entered WSU in fall 1995 knowing little about rowing until he found himself sitting in an orientation meeting listening to varsity oarsmen Mike Slotemaker and Drew Osborne make their pitch to the new recruits: "This will be one of the best things you'll ever do! The team is awesome. We race hard. We train hard. We're best friends outside the boathouse!"[66] Slotemaker and Osborne were big guys with big personalities; and their heartfelt, passionate appeal spoke to Bagnall.

Bagnall joined the team and rowed for second-year freshman/novice coach Glenn Putyrae, the former Husky who was already developing a loyal following among Cougar oarsmen. Putyrae was a technician whose crews rowed hard and well, and Bagnall spent that first year trying to break onto the first freshman eight. They were big, brash, and fast; and the undersized Bagnall bounced between the second freshman boat and the junior varsity eight for that fall and the first part of the spring, missing trips to Seattle and San Diego. In the late spring of 1996, he finally made the freshman eight just in time for the Pac-10 Championships at Redwood Shores, where they finished third behind UW and Cal Berkeley, avenging their loss to Stanford at the San Diego Crew Classic. It was one of the fastest freshman boats in WSU history—if not the fastest.

In many ways, his freshman year was the pinnacle of Bagnall's rowing career at WSU. He spent his entire sophomore year, 1996–97, trying unsuccessfully to make the varsity eight—he seemed to be perennially on the bubble without ever breaking through, an experience that later gave him insight into motivating those oarsmen who were always rowing on the edge of making the cut. The highlight of that spring for Bagnall was being elected commodore for the following year—it was no small thing that a sophomore from the junior varsity boat had been chosen by his teammates to lead them.

Bagnall finally broke onto the varsity eight during his junior year, but his achievement, he realized, was diminished by the fact that most of the strongest oarsmen from his freshman boat two years earlier had already left the team. In spring 1997, there had been discontent and grumbling on the varsity squad. The crew learned that Glenn Putyrae had been hired to coach at Gonzaga the following year and some of his former rowers had floated a petition to hire him as head coach at WSU. Putyrae didn't support their petition, nor did he want the job at WSU. He was happily bound for Gonzaga, leaving his position on good terms with Iseminger, who had been extremely supportive of Putyrae during his time in Pullman. Nevertheless, there was a large exodus of varsity rowers after the spring of 1997, and competition for the first boat dropped off dramatically by 1998.[67]

Bagnall's year as commodore was a turbulent one. Numbers were down, as was boat speed. Finances were shaky. The older alumni were still absent from the Pullman scene. The crew seemed pulled in different directions, with Aaron Starks coaching a lightweight contingent and Iseminger working with the remaining heavyweights. Jesse Wolfe, one of Iseminger's former rowers, had agreed to coach the freshman for one year, but a sense of fragility and instability permeated the club. Bryan Smith, another of Iseminger's varsity rowers, was slated to be the freshman coach for the following year, 1998–99, but that fell through. Iseminger called Bagnall in August 1998 and asked him if he would coach the freshmen. Iseminger knew that Bagnall was interested in becoming a coach—they had talked coaching a number of times—and this was a prime opportunity for him to gain experience. But Bagnall was entering his senior season and still had eligibility. Iseminger promised him they would arrange it so that he could coach while rowing on the varsity team. Bagnall agreed. Then, the other shoe dropped. Two weeks later, just before the start of classes, Iseminger told Bagnall that he was leaving for the position at Oberlin College.

Bagnall entered his senior year as the freshman coach for a team that had no head coach. That fall was pandemonium. Chris Tapfer at UREC told the club that they could not row without a coach in the launch, so Bagnall, who was already coaching, recruiting, and organizing fundraisers in his capacity as the freshman coach, now took on the varsity crew as well—his old teammates!—as a kind of informal interim head coach. He ran the launch and coached them in the mornings, worked as a cook at Swilly's during the lunch rush, and then took the freshman team down to the river in the afternoons—and somehow managed to fit in some classes. That fall, two former club rowers—Tammy and Roger Crawford—offered Bagnall advice and support. Tammy taught him how to rig boats and gave him coaching tips while Roger proved invaluable in helping him balance the books. The club was running a deficit and had no coach. Bagnall felt like the boy with his finger in the dike, just trying to avert disaster until they could find a permanent solution.[68]

The crew hired Hugh Dodd, a former UW oarsman, as head coach in February 1999. Bagnall was relieved. He could now focus on the freshman and also row with his teammates. But Dodd was not having it—either Bagnall would coach the freshmen or he would row with the varsity, but not both. It was a hard decision for Bagnall. He wanted to finish out his senior rowing season with his teammates, but by then he had already developed a strong sense of loyalty to his freshman crew. He chose coaching over rowing that year, and it was a decision he never regretted. It led to one more year as freshman coach under Hugh Dodd, and then—when Dodd left—the head coaching job fell to Bagnall. Roger Crawford and Doug Engle, now acting as de facto alumni advisers, handed the team over to Bagnall, much as Ken Abbey had handed the team over to Ken Struckmeyer following Bob Orr's departure in 1973, "after a five-minute national search."

Bagnall served for two years as head coach of Cougar Crew. His teams were never particularly big or fast, but they were competitive, and he retained his rowers. Moreover, when he handed the team over to Michelle Kistler two years later—admittedly leaving the team in the lurch—the club was no longer in debt, a fact of which he was extremely proud. Further, Cougar Crew still existed, thanks in part to his efforts. In 2001–02, his last year as head coach, he pulled an exceptionally gifted freshman into the varsity boat. That freshman, perhaps the first since Paul Enquist to row for four years in the varsity eight, was Danny Brevick, who would shortly make his own mark on the history of Cougar Crew.

Conclusion

The clashing of competitive personalities heightened the friction in Cougar Crew during the 1990s, but absent larger forces, the heat of those conflicts might have produced only temporary sparks. Instead, larger developments beyond Cougar Crew, such as Title IX, created a powder keg that exploded when touched off by those conflicts. Certainly, individual actions shaped Cougar Crew's turbulent decade. But even if the characters had been different,

Cougar Crew might still have experienced a decade of tumult. If not Ed Hall, another rower would have resisted the separation of the women from the men's club. If not Tammy Crawford, another coach charged with the responsibility of building a varsity program while sharing the same shell house with a men's club team would have garnered resentment and hostility. If not Ernie Iseminger, another coach who succeeded Ken Struckmeyer and pushed the club in a new direction would have garnered backlash from older alumni loyal to their iconic coach.

The conflicts that embroiled the crew during those years had been building for decades; they were philosophical debates over the future of the program, over how the crew would move forward into a new era, and what kind of values it would embody and represent. Would the athletic department model, where coaches were sovereign and rowers were "athletes," prevail over the club model, where students were sovereign but the club foundered permanently on the edge of financial instability? Could a student-run club yield winning boats? Was having winning boats itself a goal that fundamentally provided a more enriching experience than recreation, participation, and shared striving? If so, how did one make fast boats? In essence, what did it mean to be a "club" versus a "team"? Was Cougar Crew an assemblage of athletes or an organic community of kindred spirits? Was the financial hardship of the club experience itself a central and necessary part of the Cougar Crew experience?

These questions yielded only subjective answers, which raised even more questions and engendered more debates. Moreover, these debates offered up false dichotomies, such as club vs. team and winning vs. participation. As Mike Klier later noted, "A meaningful life experience through rowing and a race-to-win competitive spirit are not mutually exclusive."[69] They were still necessary questions that illuminated the very essence of Cougar Crew, and the answers were less important than the act of asking them and then debating them among the community, preferably at Rico's Pub well into the evening. This was Cougar Crew's never-ending debate—the ongoing conversation that animated the tribe.

Remarkably, even in the midst of turbulence and turmoil, young men and women continued to travel to the Snake River Canyon to sit on their asses and go backward. On the men's side, the real heroes of the story were the unheralded rowers of the late 1990s and early 2000s who carried the torch during the hard years when there was a new coach every two years, alumni support dropped, press coverage declined, the club disappeared from the *Chinook, The Pull Hard* ceased circulation, and Class Day became an empty ritual. The club was diminished during those years, but *still it persisted*. That was the nature of

Cougar Crew—pushing forward through adversity and hardship. Call it grit or persistence—it was the primary characteristic that united generations of rowers from 1970 to 2020. And shortly, as the twenty-first century unfolded, those generations of WSU rowers would be reunited in a reawakened club that once again brought alumni and current rowers together in a shared experience.

Tracy (Vadset) Landboe (1985–88)

Our team adviser, Ken Abbey, asked me as commodore and Sheri Schneider as vice commodore to write a proposal aimed at having women's crew accepted as a varsity sport at WSU. Sheri and I worked on a written statement on behalf of the program, which was presented to the board of regents, outlining why women's crew was an obvious choice to be selected as a varsity sport. From our perspective, it made total sense. The women's crew program was well established, with a boathouse, equipment, and a record of some success in the PAC-10 Conference. All we lacked was funds for coaching and further recruitment. We pointed out that the university could add a quality women's sport program with little capital investment. Making crew a varsity sport would ensure stability and a permanent future for the women's team—and for the program in general—at WSU. We felt the men's team would benefit indirectly from the transition of the women's team to varsity; we shared various expenses, we shared the boathouse, and perhaps more alumni support could be directed specifically to the men's program, not to mention the additional exposure a successful women's team might bring. Looking back, my years rowing at WSU crew cemented important key values into my way of approaching the world. I learned that hard work does not always result in a perfect outcome and one must persevere in those difficult times. I made lifelong friends, learned to balance tackling several activities at the same time while working at a high level. It set me up for a lifetime of achievements and adventures in water sports, a passion which has been passed on to my children.

Steve Young (1992–93)

I will never forget my days as a rower for WSU. Like Ernie—my coach at the time—said, not many of us rowed in high school, and that was true for me as well. I came to WSU wanting to play baseball, but when that didn't pan out, I had to find something else. I went to one of the informational meetings and was really interested—the exercise, the team spirit, and the opportunity to do something great fit with where I was and what I needed at that time. I joined my first fall at WSU, and I remember two things: the van rides down to the river and Ken Struckmeyer. We'd all crowd in and make the long, windy way down to Wawawai to train—it was galvanizing and one of the reasons I think kept guys in it. The other was Ken, who was an intimidating individual with a witty comment and big smile.

Through that fall and winter, we trained and sweated a lot, whether in the boat, on land, in the gym, or on the erg. It was great, and I was making progress that first year—rowing well in the novice eights. I remember the spring break I spent at WSU just training for crew—this was foreign to me, as the original plan was to spend a relaxing week at home. The next fall, I continued to improve and got onto the heavyweight boat for the second-year guys. I was the lightest but could pull with anyone, and I enjoyed the tremendous endurance that it took to row that hard for that long. My most memorable time was when we were training over in Seattle during the winter break of my second year on the team. I remember like it was yesterday how we sailed silently through Puget Sound in the early morning when all of the city lights were shining so brightly. It was a thrill for me to be on the water with such scenery and serenity. I'll never forget it.

WSU crew has impacted my life in one major way—staying fit. Even after I left crew, I could not give up the intense workouts and the feeling of satisfaction from exerting myself beyond my limits. In fact, those years in crew laid the foundation for me to pursue other athletic activities, such as running, biking, and swimming. My roommate was a runner for Ferris High School, and he got me into marathons and Ironman competitions, but I couldn't have done those things without the exposure to training and being committed to really pushing myself for crew.

CHAPTER SEVEN

The Reawakening, 2000–2017

Crew was never just about winning. Winning was important, but it was more than that. I told Michelle [Kistler] that I was fairly sure there were alumni out there who would support the crew if: 1) they knew about the crew of today, 2) knew the efforts would be directed toward the men's crew, 3) knew Struck-meyer was supportive of the efforts.... I am writing to all of you to ask a couple of favors. If you are interested in the future of Men's Cougar Crew, let it be known. Email the new head coach, Arthur Ericsson, Commodore Danny Brev-ick, or myself.... The other thing I would like to do is invite everyone to Class Day 2005, set for March 19. A great time to renew old friends and help Cougar Crew.

—Tim "Haole" Richards, *Pull Hard*, Fall 2004

I am here because I want to coach a program that has the ability to compete with the best. I know that there is a rich history for men's rowing here at WSU, and I can see the pride the team has in this legacy. It has a great impact on the energy and efforts of the men and women now involved. They have the matu-rity and work ethic to really work together as a team and achieve their fullest potential. That is what inspires me the most.... With the exception of the few varsity programs, there is not one team that I feel should be faster than WSU. WSU Men's Rowing is a "sleeping giant," and I am here to start waking it up.

—Arthur Ericsson, *Pull Hard*, Fall 2004

In fall of 2000, *The Pull Hard* published its first edition since 1990. Published sporadically in the 1970s but consistently in the 1980s during the high point of club stability and alumni activism, the newsletter had become the collective mouthpiece of the crew, an essential link between current rowers and the alumni. Its absence indicated both the club's lack of institutional strength during the 1990s and the fraying fabric of the intergenerational Cougar Crew community. Its restoration was one of the first attempts to knit that fabric back together. Editor Rich Ray recognized the "crying need for occasional data exchange between members of the WSU rowing community. No data, community kaput."[1]

The Pull Hard had disappeared during a period of institutional instability, when publishing a quarterly update about the crew took a back seat to the necessity of simply keeping the crew afloat on a daily basis—making sure the vans were running and that there was gasoline in the launch and batteries in the cox boxes. In 1998, when Roger Crawford became crew adviser, the club was rudderless. Ernie Iseminger had just left Pullman. During his time as coach, Iseminger had done most of the heavy lifting for the club—keeping boats and vans maintained, working with UREC on administrative functions, organizing travel, making sure the bills were paid. The team was managing a complex budget that included insurance as well as monthly payments to Pocock for shells purchased on installments, but the officers Roger Crawford encountered did not even know how to request a purchase order from UREC for gasoline or vehicle maintenance. Crawford, who had rowed in the early 1980s and then assisted his wife Tammy, the varsity women's coach, with boat maintenance and other sundry tasks, stepped in to help the struggling men's team in the late 1990s. He worked with Shawn Bagnall—a senior, but newly hired as the freshman coach—as well as club officers like Jason Hizer and Lucas Olona to organize the team budget, navigate the university bureaucracy, hire a new head coach (Hugh Dodd), and carry out the basic functions of the club. Those were not years of growth but of finding a way to survive.[2]

In this singular issue of the revived *Pull Hard,* Crawford pointed to the historical reasons for the crew's survival through good times and bad: remarkable student leaders like Shawn Bagnall, who "consistently provided intelligent and resourceful leadership"; assistance from UREC staffers like Chris Tapfer and Bob Stephens; and the "hours, dollars, and energy donated by Ken Struckmeyer and Ken Abbey" over the decades. "These crucial institutional and individual factors, and our collective efforts as athletes and alumni of Cougar Crew, have brought us to the point where we can state with confidence that this team is here to stay," Crawford concluded. "WSU Men's Rowing is truly student-run and is possibly the most successful and long-lived collegiate club on the West Coast."[3]

Crawford's piece was a celebration of the club's continued survival, but the fact that he had to announce to alumni that the men's crew was indeed "here to stay" suggested that, in the late 1990s, that was still an open question. In fact, the crew in the 1990s had been on the shoals and was in danger of breaking apart. By 2000, the hull was perhaps saved, but the crew was not out of peril just yet. *The Pull Hard* did not publish again for three years. Bagnall, who became head coach in 2000, served for only two years, to be succeeded by another short-term coach. The alumni were still largely absent, and Class Day would not be reconstituted until 2004.

But the forces of revival were gathering, and the people who would lead it were beginning to coalesce in the early 2000s: Danny Brevick, Peter Brevick, Tim Richards, Michelle Kistler, Ken Struckmeyer, Tom Anderson, Doug Engle, Lisa (Coble) Curtis, Tom Caudill, Rich Ray, Ernie Iseminger, and on and on. The crew self-consciously described this revival as "The Reawakening," specifically referring to the reawakening of the alumni and the revitalization of the crew itself, including *The Pull Hard*, Class Day, and a reenergized student leadership that would make its mark not only on the water, but in boardrooms, banquet rooms, and even on the Internet. If Roger Crawford could make a case for Cougar Crew being one of the strongest clubs on the West Coast in 2000, there was no doubt that by 2020, it was just that: a thriving, vibrant club that channeled the aspirations of generations of current and former rowers. How did it happen?

"Raising the Dead"

When Danny Brevick showed up at the WSU shell house in fall 2001, there were only eleven rowers on the varsity team, and that included himself, a freshman, who was pulled up to the varsity eight by Shawn Bagnall, then beginning his second and final year as head coach. Brevick arrived in the middle of a six-year span where Cougar Crew had three different head coaches—Hugh Dodd, Bagnall, and Michelle (Arganbright) Kistler. Class Day was no longer a recognizable tradition, and the thought of fielding entire eights filled with oarsmen from each class was laughable since each class in 2001 consisted of only two or three rowers.

In fact, the team had largely lost contact with many of its traditions. The club's oars, for generations emblazoned with a black chevron that separated the gray tip from the crimson base, were now painted a convenient solid crimson—not because of any deliberate break with custom, but simply because they were easier to paint and who knew that anyone even cared. The letter jackets, introduced by Bob Orr in 1972, were a thing of the past. There was no longer a banquet at the end of spring break, and if there had been, who would have showed up? The old alums were still largely absent from the Wawawai scene. The Cougar Rowing Association (CRA) and *The Pull Hard* were both defunct. Ken Abbey, the longtime administrative backbone of the team, had passed away in 1995. Other pillars of the program, most notably Ken Struckmeyer, but also former club leaders like Dave Emigh, Jim Verellen, Mike Klier, Mike Kimbrell, Jim Rudd, Bob Appleyard, Jim Austin, Gene Dowers, Doug Kee, Fred Darvill, Steve Wells, Rich Ray, Doug Engle, Tim Richards, Mike Noble,

Brett Purtzer, John Sanders, Jim Gressard, Jess O'Dell, Mike McQuaid, Dave Reeder, Ole Jorgenson, Kent McCleary, Tom Eldridge, and on and on, were estranged from the club. Some of them had walked away from the program in the 1990s. Others had simply lost contact and moved on. In 2001, Brevick and his teammates didn't even know Ken Struckmeyer.[4]

In the four short years of Danny Brevick's club tenure, from 2001 to 2005, seemingly everything that had been lost during the turbulent 1990s would be found again: Class Day, *The Pull Hard*, and the alumni themselves, returned to Pullman bigger and stronger than ever, as did a new era of coaching stability under the guidance of Arthur Ericsson. A newly chartered Cougar Crew Alumni Association rose from the ashes of the old CRA. Even the black chevron on the oars returned, signaling an important reconnection to the team's past. The past itself was something that Brevick and his teammates wanted to revive, creating a new club officer with the title of "Historian."

All these developments circled back to Danny Brevick, who put the club on his back during those pivotal years. It was not an exaggeration for Arthur Ericsson to say, in 2004, that "everyone currently involved with the team is there, at least indirectly, because of Danny." Ericsson himself was drawn to Pullman because of Danny, and his statement in 2004—"if you are in touch with Men's Rowing at WSU today, then you surely know Danny Brevick"—was remarkably still as true in 2020 as it was then.[5]

Danny Brevick was as unique as WSU freshmen come. A homeschooled kid who grew up the eldest of seven children on a family farm in Fall City, Washington, he arrived in Pullman with a strong work ethic and an appreciation for laboring in the outdoors. Beyond working on the farm, he was also a competitive endurance athlete. As a young man, Danny had developed a passion for biking, running, and mountaineering—anything that involved physical suffering and getting cold and wet. He seemed designed for Cougar Crew, especially that first year, when he joined a varsity eight with formidable oarsmen like Carl Cronk and Joey Tennison, who rowed powerfully but roughly. Danny remembers them pounding through the water and arriving back on the dock drenched even on calm days. But they worked hard and did their best during a time when the crew was treading water, keeping afloat but not advancing or growing. That was about to change. The departure of head coach Shawn Bagnall in August 2002 set into motion a series of events that led to the "Reawakening" of Cougar Crew.[6]

The unexpected departure of Bagnall thrust Danny into a leadership role in the club. Just months earlier, he was a freshman trying to figure out how to row and race, but now he was working alongside Commodore Carl Cronk and a small group of returning oarsmen to locate a new head coach. As he recalls, it was a two-step process: first they panicked, then they got lucky. Their luck indirectly involved the retirement of longtime women's coach Tammy Crawford and the arrival of new head coach, Jane LaRiviere, in the fall of 2002. LaRiviere did not retain Crawford's assistant coaches, and one of them, Michelle Kistler, a former varsity rower for Crawford, was still in Pullman pursuing a graduate degree.

Kistler was happy to take on the men's program, and the club leadership was thrilled. She brought technical expertise, recruiting prowess, and the same high expectations she had demanded of her varsity rowers, namely that every oarsman practice six days a week and lift weights three times a week. Nine workouts a week became the standard for the Kistler years, as the club adopted a less recreational and more professional approach to rowing. It was the beginning of a turnaround for the crew. It was also the beginning of Danny Brevick becoming vested in the long-term prospects of Cougar Crew. Now that he had helped hire a head coach, the crew had "wrapped its tentacles" around him for good.[7]

Kistler was the first and only female head coach in the history of Cougar Crew, a fact impossible for her young rowers not to recognize during her short two-year tenure: she interviewed in September 2002, while nine months pregnant with her first child; began coaching only two weeks after she gave birth; and was pregnant with her second child in the spring of 2004, her final season as head coach. Her oarsmen became accustomed to little Emily being rocked to the sound of whirring ergometers. To her athletes, the fact that she was pregnant or tending small children for her entire coaching tenure only served to highlight Kistler's physical and mental toughness. At Pac-10s in spring 2004, when Kistler, then six months pregnant, squatted and scooped up all eight of her crew's oars and carried them to the dock, her rowers beamed. "That's our coach!" The team fondly made T-shirts proclaiming, "I Survived My Coach's First Trimester." It was an affection born of respect for Kistler, who pushed them hard and expected them to push themselves even harder.[8]

Kistler was a no-nonsense badass who demanded that her crew not only train hard but change their mindset. As a rower and coach on the varsity side, she had noticed an air of resentment toward the women's crew emanating from the men's club. Since freshman did not arrive at the shell house with pre-ordained prejudices against the varsity women, Kistler assumed their attitude had been cultivated by previous men's coaches. That attitude was about to end. She told her team plainly, with Kistlerian directness, that their bitterness was not only misdirected, but it wasn't going to help them win. "That bullshit ends now. I don't *ever* want to hear it," she admonished them. "Bitching is not going to make you row faster." She also implored them to think of themselves as athletes. At their first team meeting, she told them, "You need to tell yourself: I am an athlete!" Immediately, several her rowers repeated her words out loud, like robots: "I am an athlete!" Kistler, surprised, looked at them and smiled to herself. She had not meant for them to *literally* voice the words but rather to change their *internal* dialogue. Is this what coaching men was like, she wondered? Would they just mindlessly follow her directives?[9]

Kistler demanded that her rowers exhibit mental toughness. She had no tolerance for "mental marshmallows," and she enforced her standards with action. For example, when she noticed that one of her rowers could not maintain even splits on the ergometer—his power waxed and waned, depending on his degree of mental focus—she told him to maintain his pace or leave. "You pull that shit one more time, you're off this erg!" When his splits went up again, she pulled him off the machine. "This is bullshit. You're wasting your time and mine. Pull your head together. Get out and go home." She had to show her team that she didn't make idle threats or false promises. It worked. He apologized, his intensity increased, and he told her later that her intervention changed his life by forcing him to push beyond his former limits. Kistler compelled a similar outcome in the mind of Peter Brevick, who initially doubted one of her workouts. She told them to row three 1,500-meter pieces on the ergometer at their target 2,000-meter race pace. Brevick thought she was mad. How could he possibly maintain his 2,000-meter race pace for three consecutive pieces that were nearly as long? But then, miraculously, he did. He surprised himself by hitting his numbers, and finally the workout made sense. Now he had the confidence to maintain his target pace for that final 500 meters of a 2,000-meter effort. She demanded a lot of them, but they complied, and in doing so, they began to exceed their own expectations.[10]

Kistler encouraged her rowers to set high goals, and when the team determined that they wanted to take a varsity four to the IRA National Championship Regatta in Camden, New Jersey, in spring 2003, she helped them do it. She told them they needed to train harder and raise more money so they could purchase a new bow-coxed four racing shell. It was an ambitious plan, but they pulled it off, raising $8,000 and purchasing an economy racing shell from a Canadian company, which they hoisted onto the University of Washington shell trailer following the Pac-10s. By the time the shell arrived in Camden, a day before their race, the crew—consisting of Joey Tennison, Chris Kanyer, Danny Brevick, Peter Brevick, and Julia Anderson—had rowed it less than a dozen times, and those practices had been disappointing and problematic. They struggled to balance the shell and, to make matters worse, if the gunnels were even slightly off-kilter, their knuckles scraped across the poorly designed winged riggers, forcing them to tape their fingers before every row. It did not inspire confidence.

At the nationals, however, the unseasoned crew buried their insecurities and exceeded their expectations. After a rough first heat, they won their semifinal and qualified for the Third Final, where they defeated a field that included Navy, Yale, Princeton, Ohio State, and Boston University, placing a respectable thirteenth out of twenty-four crews. Kistler beamed. Despite the trouble with their new racing shell, they had stayed with it, never succumbing to their fears or using the boat as an excuse. They had maintained their mental toughness, and as they glided across the finish line at a full sprint, leaving some very good crews behind, they looked brilliant. The shell was set up level and flying.

Kistler could not have been prouder. It was a satisfying conclusion to her first year as coach, and the team had high hopes for the coming year. "We experienced a higher level of rowing and are determined to become a regular part of it," declared Kistler. "We hope to race at IRAs every year from now on, and instead of having people wonder who the heck we are when we arrive, they will recognize WSU as a powerful force in collegiate club rowing."[11] Coxswain Julia Anderson, whose father Tom had rowed for WSU in the late 1970s, thought that the trip to the nationals allowed her crew to see "that there was a next level in terms of competition and technology, and that was the direction we needed to be going."[12]

For the long-term prospects of the crew, however, the most important thing to happen in the spring of 2003 was not that trip to the IRA nationals but rather the election of Danny Brevick as club commodore, a role in which he served for two consecutive years, to be followed by his younger brother Peter. Danny was a natural leader with a wholesome smile and an infectious charisma that pulled everyone around him along. "He makes a very strong impression," Arthur Ericsson later noted. "You can see that he is driven toward excellence, and it makes you want to join him in the pursuit." Growing up on the family farm as the eldest of six siblings meant that Danny understood the power of working together toward common goals. Homeschooling had also given him a unique perspective: it expanded his sense of self-efficacy as well as his expectations for himself and those around him. Danny embraced the role of commodore. "I love leading people," he said, "and I'm so proud when the team does well." Danny's leadership focused on relationships. He believed "people are more important than projects"; he professed his unyielding loyalty to his teammates, and they showed him the same in return.[13]

Danny's goals for his junior and senior years were far more ambitious and consequential than winning national championships: he vowed to reconnect the club to its estranged alumni base. In his first two seasons, the student leadership had hired a coach and raised money to purchase a shell and take it to IRA nationals, but Danny realized that the support of the alumni was crucial if the team were to reach the next level. He wanted the financial support that the alumni would bring, but more than that, he wanted their guidance when it came to fiscal management and hiring decisions. Kistler counseled him to reconnect with the older alumni who might have the time and financial stability to truly help the club.[14]

The first step was to meet with Ken Struckmeyer. Kistler had no idea that Struckmeyer was still in Pullman. When she found this out, she was dumbfounded that no one had reached out to him previously. When Danny, Peter, and Coach Kistler first met with Struckmeyer, it was like a reunion of old friends who had never met before. They talked for a couple hours, asking him questions about the history of the crew. Struckmeyer had a twinkle in his eyes. He was thrilled to reconnect with the current crew. Kistler was impressed by how much Struckmeyer knew about his former rowers—their whereabouts and doings. From the nicknames he had for them to the stories he recounted, she could tell that, for him, coaching was about far more than rowing. By the end of the long meeting, Danny and Struckmeyer were plotting how to get the alumni back on board. Struckmeyer's advice was three-fold: the crew needed to return to the traditional oar blade design, restore Class Day, and revive *The Pull Hard*. Struckmeyer also encouraged Danny to reach out directly to previous commodores, providing him a list of important contacts.[15]

Danny drafted a letter and sent it out to the club's former leaders. Peter edited a new version of *The Pull Hard*, and the club spent $1,500 sending it out to all the former rowers they could reach. Not knowing how many volumes of *The Pull Hard* had been published previously (there had been only one printed since 1990, and that had come in 2000, before Danny and Peter arrived in Pullman), Peter innocently labeled his new version "volume 2," and was thoroughly chastised by crotchety old-timers, leading him to apologize in the next edition: "Please accept my apologies for choosing a volume number that had long been surpassed. No harm was meant. To avoid infringing on former volume numbers again, this issue has been dubbed volume 10, issue 2. Last issue will be recorded as volume 10 also. I hope this clears up any confusion."[16] Of course it didn't clear up the confusion. Damn kid! Danny and Peter were dipping their toes into the placid surface of Cougar Crew's past, and they were bound to stir up sediment that contained dark matter—there were dormant grievances, hurt feelings, and internecine feuds lurking below the surface. And yet, their missives had flown into the ether and returned news that alumni lifeforms existed in other universes. They were not alone.

One former commodore who received Danny Brevick's letter was Tim "Haole" Richards. Richards, in fact, had been at the top of Struckmeyer's list of people to contact if the Brevicks and Kistler were serious about reengaging the alumni. Struckmeyer told them, "If you can get Haole on board, everyone else will follow."[17]

Richards had rowed lightweight in the late 1970s and served as commodore in 1979–80, helping to lead the team through the Cristy Cay Cook tragedy as well as Mount St. Helen's eruption. During his time in Pullman, he had been devoted to the crew both as a rower and a student leader, but like many rowers from his era, he had lost touch with the program in the 1990s after Struckmeyer's departure. Richards and other older alumni "held Coach Struckmeyer in great regard," and there was bad blood that had damaged relationships and created a rift in the crew. As Richards and other alumni walked away, news from Pullman dwindled. *The Pull Hard* stopped publishing for an entire decade. What was happening in Pullman? He had no idea.

Then, in fall 2003, he received that first student-edited *Pull Hard* in the mail. "This came as a bit of a surprise to me as I had not heard anything of the crew for many years," Richards said. "I had talked with a few of the old oarsmen and pretty much no one else had heard anything." Initially, Richards just "wrote it off" and pitched the newsletter in the trash because "it came out of the blue and with no connection."

Then a second *Pull Hard* arrived in his mail that winter, followed by a letter from Danny Brevick urging alumni to return to Pullman for Class Day 2004. Now his interest was piqued. He emailed Coach Kistler and Danny, and followed up with phone calls. He hit it off with both of them immediately. He and Kistler talked on the phone for three hours. She remembered it later as a "meeting of minds." The first time Richards called Danny Brevick, they talked for an hour and a half. Richards was impressed. Kistler and Brevick genuinely "wanted to reestablish contact with their alumni and thus their history." They were positive and insightful, understanding the obstacles they faced. Kistler had been told by another former rower that bringing the alumni back would be harder than "raising the dead," but this did not deter her or Danny. Richards was delighted to learn that they had already visited Ken Struckmeyer—"the first coach and commodore to contact him in twelve years." In a heartfelt letter published in *The Pull Hard* that fall, Richards told older alumni that "the crew we knew and worked for is there today. The feeling I received from my discussions was one of true sincerity but not knowing how to connect with us."[18]

Danny Brevick could not have sent his letter to a more receptive audience than Tim Richards. Richards had loved the athletic side of rowing. He had been a three-sport athlete in high school and was as competitive as anyone. The lightweights during his years had remarkable success, winning the Midwest Sprints and defeating UW in Pullman. He also loved the environment of the Snake River Canyon. He hailed from a cattle-ranching family in Hawaii and felt claustrophobic in Pullman. The Snake River breaks reminded him of the hills back home. But the central pull of Cougar Crew for Richards was that it gave him purpose and connected him to a community of like-minded individuals. It was the obligation to others—"you can't stop for fear of letting down the other people in the boat"—and the purpose-driven pursuit of collective goals that really motivated Richards.

Rowing was about more than athletics or exercise. It was about leadership—and Tim Richards was all about leading. He had led as club commodore; he led in the management of his veterinary practice; and he subsequently became a community leader in Hawaii. Much of his own success, he believed, had stemmed from the lessons he learned on the Snake River. He believed that Cougar Crew "set people up for success in life" and he wanted to be part of extending that experience to more students at WSU. In particular, he wanted to connect WSU student rowers to leadership opportunities. Danny Brevick, a young student leader who would likewise go on to start his own company, was on precisely the same wavelength as Richards. As a junior, he was already realizing that his actions as club commodore were more consequential and far-reaching than anything he could ever achieve on the water.[19]

Once Tim Richards was on board, he was all the way on board. He told Danny Brevick that he could not make it to their first revived Class Day in March 2004 but that he would attend in 2005 and would also encourage older alumni to come back to Pullman for the event. Meanwhile, Class Day 2004 went off as planned—a platter of Little Smokies was served to the seventeen attendees (including current rowers) in a small, windowless conference room at the Holiday Inn Express, which, much to the delight of the club officers, ran "Welcome Cougar Crew Alumni" on its reader board.[20]

The alumni could be counted on two hands: Ken Struckmeyer, Doug Engle, Ernie Iseminger, Tom Anderson, Jeff Corwin, Joel Jones, Shawn Bagnall, Kevin Harris, Carl Cronk, and Joey Tennison. Struckmeyer, Iseminger, and Bagnall, all former coaches, regaled the current rowers with tales of Cougar Crew's glorious past. "Afterwards, several alums commented that they were glad to see the revival of Class Day and hoped to see it grow into what it once was," wrote Coach Kistler in *The Pull Hard*. "Likewise, several WSU athletes commented they now felt more 'connected to a tradition' and 'enjoyed hearing the past coaches speak about WSU crew.'"[21] It was a modest gathering, but it laid the foundation for something bigger to come. It also provided a couple of choice photos to use as publicity for Class Day 2005, which was Danny Brevick's plan all along.

Tim Richards visited Pullman that October and had a face-to-face with Danny, who was now a senior serving as a second-term commodore. Richards left the meeting even more impressed with Danny and with the renewed spirit of the crew. "I saw what I had thought I would; the same attitude toward crew as in my time."[22] Richards wrote a letter to *The Pull Hard* encouraging alumni to come back. He also began twisting the arms of his old rowing buddies to get them to commit to Class Day 2005, among them Lisa (Coble) Curtis (who later organized the silent auctions at the Class Day banquets and spearheaded the founding of the Cougar Crew Booster Club), and Tom Caudill (who later spearheaded the "Power Ten" campaign). That Class Day in 2005 was memorable: more than thirty alumni attended, and the crew hosted a catered, semiformal gala in the WSU Alumni Center. It was one of Commodore Danny Brevick's proudest moments: the crew had spent $2,000 on food alone, and all the oarsmen were wearing ties. Recent graduates, and even the current rowers, were incredulous. How did we afford this? How did we pull this off? No one could stop smiling.[23] It was as if a champagne bottle of warmth and good cheer had been uncorked and served to everyone at the gathering. Something long dormant had been reawakened, and everyone could feel it.

What happened at the business meeting that Saturday was even more important than what happened in the banquet hall. About fifty people, rowers and alumni, gathered that morning in the Alumni Center's board room. Brevick presented his ambitious plan to create a new organization—the Cougar Crew Alumni Association—that would help guide the club forward. Someone asked him, "When do you plan on doing this?" He answered, "Right now. Today. Before we all leave this room."[24] Everyone quietly nodded their heads and smiled. Okay, so the kid was serious. The first step was to nominate board members. The last thing he wanted was to have someone turn down the first nomination—he feared it would let all the air out of the room. But Brevick had a ringer—Tim Richards had already agreed to serve as chairman of the board of the newly created CCAA. When nominated, he accepted. The inertia had been broken. Things were beginning to roll. If reviving the alumni was equivalent to raising the dead, Class Day 2005 was the first of many seances to follow. The Reawakening had begun.[25]

Tim Richards, as chairman, took a leading role in establishing the structure of the CCAA. This would be an organization that united current rowers and alumni around the shared mission of supporting the crew. The board itself consisted of six alumni and five rowers, and placed an emphasis on cultivating student leadership. Club officers, and commodores in particular, played a major role in formulating and pursuing club goals through the CCAA. Fundraising was important, as always, but Richards wanted to focus primarily on "building bridges and building relationships," under the assumption that if the alumni were reengaged and reconnected to the crew, financial contributions would naturally follow. He didn't want the CCAA to be a flash in the pan but rather a durable, sustainable institution with long-term vision and goals. He also wanted those goals built around cultivating student leaders rather than simply winning on the water.[26]

Brevick and the club officers had succeeded in raising the dead.[27] But perhaps Brevick's most consequential achievement as commodore was to lure Arthur Ericsson to Pullman in fall 2004, because all the new projects that were being planted—Class Day, *The Pull Hard*, the CCAA—required club stability to take root. For that, the team needed a professional, long-term coach, and while Kistler was professional, she was not a long-term option: she had already informed the crew that she was leaving after the spring of 2004. Kistler, who would herself serve on the hiring committee, told the crew that all the work they had done toward the Reawakening meant nothing if they could not find a permanent head coach who would build on their achievements.

Every other head coaching changeover since 1973 had occurred at the last minute, leaving the club unable to conduct an organized, timely search for a replacement. In 2004, they had time to shop for a new coach, but they were limited by their paltry resources. As Brevick saw it, they needed to buy a "nice used Ford pickup," but all they had was "beat-up junkyard Hyundai money."[28] When he met Ericsson, then head coach at California State University Maritime Academy (Cal Maritime), at the Pacific Coast Rowing Championships at Lake Natoma, Ericsson expressed interest in the WSU job, but when the club offered him the position that summer, he initially turned it down. Ericsson had a job and a family in Sacramento, and the WSU position was tempting but financially risky.

Brevick knew he had to act. He saw Ericsson for what he was: the deal of a lifetime—better than a used Ford pickup—like a rarely used car sitting in an old lady's garage, if only the crew could make him a deal he couldn't refuse. Brevick took his moonshot: he purchased three plane tickets on his credit card and invited Ericsson and his family to Pullman for a no-obligation, all-expenses-paid weekend to show the coach why he should take the job. Brevick rented a room at the Holiday Inn, borrowed his parent's nice Suburban to pick up Ericsson and his family from the airport in Spokane, and set out to give them a "razzle-dazzle" tour of Pullman that included the campus, the boathouse, and the grizzly bears on Farm Road (for Ericsson's four-year-old daughter Sienna). Brevick even managed to arrange a meeting between Sharon Ericsson, a professional accountant, and Wendy Peterson in the WSU finance office, so she could get a sense of what kinds of job possibilities existed at the university.

Danny Brevick's gambit worked: a couple weeks after their visit to Pullman, Ericsson called Danny to accept the position as head rowing coach for the WSU men's club at a salary of approximately $20,000. The Ericssons were willing to take their own moonshot, giving up Sharon's secure career in Sacramento to relocate their young family to Pullman so that Arthur could become the head rowing coach of a struggling club that would have to fundraise his paltry salary. Brevick knew the club had found the right person.[29]

The brilliance of Danny Brevick was his combination of enthusiasm, earnestness, self-confidence, and naivety. Like a young parent, if he had known all the potential obstacles and risks that awaited him, he might never have attempted to give birth to the Reawakening or purchase those plane tickets for Arthur Ericsson. But he didn't know enough to be afraid. When he brought the Ericssons to Pullman, Arthur asked him how they would pay his salary. "We'll do fund-raisers," Brevick responded. "What if you can't raise enough money?" asked Ericsson. "Oh, don't worry," Danny replied. "We will."[30] Just like that. With all the confidence of a twenty-one-year-old. And yet, everything worked according to plan: Ericsson came to Pullman and stayed for thirteen years, bringing the kind of stability the team had lacked since the 1980s. The role of the CCAA grew, anchored by the leadership of Tim Richards and Danny Brevick, and enriched by new generations of student leaders. *The Pull Hard* became a reliable publication once again, reaching more alumni than ever before, and Class Day continued to grow, drawing hundreds of alumni and crew supporters to Pullman every spring for lavish banquets and lucrative fundraisers. The 2000s became Cougar Crew's Renaissance after the Dark Ages of the 1990s.

The Zen Master

Arthur Ericsson took an unorthodox path into college coaching. Most university rowing coaches, with very few exceptions, rowed as undergraduates and then began coaching as assistants in college programs. Coach Ericsson, who would come to be known by his WSU rowers simply and affectionately as Arthur, never rowed in college. He took up the sport in his mid-twenties with only a vague idea of what it entailed, but he was drawn in immediately. The idea of propelling a craft swiftly through the water became an obsession for the young Ericsson, first as a successful lightweight club rower and then as a coach. Arthur was soft-spoken, unassuming, modest, and calm. However, he carried within his lean, lightweight frame a competitive athletic spirit that often surprised his rowers, most of whom he could beat on an ergometer as well as in other athletic competitions, like the Olympic-length triathlons that became a team tradition during his years as WSU's head coach, or running backward, an exercise at which he seemed to possess an uncanny talent for speed.[31]

An iconic image: Coach Arthur Ericsson pencils in boatings and finalizes the workout as his crews prepare to take the water in 2010. Photo courtesy of WSU Manuscripts, Archives, and Special Collections.

Arthur believed in finding and following one's path in life, no matter where it led. In his case, it led to Pullman. He started on his path in Portland, where he began rowing after seeing a poster on the Portland State University campus. After moving to Sacramento, he continued rowing at River City Rowing Club, and he also began teaching rowing classes to adults in a popular summer program. However, as the owner of a successful vegetarian restaurant, he found it hard to continue.

Ericsson stopped coaching for nearly a year. He missed it so much, that he began to realize how strongly his destiny was bound up with rowing, especially *coaching* rowing. He expanded his role at River City, teaching master rowers not only how to row but how to become competitive rowers. From there, seeking to challenge himself in a more competitive environment, he turned to college coaching and became head coach at Cal Maritime. It was in this capacity that he encountered Danny Brevick at Lake Natoma in spring 2004 during the Pacific Coast Rowing Championships. Arthur, interested in continuing his own journey toward a more challenging and competitive rowing environment, could see the potential in WSU's program, especially after his visit to Pullman that summer. He could sense the desire of the oarsmen, and he recognized the leadership in Danny Brevick. He was also overwhelmed by the majestic Snake River Canyon—it would be hard to find a more sublime and meditative environment in which to spend his days.[32] He took his leap of faith and headed to Pullman.

Arthur's first day on the Snake River was a gut check. He settled into the launch and watched as the varsity eight began to row. They looked good. Arthur wondered to himself if he could do this. Could he teach them anything? Could he help them? Had he made the right decision in coming to Pullman? When he cleared his mind and began to watch them row more closely, he realized he *could* help them. He could see things they needed to improve.[33] Arthur brought a "high degree of technical sophistication" to the Snake River and began to refashion the WSU style, emphasizing the finish of the stroke more than "pounding the catch," a longtime tradition on the Palouse.[34] He was also a master at designing workouts that helped his crews push their physical limits. But Arthur, in the words of Danny Brevick, "was not a high school football coach rah-rah-rah kind of a guy." He was a mature coach, quiet and methodical, whose skills and personality were extremely well-suited to the adult rowers he had coached in Sacramento but perhaps less so to young men who expected their coaches to holler and scream. Arthur was calm and quirky, more intellectual and thoughtful than his oarsmen were accustomed to from their high school days.[35] Would the relationship work?

That fall of 2004, everyone wondered what kind of coach Arthur Ericsson would be—even Danny Brevick. The moment Brevick knew that Arthur was the right choice was the first time a varsity rower skipped practice. The culprit had rowed in high school for the Sammamish Rowing Association and arrived in Pullman that fall as a freshman expecting to matriculate directly onto the varsity squad. The crew was happy to have him, but he arrived with a definite air of entitlement. He skipped one of the first practices, and when he arrived at the next—a morning weight workout—he was not very contrite. When he breezily said to Arthur, "Oh, hey, coach, sorry I missed practice," everyone's ears perked up, waiting to see how Arthur would respond. "Oh, that's no problem," said Arthur. "You have a free skip." Heads turned, eager to hear their new coach's attendance policy. "A free skip?" asked the young man. "Yes, you get one free skip for the entire team for the whole year," said Arthur, without missing a beat. "And you just used it!" Brevick smiled to himself. Alright baby, he thought, this is going to be a good match![36] Arthur was not kidding around. "WSU Men's Rowing is a 'sleeping giant,'" he had said, "and I am here to start waking it up."[37]

Arthur hit the ground running. He challenged his oarsmen "both physically and mentally from the first day of practice," said Brevick, who found Arthur both "energetic" and "no-nonsense."[38] He desired to bring a higher level of competition to the Palouse, and one of his first achievements was getting WSU admitted into the Western Intercollegiate Rowing Association (WIRA). WIRA was composed of nearly all the collegiate rowing teams on the West Coast, except the large, varsity-funded Pac-10 crew programs like UW, Cal Berkeley, Stanford, and OSU. This conference of twenty-nine western colleges and universities hosted an annual championship regatta every May on Lake Natoma, providing more competitive opportunities—and some hope—for smaller rowing programs and club teams tired of being dominated by rowing powerhouses like UW and Cal Berkeley.

Arthur had to appeal directly to the WIRA Board of Stewards, many of whom resisted the idea of allowing a Pac-10 program into their conference, since WIRA schools were themselves excluded from competing in the Pac-10 Championships. But Arthur made a persuasive case for WSU's inclusion: "I explained that we have a rich thirty-four-year history and are proud members of the PAC-10, but that we have more in common with many of their schools and we want to have the opportunity to compete against the best club teams in the western region."

WIRA coaches overwhelmingly agreed—Gonzaga advocated on WSU's behalf—and WSU joined WIRA in 2005, greatly expanding the team's competitive opportunities and shifting the rivalries of Cougar Crew away from its obsessive focus on UW and OSU toward schools like Orange Coast College, Santa Clara University, UC San Diego, UC Santa Barbara, UC Davis, UC Irvine, and, of course, Gonzaga. During Arthur's thirteen-year tenure, the club maintained its traditional races against WWU, UW, and OSU, and continued to compete at the Pacific Coast Rowing Championships and the Pac-10/Pac-12s, but it also expanded its schedule to include the WIRA Championships and, after 2008, the American Collegiate Rowing Association National Championships, or the ACRAs, which took the place of the IRAs for collegiate club programs after they were barred from participating in the IRAs in 2008.[39] Ericsson was thrilled at the new opportunities for his oarsmen. "I can guarantee that the competition will test every ounce of our rowing abilities," he promised.[40]

Arthur then turned his attention toward training his team for such competition. In a sport defined by uniformity, one of the hallmark features of Arthur's tenure was a knack for conjuring up unique, creative, and quirky workouts that engaged the bodies and the minds of his oarsmen. It was during winter workouts that his team experienced Arthur's genius for pushing them while keeping things interesting. It began with his commitment to cross-training. "On any given day, rowers could be found riding on exercise bikes, swimming in the pools, or running the hilly roads of the Palouse," described one of his rowers, Luke Jones. "There are races on the erg, there are races in the pool, there are races up and down (and up and down, and up and down) the icy stairs of Martin Stadium. There are races to the top of snow-covered hills while doing lunges with a teammate on your back."[41] There were also ergometer workouts with names like "Dante's Ergferno," "C'Erguit," and "Erg Lottery & Roulette." From there, his workouts morphed into more creative forms. If you were going to run stadiums, Arthur thought, why not throw a soccer ball or an erg or a medicine ball into the mix and see what you could come up with? Why not create teams and make each workout a competition in its own right?

One of Arthur's most notorious inventions was a competition called "Mother's Ass," where oarsmen ran from point to point on the main campus carrying an ergometer, which they then assembled and rowed for 2,000 meters before breaking it down and running to the next station. The workout was not only punishing, but it had the added benefit of publicizing the intensity and hard work of the crew to the campus community, as other students looked on in amazement while these determined young men assembled and rowed their ergometers on the CUB mall. Another competition, called the "Boston Massacre," involved a game of catch with a ten-pound medicine ball that teammates tossed through the stadium goal posts, followed by a race across the pitch to place racquetballs on cones. In essence, the workout entailed 200-meter sprints punctuated by tossing a medicine ball. "No matter how seemingly ridiculous the workout, when you were finished, you were physically spent," remembered Karl Huhta. "Arthur had a gift for making physically demanding workouts fun and interesting. It was never monotonous." Huhta, who began rowing the same year Arthur arrived on campus, later adopted many of his coach's creative workout ideas with his own teams as head coach of the Loyola Marymount University women's crew.[42]

While sometimes his rowers wondered at Arthur's unique workouts, the intention was not to be silly but rather to compel a higher level of intensity, competition, and fitness in his oarsmen without having them burn out. It was also about racing and instilling in them a competitive fire and mental focus. "I try to offer mental challenges as part of every practice so that the team will know that they can overcome just about anything," he explained. If they trained with mental intensity in land workouts, they could sustain their focus while rowing; and Arthur religiously believed, "There's never time for a careless stroke."[43]

In those first years, WSU oarsmen embraced Arthur's methods without question, and the results, both in attitude and performance, spoke for themselves. "He has strengthened our will to succeed and our thirst for competition," said Jason Lackie, who likened Arthur's creative workouts to artwork: "If winter training is a work of art, then Coach Arthur Ericsson is its artist."[44] They emerged confident from Arthur's first winter and had a strong performance in their annual erg dual with Gonzaga that February. They could not count many victories that spring, but they were close, especially to Gonzaga, whose dominance over them reached back to the distant, mythic age of 1989. Spring 2005 was a good season but also a tough one, as mere seconds separated them from winning both their Fawley Cup Regatta race and UW tanks. The team's two seniors, Danny Brevick and Brian Anderson, who had put so much work into reviving the club, never reaped the rewards of their efforts, at least in terms of victories on the water.[45]

The breakthrough came the following year, in 2005–06, signaling what was possible and inaugurating a stretch of nine years during which WSU regained its competitive form, culminating in WIRA medals for the varsity eight in 2006, 2010, and 2015. Signs of the turnabout began at the Portland LOOP Regatta in November 2005, the same month that the newly chartered CCAA met in Seattle, bringing news of the Reawakening to westside alums.

The crew arrived in Portland ready to compete, except for one important detail: as they began to rig their boats, they could not find the rigger bolts for the varsity shell, the *Struckmeyer II*. Coxswain Julia Anderson immediately began to assemble replacement parts, borrowing bolts from UW and former WSU novice coach Ginny Bradley, who was now coaching in Portland. Her crew hurriedly rigged their shell and made it to the starting line, but by then Chris Seaman, rowing two seat, found that one of the wingnuts on his foot stretcher was missing. Then, six seat Sean Martin realized his rigger needed a nut and washers. Anderson tried to keep her crew calm. She passed back a wrench so Martin could transfer the nut from his foot stretcher to his rigger.

They barely finished their adjustments before the start, and the boat was still a bit wonky; but when the race began, none of that mattered. Anderson steered a brilliant line, cutting corners on the Willamette with precision while her crew pushed the distractions aside and rowed an inspired race, walking through OSU in the final stretch and finishing third behind the top two UW boats.[46] They had displayed mental focus and fortitude. Like good Buddhists, they had stayed in the moment and transcended their material circumstances, much to the delight of Arthur, who they called the Zen Master. They headed into winter training that year "with a sense of accomplishment and determination for the spring," according to Commodore Peter Brevick. "Knowing their capabilities, the Cougars look forward to opening some eyes come spring racing."[47]

The crew that emerged the following spring was fit, confident, and stacked with some impressive oarsmen, including Brevick, Huhta, Andrew McCaffrey, Luke Jones, Pat Pursley, Chris Jantzen, Charlie Remington, and Dave Worley. In February 2006, at Ergomania, the Northwest Indoor Rowing Championships, Worley won first place in the collegiate category, pulling a 6:09, and becoming only the fourth oarsmen in the history of Cougar Crew to finish a 2,000-meter piece under 6:10.[48] It was a sign of good things to come that spring, which included a bronze at WIRAs for the varsity eight and, even more importantly, the return of the Fawley Cup to Pullman for the first time in sixteen years.

On the morning of the Fawley Cup Regatta, Arthur called his team together and told them about a dream he had the night before, where they executed their race plan and moved through Gonzaga, winning by open water. It was a prescient vision. At 500 meters, Gonzaga was up by four seats, but at the 1,000-meter mark, the Cougars took a silent power five-five-five[49] and began to move. As they took back seats, the two boats were within earshot of each other, and Julia Anderson, instead of calling out, "I have their six-man," began to call out the names of the Gonzaga rowers in those seats.

They were taking a seat with every stroke, and Anderson could see Gonzaga oarsmen look out of their boat when their names were called. Their move shocked Gonzaga. By 1,500 meters, Anderson had Gonzaga's bow ball, and her crew could now see the backs of the Gonzaga oarsmen. "We exploded with power, and with every stroke, we opened the gap even more," Anderson remembered. "When we crossed the finish line, we were four seconds ahead of GU, and we could not contain our excitement."[50]

The victory over Gonzaga in spring 2006 was an important benchmark in the club's progress during the early 2000s. When Gonzaga founded its crew program in the early 1980s, it was a club program, like WSU's. During that decade, WSU played a similar role for Gonzaga that UW had played for Cougar Crew in the 1970s: the team gave Gonzaga some old boats and some good old-fashioned drubbings. Even if WSU always remained UW's inferior, the Cougars were at least the powerhouse of *eastern* Washington. That changed in the 1990s, as Gonzaga became a well-funded and fast university-funded program, even making the finals at the Pac-10 Championships one year—the only non-Pac-10 crew allowed to compete.

As the losses to Gonzaga piled up, it became a psychological burden on WSU oarsmen, more dispiriting than losing to UW, which was understandable. But WSU could, and *should*, be able to defeat the Zags. On April 15,

The 2006 varsity boat. This motley crew brought the Fawley Cup back to Pullman for the first time in sixteen years. From left to right: Luke Jones, Peter Brevick, Pat Pursley, Chris Jantzen, coxswain Julia Anderson, Coach Arthur Ericsson (kneeling), Dave Worley, Andrew McCaffrey, Charlie Remington, Karl Huhta. Photo courtesy of Peter Brevick.

2006, the WSU varsity eight finally lifted that weight from their shoulders and proved to themselves how far they had come. In 2020, Julia (Anderson) Collins still got chills when she remembered their victory, and Peter Brevick only half-jokingly said that when the oarsmen on that boat were married, their wedding day would be only the *second* happiest day of their lives—the first would always remain April 15, 2006, the day the Fawley Cup was liberated from Gonzaga's trophy case.[51]

If the 2006 Fawley Cup was an important turning point in the crew's development, the 2010 WIRA championships were the highwater mark of the Arthur years. The Cougar varsity eight out-sprinted UC Davis in the last 500 meters to take WIRA gold for the first and only time in club history, battling a crosswind but still finishing in an impressive 6:13.0. The WSU lightweights also won gold, and the Cougars took home the overall team trophy, defeating a few athletic-department-funded programs like Gonzaga, UC San Diego, University of San Diego (USD), and Orange Coast College. Paul Ehlers, who rowed on the varsity eight that season, called it "a dramatic show

The zenith of the Arthur Ericsson era: the WSU varsity eight takes gold at the Western Intercollegiate Rowing Championships in 2010 on Lake Natoma. From left to right: Alan Scott, Jaron Lindbom, Weston Spivia, Mitch Williams, coxswain Nichole Martin, James Dorsey, Paul Ehlers, Andrew King, and Nick Estvold. Photo courtesy of David Herrick.

of depth and force." Indeed, it was a dominant performance for Cougar Crew, and Arthur was overjoyed that they had not only won "the premier varsity [coxed eight] event" but had also displayed "the depth of our varsity, novice, and lightweight teams."[52]

Fueling the depth and success of the crew during those heady years was a strong novice program led by Julia Gamache. Gamache had rowed—and won NCAA championships—at WWU. She then coached for the UW women followed by the University of Miami. The salary at Miami was nice, but she never felt comfortable with the sense of entitlement in a Division I varsity program.[53] Hailing from WWU, she understood what it meant to be a small, underfunded program, and she returned to the Pacific Northwest in 2008 to coach the WSU novices at a greatly reduced salary—she was making only $10,000 a year, while Arthur was still, remarkably, coaching for only $20,000.[54]

Gamache found that she had a gift for working with the novice men. She was tough on them and ribbed them mercilessly, but they did whatever she asked of them. Tim Richards, chair of the CCAA, was amazed at her ability to motivate young oarsmen. "She could get novice oarsmen to dig deeper within themselves by almost shaming them but also setting an expectation higher than they themselves could even imagine." Richards fondly called Gamache's coaching style "compassionately condescending," and it seemed to work miracles.[55] In 2009, her first spring in Pullman, her novices beat OSU, took bronze at WIRAs, and then finished second only to Michigan at ACRAs, the club nationals. In her three years with WSU, her crews had three consecutive top ten finishes at nationals.

Gamache worked exceptionally well with Arthur, and the two made a formidable team between 2008 and 2011. Arthur gave her complete freedom, trust, and the autonomy to work her magic. When it came to working with his assistant coaches, he had no ego. He claimed no credit for Gamache's successes and was unfailingly supportive and kind.[56] The formula for those years was simple: Gamache built fast novice crews and sent Arthur rowers who became even faster as varsity oarsmen. David Herrick, one of Gamache's novices, believed that her greatest gift was "inspiring in her athletes a love for the sport of rowing."

Herrick himself became a club officer for two years before pursuing a career in coaching at Syracuse University, University of Virginia, and, finally, OSU. He credited Gamache for a large part of the reason he continued to forge a life in rowing.[57] Unfortunately for the Cougars, and for Arthur, Gamache left Pullman in 2011. She later become head coach of the Loyola Marymount men, joining another Cougar from those years, Karl Huhta, who coached the LMU women. The Gamache story, like that of Ginny Bradley before her, underscored both how important it was to have an outstanding novice coach

The 2014 varsity eight rows to a Fawley Cup victory on a windy day at Wawawai. At 1000 meters, when this photo was taken, they were a half-length down, but they rowed through Gonzaga at 1500 meters and won by open water. From stern to bow: coxswain Ashley Vomund, John Gehring, Curtis Treiber, David Herrick, Max Vaughn, Alex Weatbrook, William Miedema, John Dorscher, Zach Jensen. Photo courtesy of David Herrick.

who worked harmoniously with the head coach and how hard it was to retain them in Pullman. It was a common thread in the club's fifty-year history.

In the years between 2011 and 2015, when WSU took home a WIRA silver in the varsity eight, expectations of WSU oarsmen were higher than ever, even if the results were uneven. But progress was not always measured in victories on the water. The team was fielding good numbers, including dozens of powerful and dedicated oarsmen; competition was fierce; and leadership was strong. Commodores during those years, such as Andy Winters (2008–09), Mitch Williams (2009–10), and Andy King (2010–12), fought for and obtained the status of "varsity sport club," which gave Cougar oarsmen priority registration, support for a full-time paid coach, and also special access to workout facilities, eventually leading to the crew's appropriation of the fourth floor of WSU's Hollingbery Fieldhouse for their erg room—a grandiose facility contrasted to the basement of the moribund agriculture laboratory used during the Iseminger years or the "closet" in the Fieldhouse given to the crew for its two ergometers during the Struckmeyer years.

The achievement of varsity sport club status and other institutional advances in Cougar Crew from 2000 to 2020 were bolstered by the reorganization of UREC, which dramatically expanded support for WSU sports clubs. In the 1990s, club sports, like all student clubs, were part of ASWSU. When the new WSU Recreation Center opened in 2001, all student activities were consolidated under UREC, which now became a university department with a larger budget and more staff to support the expansion of club sports. After 2011, club sports became part of the new Competitive Sports Division of UREC, managed by Matt Shaw. In the bargain, Cougar Crew and all WSU club sports gained privileges that other student clubs did not have, such as the use of university logos, travel budgets, and access to sports training facilities and personal trainers.[58]

Joanne Greene, who later became program director at UREC, came to the department in 1999 as a graduate assistant and participated in the expansion of resources and expectations for club sports. Greene saw the transformation of UREC and club sports as the product of increased expectations from both students and the WSU administration. In the 2000s, many students were arriving on campus with backgrounds in competitive club sports, from soccer to swimming to lacrosse to biking. They weren't recruited athletes, but they still wanted to continue their competitive growth within the context of team sports. At the same time, the WSU administration was placing more emphasis on clubs and recreation as a vehicle of student success, retention, and well-being.[59]

The result was a boon to Cougar Crew. Greene, and later Matt Shaw, supported the varsity sport club designation that recognized clubs such as Cougar Crew, which have "reached a level of budget, organization, and competition that is similar to a varsity athletic team" while still remaining "primarily self-funded." Cougar Crew was the first and only club sport to achieve this status, giving the crew greater access to resources, a higher budget allocation, more staff time from UREC, subsidy for a head coach's salary, as well as tuition waivers for graduate assistants who served as assistant coaches.[60]

No less important than these tangible benefits were the psychological benefits of the varsity sport club designation, which differentiated Cougar Crew from other student clubs and signaled that Cougar oarsmen were putting forth countless hours, competing against increasingly competitive varsity programs, and meeting standards beyond the expectations of standard-run student clubs.[61] Unlike during the Struckmeyer years, when the administrative line was always, "If we do it for you, we have to do it for the Tiddlywinks Club as well," under the leadership of Cougar Crew superfan President Elson S. Floyd and the stewardship of UREC administrators like Joanne Greene and Matt Shaw, WSU was now acknowledging the efforts and successes of Cougar Crew. The emerging self-identity of the crew was itself reflected in the unofficial motto of those years: "Club in name only."[62]

Another important development during the Arthur years was the reemergence of the women's club team. In 2009, Arthur Ericsson was laying in bed one morning with his eyes closed, and it hit him: "Lightweight women at WSU don't have a way to row—we should start a team as part of men's crew. We have boats and oars; all we need to figure out is how to provide coaching, and then we can put the word out and start recruiting, and it will enrich a whole bunch of athletes' lives and bring even more energy and support to our club team."[63]

Ericsson's idea, as idealistic and inclusive as it sounded, was supported by UREC, whose primary mission was expanding student participation in university clubs. However, the concept was initially met with disapproval by club officers, who worried about spreading the club's resources too thinly, and by the varsity women, who felt that the men's club was infringing on their turf. Of course, the varsity women did not support lightweights, so Arthur felt justified in expanding into that void, but when it became hard to recruit an entire team of just lightweight women, the women's club expanded into the open women's category in 2016, raising questions anew from some officers, recent alumni, and again from the varsity women. Some on the men's side, with their "club in name only" mentality, felt more affinity for the women's varsity than for the new women's team. Others simply worried about the new women's team carrying their own weight, similar to the concerns voiced in the 1970s over the founding of the original women's club.

Despite these concerns, Arthur was adamant that supporting a women's team was the right thing for Cougar Crew—it expanded access and partic-ipation, increased club membership, and moreover reconnected disinherited female club alumni back to the team, closing the circle in the club's unfinished history. One alumnus told him that rekindling the women's club was "like going back to our roots when we were all part of the same club."[64] Those first years saw some notable achievements on the women's team, including Breanna Trimble and Shayla Boyle winning gold and silver in the pair event at WIRAs in consecutive years—the silver medal was for the open weight event, even though they were both lightweights. "Being able to medal as lightweights was not only a huge accomplishment to us, but it proved to us that our hard work paid off," said Trimble. "All of the extra practices, all of the technical work as well as the hard effort in land workouts were all worth it."[65]

These developments—from winning on the water and achieving var-sity sport club status to forming a women's club—required ceaseless energy, enthusiasm, and leadership from the club's student athletes. They also required fundraising and more fundraising: tables and chairs, erg-a-thons, rent-a-rower, "rowpocalypse." The need was endless, and the pace was relentless. Student leaders in the 2000s were doing more than at any time in Cougar Crew his-tory. In the 1980s, for example, the vice commodore ran winter workouts.

"No rates, no rudder, no regrets!" Such was the motto of the 2015 Women's Lightweight 4+ who won a silver medal at the American Collegiate Rowing Association
(ACRA) championships in Gainesville, Georgia, despite having no functional stroke
watch and a borrowed shell with a broken rudder. They overcame their circumstances and rowed through Georgia Tech in the last 300 meters to place second.
From stern to bow: Rachel Crowther, Ashley Vu, Allison Thomas, Katie Fowler, and
coxswain Sidney Cross. Photo Credit: Catherine Weatbrook.

By the time Andy Winters was vice commodore in 2007–08, the duties for
that position alone included working with UREC to organize vans, filling out
paperwork for travel funding, managing the logistics of travel itself—including booking plane tickets and lodging—*and* organizing crew fundraising
efforts, which was itself a full-time job.[66]

The tasks of crew officers proliferated, as did the number of offices. For-
merly, the positions included commodore, vice commodore, and treasurer.
In the 2000s, four new ones were added: historian, publisher, webmaster,
and UREC liaison. The work of pushing the club forward on all fronts was
rewarding but also exhausting for the rowers and their coaches alike. As they
labored into the night to take down tents in the aftermath of home football
games, Arthur sometimes wondered how it was possible he had any rowers
left at all.[67] He and his crew wanted to focus on rowing, but it seemed there
were innumerable chores to be completed before they could take a stroke.

Fortunately, during these years of endless activity, rising expectations,
as well as increasing financial pressures, the crew benefited from greater

alumni support. Not only was the CCAA helping to bolster club initiatives, but alumni were emerging to contribute more money to take the pressure off student athletes and their coaches. In 2010, for example, Tom Caudill, who rowed lightweight with Tim Richards in the late 1970s, spearheaded the Power Ten campaign, which encouraged alumni to donate ten dollars a month so that student athletes could spend less time fundraising and more time rowing. "Given the meager compensation to our coaches, the tireless effort of the rowers, …and given the hand-me-down shells in which they race, I had a difficult time looking eye to eye with persons such as Coach Arthur Ericsson," wrote Caudill. "As an alum…I was both embarrassed and ashamed that we… cannot do more for those who strive to maintain a tradition of which we were and are a part."[68]

Class Day continued to grow during these years, attracting more alumni back to Pullman for the large banquet that culminated in a silent auction that began to yield more revenues for the crew than all its other fundraisers combined. In 2013, at the club's fortieth anniversary celebration, the club grossed $45,000 at the banquet alone—and that number continued to grow.[69] Individuals like Ernie Iseminger and Ken Struckmeyer also stepped forward to help the crew by purchasing boats or giving cash donations.

Increased funds from the alumni, however, did not solve all of Cougar Crew's problems. It was still a club whose ambitions sometimes outmatched its reach. As it always had, the crew was prone to expand and contract, get faster and slower, in cycles related to several factors, including the quality of coaching, the success of recruiting, and the enthusiasm of student leadership. Ericsson always understood the fortunes of Cougar Crew to be largely a numbers game. By 2016, the crew was healthier and stronger and more competitive than when he had arrived, but the number of novice recruits was in steady decline. A series of graduate assistants had not recruited and retained the volume of rowers needed to feed the varsity—the glory days of 2010, when Julia Gamache had more rowers than she could put in boats, seemed a distant memory. Something needed to be done.

In fall 2016, Arthur became the novice coach. He always had enjoyed teaching beginners how to row. As novice coach, he could do that and, hopefully, retain more oarsmen who would move up to varsity. The decision reflected Arthur's complete lack of ego. Not many head coaches would give up the more prestigious varsity eight to coach the novices, but Arthur cared nothing for prestige. He did care about the health of the program, and his move to novice coach might have restored the crew to top form had not the varsity crew also begun to hemorrhage rowers. Arthur was used to chopping wood and carrying water for Cougar Crew, but in his last two years, ever-greater efforts were not yielding greater results. The crew was like a giant boulder and Arthur was like Sisyphus, straining mightily but losing ground. He had been an uncomplaining servant of the crew, a calm Zen Master who maintained his Buddha smile despite circumstances. And yet, it was clear by 2016–17 that all the effort he was expending was no longer pushing the crew upwards.

Ericsson had laid the foundation for the renaissance of Cougar Crew in the 2000s, one that included on-the-water victories as well as off-the-water successes. And yet, like Struckmeyer, Iseminger, and other head coaches before him, Arthur's decisions about how to run the club became increasingly subject to the ongoing debate within the Cougar Crew community over what it meant to be a "club." The new women's team was a potent example. For Arthur, the creation of a women's lightweight team, and later an open weight club program, was about fostering more opportunities for students to row, and achieving that goal alone justified its existence. As competitive as anyone, Arthur was, at his core, more concerned with introducing students to rowing than producing fast boats (although he was motivated to do both).

For others—some of the men's officers in those years—the driving goal of the club was fielding competitive boats, not simply expanding participation (although they were motivated to do both). These were never mutually exclusive goals. Fielding competitive boats required expanding participation, something that Arthur well understood. But diverting club resources and equipment away from the men's team, with its stated purpose of winning WIRA medals, to a women's club program that seemed to be more focused on participation than competition was, to some oarsmen and recent alumni, a betrayal of the varsity sport club ethos that now defined the crew. To others it was the epitome of the club ethos. Was a club sport primarily about athletic excellence or participation? Could both approaches peacefully coexist? And what about other values, such as leadership, personal growth, and fellowship, which could be found not just on the water but in the CCAA boardroom, on the UREC club committee, and in the Fieldhouse before and after football games as club members wrestled with tables, chairs, and tents? What should be the ethos and the direction of the club?

These longstanding debates within Cougar Crew played out during the hiring process for a new head coach when Arthur decided, in the spring of 2017, to return to Sacramento and become executive director and head junior coach at the River City Rowing Club. The hiring committee—consisting of UREC representatives, club alumni, and current rowers—interviewed three candidates, and the UREC representatives supported a candidate who reflected the values of participation over competition while the alumni and current rowers gravitated toward the candidate who embodied the competitive values of the varsity club ethos. In the end, they chose the latter candidate, Peter Brevick, a former WSU rower, commodore, and novice coach, who had left WSU to gain national team coaching experience before returning as head coach.

Brevick wanted to make the crew faster, but he also understood what it meant to be a club rower at WSU. He had rowed for and coached under Arthur, for whom he had tremendous fondness and respect. "There was no one who did as good a job for as little money for as long as Arthur Ericsson," contended Brevick. It was a fitting closure to the Ericsson era, which began with one Brevick as commodore and ended with another Brevick as coach. In 2018, Coach Peter Brevick and his crew christened a new shell the *Zen Master*, named in honor of Arthur Ericsson.

Conclusion

With the hiring of Peter Brevick, the gains of the Reawakening were secure, and nothing could have been more telling of that than the hiring process itself, which involved a national search with multiple candidates. It was a professional changeover that resulted in the hiring of a professional coach who was primed to take the club to the next level. Cougar Crew had arrived at a place of professionalism and organizational stability where this was now possible. Behind it all was the unique connection between rowers and former rowers, fostered by the CCAA.

The club community was now larger and more prosperous than it had ever been. Tim Richards and the CCAA had established relationships with WSU presidents, regents, and administrators. The club had also finally developed the kind of relationship with the women's varsity team that was originally intended. Most importantly, the CCAA remained centrally committed to cultivating student leadership, not simply raising money. Cougar Crew had always been a vehicle for developing character, but now the club was more than just an athletic proving ground. It was also a crucible for the development of student leaders on multiple fronts, providing, in the words of Tim Richards, "life lessons that really matter" to hundreds of students.[70]

The Reawakening was about more than winning races or growing the club endowment. It was about identity and community—finding one's place among a tribe of kindred spirits. It gave present rowers a greater sense that this thing they were doing every day on the Snake River was more than just exercise or athletics. It was something greater than themselves. As a freshman in Arthur's first year of coaching, Karl Huhta was there at the beginning of the Reawakening. He was there at the 2005 Class Day. "I saw what it meant to rowers from the 1970s who were coming back to Pullman," he remembered. It forced him think about the importance of Cougar Crew from a broader perspective than that of a college freshman. "There is more to this than just us here right now," he realized. "This means a lot to a lot of people."[71]

Karl Huhta (2002–06)

I miss the guys I rowed with. I miss being with them every day. I do feel like I was pretty good at staying in the moment and appreciating and being grateful for the opportunity to be rowing at Washington State. You don't realize how good you have it when all you have to do is go to class and row. One thing I learned rowing at WSU is that hard work can get you everything. You don't need a lot, but if you have the right attitude and the right work ethic, you can produce a lot of really good results. The things I took away from my time with WSU Men's Crew have been life-changing. I think about everything we had to do just to be able to row, all the work that went into what we did outside of practice to be successful.

Arthur Ericsson, Head Coach (2004–17)

My thirteen years at WSU were always very rewarding. Every year, there were inevitable challenges to persevere through, but I always felt that support was available from alumni or the university. I am proud of how the team developed over the course of my time there. The challenge to make a fast program was the most important one, and we had many highlights, but it proved difficult to keep it moving in only one direction. Every season we made the best of it that we could. Each rower that finished out the season earned my respect, and for those who finished it through the end of their senior year, I am most grateful and know that they have true passion for the sport and will have an inner strength with them for the rest of their lives. I've considered myself so lucky to have been able to coach at WSU. Each rower and coxswain, male and female, has made a lasting impression on me, which I will fondly remember.

EPILOGUE

Overcoming 2020

Despite their discouragement, especially for the seniors, in not having a racing season, generally speaking they are surprisingly upbeat. They are doing virtual workouts, running, encouraging membership, and working hard to retain team members for next year. They are having ongoing conversations for recruiting this summer and into the fall. The current team is demonstrating what we all felt those years ago when we pulled a blade for the Cougs—stepping forward in the face of adversity with that inherent drive that defines Cougar Crew. It is reminiscent of a shell that lived in our shell house years ago that many of you may remember—*Against All Odds*.

—CCAA chair, Tim Richards, March 31, 2020

It's been hard to be a rowing team this past year.

—Head Coach Peter Brevick, March 20, 2021

At the end of the 1973 spring season, Cougar Crew celebrated its first banquet at Boyer Park. Dick Erickson, the legendary coach of UW, gave the keynote. "Look at what you guys have started," he told the club. "You guys come back here in fifty years and you won't believe what this has grown into."[1] In March 2020, the club planned to do just that, organizing the largest "Cougar Crew Days" celebration in its fifty-year history, a multiday event that would amount to a marathon of mixers, meals, fundraising activities, commemorative presentations, and, of course, rowing. The CCAA took an active role in organizing the multifaceted gala, creating a Cougar Crew Days program committee consisting of cochairs Shayla Boyle and Griffin Berger, both rowers from the 2010s, longtime coach Ken Struckmeyer, along with Rich Ray, Kari Ranten, and Tom Anderson from the 1970s, and Vicky O'Dell and Katie Fowler from the late 1980s.

For the banquet, the crowning event of the days-long affair, the committee assigned Dave Emigh and Tammy Crawford the task of curating history presentations that would involve at least twenty former rowers—and that was just one of the many presentations scheduled. There would also be alumni speaking on various topics—Ernie Iseminger on the crew endowment; Tim Richards on the CCAA; Bob Appleyard (a USRA rowing official) on the future of rowing; Paul Enquist and Kris Norelius on their gold medal victories; and Sean Halstead, a former WSU rower and Air Force veteran who broke his spine in a helicopter accident and became a three-time Paralympian, on his remarkable life story.

There would be speeches by WSU President Kirk Schulz as well as Trevor Vernon of the University of Washington Board of Rowing Stewards. Two families were to be recognized: the Brevicks, who have produced more WSU rowers, men and women, than any other; and the Cooks, who lost their daughter Cristy Cay in that tragic 1979 car accident. Of course, there would also be food, drinks, music, and auctions. Hundreds—*thousands*—of volunteer hours had gone into organizing what would be the grandest Cougar Crew Days celebration ever. Over six hundred rowers, alumni, and crew supporters were expected to gather in Beasley Coliseum to witness the festivities.

Then COVID-19 changed everything. Cougar Crew Days was scheduled for March 19–21, at the end of WSU's spring break. It was precisely the moment when universities across the nation began to shut down and send students home to finish their courses online. The dominoes fell quickly. Two weeks prior to the event, the WSU administration had not yet restricted large gatherings, but the signs were ominous. The Murrow Symposium, scheduled for the same weekend, was postponed. The CCAA had to decide quickly what to do. For a club that was used to facing hardship and prided itself on its competitive go-get-'em spirit, there was a desire, especially among the current athletes and younger alumni, to push forward. Let the show go on! Older members of the CCAA board were more cautious. Was it prudent to ask people to get on planes and attend a large social gathering in Washington state, which at that point was the West Coast center of the pandemic? One of the program committee members, Rich Ray, for example, had been told by his employer that if he visited Washington voluntarily, he could not return to the office for two weeks. If he was under such pressure, others would be facing similar situations, not to mention that they would be jeopardizing their own health as well as that of their families.

Beyond health concerns, there were numerous economic calculations to be made. Tim Richards was poised to ship to Pullman thousands of dollars' worth of beef, which would be a total loss if the banquet were cancelled at the last minute. The crew had rented out Beasley Coliseum at a significant cost—if they cancelled immediately, they could be reimbursed, but if they held firm, they might lose the entire amount. The debate and the vote that followed underscored the democratic nature of Cougar Crew. It was a club, which meant there *could* be a debate followed by a vote. If Cougar Crew was part of WSU's Athletic Department, there would have been no debating or voting—the team would have taken its orders from the athletic director. In the end, the vote was extremely close, but on March 9, a decision was made by the CCAA to cancel the celebration and reschedule for the following year to prevent the possibility of an unplanned, last-minute cancellation. "We are all disappointed," lamented Tim Richards in an email to the Cougar Crew community, "but this decision will ensure that our fiftieth celebration will truly be the best it can be."[2] In March 2021, Cougar Crew did indeed gather again to celebrate its shared heritage and raise money for the current program—this time on Zoom, with designated breakout rooms by decade for alumni to reconnect with their former teammates. It wasn't the same as mingling together in the CUB Ballroom or at Rico's, but it highlighted the adaptable, resilient nature of the club and its loyal alumni, who planned to finally return to Pullman and celebrate fifty years of Cougar Crew in March 2022.

For alumni who had intended to return to Pullman for the gala in March 2020, the pandemic was a disappointment and an inconvenience. But for head coach Peter Brevick and his rowers, the situation was far more impactful. In the span of two days, from Wednesday, March 11, to Friday, March 13, 2020, *all* their spring races were cancelled. That Friday, Brevick had his team on the Snake River for what turned out to be their last practice of the season. The team gathered, teary-eyed, the following morning to elect officers for the coming year, realizing it might be their last time together as a unit. For seniors, their WSU rowing career came to an abrupt and disappointing end. Practices stopped. Classes went online. Many rowers left Pullman and returned home. Brevick was characteristically undeterred. He sent them home with training plans. The team used their smart phones to maintain contact as well as to chart their workouts.

Brevick and his rowers maintained a positive attitude, but as the fall of 2020 approached, it was clear that this would be a year like none other in Cougar Crew's fifty-year history. Their fall races were cancelled. Their practices were limited. They could not row together in an eight-oared shell, which was their primary racing craft. The team could only row by household, which meant that most had to row in singles, pairs, or doubles. And coxswains got no work at all. The daily ritual of driving to the river together was lost as the crew reverted to private vehicles or bicycles to convey themselves to Wawawai. They trained mostly on ergometers placed twenty feet apart on the outdoor basketball courts behind the Student Recreation Center. It was a year filled

Because of the pandemic, the crew could not row in eights, so they took to the river in small boats, mostly doubles and singles. Pictured here is varsity coxswain Jeremiah Lee in February 2021. Coxswains had no eights and fours to pilot, so they took to the Snake River to row with their teammates. Photo courtesy of Peter Brevick.

with hardship and social isolation for Cougar rowers, who struggled to stay focused and train with intensity without the close competition and encouragement of their boatmates.[3]

Nor could Brevick's team recruit among the freshman as they normally had. Brevick and novice coach Devon McCornack understood that good recruiting was essential to maintaining a vibrant, growing program. Typically, the team recruited during the WSU ALIVE orientation sessions, using the power of real-life human interaction to entice novices to the Snake River. But when those sessions moved online, the crew had to pursue other methods, such as "tabling" for hours in strategic locations where freshmen gathered and relying on social media and direct messaging. Commodore Henry McRae spearheaded these innovative outreach methods, but the going was tough. There were less than a thousand freshmen on campus in the fall of 2020, down from five thousand in a normal year, and most of them were holed up inside their dormitories. "At times it was extremely challenging, tabling for hours and hardly talking to any freshmen," lamented McRae, "But every day there

During the pandemic, Cougar Crew adapted. They could not erg indoors, so they worked out on the basketball courts behind the WSU Student Recreation Center, even in the snow, as pictured here in February 2021. Clockwise from bottom left: Nolan Hubbell, Cedar Cunningham, Devon McCornack (assistant coach), Christian Rorie, Ryan Sander, Sean Swett, Steven Collett (whose mother, Lori Taylor, rowed in the late 1980s), Commodore Henry McRae, Don Kelly, and Jeremiah Lee. Photo courtesy of Peter Brevick.

was good effort and attitude." The positive attitude of McRae and his teammates remarkably attracted sixteen novices, but this number was far below normal. Half of them were training virtually online, and only two of them had rowed on the water as the spring of 2021 approached.[4]

Cougar Crew pushed onward nonetheless. Brevick saw opportunity in the crisis, understanding that the best crews were the most resilient ones. "Handling the COVID-19 situation is certainly an opportunity to deal with the unexpected," he reasoned, "and the team is dealing with it well."[5] Indeed, Cougar Crew weathered the storm better than any other club program on the West Coast. Many rowing clubs were shut down because of COVID-19 outbreaks or simply a lack of rowers or resources. Cougar Crew established responsible protocols and then made sure that *everyone* followed them. They tested, and they rowed with masks. In spring 2021, the team volunteered at vaccination clinics, which not only contributed to the greater good but allowed them to get their vaccines. Their efforts were rewarded when, for the first time in over a year, Cougar Crew returned to racing, conducting its Class Day event at Wawawai.

For Coach Brevick and his rowers, the pandemic was but one more challenge added to those that already existed for Cougar Crew as it moved into the 2020s. When Peter Brevick took over the team in 2017, he realized that his rowers were more burdened with obligations and more stressed out than ever before. Gone were the days when college was a relaxing time filled mostly with youthful shenanigans, punctuated by last-minute cramming sessions. Academic expectations and the demands on his rowers' time and resources seemed to be constantly on the rise. Academic programs were pushing internships, study abroad programs, and disciplinary extracurriculars of every sort. With the rising cost of tuition and a competitive job market, there was increasing pressure to maximize the academic outcomes of a college education. Many students, and their parents—who were often footing the bill—found it harder to justify seemingly superfluous activities like club rowing. Students could afford neither the time nor the money for a club sport as demanding as Cougar Crew.

Added to these stresses was the impact that smart phones and social media were having on his young rowers' overstimulated lives. Connection was good—but too much connection left precious little time for the intense focus and meditative mindset required for rowing. Brevick remembered his own experience in college, way back in the early 2000s, before everyone owned cell phones, not to mention smart phones. Life seemed simpler. It was easier to unplug, which was precisely the goal of traveling to the Snake River Canyon every day. Not only were his rowers more harried than ever, but he realized that now, despite their impressive academic achievements, they often struggled with social relationships as they happened in real time. It occurred to him that his rowers were used to resolving problems and working out personality conflicts online, but not face-to-face. This created a strange disconnect. If there was a problem in the boat, could it be resolved satisfactorily without the oarsmen addressing each other directly, in person?

There were also other disconnects: academically advanced students who could create websites but couldn't figure out how to put riggers on their racing shells. It was a strange world, full of anxiety, pressure, and obstacles to overcome.[6]

Further, there were growing concerns about diversity, equity, and inclusion as Cougar Crew looked toward extending the shared experience of club rowing to historically underrepresented groups.[7] Finally, there was the angst-producing possibility that *no one* would be rowing at Wawawai in the future if the salmon-killing lower Snake River dams, including Lower Granite, were breeched to allow the river to run free again. What would the future bring?

Fortunately for Brevick and his crew, the solution was the same as it had been for fifty years: get down to the Snake River Canyon and row. It was the great equalizer; the great cure; the central experience that unified WSU rowers across the generations. Fundamentally, Cougar Crew was still the same in 2020 as it had been in 1970. There were new challenges and more noise and interference, but the act of rowing was as important as ever—*more important*. In a society where people suffered from nature deficit disorder, where they were overwrought, where they couldn't work out their differences, Cougar Crew seemed to offer a catch-all solution to every problem: place eight unique individuals, without their smart phones, into a thin boat in the midst of a majestic river canyon and have them focus on the monotonous process of rowing in perfect symmetry, of blending their eight identities into one eight-oared organism, even if just for a fleeting moment. In a world of false cures and promises of instant happiness, rowing—a ritual of shared suffering amidst the grandeur of nature—seemed to offer one source of hope.

What better gift to give young people in an anxious age than a counter-cultural, anti-technological activity that promises to boost their capacity to work together and overcome whatever is coming next. What better education can be gained? "Harmony, balance, and rhythm. They're the three things that stay with you your whole life," said George Yeoman Pocock, the legendary Seattle boatbuilder. "Without them civilization is out of whack. And that's why an oarsman, when he goes out in life, he can fight it, he can handle life. That's what he gets from rowing."[8]

ACKNOWLEDGMENTS

I am so grateful to everyone in the Cougar Crew community who shared their stories with me. During the tumultuous year of 2020, it was truly a blessing to interview over ninety current and former WSU rowers, coaches, and administrators. Their stories saved me. Each interview renewed my faith in humanity, reminding me what diverse humans can achieve working together toward collective goals.

Each interview and every story sent to me by former rowers conveyed the passion, commitment, grit, and humor of fifty years of Cougar Crew—a reservoir of memory and experience so deep it could fill the Snake River Canyon. This is not a *definitive* history of Cougar Crew—it is an *interpretive* history that uses some stories and individuals as emblematic of a larger narrative. I am sorry that this book—already well over the word limit prescribed by my forbearing editors at WSU Press—could not include more stories from more former rowers from all the eras of Cougar Crew, for they are all deserving. I am also sorry that I cannot acknowledge here everyone who contributed to this book. There are just too many of you who helped me along the way. This manuscript was truly a community effort, but I alone am responsible for any mistakes or misinterpretations in its pages.

This book began with two lunches in Pullman in 2018. The first was with Coach Ken Struckmeyer—the backbone of Cougar Crew—who gave me his blessing, his memories, and provided lists of former rowers for me to contact. This project would have gone nowhere without his support and encouragement. The second lunch was with former rower Doug Engle, who has been a mainstay of the club's success since he arrived on the WSU campus in 1975. Doug and I began emailing in 2017 as the idea of this project took shape. He provided critical assistance, feedback, advice, and perspective throughout the entire project. I never waited more than a few hours for one of my email queries to be answered by Doug, who should have just written the book himself. Ken and Doug, along with Tim Richards, Ernie Iseminger, and Patricia Deisher also donated funds that made it possible for this book to be produced with color photographs.

Rich Ray—truly the bard of Cougar Crew—was a generous and eloquent interlocuter (likely a word I learned from him) who was willing to take my calls at all hours, listened to my ideas, and responded to my questions with grace and equipoise (another word Ray taught me). I am still waiting for his Cougar Crew memoir.

Mike Klier sent me treatises on the physics of rowing, which were far beyond my grasp, and then took the time to patiently explain them to me as he would to a child, until my brain caught a small flicker of recognition. I was the lucky beneficiary of Mike's brilliance in connecting the science of rowing with the history and philosophy of rowing, both at WSU and beyond.

Kathy (Figon) Katz gave me a window into what it was like to be a young woman in a men's sport in the mid-1970s; her valuable feedback on the manuscript helped me formulate the title and clarify my primary themes. Mo (Carrick) Kelley enthusiastically embraced my project and sent me photographs and names of people to contact, including that of her close friend Kris Norelius, whose incredible rowing odyssey beyond WSU deserves a book-length treatment. Andy Moore and Roberta "Berta" Player both helped me capture the essence of that first year of women's rowing, especially the importance of Anne Marie Dousset, whom I would have loved to meet. Jean "Snake Action" Patterson's hilarious and lively interview made me wonder if those rowers from the mid-1970s had more fun than any other generation in the history of Cougar Crew.

Paul Enquist graciously granted me hours of his time and patiently suffered my interruptions and many questions while providing me a year-by-year account of his incredible, circuitous journey to the gold medal. He was always willing to help, and I can see why his rowing partners, like John Biglow and Brad Lewis, were so fond of him.

A special thanks goes to my colleague Meg Woods, who was the only person beyond the WSU reviewers and Dave Emigh, to read and comment on the first draft of the entire manuscript. This book benefited greatly from Dave's knowledge, wisdom, encouragement, and generous feedback. Like a good coach, Dave gauged my mindset and made sure that his constructive criticisms encouraged rather than demoralized me. Dave also freely shared his personal letters and memorabilia with me, including a number of photographs that appear in this book

There are so many others who deserve mention: Jim Rudd and Jim Verellen for providing historical insights and documentation from the early years; David Yorozu for sending me his wonderful photographs; Gene and Carleen Dowers for sharing so many of their photographs and spending countless hours on their scanner; David Herrick for educating me on the recent history of the team and for his excellent work in reviving *The Pull Hard*, which is a great historical treasure for Cougar Crew; Ernie Iseminger for sending me contacts and information whenever I asked and sharing his amazing life story; Ole Jorgenson for reading the entire manuscript and convincing me that my treatment of the 1980s and 1990s was fair and balanced; Jess O'Dell for lending his even-handed perspective on both the men's and women's teams; Marietta "Ed" Hall for sharing with me her life in rowing; Kent McCleary for providing me new insights into our trip to Istanbul; Tim Richards for always being willing to take a call; Peter Brevick for making himself available to me whenever I needed a question answered and for taking me on bike rides through the Palouse, where he could simply power away from me if he tired of my continuous interrogations and speculations; and the Cougar Crew Alumni Association (CCAA) for its support and encouragement.

I could go on and on. I was delighted at how eager former rowers were to talk about their time in Cougar Crew, but I was never surprised. Each interview confirmed my thesis that Cougar Crew was, for most of us, the central experience of our college education. I was always struck by the through lines in that experience, no matter the era in which we rowed: friendship, community, shared sacrifice, personal growth, resilience, and the powerful natural backdrop of the Snake River Canyon.

Len Mills took beautiful photographs of the crew in the 1970s that reveal his generous, humanistic spirit. His images convey the comradery and verve of the early crew during the Bob Orr years and highlight the beauty of the sport and the Snake River Canyon. I cannot thank him enough for the time he spent with me, looking at photos and then scanning them, sending them, and of course, allowing me to use them. The next book needs to be a photographic essay of Cougar Crew that highlights Len's artistic documentation of the early 1970s.

Thanks to Mark O'English at WSU Libraries' Special Collections, who went above and beyond to help with my research in the time of COVID-19, which prevented me from actually visiting the archives. I also am indebted to Steve Bisch at WSU Tri-Cities Max E. Benitz Memorial Library for finding a way to get me every edition of the *Chinook* since 1990 at a moment's notice, even though my faculty library privileges had expired and I owed a small mortgage in library fees to WSU Libraries. Also thanks to Imelda Farias, who patiently helped me use the professional-grade scanner in the Columbia Basin College graphics department on multiple occasions.

Thanks to WSU Press's former managing editor, Beth DeWeese, who encouraged me from the beginning and helped me obtain a contingent contract for the book, without which I would not have pursued the project in full.

Of course, special thanks to current WSU Press editor-in-chief Linda Bathgate, who has been incredibly helpful, supportive, and delightful to work with throughout this entire process. Linda was amazingly forbearing, regardless of the situation. Perhaps it was her long kayak trip down the Snake River from Boyer Park, where she returned to Pullman late at night, exhausted but exhilarated, after which she seemed to understand us rowers as a peculiar subculture requiring certain accommodations. I am indebted to the entire staff at WSU Press for their efforts in bringing this project to fruition and also to copyeditor Christina Dubois for making this a better book (and especially for her heavy lifting on the endnotes).

A special thanks to the president of Columbia Basin College, Rebekah Woods, who granted me a sabbatical to write this book because she recognizes the power of professional growth and development through research and writing, even among community college teachers.

Finally, to my lovely wife, Arienne Arnold—whom I just cannot possibly thank enough for everything—and my mom, to whom this book is dedicated.

David Arnold
Richland, Washington
June 2021

APPENDIX A

Cougar Crew Head Coaches

Year	Men's Head Coach	Women's Club Coach
2021-22	Peter Brevick	Milos Aleksic
2020-21	Peter Brevick	Milos Aleksic
2019-20	Peter Brevick	Milos Aleksic
2018-19	Peter Brevick	Hugo Moon
2017-18	Peter Brevick	Hugo Moon
2016-17	Arthur Ericsson	Dave Kempsell
2015-16	Arthur Ericsson	Giles Dakin-White
2014-15	Arthur Ericsson	Giles Dakin-White
2013-14	Arthur Ericsson	Dan Thayer
2012-13	Arthur Ericsson	Dan Thayer
2011-12	Arthur Ericsson	Dan Thayer
2010-11	Arthur Ericsson	Ericsson/Julia Gamache/Thayer
2009-10	Arthur Ericsson	Emily Kohl
2008-09	Arthur Ericsson	No women's club
2007-08	Arthur Ericsson	No women's club
2006-07	Arthur Ericsson	No women's club
2005-06	Arthur Ericsson	No women's club
2004-05	Arthur Ericsson	No women's club
2003-04	Michelle Arganbright	No women's club
2002-03	Michelle Arganbright	No women's club
2001-02	Shawn Bagnall	No women's club
2000-01	Shawn Bagnall	No women's club
1999-00	Hugh Dodd	No women's club
1998-99	Hugh Dodd	No women's club
1997-98	Ernie Iseminger	No women's club
1996-97	Ernie Iseminger	No women's club

1995-96	Ernie Iseminger	No women's club
1994-95	Ernie Iseminger	No women's club
1993-94	Ernie Iseminger	No women's club
1992-93	Ken Struckmeyer/ Gene Dowers	No women's club
1991-92	Ken Struckmeyer	No women's club
1990-91	Ken Struckmeyer	No women's club
1989-90	Ken Struckmeyer	Jess O'Dell
1988-89	Ken Struckmeyer	Jess O'Dell
1987-88	Ken Struckmeyer	Thad O'Dell
1986-87	Ken Struckmeyer	Piotr Rylski
1985-86	Ken Struckmeyer	Gene Dowers
1984-85	Ken Struckmeyer	Bob Appleyard
1983-84	Ken Struckmeyer	Rich Ray
1982-83	Ken Struckmeyer	Rich Ray
1981-82	Ken Struckmeyer	Gene Dowers
1980-81	Ken Struckmeyer	Gene Dowers
1979-80	Ken Struckmeyer	Gene Dowers
1978-79	Ken Struckmeyer	Gene Dowers
1977-78	Ken Struckmeyer	Steve Porter
1976-77	Ken Struckmeyer	Doug Kee
1975-76	Ken Struckmeyer	Ron Neal
1974-75	Ken Struckmeyer	Anne Marie Dousset
1973-74	Ken Struckmeyer	No women's club
1972-73	Bob Orr	No women's club
1971-72	Bob Orr	No women's club
1970-71		
1969-70		

APPENDIX B

Cougar Crew Commodores

Year	Men's Commodore	Women's Commodore
2021-22	Ciara McCall	Kamira Hamilton
2020-21	Henry McRae	Sabrina Amundson
2019-20	John Michael Najarian	Anne Spellman
2018-19	Devon McCornack	Anne Spellman
2017-18	Devon McCornack	Harlow Bronstein
2016-17	August Boyle	Harlow Bronstein
2015-16	Griffin Berger	Katie Fowler
2014-15	Max Vaughn	Ashley Vu
2013-14	William Miedema	Simone Parker
2012-13	Eric DeMaris	Shayla Boyle
2011-12	Andrew King	No women's club
2010-11	Andrew King	No women's club
2009-10	Mitch Williams	No women's club
2008-09	Andrew Winters	No women's club
2007-08	Karl Huhta	No women's club
2006-07	Chris Seaman	No women's club
2005-06	Peter Brevick	No women's club
2004-05	Danny Brevick	No women's club
2003-04	Danny Brevick	No women's club
2002-03	Carl Cronk	No women's club
2001-02	Jeff Olson	No women's club
2000-01	Aaron Hustead	No women's club
1999-00	Lucas Olona	No women's club
1998-99	Jason Hizer	No women's club
1997-98	Shawn Bagnall	No women's club
1996-97	Thad Smith	No women's club

1995-96	Mike Slotemaker	No women's club
1994-95	Phil Demaray	No women's club
1993-94	Geoff Owen	No women's club
1992-93	Mike Williams	No women's club
1991-92	Sean Powers	No women's club
1990-91	Thom Eldridge	No women's club
1989-90	Dave DeLorenzo	Marietta "Ed" Hall
1988-89	Kent McCleary	Stacey (Gosney) Burge
1987-88	Ernie Iseminger	Tracy (Vadset) Landboe
1986-87	Dave Reeder	Annie (Calvin) Kendall
1985-86	Jess O'Dell	Loresa Soviskov
1984-85	Jim Gressard	Tami Gill
1983-84	John Sanders	Lisa (Stivers) Tintinger and Mary Jean Sheenstra
1982-83	Tracy Pierson	Tammy (Boggs) Crawford
1981-82	Brett Purtzer	Tammy (Boggs) Crawford
1980-81	Mike Noble	Tammy (Boggs) Crawford
1979-80	Tim Richards	Kathleen Randall
1978-79	Rich Ray	Kari (Buringrud) Ranten
1977-78	Steve Wells	Kari (Buringrud) Ranten
1976-77	Fred Darvill	Kristi Norelius and Jean Patterson
1975-76	Mike Kimbrell	Sharon McKendrick
1974-75	Jim Austin	Andrea "Andy" Moore
1973-74	Ron Neal	No women's club
1972-73	Jim Verellen	No women's club

NOTES

Introduction

1. Ken Struckmeyer, *The Pull Hard* 2, no. 1 (December 1974): 1.

2. Angela Duckworth, *Grit: The Power of Passion and Perseverance* (New York: Simon and Schuster, 2016), 7. It should be noted that a body of scholarship critiques the concept of grit, asserting most notably that students from harsh environments often do not have the social, economic, emotional, or family stability that allows them the privilege of using "grit" to succeed. See, for example, David Denby, "The Problem With Grit," *The New Yorker*, June 21, 2016, https://www.newyorker.com/culture/culture-desk/the-limits-of-grit.

3. Washington State University Rowing Club, "Constitution," 1971, private collection.

4. Rowing at WSU has always been more inclusive and accessible to non-elites than at exclusive private colleges; but, as Esha Bhattacharya writes, "The absence of racial diversity in rowing has plagued the sport since its foundation." See Esha Bhattacharya, "Diversity in Rowing, or the Lack Thereof," *Row2K*, October 8, 2020, https://www.row2k.com/features/5280/Diversity-in-Rowing--or-the-Lack-Thereof/. See also Arshay Cooper, *A Most Beautiful Thing: The True Story of America's First All-Black High School Rowing Team* (New York: Flatiron Books, 2015). Since 2020, USRowing, the national governing body of the sport, has begun to focus more attention on diversity, equity, and inclusion within the sport of rowing. See *USRowing*, "Statement on Racism and Injustice," June 2, 2020, https://usrowing.org/news/2020/6/2/general-usrowing-statement.aspx.

5. Jing Wang and Jonathan Shiveley, "The Impact of Extracurricular Activity on Student Academic Performance," California State University, Sacramento, Office of Institutional Research, 2009, https://www.cair.org/wp-content/uploads/sites/474/2015/07/Wang-Student-Activity-Report-2009.pdf; C. Moore and N. Shulock, "Student progress toward degree completion: Lessons from the research literature," California State University, Sacramento, Institute for Higher Education Leadership and Policy, September 2009, https://files.eric.ed.gov/fulltext/ED513825.pdf; G. D. Kuh, J. Kinzie, J. A. Buckley, B. K. Bridges, and J. C. Hayek, "What Matters to Student Success: A Review of the Literature," commissioned paper for NPEC, July 2006, https://nces.ed.gov/npec/pdf/kuh_team_report.pdf.

6. Roger Crawford, "Roger Reconnoiters the Correlation of Forces," *Pullhard.redux* 1.1 (Fall 2000): 1.

Chapter One

1. Rick Coffman, "In the Future," *Daily Evergreen*, January 8, 1969, 9.

2. "Student Attempt to Start Rowing Club with Meeting," *Daily Evergreen*, November 12, 1970, 5; "Rowing Club Meets Tonight," *Daily Evergreen*, December 3, 1970, 6; Dave Emigh, "Notes from Dave Emigh papers," Dave Emigh papers, private collection.

3. Pam Chaney, "Sun Begins to Shine on Cougar Crew," *Daily Evergreen*, April 25, 1974, 10.

4. "Draft Law Changes Reviewed at Meeting," *Daily Evergreen*, October 22, 1971, 1.

5. "U.S. To Mine All Vietnam Ports," *Daily Evergreen*, May 9, 1972, 1; "Anti-war Group Asks for CUB Bread Boycott," *Daily Evergreen*, May 9, 1972, 3; "Arabs Hijack Belgian Airliner," May 10, 1972, 2; "Anti-War Students to Occupy CUB," May 10, 1972, 1.

10. Emigh, "Notes."

6. Adriana Janovich, "Cougar Crew Profiles," *Washington State Magazine* (Winter 2019), "Web extra," https://magazine.wsu.edu/web-extra/cougar-crew-profiles/; Emigh, "Notes."

7. "Student Attempt to Start Rowing Club with Meeting," *Daily Evergreen*, November 12, 1970, 5.

8. "Rowing Club Meets Tonight," *Daily Evergreen*, December 3, 1970, 6.

9. Mike Klier, in discussion with author, 2019–21.

10. Emigh, "Notes."

11. David T. Pratt, "In the Beginning: Recollections of Early Days of Cougar Crew," March 25, 2010, David T. Pratt papers, private collection. At the University of Washington, Pratt had rowed for the famed Al Ulbrickson, who coached the "boys in the boat" to an Olympic gold medal at Berlin in 1936. After Pratt graduated from UW, he began active duty as a second lieutenant in the Marine Corps while coaching rowing at Seattle's Green Lake Crew Club. Because of his experience rowing and coaching, as well as his mechanical engineering degree, in 1958 Pratt was reassigned to the United States Naval Academy as an officer instructor of marine engineering and coach of the academy's lightweight crew. Pratt resigned his commission after three years to pursue graduate work at the University of California, Berkeley. After obtaining his masters at Berkeley, Pratt returned to Annapolis, this time as assistant professor of marine engineering and coach of the freshman crew. He coached the plebes through spring 1964, and then the ever-ambitious Pratt went back to Berkeley, this time for his doctorate, which he obtained just prior to arriving at WSU in fall 1968 as an assistant professor of mechanical engineering.

12. Pratt, "In the Beginning." Erickson and Pratt had rowed together at UW in the mid 1950s but had become even closer in the early 1960s when Pratt was coaching the freshmen (plebes) at the U.S. Naval Academy and Erickson was freshman coach at the Massachusetts Institute of Technology (MIT).

13. Pratt, "In the Beginning"; "Student's Design Selected For Club's Storage House," *Daily Evergreen*, May 11, 1971, 7. The latter article notes that Pratt "asked James Stanek, assistance professor of architecture, to help design the project," which was then "assigned to 60 fourth-year design students."

14. Janovich, "Cougar Crew Profiles."

15. Pratt, "In the Beginning."

16. Doug Engle, in discussion with author, 2017–21.

17. Klier, discussion.

18. Kenneth A. Struckmeyer, speech presented at the dedication of the Ken Abbey Shell House, Wawawai, WA, March 20, 2010, Ken Struckmeyer papers, private collection.

19. "Lower Granite Lock and Dam Master Plan," July 2018, U.S. Army Corps of Engineers, Walla Walla District, https://www.nww.usace.army.mil/Portals/28/181003_revised_LGMP_main.pdf.

20. Doug Engle, email correspondence with author, fall 2017.

21. Dave Emigh, "Notes on the Formation of the WSU Crew," March 20, 2013, private collection.

22. Emigh, "Notes on the Formation."

23. Emigh, "Notes on the Formation."

24. Janovich, "Cougar Crew Profiles."

25. "Rowers Get Shell; Need Shelter Next," *Daily Evergreen*, February 12, 1971, 9.

26. Pratt, "In the Beginning"; "New Building to House Shells," *Daily Evergreen*, March 26, 1971, 9.

27. Bob Orr, in discussion with author, 2019; Janovich, "Cougar Crew Profiles."

28. Len Mills, in discussion with author, 2019–21.

29. Bob Appleyard, in discussion with author, 2020.

30. Jim Verellen, in discussion with author, 2020.

31. Appleyard, discussion.

32. Dave Emigh, in discussion with author, 2019–21.

33. Appleyard, discussion.

34. Orr, discussion.

35. Klier, discussion.

36. Jim Rudd, in discussion with author, 2019.

37. Emigh, discussion.

38. Pam Chaney, "Sun Begins to Shine on Cougar Crew," *Daily Evergreen*, April 25, 1974, 10.

39. "Gone with the Wind," *Daily Evergreen*, January 13, 1972, 1.

40. Appleyard, discussion.

41. "Rowing Club Sticks Together after Wind Loss," *Daily Evergreen*, February 4, 1972, 11; "Button Sale Aids in Replacement of Club's Losses," *Daily Evergreen*, February 15, 1972, 3.

42. Orr, discussion.

43. Klier, discussion. On the *Loyal Shoudy*'s namesake, see Daniel James Brown, *The Boys in the Boat: Nine Americans and Their Epic Quest for Gold at the 1936 Berlin Olympics* (New York: Viking, 2013), 112–13; 264; 284.

44. Orr, discussion.

45. "Wind Storm Doesn't Stop Crew," *Daily Evergreen*, March 30, 1972, 5.

46. "Interclass Meet for Rowing Club on Saturday," *Daily Evergreen*, April 21, 1972, 8.

47. "Sports Roundup," *Daily Evergreen*, April 26, 1972, 8.

48. Klier, discussion.

49. "Happenings," *Daily Evergreen*, April 26, 1972, 7.

50. Appleyard, discussion.

51. "Rowers Thirteenth in Corvallis Regatta," *Daily Evergreen*, May 2, 1972, 8.

52. Bill Knight, "Husky Crew Wins," *Seattle Post-Intelligencer*, May 14, 1972, G5; "Crew Finishes Fifth," *Daily Evergreen*, May 16, 1972, 12.

53. Jim Austin, in discussion with author, 2020.

54. "Crew to Row in Seattle," *Daily Evergreen*, November 11, 1972, 2; "Error Costs Crew Second," *Daily Evergreen*, November 14, 1972, 6.

55. "Cougar Crew Gains Respect," *Hilltopics* (June 1973): 24.

56. Steve Rowlett, email correspondence with author, August 2019.

57. "Crew to Row in Seattle," *Daily Evergreen*, November 11, 1972, 2.

58. Bob Orr, "The 1973 Rowing Season in Review," *The Pull Hard* 1, no. 1 (1973–74): 1.

59. "Crew Announces Schedule; Season Begins March 31," *Daily Evergreen*, March 8, 1973, 8.

60. Doug McBride, "WSU Crew—Black Thursday, Spring 1973." Doug McBride papers, private collection.

61. McBride, "WSU Crew."

62. Klier, discussion; Mike Kimbrell, in discussion with author, 2019.

63. Philip Irvin, "Black Thursday–I was there," *WSU Cougar Crew*, The 1970s, Where it all Began, https://www.cougarcrew.com/history/1970s.html; Mike Klier, email correspondence with author, June 2020.

64. Doug Kee, in discussion with author, 2020.

65. Appleyard, discussion.

66. Orr, "The 1973 Rowing Season," 2.

67. Orr, "The 1973 Rowing Season," 2; Orr, discussion.

68. Orr, "The 1973 Rowing Season," 3.

69. Orr, "The 1973 Rowing Season," 3.

70. Janovich, "Cougar Crew Profiles."

71. "Cougar Crew Gains Respect," *Hilltopics* (June 1973): 24.

72. Appleyard, discussion.

73. Orr, discussion; Janovich, "Cougar Crew Profiles."

Chapter Two

1. Steve Wells, in discussion with author, 2019.

2. Ken Struckmeyer, in discussion with author, 2019–21.

3. Ken Struckmeyer, "Memorandum to All Returning WSU Oarsmen and Cox'ns," June 29, 1973, 1. Doug Engle papers, private collection.

4. Doug Engle, email correspondence with author, 2017.

5. Struckmeyer, "Memorandum."

6. Wells, discussion.

7. Struckmeyer, discussion.

8. Pam Chaney, "Cougar Crew Hosts Regatta on Lake Bryan," *Daily Evergreen*, March 21, 1974, 8.

9. "Varsity Oarsmen Sweep to Easy Wins," *Daily Evergreen*, March 26, 1974, 6.

10. Ken Struckmeyer, "Struckmeyer Takes Over," *The Pull Hard* 1, no.1 (1973–74): 3.

11. Pam Chaney, "Sun Begins to Shine on Cougar Crew," *Daily Evergreen*, April 25, 1974, 10.

12. Jim Rudd, in discussion with author, 2019.

13. Brad Sleeper, in discussion with author, 2020.

14. Jim Austin, in discussion with author, 2020.

15. Struckmeyer, discussion.

16. "Crew Team has Strong Showings," *Daily Evergreen*, May 1, 1974, 8.

17. Ken Struckmeyer in *The Pull Hard* 2, no.1 (December 1974): 2.

18. Struckmeyer, discussion.

19. "Lightweight Oarsmen Edge Huskies," *Daily Evergreen*, May 7, 1974, 6.

20. Bob Appleyard in discussion with author, 2020.

21. Wikipedia contributors, "Lightweight Rowing," *Wikipedia: The Free Encyclopedia*, https://en.wikipedia.org/wiki/Lightweight_rowing (accessed May 7, 2021).

22. "Rowers Seek New Members," *Daily Evergreen*, February 13, 1974, 7; "Crew Needs Heavyweights," *Daily Evergreen*, October 15, 1975, 6; "Wanted," *Daily Evergreen*, October 20, 1976, 2.

23. Doug Engle, in discussion with author, 2017–21.

24. Kathy (Figon) Katz, in discussion with author, 2019.

25. "Crew Team has Strong Showings."

26. Rudd, discussion.

27. Appleyard, discussion.

28. "Lightweight Oarsmen Edge Huskies," *Daily Evergreen*, May 7, 1974, 6.

29. Rudd, discussion.

30. Ken Struckmeyer, "Vance Smith," *The Pull Hard* 2, no. 2 (September 1975): 7–8.

31. Fred Darvill, in discussion with author, 2020; Sleeper, discussion; Appleyard, discussion; Rudd, discussion; and Wells, discussion.

32. Dave Yorozu, in discussion with author, 2020; Struckmeyer, discussion; and Doug Kee, in discussion with author, 2020.

33. Appleyard, discussion.

34. Sleeper, discussion.

35. Darvill, discussion.

36. Kee, discussion.

37. Darvill, discussion; and Yorozu discussion.

38. Sleeper, discussion.

39. Sleeper, discussion.

40. Sleeper, discussion; Darvill, discussion; and Yorozu, discussion.

41. Ken Struckmeyer, "Western Washington—Clarkston," *The Pull Hard* 2, no. 2 (September 1975): 2; Appleyard, discussion; Sleeper, discussion; Yorozu, discussion; and Darvill, discussion.

42. "Cougars 'Scare' Husky Rowers," *Daily Evergreen*, April 15, 1975, 9.

43. Sleeper, discussion; Darvill, discussion.

44. Ken Struckmeyer, "Steward's Cup—Seattle," *The Pull Hard* 2, no. 2 (September 1975): 3; Appleyard, discussion.

45. Appleyard, discussion.

46. Ken Struckmeyer, "Western Sprints—Long Beach," *The Pull Hard* 2, no. 2 (September 1975): 3.

47. Darvill, discussion.

48. Doug Engle, email correspondence with author, 2019.

49. Engle, email, 2019.

50. Jim Carberry, "Crew: Months of Dedication," *Daily Evergreen*, May 19, 1976, 6.

51. Bob Condotta, "Respect," *Chinook '85* (Pullman: Washington State University, 1985), 36.

52. Ken Struckmeyer, "Budgets," *The Pull Hard* 2, no. 2 (September 1975): 8.

53. "Chapter 13 – Dear Pullman…." *Dr. Frank Writes* (blog), November 16, 2015, http://doctorfrankwrites.blogspot.com/2015/11/chapter-13-dear-pullman.html.

54. Ken Struckmeyer, "Western Sprints—Long Beach," and "Summer News," *The Pull Hard* 2, no. 2 (September 1975): 4, 6.

55. "Crew Left Disappointed by High Winds and Huskies," *Daily Evergreen*, April 14, 1976, 8.

56. "Crew Nips UW," *Daily Evergreen*, May 5, 1976, 6.

57. "Chapter 13."

58. Gene Dowers, in discussion with author, 2020–21.

59. Engle, email, fall 2017.

60. Jim Carberry, "Cougar Crew: California or Bust," *Daily Evergreen*, May 1, 1976, 6.

61. Carberry, "Cougar Crew."

62. Rich Ray, email correspondence with author, 2020.

63. Ray, email.

64. "Rowers Second to UW," *Daily Evergreen*, April 12, 1977, 9; "Crew," *Daily Evergreen*, April 26, 1977, 6.

65. "Crew Finishes Third," *Daily Evergreen*, May 3, 1977, 6; "New Record Set by Crew Heavies," *Daily Evergreen*, May 12, 1977, 8.

66. Steve Porter, email correspondence with author, March 2020.

67. "Oarsmen Row to Fourth," *Daily Evergreen*, May 24, 1977, 8.

68. "Men's Crew: Second in Northwest," *Chinook '77* (Pullman: Washington State University, 1977), 204.

69. *American Experience: The Boys of '36*, PBS documentary (2016), directed by Margaret Grossi, written by Aaron R. Cohen, featuring Oliver Platt, Timothy Egan, and others.

70. Engle, email, fall 2017.

71. Engle, discussion.

72. Dave Emigh, in discussion with author, 2019–21.

73. Rich Ray, "Meatwagon, Part 1: The Two Man Learns How to Take It Easy," Rich Ray papers, private collection; Rich Ray, in discussion with author, 2019–20.

74. Wells, discussion.

75. Engle, email, fall 2017.

76. Emigh, discussion.

77. Emigh, discussion.

78. "Seniors Top Rest in Crew Races," *Daily Evergreen*, March 20, 1979, 9.

79. "Oarsmen Stun Highly-Rated B.C. Crew," *Daily Evergreen*, April 3, 1979, 6.

80. "Crew Third in Pac-10," *Daily Evergreen*, May 22, 1979, 8.

81. "Oarsmen Going to Nationals," *Daily Evergreen*, May 24, 1979, 6.

82. Emigh, discussion.

83. Engle, email, fall 2017.

84. Engle, email, fall 2017.

85. Doug Engle, email correspondence with author, spring 2020.

86. "UW Takes 8 of 11 in Crew," *Daily Evergreen*, April 24, 1979, 6.

87. "Oarsmen Going to Nationals," *Daily Evergreen*, May 24, 1979, 6.

88. Emigh, discussion.

89. David Halberstam, *The Amateurs: The Story of Four Young Men and their Quest for an Olympic Gold Medal* (New York: Random House, 1985), 40.

90. Halberstam, *The Amateurs*.

91. "Crew Wins Semifinal Heat," *Daily Evergreen*, June 1, 1979, 6.

92. "Varsity Fours With," *Rowing Magazine* (June 1979), in "Meatwagon Paper Trail," Cougar Crew Shared Google Drive, CCAA.

93. Richard Ray to Ken and Marj Struckmeyer, March 12, 2014, Ken Struckmeyer papers, private collection.

94. William N. Wallace, "20,000 Fans Turn Out for I.R.A.'s Regatta," *New York Times*, June 2, 1979, in "Meatwagon Paper Trail," Cougar Crew Shared Google Drive, CCAA.

95. "Washington State Crew? IRA Champs," n.d., in "Meatwagon Paper Trail," Cougar Crew Shared Google Drive, CCAA.

96. Georg N. Meyers, "The Sporting Thing," *Seattle Times*, June 8, 1979, in "Meatwagon Paper Trail," Cougar Crew Shared Google Drive, CCAA.

97. "WSU Crew Cited as Team of the Week," in "Meatwagon Paper Trail," Cougar Crew Shared Google Drive, CCAA.

98. "Cougar Crew Claims National Rowing Title," *Hilltopics* (July 1979): 21.

99. Kenneth Struckmeyer to Sam Jankovich, memorandum, June 22, 1979, 2, Crew (Rowing) Records, 1975–2011 (Archives 359, box 1, folder 9), MASC, WSU.

100. Struckmeyer to Jankovich, 6.

101. Struckmeyer to Jankovich, 5.

102. Bill Roberts, "Cougar Crew: A Champion Team Grasps for Money," *Daily Evergreen*, September 20, 1979, C1.

103. Roberts, "Cougar Crew."

104. Roberts, "Cougar Crew."

105. Stephanie Anacker, "Dedication Spurs on Crew Team," *Daily Evergreen*, September 26, 1983, 10.

Chapter Three

1. Kris Norelius, in discussion with author, 2020.

2. Norelius, discussion.

3. Norelius, discussion.

4. Daniel J. Boyne, *The Red Rose Crew: A True Story of Women, Winning, and the Water* (Guilford, CT: The Lyons Press, 2005), 197–98; Ginny Gilder, *Course Correction: A Story of Rowing and Resilience in the Wake of Title IX* (Boston: Beacon Press, 2015), 44–55.

5. Gilder, *Course Correction*, 36.

6. Norelius, discussion.

7. Norelius, discussion; Peg Staeheli, in discussion with author, 2020.

8. Gary Akizuki, "Women's Crew Making Strides," *Daily Evergreen*, May 25, 1977, 6.

9. Boyne, *Red Rose Crew*, 28–29.

10. Akizuki, "Women's Crew Making Strides."

11. Norelius, discussion.

12. Akizuki, "Women's Crew Making Strides."

13. Norelius, discussion; Bob Ernst, in discussion with author, 2020.

14. Norelius, discussion.

15. Peter Mallory, "Rowing History: Women in the 1970s" (January 17, 2011), *The Sport of Rowing: A Comprehensive History* (Row2k Book exclusives, 2011), 1607, https://www.row2k.com/features/books/tsor/.

16. Norelius, discussion.

17. Norelius, discussion.

18. Andrea Moore, in discussion with author, 2019–20.

19. Doug Kee, in discussion with author, 2020; Jim Austin, in discussion with author, 2020; Bob Appleyard, in discussion with author, 2020.

20. Gene Dowers, in discussion with author, 2020–21.

21. Moore, discussion.

22. Amanda Nicole Schweinbenz, "Paddling against the Current: A History of Women's Competitive International Rowing between 1954 and 2003." (PhD diss., University of British Columbia, 2007), 6, doi:http://dx.doi.org/10.14288/1.0077008.

23. Daniel J. Boyne, *Kelly: A Father, A Son, An American Quest* (New York: Lyons Press, 2012), 81.

24. Endicott Peabody, "School Patriotism," *The School Review* 3, no. 8 (October 1895): 502–4; on notions of Victorian manhood, sports, and amateurism, see Bruce Haley, *The Healthy Body and Victorian Culture* (Boston: Harvard University Press, 1978); J. A. Mangan and James Walvin, eds., *Manliness and Morality: Middle-Class Masculinity in Britain and America, 1800–1940* (New York: St. Martin's Press, 1987); E. Anthony Rotundo, *American Manhood: Transformations in Masculinity from the Revolution to the Modern Era* (New York: Basic Books, 1993).

25. Peabody, "School Patriotism."

26. Lisa Taylor, "From Pleasure Rows and Plashing Sculls to Amateur Oarswomanship: The Evolution of Women's Amateur Rowing in Britain," *The International Journal of the History of Sport* 35, no. 14 (2018): 1491.

27. Schweinbenz, "Paddling Against the Current," 6–10.

28. Boyne, *Red Rose Crew*, 41.

29. Taylor, "From Pleasure Rows," 1502.

30. Roberta Player, in discussion with author, 2020; "Pretty Maids…Minerva Takes Her Toll," *Daily Evergreen*, May 16, 1972, 6.

31. "'High Priests' Offer 200 Wet Women to Minerva," *Daily Evergreen*, May 9, 1974, 1.

32. Brad Sleeper, in discussion with author, 2020; Fred Darvill, in discussion with author, 2020; Mike Klier, in discussion with author, 2019–21; Moore, discussion; Player, discussion; Staeheli, discussion; Jean Patterson, in discussion with author, 2020; and Kee, discussion. On previous efforts to begin a women's program, see "People, Places, Things," *Daily Evergreen*, March 7, 1973, 3; "People, Places, Things," *Daily Evergreen*, March 14, 1973, 3.

33. Darvill, discussion; Sleeper, discussion; Klier, discussion; Moore, discussion; Player, discussion; Staeheli, discussion; Patterson, discussion; and Kee, discussion.

34. Moore, discussion; Player, discussion; Staeheli, discussion; and Patterson, discussion.

35. Sleeper, discussion; Klier, discussion; and Darvill, discussion.

36. Dowers, discussion.

37. Ken Struckmeyer, in discussion with author, 2019–21.

38. Player, discussion.

39. Dowers, discussion.

40. Dowers, discussion.

41. Roberta Player, speech prepared for the Cougar Days Fiftieth Anniversary Celebration, Pullman, WA, March 21, 2020, cancelled because of the COVID-19 pandemic, private collection.

42. "Crew Women Place Sixth in Regatta," *Daily Evergreen*, May 14, 1975, 6.

43. Ken Struckmeyer, *The Pull Hard* 2, no. 2 (September, 1975): 1.

44. Struckmeyer, discussion.

45. Darvill, discussion.

46. Patterson, discussion; Moore, discussion; Staeheli, discussion; and Player, discussion.

47. Staeheli, discussion.

48. Patterson, discussion.

49. Mo (Carrick) Kelley, email correspondence with author, 2020.

50. Kelley, email.

51. Staeheli, discussion.

52. WSU Women's Cougar Crew, letter to the editor, "Women's Crew Still in Need of Support," *Daily Evergreen*, November 19, 1975, 4.

53. "Shell Loss Hurts Women's Crew," *Chinook '76* (Pullman: Washington State University, 1976), 133.

54. Sleeper, discussion.

55. Patterson, discussion.

56. Akizuki, "Women's Crew Making Strides."

57. Doug Engle, in email correspondence with author, February 2020.

58. Kari Buringrud, "Women's Crew," *The Pull Hard* 3, no. 1 (January 1978): 4.

59. Kathy (Figon) Katz, in discussion with author, 2019.

60. Jim Lefebvre, "UW Dominates Midwest Racing," *Wisconsin State Journal*, May 1, 1977, 1 (in Dave Emigh papers, private collection). Also see Bradley F. Taylor, *Wisconsin Where They Row: A History of Varsity Rowing* (Madison: University of Wisconsin Press, 2005).

61. "Crew Travels to Wisconsin," *Daily Evergreen*, April 27, 1978, 8.

62. Kari (Buringrud) Ranten, in discussion with author, 2020.

63. Kari Buringrud, "Cougar Crew Season Finale 'Disappointing,'" *Daily Evergreen*, May 25, 1978, 8.

64. See, for example, Akizuki, "Women's Crew Making Strides," 6, which covered the women's performance at Pac-8s, while the men's team was covered separately: "Oarsmen Row to Fourth," *Daily Evergreen*, May 24, 1977, 8.

65. "Seniors Top Rest in Crew Races," *Daily Evergreen*, March 20, 1979, 9.

66. "Oarsmen Sink SPU," *Daily Evergreen*, April 25, 1978, 6.

67. Ranten, discussion.

68. Sheri (Van Cleef) Bodman, in discussion with author, 2020.

69. Ranten, discussion.

70. Kathleen Randall, in discussion with author, 2020.

71. Susan Ernsdorff, in discussion with author, 2020.

72. Kerin McKellar, in discussion with author, 2020.

73. Randall, discussion; and McKellar, discussion. Both of these slogans were most likely coined by coxswain Kerin McKellar.

74. Rich Ray, in discussion with author, 2019–21.

75. "Rowers tryout begin [*sic*] Saturday," *Daily Evergreen*, September 28, 1979, 18.

76. Dowers, discussion.

77. Deb Julian, in discussion with author, 2020; Kathy Murphy, in discussion with author, 2020.

78. McKellar, discussion; Dowers, discussion; and Murphy, discussion.

79. "Hurt Crew Members Recovering," *Daily Evergreen*, November 9, 1979, 1; "Injured Woman Returns," *Daily Evergreen*, November 16, 1979, 1.

80. Tim Richards, in discussion with author, 2019–21.

81. Sandy (Schively) Buckley and Mike Buckley, in discussion with author, 2020; and Kathleen Randall, in discussion with author, 2020.

82. Dowers, discussion.

83. Sandy Buckley, discussion; Bodman, discussion; Richards, discussion; and McKellar, discussion.

84. "Christy" [*sic*], *Chinook '80* (Pullman: Washington State University, 1980), 208.

85. Richards, discussion.

86. "Olympic Hopefuls: University Student, Town Resident Try Out," *Daily Evergreen*, June 25, 1980, 7.

Chapter Four

1. "Paul 'Zenquist' – The Quad That Could Have Been," *The Rowing Podcast*, May 3, 2020, https://podcasts.apple.com/us/podcast/paul-zenquist-the-quad-that-could-have-been/id1508639477?i=1000473484552.

2. Brad Alan Lewis, *Assault on Lake Casitas* (Newport, CA.: Shark Press, 2011), 213–14.

3. "Paul 'Zenquist,'" *The Rowing Podcast*.

4. Lewis, *Assault*, 215.

5. "Paul 'Zenquist,'" *The Rowing Podcast*.

6. Lewis, *Assault*, 215.

7. Christopher Dodd, *The Story of World Rowing* (London: Stanley Paul & Co., 1992), 209.

8. "Paul 'Zenquist,'" *The Rowing Podcast*.

9. Lewis, *Assault*, 88.

10. Peter Mallory, "Rowing History: The Amateurs" (October 25, 2010), *The Sport of Rowing: A Comprehensive History* (Row2k Book exclusives, 2011), 1970, https://www.row2k.com/features/books/tsor/.

11. Paul Enquist, in discussion with author, 2019–21.

12. Enquist, discussion.

13. Mallory, "Rowing History: The Amateurs," 1993.

14. David Halberstam, *The Amateurs: The Story of Four Young Men and Their Quest for an Olympic Gold Medal* (New York: Random House, 1985), 174.

15. Enquist, discussion.

16. Brad Sleeper, in discussion with author, 2020.

17. Mike Klier, in discussion with author, 2019–21.

18. Klier, discussion; Mike Kimbrell, in discussion with author, 2019.

19. Doug Engle, email correspondence with author, fall 2017.

20. Rich Ray, in discussion with author, 2019–21.

21. Ray Wittmier, in discussion with author, 2020.

22. Engle, email, fall 2017.

23. Wittmier, discussion.

24. Enquist, discussion.

25. Paul Enquist, "Letter of Appreciation for Ken Struckmeyer," 2013, Ken Struckmeyer papers, private collection.

26. Engle, email, fall 2017.

27. Paul Enquist, email correspondence with author, June 2020.

28. Steve Wells, in discussion with author, 2019.

29. Brad Alan Lewis, in discussion with author, 2020.

30. "Paul 'Zenquist,'" *The Rowing Podcast*; Enquist, discussion.

31. Bob Ernst, in discussion with author, 2020.

32. Ernst, discussion.

33. Halberstam, *Amateurs*, 174.

34. Dave Emigh, in discussion with author, 2019–21.

35. Lewis, *Cassitas*, 89.

36. Ernst, discussion.

37. Halberstam, *Amateurs*, 21; Craig Lambert, *Mind Over Water: Lessons on Life from the Art of Rowing* (New York: Houghton Mifflin, 1999), 166.

38. Ernst, discussion.

39. Enquist, discussion.

40. Mallory, "Rowing History: The Amateurs," 1937.

41. Enquist, discussion.

42. Paul Enquist to Ken Struckmeyer, September 26, 1979, Ken Struckmeyer papers, private collection.

43. Paul Enquist to Dave and Jill Emigh, August 17, 1980, Dave Emigh papers, private collection.

44. Paul Enquist to Dave and Jill Emigh, July 21, 1981. Dave Emigh papers, private collection.

45. Enquist, discussion.

46. "Paul 'Zenquist,'" *The Rowing Podcast*.

47. Lewis, *Assault*, 88.

48. Mallory, "Rowing History: The Amateurs," 1973.

49. Enquist, discussion.

50. Halberstam, *Amateurs*, 175.

51. Enquist, discussion.

52. Lewis, *Assault*, 17.

53. Lewis, *Assault*, 17.

54. John Biglow, in discussion with author, 2020.

55. Stephen Kiesling, *The Shell Game: Reflection on Rowing and the Pursuit of Excellence* (Ashland, OR: Nordic Knight Press, 1982), 20–21; Halberstam, *Amateurs*, 46–47.

56. Craig Smith, "Seattle Rowing Icon Frank Cunningham Dies at 91," *Seattle Times*, March 8, 2013, last updated March 8, 2013, https://www.seattletimes.com/sports/other-sports/seattle-rowing-icon-frank-cunningham-dies-at-91/.

57. Halberstam, *Amateurs*, 79.

58. Biglow, discussion.

59. Biglow, discussion; also Mallory, "Rowing History: The Amateurs," 1937.

60. Enquist, discussion.

61. Mallory, "Rowing History: The Amateurs," 1937.

62. Mallory, "Rowing History: The Amateurs," 1931.

63. Biglow, discussion.

64. Halberstam, *Amateurs*, 39.

65. Biglow, discussion; Mallory, "Rowing History: The Amateurs," 1940.

66. Biglow, discussion; Halberstam, 44.

67. Biglow, discussion; Mallory, "Rowing History: The Amateurs," 1975; Enquist, discussion; "Paul 'Zenquist,'" *The Rowing Podcast*, May 3, 2020.

68. Biglow, discussion.

69. Mallory, "Rowing History: The Amateurs," 1932.

70. Frank Cunningham, *The Sculler at Ease* (Seattle: Vanguard Press, 1999), 142–44.

71. Mallory, "Rowing History: The Amateurs," 1978.

72. Halberstam, *Amateurs*, 15.

73. Halberstam, *Amateurs*, 100–101.

74. Lewis, discussion.

75. Mallory, "Rowing History: The Amateurs," 1970.

76. Brad Alan Lewis, *Lido for Time: 1439* (Newport, CA.: Shark Press, 2011), 79; 23–24; Lewis, *Assault*, 85–109; Lewis, discussion; Enquist, discussion.

77. Lewis, *Lido for Time*, 79–80; Enquist, discussion; Mallory, "Rowing History: The Amateurs," *The Sport of Rowing*, 1986.

78. Mallory, "Rowing History: The Amateurs," 1987.

79. Halberstam, *Amateurs*, 160; Paul Enquist's journal in Lewis, *Lido for Time*, 84.

80. Lewis, *Assault*, 92.

81. Lewis, *Lido for Time*, 84.

82. Enquist, discussion.

83. Lewis, *Lido for Time*, 58.

84. Lewis, *Assault*, 149.

85. Enquist, discussion.

86. Mallory, "Rowing History: The Amateurs," 1992.

87. Lewis, *Assault*, 186–93.

88. Enquist, discussion.

89. Lewis, *Assault*, 199–200.

90. Enquist, discussion.

91. Ernst, discussion.

92. Harry Parker to Paul Enquist, Winter 1984–85. Paul Enquist papers, private collection.

93. Michael McLaughlin, "Where Are They Now: Paul Enquist, Fisherman's Son Took Watery Route to Gold from Unlikely Place," *Seattle Post-Intelligencer*, March 30, 2004, last updated March 15, 2011, https://www.seattlepi.com/sports/article/Where-Are-They-Now-Paul-Enquist-1140950.php.

Chapter Five

1. Dave Brumbaugh, "Coach Struckmeyer Honored," *Daily Evergreen*, February 9, 1979, 19.

2. Ken Struckmeyer, in discussion with author, 2019-21.

3. Paul Enquist to Ken Struckmeyer, September 26, 1979, Ken Struckmeyer papers, private collection.

4. Ken Struckmeyer. "Letter to Oarsmen and Oarsladies," August 6, 1979, Ken Struckmeyer papers, private collection.

5. Bill Roberts, "Crew Practices Despite Adversity," *Daily Evergreen*, December 14, 1979, 14.

6. Bill Roberts, "Cougar Crew: A Champion Team Grasps for Money," *Daily Evergreen*, September 20, 1979, C1.

7. Ken Struckmeyer, "A Word from Struckmeyer," *The Pull Hard*, no. 2 (Summer 1983): 1.

8. Struckmeyer, "A Word from Struckmeyer."

9. Struckmeyer, "A Word from Struckmeyer."

10. Struckmeyer, "A Word from Struckmeyer."

11. "Cougar Tracks," *Daily Evergreen*, July 2, 1980, 6.

12. "Crew Wins Varsity Pairs w/Coxswain Title," *Daily Evergreen*, June 4, 1980, 10.

13. Rich Ray, "Several Errors in Story," *Daily Evergreen*, April 4, 1980, 4.

14. Struckmeyer, discussion.

15. Rich Ray, "Portland Row," *The Pull Hard* 3, no. 1 (January 1978): 2.

16. Doug Engle, in correspondence with author, 2017.

17. Ray, "Portland Row."

18. Greg Johns, "Cougar Crew in Over Their Heads on Mighty Snake," *Daily Evergreen*, September 21, 1978, 4.

19. Rich Ray and Doug Engle, "Open Letter to Cougar Crew," July 3, 1981, Rich Ray papers, private collection.

20. Doug Engle and Rich Ray, email correspondence with author, December 2019.

21. Ken Struckmeyer, *The Pull Hard* 2, no. 1 (December 1974): 4.

22. Bob Appleyard, "Cougar Rowing Association," *The Pull Hard* 5, no. 1 (October 1981): 2.

23. "CRA Members Pull Together," *The Pull Hard* (Summer 1987): 1.

24. "First Annual CRF Charter Ready for Take-off!" and "Better Than Ever: Class Day '89," *The Pull Hard* 5, no. 1 (Spring 1989): 1.

25. "Record Class Day Turnout," *The Pull Hard* 6, no. 2 (Summer 1988): 1.

26. Ray and Engle, "Open Letter"; Doug Engle, in discussion with author, 2017–21.

27. "Liberty Lake Regatta," *The Pull Hard* (Spring 1983): 1.

28. "Crew Championship Slated for Spokane," *Daily Evergreen*, December 7, 1983; "Cougars to Host Crew Regatta Near Spokane," *Daily Evergreen*, May 10, 1984, 8.

29. Ken Abbey, "Improvements on the Way," *The Pull Hard* 5, no. 1 (October 1981): 4.

30. "It's the House," *The Pull Hard* (Spring 1985): 1.

31. Paul Enquist, letter to the editor, *The Pull Hard* (Summer 1985): 2.

32. "News Briefs," *The Pull Hard*, 5, no. 3 (Winter 1988): 1.

33. Kim Heggerness, "Message from a Director," *The Pull Hard* 6, no. 1 (Winter/Spring 1990): 2.

34. Mike McQuaid, in discussion with author, 2019–20.

35. John Holtman, in discussion with author, 2020.

36. McQuaid, discussion.

37. "Crew Beats Three for Columbia Cup," *Daily Evergreen*, April 29, 1985, 10; "Crew Meets with Split Decision in Columbia Rowing Regatta," *Daily Evergreen*, April 29, 1986, 8.

38. Dan Ivanis, "Strokin' It: Lightweights Outshine Varsity Boat, Grab Second Place," *Chinook '86* (Pullman: Washington State University, 1986), 192.

39. Arthur Ericsson, in discussion with author, 2019. As head coach in the 2000s, Ericsson occasionally had Struckmeyer join him in the coaching launch and was impressed with his eye for technique.

40. Jim Austin, in discussion with author, 2020.

41. Stephanie Anacker, "Cougar Crew Plans More Surprises," *Daily Evergreen*, September 19, 1985, 13.

42. David Halberstam, *The Amateurs: The Story of Four Young Men and their Quest for an Olympic Gold Medal* (New York: Random House, 1985), 85–86.

43. Bob Ernst, in discussion with author, 2020.

44. Holtman, discussion.

45. Paul Enquist, in discussion with author, 2019–21.

46. Holtman, discussion.

47. Eric Weseman, in discussion with author, 2020–21.

48. Ken Struckmeyer, discussion.

49. Dave Emigh, in discussion with author, 2019–21.

50. "Sagebrush Navy: Washington State Crew Still Suffers from an Identity Crisis," *Los Angeles Times*, 17 May 1987. https://www.latimes.com/archives/la-xpm-1987-05-17-sp-800-story.html.

51. Mike Noble, in discussion with author, 2019.

52. Noble, discussion.

53. Noble, discussion; Tom Anderson, in discussion with author, 2019; "Oarsmen Winners Over Cal," *Daily Evergreen*, April 28, 1981; Dave Emigh, "Life in the Fast Lane," *The Pull Hard* 5, no. 1 (October 1981): 3.

54. Stephanie Anacker, "Crew Hosts Mighty UW," *Daily Evergreen*, April 19, 1985, 16A.

55. Jess O'Dell, in discussion with author, 2019–21.

56. O'Dell, discussion.

57. Stephanie Anacker, "Cougar Crew Plans More Surprises," *Daily Evergreen*, September 19, 1985, 13.

58. Jim Gressard, in discussion with author, 2020.

59. "Lightweights Upset Huskies," *The Pull Hard* (Summer 1986): 1.

60. Del Hays, in discussion with author, 2020.

61. Dan Ivanis, "Strokin' It: Lightweights Outshine Varsity Boat, Grab Second Place," *Chinook '86* (Pullman: Washington State University, 1986), 192.

62. Tammy (Boggs) Crawford, in discussion with author, 2019–21.

63. Stephanie Anacker, "Dedication Spurs on Crew," *Daily Evergreen*, September 26, 1983, 10.

64. Sandy (Schively) Buckley, in discussion with author, 2020.

65. Rich Ray, in discussion with author, 2019–21.

66. Gene Dowers, "Women's 1981 Season," *The Pull Hard* 5, no. 1 (October 1981): 6.

67. Brenda Frederick, email correspondence with author, 2019.

68. Tracy (Vadset) Landboe, in discussion with author, 2020.

69. Stacy Jenkins, in discussion with author, 2020.

70. Landboe, discussion; Jenkins, discussion; Pam (Ware) Single, in discussion with author, 2020; Crawford, discussion.

71. Dan Ivanis, "New Heights: Women's Crew Qualifies Four Boats for Championship Heats," *Chinook '86* (Pullman: Washington State University, 1986), 194.

72. Ivanis, "New Heights."

73. "New Coaches Join Cougs," *The Pull Hard* (Winter 1986): 1.

74. Jenkins, discussion; Annie (Calvin) Kendall, in discussion with author, 2020–21.

75. Amy Barnes, "Women Look to Row by Opposition," *Daily Evergreen*, February 24, 1987, 14.

76. Pam Ware, "Women's Commodore's Report," *The Pull Hard* 5, no. 3 (Winter 1988): 1.

77. "Crew Makes Splash in Tri-City Regatta," *Daily Evergreen*, April 25, 1989, 9.

78. "Cougar Crew in Istanbul," *The Pull Hard* (Winter 1986): 1.

79. Jess O'Dell, "Anatolian Adventure," *The Pull Hard* 4, no. 3 (Fall 1988): 1–3.

Chapter Six

1. Marietta Hall, in discussion with author, 2019–20.

2. Susan Parkman, "Rowing in Alaska: The Kenai Crewsers Conquer the Gold," *USRowing*, January–February 1998, 18–19.

3. Hall, discussion.

4. Tracy (Vadset) Landboe, in discussion with author, 2020.

5. *Title IX of the Education Amendments of 1972*, 20 U.S.C. Ð 1681 – 1688. Pub. L. 92–318, title IX, § 901, June 23, 1972, 86 Stat. 373, last updated November 13, 2000, https://www.justice. gov/crt/title-ix-education-amendments-1972.

6. *Blair v. Washington State University*, 108 Wn.2d 558 (1987), 740 P.2d 1379, https://law.justia. com/cases/washington/supreme-court/1987/50591-8-1.html; Richard B. Fry, *The Crimson and the Gray: 100 Years with the WSU Cougars* (Pullman: WSU Press, 1989), 315–20; Joanne Washburn, "Women's Athletics," *Chinook '80* (Pullman: Washington State University, 1980), 136; Hannelore Sudermann, "History Was Made…The Fight for Equity for Women's Athletics in Washington," *Washington State Magazine* (Winter 2007): 15–17.

7. "WSU to Add Women's Sports," *Daily Evergreen*, September 21, 1988, 1; Dan A. Nelson, "WSU Must Add Women's Sports or Risk Loss of Pac-10 Standing," *Daily Evergreen*, November 8, 1988, 2.

8. Greg Walker, "WSU May Not Add Another Women's Sport this Year," *Daily Evergreen*, October 18, 1989, 9; Greg Walker, "Women's Sport on Hold at Least a Year," *Daily Evergreen*, March 12, 1990, 1.

9. Fry, *The Crimson and the Gray*, 315.

10. Trevor Panger, "WSU Women's Crew Joins Varsity Program," *Daily Evergreen*, June 11, 1990, 9.

11. "UW Assistant Hired as WSU Women's Crew Coach," *Daily Evergreen*, June 19, 1990, 1.

12. "UW Assistant Hired," 7.

13. Tammy (Boggs) Crawford, in discussion with author, 2019–21.

14. Rich Ray, "Boggs Coaches Big League," *The Pull Hard* 6, no. 2 (Summer 1988): 1.

15. Ray, "Boggs Coaches Big League."

16. Crawford, discussion.

17. Mikki Mahan, "Decision Still Pending on Women's Sports," *Daily Evergreen*, April 26, 1990, 1.

18. Hall, discussion.

19. Trevor Panger, "WSU Women's Crew Joins Varsity Program," *Daily Evergreen*, June 11, 1990, 9.

20. Hall, discussion.

21. Tammy Crawford to Felicia Beluche, May 6, 1991, Marietta Hall papers, private collection. In response to one such distraction, Crawford told a former WSU rower that her criticisms of Crawford's coaching were "worthless" and a waste of her time. "On a day when I have already spent nine hours on the water, one hour in the erg room, and two hours in the office, I now must spend additional time responding to your warped opinions."

22. Hall, discussion.

23. Hall, discussion.

24. Ken Abbey, "Soccer Selected as First Women's Sport: Women's Crew and Entry into the Athletic Department," *The Pull Hard* 5, no. 2 (Summer 1989): 5.

25. Ken Struckmeyer, in discussion with author, 2019–21.

26. Crawford, discussion.

27. Jess O'Dell, in discussion with author, 2019–21.

28. O'Dell, discussion.

29. Crawford, discussion.

30. O'Dell, discussion.

31. Lisa (Stivers) Tintinger, in discussion with author, 2019.

32. Sandy (Schively) Buckley, in discussion with author, 2020; Kari (Buringrud) Ranten, in discussion with author, 2020; Kathleen Randall, in discussion with author, 2020; Hall, discussion; Sheri (Van Cleef) Bodman, in discussion with author, 2020; Susan Ernsdorff, in discussion with author, 2020; Peg Staeheli, in discussion with author, 2020; and Tintinger, discussion.

33. Thom Eldridge, in discussion with author, 2020.

34. Ernie Iseminger, in discussion with author, 2019–21.

35. Doug Wordell, in discussion with author, 2020; Bob Barton, in discussion with author, 2020; Iseminger, discussion.

36. Frank Hill, "Rowers Look for New Crew," *Daily Evergreen*, August 27, 1991, 9.

37. Wordell, discussion.

38. "Sagebrush Navy: Washington State Crew Still Suffers from an Identity Crisis," *Los Angeles Times*, May 17, 1987. https://www.latimes.com/archives/la-xpm-1987-05-17-sp-800-story.html.

39. Iseminger, discussion.

40. Iseminger, discussion.

41. Iseminger, discussion.

42. Garrett Riddle, "Men's Crew Has Huskies' Respect in 1992 Season," *Daily Evergreen*, September 10, 1992, 8.

43. Rich Waters, "Men Excel on Land Too," *Daily Evergreen*, October 22, 1992, 12.

44. Jason Smith, "Men's Novice Crew," *Daily Evergreen*, April 6, 1993, 8.

45. Jason Smith, "Club Round Up," *Daily Evergreen*, April 13, 1993, 9.

46. Geoff Owen, in discussion with author, 2019.

47. Eldridge, discussion.

48. Frank Hill, "Crew Club Rows to Win in Regatta," *Daily Evergreen*, October 22, 1991, 6.

49. Riddle, "Men's Crew Has Huskies' Respect."

50. "Men's Crew Faces UW," *Daily Evergreen*, October 23, 1992, 13.

51. Mike Williams, in discussion with author, 2020; Gene Dowers, in discussion with author, 2020–21; Del Hayes, in discussion with author, 2020; Iseminger, discussion; Struckmeyer, discussion; and Jim Gressard, in discussion with author, 2020. Gressard rowed with Paul Hensel in the 1980s, and in the late 1980s, Hensel approached Gressard several times with the idea of alumni contributing to bring in another full-time coach to replace Struckmeyer. Senior Mike "Ivan" Kettel, who had rowed under Struckmeyer and then witnessed Struckmeyer's dismissal by the club officers, later described the affair as a "coups," since Iseminger's former rowers stacked the club leadership positions and then organized the ouster. Mike Kettel, in discussion with author, 2021.

52. Randall, discussion.

53. Jim Rudd, in discussion with author, 2019.

54. Iseminger, discussion. According to Iseminger, *The Pull Hard* was being produced during the decade, but apparently not widely circulated.

55. Hayes, discussion.

56. Dowers, discussion; Kettel, discussion.

57. "Men Split Races with Some Top-Notch Competition," *Daily Evergreen*, April 18, 1995, 7.

58. "Men Split Races"; Mike V. Williams, "Crew Previews Showdown at Portland in Two Weeks," *Daily Evergreen*, October 26, 1993, 6; "Men's Crew Rows in Hawaii," *Daily Evergreen*, January 19, 1996, 13.

59. Thad Smith, in discussion with author, 2020.

60. Chris Stratton, "Men's Crew," *Daily Evergreen*, March 26, 1997, 8.

61. Smith, discussion.

62. Gus Kravas and Connie Kravas, in discussion with author, 2020; Glenn Putyrae, in discussion with author, 2020; Iseminger, discussion.

63. Shawn Bagnall, in discussion with author, 2019.

64. Greg Sheridan, in discussion with author, 2021.

65. Bagnall, discussion; "Shawn Bagnall," US Naval Academic Athletics, Men's Lightweight Rowing (website), accessed May 10, 2021, https://navysports.com/sports/mens-lightweight-rowing/roster/coaches/shawn-bagnall/275.

66. Bagnall, discussion.

67. Bagnall, discussion; Putyrae, discussion; Brian Cardwell, "Gonzaga Glides by WSU Crew Team," *Daily Evergreen*, February 10, 1998, 10.

68. Roger Crawford, in discussion with author, 2020; Bagnall, discussion.

69. Mike Klier, manuscript reader response for "Pull Hard" submission to WSU Press, December 2020, private collection.

Chapter Seven

1. Rich Ray, "Redux," *Pullhard.redux* 1.1 (Fall 2000), 2.

2. Roger Crawford, in discussion with author, 2020; Shawn Bagnall, in discussion with author, 2019.

3. Roger Crawford, "Roger Reconnoiters the Correlation of Forces," *Pullhard.redux* 1.1 (Fall 2000), 1, 4.

4. Danny Brevick, in discussion with author, 2019–20.

5. Arthur Ericsson, "A Good Oar & Rudder," *The Pull Hard* 11, no. 1 (Fall 2004): 5.

6. Danny Brevick, discussion.

7. Danny Brevick, discussion; Michelle (Arganbright) Kistler, in discussion with author, 2020.

8. Kistler, discussion; Danny Brevick, discussion; Peter Brevick, in discussion with author, 2019–21.

9. Kistler, discussion.

10. Kistler, discussion; Peter Brevick, discussion.

11. Michelle Arganbright, "The Road to the IRA's 2003," *The Pull Hard* 2, no. 1 (November 2003): 4–5.

12. Julia (Anderson) Collins, in discussion with author, 2020.

13. Ericsson, "A Good Oar & Rudder."

14. Danny Brevick, discussion; Kistler, discussion.

15. Ken Struckmeyer, in discussion with author, 2019–21; Kistler, discussion; Danny Brevick, discussion.

16. Peter Brevick, "Editor's Comments," *The Pull Hard* 10, no. 2 (Winter 2004): 8.

17. Kistler, discussion.

18. Tim Richards, "Letter to Fellow Crew Members," *The Pull Hard* 11, no. 1 (Fall 2004): 2–3; Tim Richards, in discussion with author, 2019–21; Danny Brevick, discussion; Michelle (Arganbright) Kistler, email correspondence with author, July 2020.

19. Richards, discussion; Danny Brevick, discussion.

20. Danny Brevick, discussion; Kistler, discussion.

21. Michelle Arganbright, "Class Day Returns!" *The Pull Hard* 10, no. 3 (Spring 2004): 4.

22. Tim Richards, "Letter to Fellow Crew Members," The *Pull Hard* 11, no. 1 (Fall 2004): 2–3; Richards, discussion.

23. Danny Brevick, discussion.

24. Danny Brevick, discussion.

25. Danny Brevick, discussion; Richards, discussion.

26. Richards, discussion. Richards's ideas about leadership and how to build successful organizations that can achieve long-term goals were influenced by management guru Jim Collins's book: *Good to Great: Why Some Companies Make the Leap... And Others Don't* (New York: Harper Collins, 2001).

27. Of course, aided by many others, including Michelle Kistler, Ken Struckmeyer, Peter Brevick, Tom Anderson, Julia (Anderson) Collins, Lisa (Coble) Curtis, Tom Caudill, Ernie Iseminger, and on and on, not to mention all the members of the crew itself.

28. Danny Brevick, discussion.

29. Danny Brevick, discussion; Arthur Ericsson, in discussion with author, 2019.

30. Danny Brevick, discussion; Ericsson, discussion.

31. Danny Brevick, discussion; Ericsson, discussion; Peter Brevick, discussion; David Herrick, in discussion with author, 2019–21; and Karl Huhta, in discussion with author, 2019–20.

32. Ericsson, discussion.

33. Ericsson, discussion.

34. Danny Brevick, "A New Face at the Helm," *The Pull Hard* 11, no. 1 (Fall 2004): 1; Herrick, discussion.

35. Danny Brevick, discussion.

36. Danny Brevick, discussion; Peter Brevick, discussion.

37. Brevick, "A New Face at the Helm."

38. Brevick, "A New Face at the Helm."

39. Ed Hewitt, "IRA Location, Format, Eligibility to Change for 2009 Regatta," *Row2K*, June 8, 2008, https://www.row2k.com/news/6-8-2008/IRA-Location--Format--Eligibility-to-Change-for-2009-Regatta/38292/; and Ed Hewitt, "The 40-Year Storm: Change Comes to the 106th (or 107th) IRA Regatta," *Row2K*, February 15, 2008, https://www.row2k.com/features/358/The-40-Year-Storm--Change-Comes-to-the-106th--or-107th--IRA-Regatta/.

40. Arthur Ericsson, "WSU Men Join Second Conference," *The Pull Hard* 11, no. 2 (Winter 2005): 1, 4; Nick Eaton, "New Faces, New Blisters, New Glory," *The Pull Hard* 11, no. 1 (Fall 2004): 8.

41. Luke Jones, "Winter Work Brings Spring Success," *The Pull Hard* 12, no. 2 (Winter 2006): 8.

42. Huhta, discussion; Collins, discussion; Peter Brevick, discussion; and Ericsson, discussion.

43. Brevick, "A New Face at the Helm."

44. Jason Lackie, "I Love Winter Training," *The Pull Hard* 11, no. 2 (Winter 2005): 10.

45. Peter Brevick, discussion.

46. Julia Anderson, "Portland Loop: A Day No One in the Varsity 8+ Will Ever Forget," *The Pull Hard* 12, no. 2 (Winter 2006): 3, 7.

47. Peter Brevick, "Fall Racing Recap," *The Pull Hard* 12, no. 2 (Winter 2006): 3.

48. "Worley Eyes Sub-6:00 2K," *The Pull Hard* 12, no. 2 (Winter 2006): 6.

49. A power piece is a set of strokes designated to draw maximum focus and power from the rowers, so that the boat begins to "swing" and "move through" or away from an opponent.

50. Julia (Anderson) Collins, speech prepared for the Cougar Days Fiftieth Anniversary Celebration, Pullman, WA, March 21, 2020, cancelled because of the COVID-19 pandemic, private collection; Collins, discussion.

51. Peter Brevick, discussion; Collins, discussion; and Huhta, discussion.

52. Paul Ehlers, "V8+ Wins WIRA Conference Championship," *The Pull Hard* 17, no. 5 (Summer 2010): 3–5.

53. Julia Gamache, in discussion with author, 2020.

54. Tom Caudill, "Power Ten Campaign," *The Pull Hard* 17, no. 5 (Summer 2010): 11–13.

55. Richards, discussion.

56. Gamache, discussion.

57. Herrick, discussion.

58. Joanne Greene and Matt Shaw, in discussion with author, 2021.

59. Greene and Shaw, discussion.

60. UREC, "Sport Club Federation Tier System," 2021; Greene and Shaw, discussion.

61. Andy King, in discussion with author, 2020; Herrick, discussion; Peter Brevick, discussion.

62. Herrick, discussion; Peter Brevick, discussion.

63. Arthur Ericsson, "Cougar Lightweights: Men (and Women) Wanted," *The Pull Hard* 16, no. 3 (Spring 2009): 6.

64. Ericsson, "Cougar Lightweights."

65. David Herrick, "WIRA Success," *The Pull Hard* 19, no. 5 (Summer 2012): 5.

66. King, discussion.

67. Ericsson, discussion.

68. Caudill, "Power Ten Campaign."

69. Eric Demaris, "Cougar Crew Days Success!" *The Pull Hard* (Spring 2013): 8.

70. Richards, discussion.

71. Huhta, discussion.

Epilogue

1. Bob Orr, in discussion with author, August 2019; Adriana Janovich, "Cougar Crew Profiles," *Washington State Magazine* (Winter 2019), "Web extra," accessed April 16, 2021, https://magazine.wsu.edu/web-extra/cougar-crew-profiles/.

2. Tim Richards, "Cougar Crew Days 2020 and COVID-19: A Message from Cougar Crew Alumni Association Chair Tim Richards," email to Cougar Crew community, March 9, 2020.

3. Peter Brevick, in discussion with author, 2019–21.

4. Henry McRae, "Recruitment in the Pandemic," *The Pull Hard* (Fall 2020): 7; Brevick, discussion.

5. Peter Brevick, "A Letter from the Head Coach," *The Pull Hard* (Winter 2020): 6.

6. Brevick, discussion.

7. Brevick, discussion; Rich Ray to Elson Floyd, March 31, 2009, Rich Ray papers, private collection. Brevick joined others, like alumnus Rich Ray, who were increasingly interested in recruiting racially diverse students into the crew. In 2009, Ray appealed directly to WSU President Elson Floyd, who was an ardent supporter of Cougar Crew. Noting that "rowing has a reputation for WASPishness which it no longer deserves," Ray asked Floyd to "assist us in broadening our social base across the whole student body."

8. Daniel James Brown, *The Boys in the Boat: Nine Americans and Their Epic Quest for Gold at the 1936 Berlin Olympics* (New York: Viking, 2013), 357.

SOURCES

This book rests heavily on the oral interviews I conducted with former rowers, coaches, and administrators. It also relies on unpublished documents and testimonies sent to me directly by the participants themselves. I am donating those materials to the WSU Libraries Manuscripts, Archives, and Special Collections to make them accessible to interested readers and researchers, who can also explore the digitized versions of the *Daily Evergreen*, the *Chinook*, and *The Pull Hard* to gain more context on the history of Cougar Crew.

Collections

Washington State University Cougar Crew newsletter. https://cougarcrew. com/pullhard/pullhard.html. Digitized versions of the Cougar Crew newsletter—variously, *Pullhard, The Pullhard, The Pull Hard,* and *Pullhard. redux*—are accessible through this portal.

Washington State University Libraries Digital Collections. Washington State University. Pullman, WA. https://content.libraries.wsu.edu/digital/. Digitized versions of the *Daily Evergreen, Washington State Magazine, Hilltopics,* and the *Chinook* annual yearbook are accessible through this portal.

Washington State University Libraries Manuscripts, Archives, and Special Collections, Washington State University, Pullman, WA.

Documents and Other Unpublished Materials

Collins, Julia (Anderson). Speech prepared for the Cougar Days Fiftieth Anniversary Celebration, Pullman, WA, March 21, 2020, cancelled because of the COVID-19 pandemic. Private collection.

Crawford, Tammy (Boggs). Speech presented at the dedication of the Ken Abbey Shell House, Wawawai, WA, March 20, 2010. Tammy Crawford papers, private collection.

Emigh, Dave. Personal correspondence. Dave Emigh papers, private collection.

———. "Notes from Dave Emigh papers." Dave Emigh papers, private collection.

———. "Notes on the Formation of the WSU Crew," March 20, 2013. Private collection.

Enquist, Paul. "Letter of Appreciation for Ken Struckmeyer," ca. 2013. Ken Struckmeyer papers, private collection.

Klier, Mike. Manuscript reader response for "Pull Hard" submission to WSU Press, December 2020. Private collection.

McBride, Doug. "WSU Crew—Black Thursday, Spring 1973." Doug McBride papers, private collection.

Player, Roberta. Speech prepared for the Cougar Days Fiftieth Anniversary Celebration, Pullman, WA, March 21, 2020, cancelled because of the COVID-19 pandemic. Private collection.

Pratt, David T. "In the Beginning: Recollections of Early Days of Cougar Crew." March 25, 2010. David T. Pratt papers, private collection.

Ray, Rich. "Meatwagon, Part 1: The Two Man Learns How to Take It Easy." Rich Ray papers, private collection.

———. Personal correspondence. Rich Ray papers, private collection.

Ray, Rich, and Doug Engle. "Open Letter to Cougar Crew," July 3, 1981. Rich Ray papers, private collection.

Richards, Tim. "Cougar Crew Days 2020 and COVID-19: A Message from Cougar Crew Alumni Association Chair Tim Richards," email to Cougar Crew community, March 9, 2020.

"Sport Club Federation Tier System" (internal document, University Recreation, WSU, 2021).

Struckmeyer, Ken. "Letter to Oarsmen and Oarsladies," August 6, 1979. Ken Struckmeyer papers, private collection.

———. "Memorandum to All Returning WSU Oarsmen and Cox'ns," June 29, 1973. Doug Engle papers, private collection.

———. Personal correspondence. Ken Struckmeyer papers, private collection.

———. Speech presented at the dedication of the Ken Abbey Shell House, Wawawai, WA, March 20, 2010. Ken Struckmeyer papers, private collection.

Struckmeyer, Kenneth, to Sam Jankovich, memorandum, June 22, 1979. Crew (Rowing) Records, 1975–2011 (Archives 359, box 1, folder 9). Manuscripts, Archives, and Special Collections, Washington State University Libraries, Pullman, WA.

Washington State University Rowing Club, "Constitution," 1971. Private collection.

Interviews

The date ranges in parentheses refer to the years the interviewee rowed or coached for WSU and, in some instances, rowed and then returned to coach. The interview years reflect the span of time during which multiple in-person, telephone, and/or email conversations as well as text message exchanges took place with many of the interviewees.

Tom Anderson (1976–80), 2019

Bob Appleyard (1971–75), 2020

Jim Austin (1972–75), 2020

Shawn Bagnall (1995–2000; men's head coach, 2000–2002), 2019

Bob Barton (1984–88), 2020

Felly Bergano (1976–78), 2020

John Biglow (Olympic rower), 2020

Sheri (Van Cleef) Bodman (1978–80), 2020

Danny Brevick (2001–05), 2019–20

Peter Brevick (2002–06; men's head coach, 2017–present), 2019–21

Mike Buckley (1977–81), 2020

Sandy (Schively) Buckley (1978–81), 2020

Julia (Anderson) Collins (2002–06), 2020

Roger Crawford (1982–85), 2020

Tammy (Boggs) Crawford (1980–84; women's head coach, 1990–2002), 2019–21

Dave Curran (1982–86), 2019

Fred Darvill (1973–77), 2020

Gene Dowers (1974–78; women's head coach, 1979–82, 1985–86; men's coach, 1993), 2020–21

Ingrid Jennings Durenburger (1980–82), 2020

Thom Eldridge (1987–91), 2020

Dave Emigh (1971–73), 2019–21

Doug Engle (1975–79), 2017–21

Paul Enquist (1973–77), 2019–21

Arthur Ericsson (men's head coach, 2004–17), 2019

Susan Ernsdorff (1977–81), 2020

Bob Ernst (UW and U.S. Rowing coach), 2020

Brenda Frederick (1982–86), 2019–21

Julia Gamache (men's novice coach, 2008–11), 2020

Joanne Greene (UREC, 1999–present), 2021

Jim Gressard (1982–86), 2020

Marietta "Ed" Hall (1987–91), 2019–20

Del Hays (SDSU lightweight, 1982–86), 2020

David Herrick (2010–14), 2019–21

John "Yumbo" Holtman (1977–81), 2020

Karl Huhta (2004–08), 2019–20

Ernie Iseminger (1984–88; men's head coach, 1993–98), 2019–21

Stacy Jenkins (1985–87), 2020

Deb Julian (1979–81), 2020

Kathy (Figon) Katz (1972–74), 2019

Doug Kee (1971–77), 2020

Mo (Carrick) Kelley (1975–78), 2020–21

Annie (Calvin) Kendall (1983–87), 2020–21

Steve "Ivan" Kettel (1989–95), 2021

Mike Kimbrell (1972–76), 2019

Andy King (2005–09), 2020

Michelle (Arganbright) Kistler (men's head coach, 2002–04), 2020

Mike Klier (1971–75), 2019–21

Connie Kravas (WSU vice president for university advancement, 1990s), 2020

Gus Kravas (WSU vice provost for student affairs, 1990s), 2020

Tracy (Vadset) Landboe (1985–88), 2020

Brad Alan Lewis (Olympic gold medal oarsman), 2020

Devon McCornack (2015–19), 2019

Kerin McKellar (1978–83), 2020

Mike McQuaid (1982–86), 2019–20

Len Mills (photographer, 1971–73), 2019–21

Andrea "Andy" Moore (1975–78), 2019–20

Kathy Murphy (1979–81), 2020

Bob Nehring (1982–86), 2019–20

Mike Noble (1977–81), 2019

Kris Norelius (1975–77), 2020

Jess O'Dell (1982–87; women's head coach, 1988–90), 2019–21

Thad O'Dell (1983–87; women's head coach, 1988), 2020

Jeff Olsen (1999–2002), 2019

Bob Orr (men's head coach, 1971–73), 2019

Geoff Owen (1992–94), 2019

Jean "Snake Action" Patterson (1975–78), 2020

Roberta "Berta" Player (1975–77), 2020

Steve Porter (1973–77), 2020

Glenn Putyrae (men's novice coach, 1994–97), 2020

Kathleen Randall (1977–81), 2020

Kari (Buringrud) Ranten (1976–80), 2020

Rich "Flip" Ray (1976–80; women's head coach, 1982–84), 2019–21

David Reeder (1984–88), 2020

Tim Richards (1977–80), 2019–21

Jim Rudd (1971–75), 2019

Matt Shaw (UREC, 2011–present), 2021

Greg Sheridan (WSU Foundation, 1994–2002), 2021

Pam (Ware) Single (1985–88), 2020

Brad Sleeper (1973–77), 2020

Martha (Witt) Sleeper (1976–78), 2020

Thad Smith (1993–97), 2020

Peg Staeheli (1975–77), 2020

Ken Struckmeyer (men's head coach, 1973–93), 2019–21

Lisa (Stivers) Tintinger (1982–86), 2019

Jim Verellen (1971–73), 2020

Steve Wells (1974–78), 2019

Eric Weseman (1983–87), 2020–21

Mike Williams (1990–93), 2020

Andy Winters (2005–09), 2020

Ray Wittmier (1973–77), 2020

Doug Wordell (1983–87), 2020

Lori (Haugen) Wordell (1984–87), 2020

David Yorozu (1974–77), 2020

Articles

Abbey, Ken. "Improvements on the Way." *The Pull Hard* 5, no. 1 (October 1981): 4.

———. "Soccer Selected as First Women's Sport: Women's Crew and Entry into the Athletic Department." *The Pull Hard* 5, no. 2 (Summer 1989): 5.

Akizuki, Gary. "Women's Crew Making Strides." *Daily Evergreen*, May 25, 1977, 6.

Anacker, Stephanie. "Cougar Crew Plans More Surprises." *Daily Evergreen*, September 19, 1985, 13.

———. "Crew Hosts Mighty UW." *Daily Evergreen*, April 19, 1985, 16A.

———. "Dedication Spurs on Crew Team." *Daily Evergreen*, September 26, 1983, 10.

Anderson, Julia. "Portland Loop: A Day No One in the Varsity 8+ Will Ever Forget." *The Pull Hard* 12, no. 2 (Winter 2006): 3, 7.

"Anti-war group asks for CUB bread boycott." *Daily Evergreen*, May 9, 1972, 3.

"Anti-war Students to Occupy CUB." *Daily Evergreen*, May 10, 1972, 1.

Appleyard, Bob. "Cougar Rowing Association." *The Pull Hard* 5, no. 1 (October 1981): 2.

"Arabs Hijack Belgian Airliner." *Daily Evergreen*, May 10, 1972, 2.

Arganbright, Michelle. "Class Day Returns!" *The Pull Hard* 10, no. 3 (Spring 2004): 4.

———. "The Road to the IRA's 2003." *The Pull Hard* 2, no. 1 (November 2003): 4–5.

Barnes, Amy. "Women Look to Row by Opposition." *Daily Evergreen*, February 24, 1987, 14.

"Better Than Ever: Class Day '89." *The Pull Hard* 5, no. 1 (Spring 1989): 1.

Brevick, Danny. "A New Face at the Helm." *The Pull Hard* 11, no. 1 (Fall 2004): 1.

Brevick, Peter. "Editor's Comments." *The Pull Hard* 10, no. 2 (Winter 2004): 8.

———. "Fall Racing Recap." *The Pull Hard* 12, no. 2 (Winter 2006): 3.

———. "A Letter from the Head Coach." *The Pull Hard* (Winter 2020): 6.

Brumbaugh, Dave. "Coach Struckmeyer Honored." *Daily Evergreen*, February 9, 1979, 19.

Buringrud, Kari. "Cougar Crew Season Finale 'Disappointing.'" *Daily Evergreen*, May 25, 1978, 8.

———. "Women's Crew." *The Pull Hard* 3, no. 1 (January 1978): 4.

"Button Sale Aids in Replacement of Club's Losses." *Daily Evergreen*, February 15, 1972, 3.

Carberry, Jim. "Cougar Crew: California or Bust." *Daily Evergreen*, May 1, 1976, 6.

———. "Crew: Months of Dedication." *Daily Evergreen*, May 19, 1976, 6.

Cardwell, Brian. "Gonzaga Glides by WSU Crew Team." *Daily Evergreen*, February 10, 1998, 10.

Caudill, Tom. "Power Ten Campaign." *The Pull Hard* 17, no. 5 (Summer 2010): 11–13.

Chaney, Pam. "Cougar Crew Hosts Regatta on Lake Bryan." *Daily Evergreen*, March 21 1974, 8.

———. "Sun Begins to Shine on Cougar Crew." *Daily Evergreen*, April 25, 1974, 10.

"Christy" [sic]. *Chinook '80*. Pullman: Washington State University, 1980: 208.

Coffman, Rick. "In the Future." *Daily Evergreen*, January 8, 1969, 9.

Condotta, Bob. "Respect." *Chinook '85*. Pullman: Washington State University, 1985: 34–37.

"Cougar Crew Claims National Rowing Title," *Hilltopics* (July 1979): 21.

"Cougar Crew Gains Respect." *Hilltopics* (June 1973): 24.

"Cougar Crew in Istanbul." *The Pull Hard* (Winter 1986): 1.

"Cougar Tracks." *Daily Evergreen*, July 2, 1980, 6.

"Cougars 'Scare' Husky Rowers." *Daily Evergreen*, April 15, 1975, 9.

"Cougars to Host Crew Regatta Near Spokane." *Daily Evergreen*, May 10, 1984, 8.

"CRA Members Pull Together." *The Pull Hard* (Summer 1987): 1.

Crawford, Roger. "Roger Reconnoiters the Correlation of Forces." *Pullhard.redux* 1.1 (Fall 2000): 1.

"Crew Announces Schedule; Season Begins March 31." *Daily Evergreen*, March 8, 1973, 8.

"Crew Beats Three for Columbia Cup." *Daily Evergreen*, April 29, 1985: 10.

"Crew Championship Slated for Spokane." *Daily Evergreen*, December 7, 1983, 8.

"Crew Finishes Fifth." *Daily Evergreen*, May 16, 1972, 12.

"Crew Finishes Third." *Daily Evergreen*, May 3, 1977, 6.

"Crew Left Disappointed by High Winds and Huskies." *Daily Evergreen*, April 14, 1976, 8.

"Crew Makes Splash in Tri-City Regatta." *Daily Evergreen*, April 25, 1989, 9.

"Crew Meets with Split Decision in Columbia Rowing Regatta." *Daily Evergreen*, April 29, 1986, 8.

"Crew Needs Heavyweights." *Daily Evergreen*, October 15, 1975, 6.

"Crew Needs Heavyweights." *Daily Evergreen*, October 26, 1976, 2.

"Crew Nips UW." *Daily Evergreen*, May 5, 1976, 6.

"Crew Team has Strong Showings." *Daily Evergreen*, May 1, 1974, 8.

"Crew Third in Pac-10." *Daily Evergreen*, May 22, 1979, 8.

"Crew to Row in Seattle." *Daily Evergreen*, November 11, 1972, 2.

"Crew Travels to Wisconsin." *Daily Evergreen*, April 27, 1978, 8.

"Crew Wins Semifinal Heat." *Daily Evergreen*, June 1, 1979, 6.

"Crew Wins Varsity Pairs w/Coxswain Title." *Daily Evergreen*, June 4, 1980, 10.

"Crew Women Place Sixth in Regatta." *Daily Evergreen*, May 14, 1975, 6.

"Crew." *Daily Evergreen*, April 26, 1977, 6.

Demaris, Eric. "Cougar Crew Days Success!" *The Pull Hard* (Spring 2013): 8.

"Draft Law Changes Reviewed at Meeting." *Daily Evergreen*, October 22, 1971, 1.

Eaton, Nick. "New Faces, New Blisters, New Glory." *The Pull Hard* 11, no. 1 (Fall 2004): 8.

Ehlers, Paul. "V8+ Wins WIRA Conference Championship." *The Pull Hard* 17, no. 5 (Summer 2010): 3–5.

Emigh, Dave. "Life in the Fast Lane." *The Pull Hard* 5, no. 1 (October 1981): 3.

———. Letter to the editor. *The Pull Hard* (Summer 1985): 2.

Ericsson, Arthur. "Cougar Lightweights: Men (and Women) Wanted." *The Pull Hard* 16, no. 3 (Spring 2009): 6.

———. "A Good Oar & Rudder." *The Pull Hard* 11, no. 1 (Fall 2004): 5.

———. "WSU Men Join Second Conference." *The Pull Hard* 11, no. 2 (Winter 2005): 1, 4.

"Error Costs Crew Second." *Daily Evergreen*, November 14, 1972, 6.

"First Annual CRF Charter Ready for Take-off!" *The Pull Hard* 5, no. 1 (Spring 1989): 1.

"Gone with the Wind." *Daily Evergreen*, January 13, 1972, 1.

"Happenings." *Daily Evergreen*, April 26, 1972, 7.

Heggerness, Kim, "Message from a Director," *The Pull Hard* 6, no. 1 (Winter/Spring 1990): 2.

Herrick, David. "WIRA Success." *The Pull Hard* 19, no. 5 (Summer 2012): 5.

"High Priests' Offer 200 Wet Women to Minerva." *Daily Evergreen*, May 9, 1974, 1.

Hill, Frank. "Crew Club Rows to Win in Regatta." *Daily Evergreen*, October 22, 1991, 6.

———. "Rowers Look for New Crew." *Daily Evergreen*, August 27, 1991, 9.

"Hurt Crew Members Recovering." *Daily Evergreen*, November 9, 1979, 1.

"Injured Woman Returns." *Daily Evergreen*, November 16, 1979, 1.

"Interclass Meet for Rowing Club on Saturday." *Daily Evergreen*, April 21, 1972, 8.

"It's the House." *The Pull Hard* (Spring 1985): 1.

Ivanis, Dan. "New Heights: Women's Crew Qualifies Four Boats for Championship Heats." *Chinook '86*. Pullman: Washington State University, 1986: 194.

———. "Strokin' It: Lightweights Outshine Varsity Boat, Grab Second Place." *Chinook '86*. Pullman: Washington State University, 1986: 192.

Johns, Greg. "Cougar Crew in Over Their Heads on Mighty Snake." *Daily Evergreen*, September 21, 1978, 4.

Jones, Luke. "Winter Work Brings Spring Success." *The Pull Hard* 12, no. 2 (Winter 2006): 8.

Knight, Bill. "Husky Crew Wins." *Seattle Post-Intelligencer*, May 14, 1972, G5.

Lackie, Jason. "I Love Winter Training." *The Pull Hard* 11, no. 2 (Winter 2005): 10.

Lefebvre, Jim. "UW Dominates Midwest Racing." *Wisconsin State Journal*, May 1, 1977, 1 (in Dave Emigh papers).

"Liberty Lake Regatta." *The Pull Hard* (Spring 1983): 1.

"Lightweight Oarsmen Edge Huskies." *Daily Evergreen*, May 7, 1974, 6.

"Lightweights Upset Huskies." *The Pull Hard* (Summer 1986): 1.

Mahan, Mikki. "Decision Still Pending on Women's Sports." *Daily Evergreen*, April 26, 1990, 1.

McLaughlin, Michael. "Where Are They Now: Paul Enquist, Fisherman's Son Took Watery Route to Gold from Unlikely Place." *Seattle Post-Intelligencer*, March 30, 2004. Last updated March 15, 2011. https://www.seattlepi.com/sports/article/Where-Are-They-Now-Paul-Enquist-1140950.php.

McRae, Henry. "Recruitment in the Pandemic." *The Pull Hard* (Fall 2020): 7.

"Men Split Races with Some Top-Notch Competition." *Daily Evergreen*, April 18, 1995, 7.

"Men's Crew: Second in Northwest." *Chinook '77*. Pullman: Washington State University, 1977: 204.

"Men's Crew Faces UW." *Daily Evergreen*, October 23, 1992, 13.

"Men's Crew Rows in Hawaii." *Daily Evergreen*, January 19, 1996, 13.

Meyers, Georg N. "The Sporting Thing." *Seattle Times*, June 8, 1979.

Nelson, Dan A. "WSU Must Add Women's Sports or Risk Loss of Pac-10 Standing." *Daily Evergreen*, November 8, 1988, 2.

"New Building to House Shells." *Daily Evergreen*, March 26, 1971, 9.

"New Coaches Join Cougs." *The Pull Hard* (Winter 1986): 1.

"New Record Set by Crew Heavies." *Daily Evergreen*, May 12, 1977, 8.

"News Briefs." *The Pull Hard* 5, no. 3 (Winter 1988): 1.

O'Dell, Jess. "Anatolian Adventure." *The Pull Hard* 4, no. 3 (Fall 1988): 1–3.

"Oarsmen Going to Nationals." *Daily Evergreen*, May 24, 1979, 6.

"Oarsmen Row to Fourth." *Daily Evergreen*, May 24, 1977, 8.

"Oarsmen Sink SPU." *Daily Evergreen*, April 25, 1978, 6.

"Oarsmen Stun Highly-Rated B.C. Crew." *Daily Evergreen*, April 3, 1979, 6.

"Oarsmen Winners Over Cal." *Daily Evergreen*, April 28, 1981, 6.

"Olympic Hopefuls: University Student, Town Resident Try Out." *Daily Evergreen*, June 25, 1980, 7.

Orr, Bob. "The 1973 Rowing Season in Review." *The Pull Hard* 1, no. 1 (1973–74): 1.

Panger, Trevor. "WSU Women's Crew Joins Varsity Program." *Daily Evergreen*, June 11, 1990, 9.

Parkman, Susan. "Rowing in Alaska: The Kenai Crewsers Conquer the Gold." *USRowing*, January–February 1998: 18–19.

Peabody, Endicott. "School Patriotism." *The School Review* 3, no. 8 (October 1895): 502–504.

"People, Places, Things." *Daily Evergreen*, March 14, 1973, 3.

"People, Places, Things." *Daily Evergreen*, March 7, 1973, 3.

"Pretty Maids…Minerva Takes her Toll." *Daily Evergreen*, May 16, 1972, 6.

Ray, Rich. "Boggs Coaches Big League." *The Pull Hard* 6, no. 2 (Summer 1988): 1.

———. "Portland Row." *The Pull Hard* 3, no. 1 (January 1978): 2.

———. "Redux." *Pullhard.redux* 1.1 (Fall 2000): 2.

———. "Several Errors in Story." *Daily Evergreen*, April 4, 1980, 4.

"Record Class Day Turnout." *The Pull Hard* 6, no. 2 (Summer 1988): 1.

Richards, Tim. "Letter to Fellow Crew Members." *The Pull Hard* 11, no. 1 (Fall 2004): 2–3.

Riddle, Garrett. "Men's Crew Has Huskies' Respect in 1992 Season." *Daily Evergreen*, September 10, 1992, 8.

Roberts, Bill. "Cougar Crew: A Champion Team Grasps for Money." *Daily Evergreen*, September 20, 1979, C1.

———. "Crew Practices Despite Adversity." *Daily Evergreen*, December 14, 1979, 14.

"Rowers Get Shell; Need Shelter Next." *Daily Evergreen*, February 12, 1971, 9.

"Rowers Second to UW." *Daily Evergreen*, April 12, 1977, 9.

"Rowers Seek New Members." *Daily Evergreen*, February 13, 1974, 7.

"Rowers Thirteenth in Corvallis Regatta." *Daily Evergreen*, May 2, 1972, 8.

"Rowers Tryout Begin [sic] Saturday." *Daily Evergreen*, September 28, 1979, 18.

"Rowing Club Meets Tonight." *Daily Evergreen*, December 3, 1970, 6.

"Rowing Club Sticks Together after Wind Loss." *Daily Evergreen*, February 4, 1972, 11.

"Sagebrush Navy: Washington State Crew Still Suffers from an Identity Crisis." *Los Angeles Times*, May 17, 1987. Accessed May 27, 2021. https://www.latimes.com/archives/la-xpm-1987-05-17-sp-800-story.html.

"Seniors Top Rest in Crew Races." *Daily Evergreen*, March 20, 1979, 9.

"Shell Loss Hurts Women's Crew." *Chinook '86*. Pullman: Washington State University, 1986: 133.

Smith, Craig. "Seattle Rowing Icon Frank Cunningham Dies at 91." *Seattle Times*, March 8, 2013. Last updated March 8, 2013. https://www.seattletimes.com/sports/other-sports/seattle-rowing-icon-frank-cunningham-dies-at-91/.

Smith, Jason. "Club Round Up." *Daily Evergreen*, April 13, 1993, 9.

———. "Men's Novice Crew." *Daily Evergreen*, April 6, 1993, 8.

"Sports Roundup." *Daily Evergreen*, April 26, 1972, 8.

Stratton, Chris. "Men's Crew." *Daily Evergreen*, March 26, 1997, 8.

Struckmeyer, Ken. *The Pull Hard* 2, no. 1 (December 1974).

———. *The Pull Hard* 2, no. 2 (September 1975).

———. "Struckmeyer Takes Over," *The Pull Hard* 1, no.1 (1973–1974): 3.

———. "A Word from Struckmeyer," *The Pull Hard* (Summer 1983): 1.

"Student Attempt to Start Rowing Club with Meeting." *Daily Evergreen*, November 12, 1970, 5.

"Student's Design Selected for Club's Storage House." *Daily Evergreen*, May 11, 1971, 7.

Sudermann, Hannelore, "History Was Made...The Fight for Equity for Women's Athletics in Washington," *Washington State Magazine* (Winter 2007): 15–17.

Taylor, Lisa. "From Pleasure Rows and Plashing Sculls to Amateur Oarswomanship: The Evolution of Women's Amateur Rowing in Britain." *The International Journal of the History of Sport* 35, no. 14 (2018): 1491.

"U.S. To Mine All Vietnam Ports." *Daily Evergreen*, May 9, 1972, 1.

"UW Assistant Hired as WSU Women's Crew Coach." *Daily Evergreen*, June 19, 1990, 1.

"UW Takes 8 of 11 in Crew." *Daily Evergreen*, April 24, 1979, 6.

"Varsity Fours With." *Rowing* (June 1979), in "Meatwagon Paper Trail," Cougar Crew Shared Google Drive, CCAA.

"Varsity Oarsmen Sweep to Easy Wins." *Daily Evergreen*, March 26, 1974, 6.

Walker, Greg. "Women's Sport on Hold at Least a Year." *Daily Evergreen*, March 12, 1990, 1.

———. "WSU May Not Add Another Women's Sport this Year." *Daily Evergreen*, October 18, 1989, 9.

Wallace, William N. "20,000 Fans Turn Out for I.R.A.'s Regatta." *New York Times*, June 2, 1979.

Ware, Pam. "Women's Commodore's Report." *The Pull Hard* 5, no. 3 (Winter 1988): 1.

Washburn, Joanne. "Women's Athletics." *Chinook '80*. Pullman, Washington State University, 1980: 136.

"Washington State Crew? IRA Champs." "Meatwagon Paper Trail," Cougar Crew Shared Google Drive, CCAA.

Waters, Rich. "Men Excel on Land Too." *Daily Evergreen*, October 22, 1992, 12.

Williams, Mike V. "Crew Previews Showdown at Portland in Two Weeks." *Daily Evergreen*, October 26, 1993, 6.

"Wind Storm Doesn't Stop Crew." *Daily Evergreen*, March 30, 1972, 5.

"Worley Eyes Sub-6:00 2K." *The Pull Hard* 12, no. 2 (Winter 2006): 6.

"WSU Crew Cited as Team of the Week." "Meatwagon Paper Trail," Cougar Crew Shared Google Drive, CCAA.

"WSU to Add Women's Sports." *Daily Evergreen*, September 21, 1988, 1.

WSU Women's Cougar Crew. Letter to the editor, "Women's Crew Still In Need of Support." *Daily Evergreen*, November 19, 1975, 4.

Books and Films

American Experience: The Boys of '36. PBS documentary (2016). Directed by Margaret Grossi, written by Aaron R. Cohen, featuring Oliver Platt, Timothy Egan, and others.

Boyne, Daniel J. *Kelly: A Father, A Son, An American Quest.* New York: Lyons Press, 2012.

———. *The Red Rose Crew: A True Story of Women, Winning, and the Water.* Guilford, CT: The Lyons Press, 2005.

Brown, Daniel James. *The Boys in the Boat: Nine Americans and Their Epic Quest for Gold at the 1936 Berlin Olympics.* New York: Viking, 2013.

Cooper, Arshay. *A Most Beautiful Thing: The True Story of America's First All-Black High School Rowing Team.* New York: Flatiron Books, 2015.

Cunningham, Frank. *The Sculler at Ease.* Seattle: Vanguard Press, 1999.

Dodd, Christopher. *The Story of World Rowing.* London: Stanley Paul & Co., 1992.

Duckworth, Angela. *Grit: The Power of Passion and Perseverance.* New York: Simon and Schuster, 2016.

Fry, Richard B. *The Crimson and the Gray: 100 Years with the WSU Cougars.* Pullman: Washington State University Press, 1989.

Gilder, Ginny. *Course Correction: A Story of Rowing and Resilience in the Wake of Title IX.* Boston: Beacon Press, 2015.

Haley, Bruce. *The Healthy Body and Victorian Culture.* Boston: Harvard University Press, 1978.

Halberstam, David. *The Amateurs: The Story of Four Young Men and their Quest for an Olympic Gold Medal.* New York: Random House, 1985.

Kiesling, Stephen. *The Shell Game: Reflection on Rowing and the Pursuit of Excellence.* Ashland, OR: Nordic Knight Press, 1982.

Lambert, Craig. *Mind Over Water: Lessons on Life from the Art of Rowing.* New York: Houghton Mifflin, 1999.

Lewis, Brad Alan. *Assault on Lake Casitas.* Newport, CA: Shark Press, 2011.

———. *Lido for Time: 1439.* Newport, CA: Shark Press, 2011.

Mangan, J. A., and James Walvin, eds., *Manliness and Morality: Middle-Class Masculinity in Britain and America, 1800–1940.* New York: St. Martin's Press, 1987.

Newell, Gordon. *Ready All! George Yeoman Pocock and Crew Racing.* Seattle: University of Washington Press, 1987.

Rinehart, Rick. *Men of Kent: Ten Boys, A Fast Boat, and the Coach Who Made Them Champions.* Guilford, Connecticut: Lyons Press, 2010.

Rotundo, E. Anthony. *American Manhood: Transformations in Masculinity from the Revolution to the Modern Era.* New York: Basic Books, 1993.

Taylor, Bradley F. *Wisconsin Where They Row: A History of Varsity Rowing at the University of Wisconsin* (Madison: University of Wisconsin Press, 2005).

Electronic Sources

Bhattacharya, Esha. "Diversity in Rowing, or the Lack Thereof." *Row2K.* October 8, 2020. https://www.row2k.com/features/5280/Diversity-in-Rowing--or-the-Lack-Thereof/.

Blair v. Washington State University, 108 Wn.2d 558 (1987), 740 P.2d 1379. https://law.justia.com/cases/washington/supreme-court/1987/50591-8-1.html.

"Chapter 13 – Dear Pullman…." *Dr. Frank Writes* (blog), November 16, 2015. http://doctorfrankwrites.blogspot.com/2015/11/chapter-13-dear-pullman.html.

Hewitt, Ed. "IRA Location, Format, Eligibility to Change for 2009 Regatta." *Row2K.* June 8, 2008. https://www.row2k.com/news/6-8-2008/IRA-Location--Format--Eligibility-to-Change-for-2009-Regatta/38292/.

———. "The 40-Year Storm: Change Comes to the 106th (or 107th) IRA Regatta." *Row2K.* February 15, 2008. https://www.row2k.com/features/358/The-40-Year-Storm--Change-Comes-to-the-106th--or-107th--IRA-Regatta/.

Irvin, Philip. "Black Thursday–I was there." WSU Cougar Crew (website). The "History" section: "The 1970s: Where it all began." Accessed April 16, 2021. https://www.cougarcrew.com/history/1970s.html.

Janovich, Adriana. "Cougar Crew Profiles." *Washington State Magazine* (Winter 2019). "Web extra." https://magazine.wsu.edu/web-extra/cougar-crew-profiles/.

Kuh, G. D., J. Kinzie, J. A. Buckley, B. K. Bridges, and J. C. Hayek. "What Matters to Student Success: A Review of the Literature." Commissioned paper for the National Postsecondary Education Cooperative, July 2006. https://nces.ed.gov/npec/pdf/Kuh_Team_Report.pdf.

"Lower Granite Lock and Dam Master Plan," July 2018. U.S. Army Corps of Engineers, Walla Walla District (website). https://www.nww.usace.army.mil/Portals/28/181003_revised_LGMP_main.pdf.

Mallory, Peter. *The Sport of Rowing: A Comprehensive History.* Row2k Book exclusives (2011). https://www.row2k.com/features/books/tsor/.

Moore, C. and N. Shulock. "Student progress toward degree completion: Lessons from the research literature." California State University, Sacramento, Institute for Higher Education Leadership and Policy, September 2009. https://files.eric.ed.gov/fulltext/ED513825.pdf.

"Paul 'Zenquist' – The Quad That Could Have Been." *The Rowing Podcast*, May 3, 2020, produced by Matt Rung, podcast, MP3 audio, 39:00. https://podcasts. apple.com/us/podcast/paul-zenquist-the-quad-that-could-have-been/ id1508639477?i=1000473484552.

"Shawn Bagnall." US Naval Academy Men's Lightweight Rowing website, head coach profile. Accessed May 10, 2021. https://navysports.com/sports/mens-lightweight-rowing/roster/coaches/shawn-bagnall/921.

"Statement on Racism and Injustice." *USRowing*. June 2, 2020, https://usrowing.org/ news/2020/6/2/general-usrowing-statement.aspx.

Title IX of the Education Amendments of 1972, 20 U.S.C. Ð 1681 – 1688. Pub. L. 92–318, title IX, § 901, June 23, 1972, 86 Stat. 373. Updated November 13, 2000. https://www.justice.gov/crt/title-ix-education-amendments-1972.

Wang, Jing, and Jonathan Shiveley. "The Impact of Extracurricular Activity on Student Academic Performance." California State University, Sacramento, Office of Institutional Research, 2009. https://www.cair.org/wp-content/uploads/ sites/474/2015/07/Wang-Student-Activity-Report-2009.pdf.

INDEX

Page numbers in italics refer to photographs.

ABOUT THE AUTHOR

David Arnold received a bachelor's degree in history at Washington State University in 1988, having spent more time on the Snake River rowing than in the library studying. He then earned a master's degree and doctorate in history from UCLA and returned to eastern Washington, where he has taught at Columbia Basin College since 1998. His first book, *The Fishermen's Frontier: People and Salmon in Southeast Alaska*, is also about men and women in boats.